Models for Dynamic Macroeconomics

Models for Dynamic Macroeconomics

Fabio-Cesare Bagliano

Giuseppe Bertola

OXFORD
UNIVERSITY PRESS

This book has been printed digitally and produced in a standard specification in order to ensure its continuing availability

OXFORD
UNIVERSITY PRESS

Great Clarendon Street, Oxford OX2 6DP
Oxford University Press is a department of the University of Oxford.
It furthers the University's objective of excellence in research, scholarship,
and education by publishing worldwide in
Oxford New York
Auckland Cape Town Dar es Salaam Hong Kong Karachi
Kuala Lumpur Madrid Melbourne Mexico City Nairobi
New Delhi Shanghai Taipei Toronto
With offices in
Argentina Austria Brazil Chile Czech Republic France Greece
Guatemala Hungary Italy Japan South Korea Poland Portugal
Singapore Switzerland Thailand Turkey Ukraine Vietnam

Oxford is a registered trade mark of Oxford University Press
in the UK and in certain other countries
Published in the United States
by Oxford University Press Inc., New York

ISBN 978-0-19-922832-4

☐ PREFACE TO PAPERBACK EDITION

The impact of macroeconomics on daily life is less tangible than that of micro-economics. Everyone has to deal with rising supermarket prices, fluctuations in the labor market, and other microeconomic problems. Only a handful of policymakers and government officials really need to worry about fiscal and monetary policy, or about a country's overall competitiveness. The highly sim-plified, and unavoidably controversial nature of theories used to represent the complex phenomena resulting from the interaction of millions of individuals, tends to make macroeconomics appear to be a relatively arcane and technical branch of the social sciences. Its focus is on issues more likely to be of interest to specialists than the general public.

Yet, macroeconomics and the problems it attempts to deal with are extremely important, even if they are sometimes difficult to grasp. It cannot be denied that macroeconomic analysis has become more technical over the last few decades. The formal treatment of expectations and of inter-temporal interactions is nowadays an essential ingredient of any model meant to address practical and policy problems. But, at the same time, it has also become more pragmatic because modern macroeconomics is firmly rooted in individual agents' day-to-day decisions. To understand and appreciate scientific research papers, the modern macroeconomist has to master the dynamic optimization tools needed to represent the solution of real, live individuals' problems in terms of optimization, equilibrium and dynamic accumulation relationships, expectations and uncertainty. The macroeconomist, unlike most microecono-mists, also needs to know how to model and interpret the interactions of individual decisions that, in different ways and at different levels, make an economy's dynamic behavior very different from the simple juxtaposition of its inhabitant's actions and objectives.

This book offers its readers a step-by-step introduction to aspects of macroeconomic engineering, individual optimization techniques and modern approaches to macroeconomic equilibrium modeling. It applies the relevant formal analysis to some of the standard topics covered less formally by all intermediate macroeconomics course: consumption and investment, employ-ment and unemployment, and economic growth. Aspects of each topic are treated in more detail by making use of advanced mathematics and setting them in a broader context than is the case in standard undergraduate text-books. The book is not, however, as technically demanding as some other graduate textbooks. Readers require no more mathematical expertise than is provided by the majority of undergraduate courses. The exposition seeks to develop economic intuition as well as technical know-how, and to prepare students for hands-on solutions to practical problems rather than providing fully rigorous theoretical analysis. Hence, relatively advanced concepts (such as integrals and random variables) are introduced in the context of economic arguments and immediately applied to the solution of economic problems, which are accurately characterized without an in-depth discussion of the theoretical aspects of the mathematics involved. The style and coverage of the material bridges the gap between basic textbooks and modern applied macroeconomic research, allowing readers to approach research in leading journals and understand research practiced in central banks and international research institutions as well as in academic departments.

How to Use This Book

Models for Dynamic Macroeconomics is suitable for advanced undergraduate and first-year graduate courses and can be taught in about 60 lecture hours. When complemented by recent journal articles, the individual chapters—which differ slightly in the relative emphasis given to analytical techniques and empirical perspective—can also be used in specialized topics courses. The last section of each chapter often sketches more advanced material and may be omitted without breaking the book's train of thought, while the chapters' appendices introduce technical tools and are essential reading. Some exercises are found within the chapters and propose extensions of the model discussed in the text. Other exercises are found at the end of chapters and should be used to review the material. Many technical terms are contained in the index, which can be used to track down definitions and sample applications of possibly unfamiliar concepts.

The book's five chapters can to some extent be read independently, but are also linked by various formal and substantive threads to each other and to the macroeconomic literature they are meant to introduce. Discrete-time optimization under uncertainty, introduced in Chapter 1, is motivated and discussed by applications to consumption theory, with particular attention to empirical implementation. Chapter 2 focuses on continuous-time optimization techniques, and discusses the relevant insights in the context of partial-equilibrium investment models. Chapter 3 revisits many of the previous chapters' formal derivations with applications to dynamic labor demand, in analogy to optimal investment models, and characterizes labor market equilibrium when not only individual firms' labor demand is subject to adjustment costs, but also individual labor supply by workers faces dynamic adjustment problems. Chapter 4 proposes broader applications of methods introduced by the previous chapters, and studies continuous-time equilibrium dynamics of representative-agent economies featuring both consumption and investment choices, with applications to long-run growth frameworks of analysis. Chapter 5 illustrates the role of decentralized trading in determining aggregate equilibria, and characterizes aggregate labor market dynamics in the presence of frictional unemployment. Chapters 4 and 5 pay particular attention to strategic interactions and externalities: even when each agent correctly solves his or her individual dynamic problem, modern micro-founded macroeconomic models recognize that macroeconomic equilibrium need not have unambiguously desirable properties.

Brief literature reviews at the end of each chapter outline some recent directions of progress, but no book can effectively survey a literature as wide-ranging, complex, and evolving as the macroeconomic one. In the interests of time and space this book does not cover all of the important analytical and empirical issues within the topics it discusses. Overlapping generation dynamics and real and monetary business cycle fluctuations, as well as more technical aspects, such as those relevant to the treatment of asymmetric information and to more sophisticated game-theoretic and decision-theoretic approaches are not covered. It would be impossible to cover all aspects of all relevant topics in one compact and accessible volume and the intention is to complement rather than compete with some of the other texts currently available.[*] The positive reception of the hardback edition, however, would seem to confirm that the book does succeed in its intended purpose of covering the essential elements of a modern macroeconomist's toolkit. It also enables readers to knowledgeably approach further relevant research. It is hoped that this paperback edition will continue to fulfil that purpose even more efficiently for a number of years to come.

The first hardback edition was largely based on Metodi Dinamici e Fenomeni Macroeconomici (il Mulino, Bologna, 1999), translated by Fabio Bagliano (ch.1), Giuseppe Bertola (ch. 2), Marcel Jansen (chs. 3, 4, 5, edited by Jessica Moss Spataro and Giuseppe Bertola). For helpful comments the authors are indebted to many colleagues (especially Guido Ascari, Onorato

---

[*]*Foundations of Modern Macroeconomics*, by Ben J. Heijdra and Frederick van der Ploeg (Oxford University Press, 2002) is more comprehensive and less technical; the two books can to some extent complement each other on specific topics. This book offers more technical detail and requires less mathematical knowledge than *Lectures on Macroeconomics*, by Olivier J. Blanchard and Stanley Fischer (MIT Press, 1989), and offers a more up to date treatment of a more limited range of topics. It is less wide ranging than *Advanced Macroeconomics*, by David Romer (McGraw-Hill 3rd rev. edn. 2005) but provides more technical and rigorous hands-on treatment of more advanced techniques. By contrast, *Recursive Macroeconomic Theory*, by Lars Ljungqvist and Thomas J. Sargent (MIT Press, 2nd edn. 2004) offers a more rigorous but not as accessible formal treatment of a broad range of topics, and a narrower range of technical and economic insights.

Castellino, Elsa Fornero, Pietro Garibaldi, Giulio Fella, Vinicio Guidi, Claudio Morana) and to the anonymous reviewers. The various editions of the book have also benefited enormously from the input of the students and teaching assistants (especially Alberto Bucci, Winfried Koeniger, Juana Santamaria, Mirko Wiederholt) over many years at the CORIPE Master program in Turin, at the European University Institute, and elsewhere. Any remaining errors and all shortcomings are of course the authors' own.

☐ CONTENTS

☐ DETAILED CONTENTS

☐ LIST OF FIGURES

1 Dynamic Consumption Theory

Optimizing models of intertemporal choices are widely used by theoretical and empirical studies of consumption. This chapter outlines their basic analytical structure, along with some extensions. The technical tools introduced here aim at familiarizing the reader with recent applied work on consumption and saving, but they will also prove useful in the rest of the book, when we shall study investment and other topics in economic dynamics.

The chapter is organized as follows. Section 1.1 illustrates and solves the basic version of the intertemporal consumption choice model, deriving theoretical relationships between the dynamics of permanent income, current income, consumption, and saving. Section 1.2 discusses problems raised by empirical tests of the theory, focusing on the excess sensitivity of consumption to expected income changes and on the excess smoothness of consumption following unexpected income variations. Explanations of the empirical evidence are offered by Section 1.3, which extends the basic model by introducing a precautionary saving motive. Section 1.4 derives the implications of optimal portfolio allocation for joint determination of optimal consumption when risky financial assets are available. The Appendix briefly introduces dynamic programming techniques applied to the optimal consumption choice. Bibliographic references and suggestions for further reading bring the chapter to a close.

1.1. Permanent Income and Optimal Consumption

The basic model used in the modern literature on consumption and saving choices is based on two main assumptions:

1. Identical economic agents maximize an *intertemporal utility function*, defined on the consumption levels in each period of the optimization horizon, subject to the constraint given by overall available resources.

2. Under uncertainty, the maximization is based on *expectations* of future relevant variables (for example, income and the rate of interest) formed *rationally* by agents, who use optimally all information at their disposal.

We will therefore study the optimal behavior of a *representative agent* who lives in an uncertain environment and has rational expectations. Implications of the theoretical model will then be used to interpret aggregate data. The representative consumer faces an infinite horizon (like any aggregate economy), and solves at time t an intertemporal choice problem of the following general form:

$$\max_{\{c_{t+i}; i=0,1,\dots\}} U(c_t, c_{t+1}, \dots) \equiv U_t,$$

subject to the constraint (for $i = 0, \dots, \infty$)

$$A_{t+i+1} = (1 + r_{t+i}) A_{t+i} + y_{t+i} - c_{t+i},$$

where A_{t+i} is the stock of financial wealth at the beginning of period $t + i$; r_{t+i} is the real rate of return on financial assets in period $t + i$; y_{t+i} is *labor* income earned at the end of period $t + i$, and c_{t+i} is consumption, also assumed to take place at the end of the period. The constraint therefore accounts for the evolution of the consumer's financial wealth from one period to the next.

Several assumptions are often made in order easily to derive empirically testable implications from the basic model. The main assumptions (some of which will be relaxed later) are as follows.

- *Intertemporal separability (or additivity over time)* The generic utility function $U_t(\cdot)$ is specified as

$$U_t(c_t, c_{t+1}, \dots) = v_t(c_t) + v_{t+1}(c_{t+1}) + \dots$$

  (with $v'_{t+i} > 0$ and $v''_{t+i} < 0$ for any $i \geq 0$), where $v_{t+i}(c_{t+i})$ is the valuation at t of the utility accruing to the agent from consumption c_{t+i} at $t + i$. Since v_{t+i} depends only on consumption at $t + i$, the ratio of marginal utilities of consumption in any two periods is independent of consumption in any other period. This rules out goods whose effects on utility last for more than one period, either because the goods themselves are durable, or because their consumption creates long-lasting habits. (*Habit formation phenomena* will be discussed at the end of this chapter.)

- *A way of discounting utility in future periods that guarantees intertemporally consistent choices.* Dynamic inconsistencies arise when the valuation at time t of the relative utility of consumption in any two *future* periods, $t + k_1$ and $t + k_2$ (with $t < t + k_1 < t + k_2$), differs from the valuation of the same relative utility at a different time $t + i$. In this case the optimal levels of consumption for $t + k_1$ and $t + k_2$ originally chosen at t may not be considered optimal at some later date: the consumer would then wish to reconsider his original choices simply because time has passed, even if no new information has become available. To rule out this phenomenon, it is necessary that the ratios of discounted marginal utilities of consumption in $t + k_1$ and $t + k_2$ depend, in addition to c_{t+k_1} and c_{t+k_2}, only on the distance $k_2 - k_1$, and not also on the moment in time when the optimization problem is solved. With a discount factor for the utility of consumption in $t + k$ of the form $(1 + \rho)^{-k}$ (called "*exponential discounting*"), we can write

$$v_{t+k}(c_{t+k}) = \left(\frac{1}{1+\rho}\right)^k u(c_{t+k}),$$

and dynamic consistency of preferences is ensured: under certainty, the agent may choose the optimal consumption plan once and for all at the beginning of his planning horizon.[1]

- *The adoption of expected utility as the objective function under uncertainty (additivity over states of nature)* In discrete time, a *stochastic process* specifies a random variable for each date t, that is a real number associated to the realization of a *state of nature*. If it is possible to give a probability to different states of nature, it is also possible to construct an expectation of future income, weighting each possible level of income with the probability of the associated state of nature. In general, the probabilities used depend on available information, and therefore change over time when new information is made available. Given her information set at t, I_t, the consumer maximizes expected utility conditional on I_t: $U_t = E\left(\sum_{i=0}^{\infty} v_{t+i}(c_{t+i}) \mid I_t\right)$. Together with the assumption of intertemporal separability (additivity over periods of time), the adoption of expected utility entails an inverse relationship between the degree of intertemporal substitutability, measuring the agent's propensity to substitute current consumption with future consumption *under certainty*, and risk aversion, determining the agent's choices among different consumption levels *under uncertainty* over the state of nature: the latter, and the inverse of the former, are both measured in absolute terms by $-v_t''(c)/v_t'(c)$ at time t and for consumption level c. (We will expand on this point on page 6.)

- Finally, we make the simplifying assumption that *there exists only one financial asset with certain and constant rate of return r*. Financial wealth A is the stock of the safe asset allowing the agent to transfer resources through time in a perfectly forecastable way; the only uncertainty is on the (exogenously given) future labor incomes y. Stochastic rates of return on n financial assets are introduced in Section 1.4 below.

Under the set of hypotheses above, the consumer's problem may be specified as follows:

$$\max_{\{c_{t+i}, i=0,1,\ldots\}} U_t = E_t \left[\sum_{i=0}^{\infty} \left(\frac{1}{1+\rho}\right)^i u(c_{t+i})\right] \tag{1.1}$$

---

[1] A strand of the recent literature (see the last section of this chapter for references) has explored the implications of a different discount function: a "*hyperbolic*" discount factor declines at a relatively higher rate in the short run (consumers are relatively "impatient" at short horizons) than in the long run (consumers are "patient" at long horizons, implying dynamic inconsistent preferences).

subject to the constraint (for $i = 0, \ldots, \infty$):[2]

$$A_{t+i+1} = (1+r)A_{t+i} + y_{t+i} - c_{t+i}, \qquad A_t \text{ given.} \qquad (1.2)$$

In (1.1) ρ is the consumer's intertemporal rate of time preference and $E_t[\cdot]$ is the (rational) expectation formed using information available at t: for a generic variable x_{t+i} we have $E_t x_{t+i} = E(x_{t+i} \mid I_t)$. The hypothesis of rational expectations implies that the forecast error $x_{t+i} - E(x_{t+i} \mid I_t)$ is uncorrelated with the variables in the information set $I_t : E_t(x_{t+i} - E(x_{t+i} \mid I_t)) = 0$ (we will often use this property below). The value of current income y_t in included in I_t.

In the constraint (1.2) financial wealth A may be negative (the agent is not liquidity-constrained); however, we impose the restriction that the consumer's debt cannot grow at a rate greater than the financial return r by means of the following condition (known as the *no-Ponzi-game condition*):

$$\lim_{j \to \infty} \left(\frac{1}{1+r} \right)^j A_{t+j} \geq 0. \qquad (1.3)$$

The condition in (1.3) is equivalent, in the infinite-horizon case, to the non-negativity constraint $A_{T+1} \geq 0$ for an agent with a life lasting until period T: in the absence of such a constraint, the consumer would borrow to finance infinitely large consumption levels. Although in its general formulation (1.3) is an inequality, if marginal utility of consumption is always positive this condition will be satisfied as an equality. Equation (1.3) with strict equality is called *transversality condition* and can be directly used in the problem's solution.

Similarly, without imposing (1.3), interests on debt could be paid for by further borrowing on an infinite horizon. Formally, from the budget constraint (1.2) at time t, repeatedly substituting A_{t+i} up to period $t + j$, we get the following equation:

$$\frac{1}{1+r} \sum_{i=0}^{j-1} \left(\frac{1}{1+r} \right)^i c_{t+i} + \left(\frac{1}{1+r} \right)^j A_{t+j} = \frac{1}{1+r} \sum_{i=0}^{j-1} \left(\frac{1}{1+r} \right)^i y_{t+i} + A_t.$$

The present value of consumption flows from t up to $t + j - 1$ can exceed the consumer's total available resources, given by the sum of the initial financial wealth A_t and the present value of future labor incomes from t up to $t + j - 1$. In this case $A_{t+j} < 0$ and the consumer will have a stock of debt at the beginning of period $t + j$. When the horizon is extended to infinity, the constraint (1.3) stops the agent from consuming more than his lifetime resources, using further borrowing to pay the interests on the existing debt in any period up to infinity. Assuming an infinite horizon and using (1.3) with equality, we get

---

2 In addition, a non-negativity constraint on consumption must be imposed: $c_{t+i} \geq 0$. We assume that this constraint is always fulfilled.

the consumer's *intertemporal budget constraint* at the beginning of period t (in the absence of liquidity constraints that would rule out, or limit, borrowing):

$$\frac{1}{1+r}\sum_{i=0}^{\infty}\left(\frac{1}{1+r}\right)^i c_{t+i} = \frac{1}{1+r}\sum_{i=0}^{\infty}\left(\frac{1}{1+r}\right)^i y_{t+i} + A_t. \quad (1.4)$$

1.1.1. OPTIMAL CONSUMPTION DYNAMICS

Substituting the consumption level derived from the budget constraint (1.2) into the utility function, we can write the consumer's problem as

$$\max U_t = E_t \sum_{i=0}^{\infty}\left(\frac{1}{1+\rho}\right)^i u((1+r)A_{t+i} - A_{t+i+1} + y_{t+i})$$

with respect to wealth A_{t+i} for $i = 1, 2, \ldots$, given initial wealth A_t and subject to the transversality condition derived from (1.3). The first-order conditions

$$E_t u'(c_{t+i}) = \frac{1+r}{1+\rho} E_t u'(c_{t+i+1})$$

are necessary and sufficient if utility $u(c)$ is an increasing and concave function of consumption (i.e. if $u'(c) > 0$ and $u''(c) < 0$). For the consumer's choice in the first period (when $i = 0$), noting that $u'(c_t)$ is known at time t, we get the so-called *Euler equation*:

$$u'(c_t) = \frac{1+r}{1+\rho} E_t u'(c_{t+1}). \quad (1.5)$$

At the optimum the agent is indifferent between consuming immediately one unit of the good, with marginal utility $u'(c_t)$, and saving in order to consume $1 + r$ units in the next period, $t + 1$. The same reasoning applies to any period t in which the optimization problem is solved: the Euler equation gives the dynamics of marginal utility in any two successive periods.[3]

[3] An equivalent solution of the problem is found by maximizing the Lagrangian function:

$$\mathcal{L}_t = E_t \sum_{i=0}^{\infty}\left(\frac{1}{1+\rho}\right)^i u(c_{t+i})$$

$$- \lambda\left[\sum_{i=0}^{\infty}\left(\frac{1}{1+r}\right)^i E_t c_{t+i} - (1+r)A_t - \sum_{i=0}^{\infty}\left(\frac{1}{1+r}\right)^i E_t y_{t+i}\right],$$

where λ is the Lagrange multiplier associated with the intertemporal budget constraint (here evaluated at the end of period t). From the first-order conditions for c_t and c_{t+1}, we derive the Euler equation (1.5). In addition, we get $u'(c_t) = \lambda$. The shadow value of the budget constraint, measuring the increase of maximized utility that is due to an infinitesimal increase of the resources available at the end of period t, is equal to the marginal utility of consumption at t. At the optimum, the Euler equation holds: the agent is indifferent between consumption in the current period and consumption in any

The evolution over time of marginal utility and consumption is governed by the difference between the rate of return r and the intertemporal rate of time preference ρ. Since $u''(c_t) < 0$, lower consumption yields higher marginal utility: if $r > \rho$, the consumer will find it optimal to increase consumption over time, exploiting a return on saving higher than the utility discount rate; when $r = \rho$, optimal consumption is constant, and when $r < \rho$ it is decreasing. The shape of marginal utility as a function of c (i.e. the concavity of the utility function) determines the magnitude of the effect of $r - \rho$ on the time path of consumption: if $|u''(c)|$ is large relative to $u'(c)$, large variations of marginal utility are associated with relatively small fluctuations in consumption, and then optimal consumption shows little changes over time even when the rate of return differs substantially from the utility discount rate.

Also, the agent's degree of risk aversion is determined by the concavity of the utility function. It has been already mentioned that our assumptions on preferences imply a negative relationship between risk aversion and intertemporal substitutability (where the latter measures the change in consumption between two successive periods owing to the difference between r and ρ or, if r is not constant, to changes in the rate of return). It is easy to find such relationship for the case of a *CRRA* (*constant relative risk aversion*) utility function, namely:

$$u(c_t) = \frac{c_t^{1-\gamma} - 1}{1 - \gamma}, \qquad \gamma > 0,$$

with $u'(c) = c^{-\gamma}$. The degree of relative risk aversion—whose general measure is the absolute value of the elasticity of marginal utility, $-u''(c)\,c/u'(c)$—is in this case independent of the consumption level, and is equal to the parameter γ.[4] The measure of intertemporal substitutability is obtained by solving the consumer's optimization problem under certainty. The Euler equation corresponding to (1.5) is

$$c_t^{-\gamma} = \frac{1+r}{1+\rho}c_{t+1}^{-\gamma} \quad \Rightarrow \quad \left(\frac{c_{t+1}}{c_t}\right)^{\gamma} = \frac{1+r}{1+\rho}.$$

Taking logarithms, and using the approximations $\log(1 + r) \simeq r$ and $\log(1 + \rho) \simeq \rho$, we get

$$\Delta \log c_{t+1} = \frac{1}{\gamma}(r - \rho).$$

future period, since both alternatives provide additional utility given by $u'(c_t)$. In the Appendix to this chapter, the problem's solution is derived by means of dynamic programming techniques.

  [4] The denominator of the CRRA utility function is zero if $\gamma = 1$, but marginal utility can nevertheless have unitary elasticity: in fact, $u'(c) = c^{-\gamma} = 1/c$ if $u(c) = \log(c)$. The presence of the constant term "-1" in the numerator makes utility well defined also when $\gamma \to 1$. This limit can be computed, by l'Hôpital's rule, as the ratio of the limits of the numerator's derivative, $dc^{1-\gamma}/d\gamma = -\log(c)c^{1-\gamma}$, and the denominator's derivative, which is -1.

The elasticity of intertemporal substitution, which is the effect of changes in the interest rate on the growth rate of consumption $\Delta \log c$, is constant and is measured by the reciprocal of the coefficient of relative risk aversion γ.

1.1.2. CONSUMPTION LEVEL AND DYNAMICS

Under uncertainty, the expected value of utility may well differ from its realization. Letting

$$u'(c_{t+1}) - E_t u'(c_{t+1}) \equiv \eta_{t+1},$$

we have by definition that $E_t \eta_{t+1} = 0$ under the hypothesis of rational expectations. Then, from (1.5), we get

$$u'(c_{t+1}) = \frac{1+\rho}{1+r} u'(c_t) + \eta_{t+1}. \tag{1.6}$$

If we assume also that $r = \rho$, the stochastic process describing the evolution over time of marginal utility is

$$u'(c_{t+1}) = u'(c_t) + \eta_{t+1}, \tag{1.7}$$

and the change of marginal utility from t to $t + 1$ is given by a stochastic term unforecastable at time t ($E_t \eta_{t+1} = 0$).

In order to derive the implications of the above result for the dynamics of consumption, it is necessary to specify a functional form for $u(c)$. To obtain a linear relation like (1.7), directly involving the level of consumption, we can assume a quadratic utility function $u(c) = c - (b/2)c^2$, with linear marginal utility $u'(c) = 1 - bc$ (positive only for $c < 1/b$). This simple and somewhat restrictive assumption lets us rewrite equation (1.7) as

$$c_{t+1} = c_t + u_{t+1}, \tag{1.8}$$

where $u_{t+1} \equiv -(1/b)\eta_{t+1}$ is such that $E_t u_{t+1} = 0$. If marginal utility is linear in consumption, as is the case when the utility function is quadratic, the process (1.8) followed by the level of consumption is a martingale, or a random walk, with the property:[5]

$$E_t c_{t+1} = c_t. \tag{1.9}$$

This is the main implication of the intertemporal choice model with rational expectations and quadratic utility: the best forecast of next period's consumption is current consumption. The consumption change from t to $t + 1$

---

[5] A *martingale* is a stochastic process x_t with the property $E_t x_{t+1} = x_t$. With $r = \rho$, marginal utility and, under the additional hypothesis of quadratic utility, the level of consumption have this property. No assumptions have been made about the distribution of the process $x_{t+1} - x_t$, for example concerning time-invariance, which is a feature of a random walk process.

cannot be forecast on the basis of information available at t: formally, u_{t+1} is *orthogonal* to the information set used to form the expectation E_t, including all variables known to the consumer and dated $t, t-1, \ldots$ This implication has been widely tested empirically. Such *orthogonality tests* will be discussed below.

The solution of the consumer's intertemporal choice problem given by (1.8) cannot be interpreted as a consumption function. Indeed, that equation does not link consumption in each period to its determinants (income, wealth, rate of interest), but only describes the dynamics of consumption from one period to the next. The assumptions listed above, however, make it possible to derive the *consumption function*, combining what we know about the dynamics of optimal consumption and the intertemporal budget constraint (1.4). Since the realizations of income and consumption must fulfill the constraint, (1.4) holds also with expected values:

$$\frac{1}{1+r} \sum_{i=0}^{\infty} \left(\frac{1}{1+r}\right)^i E_t c_{t+i} = \frac{1}{1+r} \sum_{i=0}^{\infty} \left(\frac{1}{1+r}\right)^i E_t y_{t+i} + A_t. \qquad (1.10)$$

Linearity of the marginal utility function, and a discount rate equal to the interest rate, imply that the level of consumption expected for any future period is equal to current consumption. Substituting $E_t c_{t+i}$ with c_t on the left-hand side of (1.10), we get

$$\frac{1}{r} c_t = A_t + \frac{1}{1+r} \sum_{i=0}^{\infty} \left(\frac{1}{1+r}\right)^i E_t y_{t+i} \equiv A_t + H_t. \qquad (1.11)$$

The last term in (1.11), the present value at t of future expected labor incomes, is the consumer's "human wealth" H_t. The consumption function can then be written as

$$c_t = r(A_t + H_t) \equiv y_t^P \qquad (1.12)$$

Consumption in t is now related to its determinants, the levels of financial wealth A_t and human wealth H_t. The consumer's overall wealth at the beginning of period t is given by $A_t + H_t$. Consumption in t is then the annuity value of total wealth, that is the return on wealth in each period: $r(A_t + H_t)$. That return, that we define as *permanent income* (y_t^P), is the flow that could be earned for ever on the stock of total wealth. The conclusion is that the agent chooses to consume in each period exactly his *permanent income*, computed on the basis of expectations of future labor incomes.

1.1.3. DYNAMICS OF INCOME, CONSUMPTION, AND SAVING

Given the consumption function (1.12), we note that the evolution through time of consumption and permanent income coincide. Leading (1.12) one period, we have

$$y_{t+1}^P = r(A_{t+1} + H_{t+1}). \tag{1.13}$$

Taking the expectation at time t of y_{t+1}^P, subtracting the resulting expression from (1.13), and noting that $E_t A_{t+1} = A_{t+1}$ from (1.2), since realized income y_t is included in the consumer's information set at t, we get

$$y_{t+1}^P - E_t y_{t+1}^P = r(H_{t+1} - E_t H_{t+1}). \tag{1.14}$$

Permanent income calculated at time $t + 1$, conditional on information available at that time, differs from the expectation formed one period earlier, conditional on information at t, only if there is a "surprise" in the agent's human wealth at time $t + 1$. In other words, the "surprise" in permanent income at $t + 1$ is equal to the annuity value of the "surprise" in human wealth arising from new information on future labor incomes, available only at $t + 1$.

Since $c_t = y_t^P$, from (1.9) we have

$$E_t y_{t+1}^P = y_t^P.$$

All information available at t is used to calculate permanent income y_t^P, which is also the best forecast of the next period's permanent income. Using this result, the evolution over time of permanent income can be written as

$$y_{t+1}^P = y_t^P + r\left[\frac{1}{1+r}\sum_{i=0}^{\infty}\left(\frac{1}{1+r}\right)^i (E_{t+1} - E_t)y_{t+1+i}\right],$$

where the "surprise" in human wealth in $t + 1$ is expressed as the revision in expectations on future incomes: y^P can change over time only if those expectations change, that is if, when additional information accrues to the agent in $t + 1$, $(E_{t+1} - E_t)y_{t+1+i} \equiv E_{t+1}y_{t+1+i} - E_t y_{t+1+i}$ is not zero for all i. The evolution over time of consumption follows that of permanent income, so that we can write

$$c_{t+1} = c_t + r\left[\frac{1}{1+r}\sum_{i=0}^{\infty}\left(\frac{1}{1+r}\right)^i (E_{t+1} - E_t)y_{t+1+i}\right]$$
$$= c_t + u_{t+1}. \tag{1.15}$$

It can be easily verified that the change of consumption between t and $t + 1$ cannot be foreseen as of time t (since it depends only on information available in $t + 1$): $E_t u_{t+1} = 0$. Thus, equation (1.15) enables us to attach a well defined economic meaning and a precise measure to the error term u_{t+1} in the Euler equation (1.8).

Intuitively, permanent income theory has important implications not only for the optimal consumption path, but also for the behavior of the agent's *saving*, governing the accumulation of her financial wealth. To discover these implications, we start from the definition of *disposable income* y^D, the sum of labor income, and the return on the financial wealth:

$$y_t^D = r A_t + y_t.$$

Saving s_t (the difference between disposable income and consumption) is easily derived by means of the main implication of permanent income theory ($c_t = y_t^P$):

$$s_t \equiv y_t^D - c_t = y_t^D - y_t^P = y_t - r H_t. \qquad (1.16)$$

The level of saving in period t is then equal to the difference between current (labor) income y_t and the annuity value of human wealth $r H_t$. Such a difference, being *transitory* income, does not affect consumption: if it is positive it is entirely saved, whereas, if it is negative it determines a decumulation of financial assets of an equal amount. Thus, the consumer, faced with a variable labor income, changes the stock of financial assets so that the return earned on it ($r A$) allows her to keep consumption equal to permanent income.

Unfolding the definition of human wealth H_t in (1.16), we can write saving at t as

$$
\begin{aligned}
s_t = y_t &- \frac{r}{1+r} \sum_{i=0}^{\infty} \left(\frac{1}{1+r} \right)^i E_t y_{t+i} \\
&= \frac{1}{1+r} y_t - \left[\frac{1}{1+r} - \left(\frac{1}{1+r} \right)^2 \right] E_t y_{t+1} \\
&\quad - \left[\left(\frac{1}{1+r} \right)^2 - \left(\frac{1}{1+r} \right)^3 \right] E_t y_{t+2} + \dots \\
&= - \sum_{i=1}^{\infty} \left(\frac{1}{1+r} \right)^i E_t \Delta y_{t+i}, \qquad (1.17)
\end{aligned}
$$

where $\Delta y_{t+i} = y_{t+i} - y_{t+i-1}$. Equation (1.17) sheds further light on the motivation for saving in this model: the consumer saves, accumulating financial assets, to face expected future declines of labor income (a "*saving for a rainy day*" behavior). Equation (1.17) has been extensively used in the empirical literature, and its role will be discussed in depth in Section 1.2.

1.1.4. CONSUMPTION, SAVING, AND CURRENT INCOME

Under certainty on future labor incomes, permanent income does not change over time. As a consequence, with $r = \rho$, consumption is constant and unrelated to current income y_t. On the contrary, when future incomes are uncertain, permanent income changes when new information causes a revision in expectations. Moreover, there is a link between current income and consumption if changes in income cause revisions in the consumer's expected permanent income. To explore the relation between current and permanent income, we assume a simple first-order autoregressive process generating income y:

$$y_{t+1} = \lambda y_t + (1 - \lambda)\bar{y} + \varepsilon_{t+1}, \qquad E_t \varepsilon_{t+1} = 0, \qquad (1.18)$$

where $0 \le \lambda \le 1$ is a parameter and $\bar{y}$ denotes the unconditional mean of income. The stochastic term ε_{t+1} is the component of income at $t + 1$ that cannot be forecast on the basis of information available at t (i.e. the income innovation). Suppose that the stochastic process for income is in the consumer's information set. From (1.18) we can compute the revision, between t and $t + 1$, of expectations of future incomes caused by a given realization of the stochastic term ε_{t+1}. The result of this calculation will then be substituted into (1.15) to obtain the effect on consumption c_{t+1}.

The revision in expectations of future incomes is given by

$$E_{t+1}y_{t+1+i} - E_t y_{t+1+i} = \lambda^i \varepsilon_{t+1}, \qquad \forall i \ge 0.$$

Substituting this expression into (1.15) for each period $t + 1 + i$, we have

$$r \left[\frac{1}{1+r} \sum_{i=0}^{\infty} \left(\frac{1}{1+r}\right)^i \lambda^i \varepsilon_{t+1} \right] = \left[\varepsilon_{t+1} \frac{r}{1+r} \sum_{i=0}^{\infty} \left(\frac{\lambda}{1+r}\right)^i \right], \qquad (1.19)$$

and solving the summation, we get[6]

$$c_{t+1} = c_t + \left(\frac{r}{1+r-\lambda}\right) \varepsilon_{t+1}, \qquad (1.20)$$

which directly links current income innovation ε_{t+1} to current consumption c_{t+1}. Like equation (1.8), (1.20) is a Euler equation; the error term is the innovation in permanent income, here expressed in terms of the current income innovation. Given an unexpected increase of income in period $t + 1$ equal to ε_{t+1}, the consumer increases consumption in $t + 1$ and expected consumption in all future periods by the annuity value of the increase in human wealth,

---

[6] The right-hand side expression in (1.19) can be written $\varepsilon_{t+1}(r/1 + r)S_\infty(\lambda/1 + r)$ if we denote by $S_N(a)$ a *geometric series* with parameter a, of order N. Since $S_N(a) - aS_N(a) = (1 + a + a^2 + \ldots + a^N) - (a + a^2 + a^3 + \ldots + a^{N+1}) = 1 + a^{N+1}$, such a series takes values $S_N(a) = (1 + a^{N+1})/(1 - a)$ and, as long as $a < 1$, converges to $S_\infty(a) = (1 - a)^{-1}$ as N tends to infinity. Using this formula in (1.19) yields the result.

$r\varepsilon_{t+1}/(1+r-\lambda)$. The portion of additional income that is not consumed, i.e.

$$\varepsilon_{t+1} - \frac{r}{1+r-\lambda}\varepsilon_{t+1} = \frac{1-\lambda}{1+r-\lambda}\varepsilon_{t+1},$$

is saved and added to the outstanding stock of financial assets. Starting from the next period, the return on this saving will add to disposable income, enabling the consumer to keep the higher level of consumption over the whole infinite future horizon.

It is important to notice that the magnitude of the consumption change between t and $t+1$ resulting from an innovation in current income ε_{t+1} depends, for a given interest rate r, on the parameter λ, capturing the degree of persistence of an innovation in $t+1$ on future incomes. To see the role of this parameter, it is useful to consider two polar cases.

1. $\lambda = 0$. In this case $y_{t+1} = \bar{y} + \varepsilon_{t+1}$. The innovation in current income is purely *transitory* and does not affect the level of income in future periods. Given an innovation ε_{t+1}, the consumer's human wealth, calculated at the beginning of period $t+1$, changes by $\varepsilon_{t+1}/(1+r)$. This change in H_{t+1} determines a variation of permanent income—and consumption— equal to $r\varepsilon_{t+1}/(1+r)$. In fact, from (1.20) with $\lambda = 0$, we have

$$c_{t+1} = c_t + \left(\frac{r}{1+r}\right)\varepsilon_{t+1}. \tag{1.21}$$

2. $\lambda = 1$. In this case $y_{t+1} = y_t + \varepsilon_{t+1}$. The innovation in current income is *permanent*, causing an equal change of all future incomes. The change in human wealth is then ε_{t+1}/r and the variation in permanent income and consumption is simply ε_{t+1}. From (1.20), with $\lambda = 1$, we get

$$c_{t+1} = c_t + \varepsilon_{t+1}.$$

Exercise 1 *In the two polar cases $\lambda = 0$ and $\lambda = 1$, find the effect of ε_{t+1} on saving in $t+1$ and on saving and disposable income in the following periods.*

Exercise 2 *Using the stochastic process for labor income in (1.18), prove that the consumption function that holds in this case (linking c_t to its determinants A_t, y_t, and $\bar{y}$) has the following form:*

$$c_t = r A_t + \frac{r}{1+r-\lambda}y_t + \frac{1-\lambda}{1+r-\lambda}\bar{y}.$$

What happens if $\lambda = 1$ and if $\lambda = 0$?

1.2. **Empirical Issues**

The dynamic implications of the permanent income model of consumption illustrated above motivated many recent empirical studies on consumption. Similarly, the life-cycle theory of consumption developed mainly by F. Modigliani has been subjected to empirical scrutiny. The partial-equilibrium perspective of this chapter makes it difficult to discuss the relationship between long-run saving and growth rates at the aggregate level: as we shall see in Chapter 4, the link between income growth and saving depends also on the interest rate, and becomes more complicated when the assumption of an exogenously given income process is abandoned. But even empirical studies based on *cross-sectional* individual data show that saving, if any, occurs only in the middle and old stages of the agent's life: consumption tracks income too closely to explain wealth accumulation only on the basis of a life-cycle motive.

As regards aggregate short-run dynamics, the first empirical test of the fundamental implication of the permanent income/rational expectations model of consumption is due to R. E. Hall (1978), who tests the orthogonality of the error term in the Euler equation with respect to past information. If the theory is correct, no variable known at time $t - 1$ can explain changes in consumption between $t - 1$ and t. Formally, the test is carried out by evaluating the statistical significance of variables dated $t - 1$ in the Euler equation for time t. For example, augmenting the Euler equation with the income change that occurred between $t - 2$ and $t - 1$, we get

$$\Delta c_t = a\Delta y_{t-1} + e_t, \tag{1.22}$$

where $a = 0$ if the permanent income theory holds. Hall's results for the USA show that the null hypothesis cannot be rejected for several past aggregate variables, including income. However, some lagged variables (such as a stock index) are significant when added to the Euler equation, casting some doubt on the validity of the model's basic version.

Since Hall's contribution, the empirical literature has further investigated the dynamic implications of the theory, focusing mainly on two empirical regularities apparently at variance with the model: the consumption's *excess sensitivity* to current income changes, and its *excess smoothness* to income innovations. The remainder of this section illustrates these problems and shows how they are related.

1.2.1. EXCESS SENSITIVITY OF CONSUMPTION TO CURRENT INCOME

A different test of the permanent income model has been originally proposed by M. Flavin (1981). Flavin's test is based on (1.15) and an additional equation for the stochastic process for income y_t. Consider the following stochastic process for income (AR(1) in first differences):

$$\Delta y_t = \mu + \lambda \Delta y_{t-1} + \varepsilon_t, \qquad (1.23)$$

where ε_t is the change in current income, Δy_t, that is unforecastable using past income realizations. According to the model, the change in consumption between $t - 1$ and t is due to the revision of expectations of future incomes caused by ε_t. Letting θ denote the intensity of this effect, the behavior of consumption is then

$$\Delta c_t = \theta \varepsilon_t. \qquad (1.24)$$

Consumption is *excessively sensitive* to current income if c_t reacts to changes of y_t by more than is justified by the change in permanent income, measured by $\theta \varepsilon_t$.

Empirically, the Excess Sensitivity Hypothesis is formalized by augmenting (1.24) with the change in current income,

$$\Delta c_t = \beta \Delta y_t + \theta \varepsilon_t + v_t, \qquad (1.25)$$

where β (if positive) measures the overreaction of consumption to a change in current income, and v_t captures the effect on consumption of information about permanent income, available to agents at t but unrelated to current income changes.

According to the permanent income model, an increase in current income causes a change in consumption only by the amount warranted by the revision of permanent income. Only *innovations* (that is, unpredictable changes) in income cause consumption changes: the term $\theta \varepsilon_t$ in (1.25) captures precisely this effect. An estimated value for β greater than zero is then interpreted as signaling an overreaction of consumption to *anticipated* changes in income.

The test on β in (1.25) is equivalent to Hall's orthogonality test in (1.22). In fact, substituting the stochastic process for income (1.23) into (1.25), we get

$$\Delta c_t = \beta \mu + \beta \lambda \, \Delta y_{t-1} + (\theta + \beta) \varepsilon_t + v_t. \qquad (1.26)$$

From this expression for the consumption change, we note that the hypothesis $\beta = 0$ in (1.25) implies that $\alpha = 0$ in (1.22): if consumption is excessively sensitive to income, then the orthogonality property of the error term in the equation for Δc_t does not hold. Equation (1.26) highlights a potential difficulty with the orthogonality test. Indeed, Δc_t may be found to be uncorrelated with Δy_{t-1} if the latter does not forecast future income changes. In this case $\lambda = 0$ and the orthogonality test fails to reject the theory, even though consumption is excessively sensitive to predictable changes in income. Thus, differently from Hall's test, the approach of Flavin provides an estimate of the excess sensitivity of consumption, measured by β, which is around 0.36 on US quarterly data over the 1949–79 period.[7]

Among the potential explanations for the excess sensitivity of consumption, a strand of the empirical literature focused on the existence of *liquidity constraints*, which limit the consumer's borrowing capability, thus preventing the realization of the optimal consumption plan. With binding liquidity constraints, an increase in income, though perfectly anticipated, affects consumption only when it actually occurs.[8] A different rationale for excess sensitivity, based on the precautionary saving motive, will be analyzed in Section 1.3.[9]

1.2.2. RELATIVE VARIABILITY OF INCOME AND CONSUMPTION

One of the most appealing features of the permanent income theory, since the original formulation due to M. Friedman, is a potential explanation of why consumption typically is *less volatile* than current income: even in simple textbook Keynesian models, a marginal propensity to consume $c < 1$ in aggregate consumption functions of the form $C = \bar{c} + cY$ is crucial in obtaining the basic concept of multiplier of autonomous expenditure. By relating consumption not to current but to permanent, presumably less volatile, income, the limited reaction of consumption to changes in current income is theoretically motivated. The model developed thus far, adopting the framework of intertemporal optimization under rational expectations, derived the implications of this original intuition, and formalized the relationship between current income, consumption, and saving. (We shall discuss in the next chapter formalizations of simple textbook insights regarding investment dynamics: investment, like changes in consumption, is largely driven by revision of expectations regarding future variables.)

In particular, according to theory, the agent chooses current consumption on the basis of all available information on future incomes and changes optimal consumption over time only in response to unanticipated changes (innovations) in current income, causing revisions in permanent income.

---

[7] However, Flavin's test cannot provide an estimate of the change in permanent income resulting from a current income innovation θ, if ε and v in (1.26) have a non-zero covariance. Using aggregate data, any change in consumption due to v_t is also reflected in innovations in current income ε_t, since consumption is a component of aggregate income. Thus, the covariance between ε and v tends to be positive.

[8] Applying instrumental variables techniques to (1.25), Campbell and Mankiw (1989, 1991) directly interpret the estimated β as the fraction of liquidity-constrained consumers, who simply spend their current income.

[9] While we do not focus in this chapter on aggregate equilibrium considerations, it is worth mentioning that binding liquidity constraints and precautionary savings both tend to increase the aggregate saving rate: see Aiyagari (1994), Jappelli and Pagano (1994).

Therefore, on the empirical level, it is important to analyze the relationship between current income innovations and changes in permanent income, taking into account the degree of persistence over time of such innovations.

The empirical research on the properties of the stochastic process generating income has shown that income y is *non-stationary*: an innovation at time t does not cause a temporary deviation of income from trend, but has permanent effects on the level of y, which does not display any tendency to revert to a deterministic trend. (For example, in the USA the estimated long-run change in income is around 1.6 times the original income innovation.[10]) The implication of this result is that consumption, being determined by permanent income, should be *more* volatile than current income.

To clarify this point, consider again the following process for income:

$$\Delta y_{t+1} = \mu + \lambda \Delta y_t + \varepsilon_{t+1}, \tag{1.27}$$

where μ is a constant, $0 < \lambda < 1$, and $E_t \varepsilon_{t+1} = 0$. The income *change* between t and $t+1$ follows a stationary autoregressive process; the income *level* is permanently affected by innovations ε.[11] To obtain the effect on permanent income and consumption of an innovation ε_{t+1} when income is governed by (1.27), we can apply the following property of ARMA stochastic processes, which holds whether or not income is stationary (Deaton, 1992). For a given stochastic process for y of the form

$$a(L)y_t = \mu + b(L)\varepsilon_t,$$

where $a(L) = a_0 + a_1 L + a_2 L^2 + \dots$ and $b(L) = b_0 + b_1 L + b_2 L^2 + \dots$ are two polynomials in the lag operator L (such that, for a generic variable x, we have $L^i x_t = x_{t-i}$), we derive the following expression for the variance of the change in permanent income (and consequently in consumption):[12]

$$\frac{r}{1+r} \sum_{i=0}^{\infty} \left(\frac{1}{1+r}\right)^i (E_{t+1} - E_t)y_{t+1+i} = \frac{r}{1+r} \frac{\sum_{i=0}^{\infty} \left(\frac{1}{1+r}\right)^i b_i}{\sum_{i=0}^{\infty} \left(\frac{1}{1+r}\right)^i a_i} \varepsilon_{t+1}. \tag{1.28}$$

In the case of (1.27), we can write

$$y_t = \mu + (1+\lambda)y_{t-1} - \lambda y_{t-2} + \varepsilon_t;$$

---

[10] The feature of non-stationarity of income (in the USA and in other countries as well) is still an open issue. Indeed, some authors argue that, given the low power of the statistical tests used to assess the non-stationarity of macroeconomic time series, it is impossible to distinguish between non-stationarity and the existence of a deterministic time trend on the basis of available data.

[11] A stochastic process of this form, with $\lambda = 0.44$, is a fairly good statistical description of the (aggregate) income dynamics for the USA, as shown by Campbell and Deaton (1989) using quarterly data for the period 1953–84.

[12] The following formula can also be obtained by computing the revisions in expectations of future incomes, as has already been done in Section 1.1.

hence we have $a(L) = 1 - (1 + \lambda)L + \lambda L^2$ and $b(L) = 1$. Applying the general formula (1.28) to this process, we get

$$\Delta c_{t+1} = \frac{r}{1+r} \left(\frac{r(1+r-\lambda)}{(1+r)^2} \right)^{-1} \varepsilon_{t+1} = \frac{1+r}{1+r-\lambda} \varepsilon_{t+1}.$$

This is formally quite similar to (1.20), but, because the income process is stationary only in first differences, features a different numerator on the right-hand side: the relation between the innovation ε_{t+1} and the change in consumption Δc_{t+1} is linear, but the slope is greater than 1 if $\lambda > 0$ (that is if, as is realistic in business-cycle fluctuations, above-average growth tends to be followed by still fast—if mean-reverting—growth in the following period). The same coefficient measures the ratio of the variability of consumption (given by the standard deviation of the consumption change) and the variability of income (given by the standard deviation of the innovation in the income process):

$$\frac{\sigma_{\Delta c}}{\sigma_\varepsilon} = \frac{1+r}{1+r-\lambda}.$$

For example, $\lambda = 0.44$ and a (quarterly) interest rate of 1% yield a coefficient of 1.77. The implied variability of the (quarterly) change of consumption would be 1.77 times that of the income innovation. For non-durable goods and services, Campbell and Deaton (1989) estimate a coefficient of only 0.64. Then, the response of consumption to income innovations seems to be at variance with the implications of the permanent income theory: the reaction of consumption to unanticipated changes in income is too smooth (this phenomenon is called *excess smoothness*). This conclusion could be questioned by considering that the estimate of the income innovation, ε, depends on the variables included in the econometric specification of the income process. In particular, if a *univariate* process like (1.27) is specified, the information set used to form expectations of future incomes and to derive innovations is limited to past income values only. If agents form their expectations using additional information, not available to the econometrician, then the "true" income innovation, which is perceived by agents and determines changes in consumption, will display a smaller variance than the innovation estimated by the econometrician on the basis of a limited information set. Thus, the observed *smoothness* of consumption could be made consistent with theory if it were possible to measure the income innovations perceived by agents.[13]

A possible solution to this problem exploits the essential feature of the permanent income theory under rational expectations: agents choose optimal consumption (and saving) using all available information on future incomes.

---

[13] Relevant research includes Pischke (1995) and Jappelli and Pistaferri (2000).

It is the very behavior of consumers that reveals their available information. If such behavior is observed by the econometrician, it is possible to use it to construct expected future incomes and the associated innovations. This approach has been applied to saving, which, as shown by (1.17), depends on expected future changes in income.

To formalize this point, we start from the definition of saving and make explicit the information set used by agents at time t to forecast future incomes, I_t:

$$s_t = - \sum_{i=1}^{\infty} \left(\frac{1}{1+r} \right)^i E(\Delta y_{t+i} \mid I_t).$$ (1.29)

The information set available to the econometrician is Ω_t, with $\Omega_t \subseteq I_t$ (agents know everything the econometrician knows but the reverse is not necessarily true). Moreover, we assume that saving is observed by the econometrician: $s_t \in \Omega_t$. Then, taking the expected value of both sides of (1.29) with respect to the information set Ω_t and applying the "law of iterated expectations," we get

$$E(s_t \mid \Omega_t) = - \sum_{i=1}^{\infty} \left(\frac{1}{1+r} \right)^i E\left[E(\Delta y_{t+i} \mid I_t) \mid \Omega_t \right]$$

$$\Longrightarrow s_t = - \sum_{i=1}^{\infty} \left(\frac{1}{1+r} \right)^i E(\Delta y_{t+i} \mid \Omega_t),$$ (1.30)

where we use the assumption that saving is included in Ω_t. According to theory, then, saving is determined by the discounted future changes in labor incomes, even if they are forecast on the basis of the smaller information set Ω_t.

Since saving choices, according to (1.29), are made on the basis of all information available to agents, it is possible to obtain predictions on future incomes that do not suffer from the limited information problem typical of the univariate models widely used in the empirical literature. Indeed, predictions can be conditioned on past saving behavior, thus using the larger information set available to agents. This is equivalent to forming predictions of income changes Δy_t by using not only past changes, Δy_{t-1}, but also past saving, s_{t-1}.

In principle, this extension of the forecasting model for income could reduce the magnitude of the estimated innovation variance σ_ε. In practice, as is shown in some detail below, the evidence of excess smoothness of consumption remains unchanged after this extension.

1.2.3. JOINT DYNAMICS OF INCOME AND SAVING

Studying the implications derived from theory on the joint behavior of income and saving usefully highlights the connection between the two empirical puzzles mentioned above (*excess sensitivity* and *excess smoothness*). Even though the two phenomena focus on the response of consumption to income changes of a different nature (consumption is excessively sensitive to *anticipated* income changes, and excessively smooth in response to *unanticipated* income variations), it is possible to show that the excess smoothness and excess sensitivity phenomena are different manifestations of the same empirical anomaly.

To outline the connection between the two, we proceed in three successive steps.

1. First, we assume a stochastic process *jointly* governing the evolution of income and saving over time and derive its implications for equations like (1.22), used to test the orthogonality property of the consumption change with respect to lagged variables. (Recall that the violation of the orthogonality condition entails excess sensitivity of consumption to predicted income changes.)

2. Then, given the expectations of future incomes based on the assumed stochastic process, we derive the behavior of saving implied by theory according to (1.17), and obtain the restrictions that must be imposed on the estimated parameters of the process for income and saving to test the validity of the theory.

3. Finally, we compare such restrictions with those required for the orthogonality property of the consumption change to hold.

We start with a simplified representation of the bivariate stochastic process governing income—expressed in first differences as in (1.27) to allow for non-stationarity, and imposing $\mu = 0$ for simplicity—and saving:

$$\Delta y_t = a_{11} \Delta y_{t-1} + a_{12} s_{t-1} + u_{1t}, \tag{1.31}$$

$$s_t = a_{21} \Delta y_{t-1} + a_{22} s_{t-1} + u_{2t}. \tag{1.32}$$

With s_{t-1} in the model, it is now possible to generate forecasts on future income changes by exploiting the additional informational value of past saving. Inserting the definition of saving ($s_t = r A_t + y_t - c_t$) into the accumulation constraint (1.2), we get

$$A_{t+1} = A_t + (r A_t + y_t - c_t) \Rightarrow s_t = A_{t+1} - A_t. \tag{1.33}$$

Obviously, the flow of saving is the change of the stock of financial assets from one period to the next, and this makes it possible to write the change in consumption by taking the first difference of the definition of saving used above:

$$\Delta c_t = \Delta y_t + r \Delta A_t - \Delta s_t$$
$$= \Delta y_t + r s_{t-1} - s_t + s_{t-1}$$
$$= \Delta y_t + (1 + r)s_{t-1} - s_t. \qquad (1.34)$$

Finally, substituting for Δy_t and s_t from (1.31) and (1.32), we obtain the following expression for the consumption change Δc_t:

$$\Delta c_t = \gamma_1 \Delta y_{t-1} + \gamma_2 s_{t-1} + v_t, \qquad (1.35)$$

where

$$\gamma_1 = a_{11} - a_{21}, \qquad \gamma_2 = a_{12} - a_{22} + (1 + r), \qquad v_t = u_{1t} - u_{2t}.$$

The implication of the permanent income theory is that the consumption change between $t - 1$ and t cannot be predicted on the basis of information available at time $t - 1$. This entails the *orthogonality* restriction $\gamma_1 = \gamma_2 = 0$, which in turn imposes the following restrictions on the coefficients of the joint process generating income and savings:

$$a_{11} = a_{21}, \qquad a_{22} = a_{12} + (1 + r). \qquad (1.36)$$

If these restrictions are fulfilled, the consumption change $\Delta c_t = u_{1t} - u_{2t}$ is unpredictable using lagged variables: the change in consumption (and in permanent income) is equal to the current income innovation (u_{1t}) less the innovation in saving (u_{2t}), which reflects the revision in expectations of future incomes calculated by the agent on the basis of all available information. Now, from the definition of savings (1.17), using the expectations of future income changes derived from the model in (1.31) and (1.32), it is possible to obtain the restrictions imposed by the theory on the stochastic process governing income and savings. Letting

$$\mathbf{x}_t \equiv \begin{pmatrix} \Delta y_t \\ s_t \end{pmatrix}, \qquad \mathbf{A} \equiv \begin{pmatrix} a_{11} & a_{12} \\ a_{21} & a_{22} \end{pmatrix}, \qquad \mathbf{u}_t = \begin{pmatrix} u_{1t} \\ u_{2t} \end{pmatrix},$$

we can rewrite the process in (1.31)–(1.32) as

$$\mathbf{x}_t = \mathbf{A}\mathbf{x}_{t-1} + \mathbf{u}_t. \qquad (1.37)$$

From (1.37), the expected values of Δy_{t+i} can be easily derived:

$$E_t \mathbf{x}_{t+i} = \mathbf{A}^i \mathbf{x}_t, \qquad i \geq 0;$$

hence (using a matrix algebra version of the geometric series formula)

$$-\sum_{i=1}^{\infty}\left(\frac{1}{1+r}\right)^i E_t \mathbf{x}_{t+i} = -\sum_{i=1}^{\infty}\left(\frac{1}{1+r}\right)^i \mathbf{A}^i \mathbf{x}_t$$

$$= -\left[\left(\mathbf{I} - \frac{1}{1+r}\mathbf{A}\right)^{-1} - \mathbf{I}\right]\mathbf{x}_t. \qquad (1.38)$$

The element of vector x we are interested in (saving s) can be "extracted" by applying to $\mathbf{x}$ a vector $e_2 \equiv (0 \quad 1)'$, which simply selects the second element of x. Similarly, to apply the definition in (1.17), we have to select the first element of the vector in (1.38) using $e_1 \equiv (1 \quad 0)'$. Then we get

$$\mathbf{e}_2' \mathbf{x}_t = -\mathbf{e}_1'\left[\left(\mathbf{I} - \frac{1}{1+r}\mathbf{A}\right)^{-1} - \mathbf{I}\right]\mathbf{x}_t \Rightarrow \mathbf{e}_2' = -\mathbf{e}_1'\left[\left(\mathbf{I} - \frac{1}{1+r}\mathbf{A}\right)^{-1} - \mathbf{I}\right],$$

yielding the relation

$$\mathbf{e}_2' = (\mathbf{e}_2' - \mathbf{e}_1')\frac{1}{1+r}\mathbf{A}. \qquad (1.39)$$

Therefore, the restrictions imposed by theory on the coefficients of matrix **A** are

$$a_{11} = a_{21}, \qquad a_{22} = a_{12} + (1+r). \qquad (1.40)$$

These restrictions on the joint process for income and saving, which rule out the excess smoothness phenomenon, are exactly the same as those—in equation (1.35)—that must be fulfilled for the orthogonality property to hold, and therefore also ensure elimination of excess sensitivity.[14] Summarizing, the phenomena of excess sensitivity and excess smoothness, though related to income changes of a different nature (anticipated and unanticipated, respectively), signal the same deviation from the implications of the permanent income theory. If agents excessively react to expected income changes, they must necessarily display a lack of reaction to unanticipated income changes. In fact, any variation in income is made up of a predicted component and a (unpredictable) innovation: if the consumer has an "excessive" reaction to the former component, the intertemporal budget constraint forces him to react in an "excessively smooth" way to the latter component of the change in current income.

---

[14] The coincidence of the restrictions necessary for orthogonality and for ruling out excess smoothness is obtained only in the special case of a first-order stochastic process for income and saving. In the more general case analyzed by Flavin (1993), the orthogonality restrictions are nested in those necessary to rule out excess smoothness. Then, in general, orthogonality conditions analogous to (1.36) imply—but are not implied by—those analogous to (1.40).

1.3. **The Role of Precautionary Saving**

Recent developments in consumption theory have been aimed mainly at solving the empirical problems illustrated above. The basic model has been extended in various directions, by relaxing some of its most restrictive assumptions. On the one hand, as already mentioned, liquidity constraints can prevent the consumer from borrowing as much as required by the optimal consumption plan. On the other hand, it has been recognized that in the basic model saving is motivated only by a rate of interest higher than the rate-of-time preference and/or by the need for redistributing income over time, when current incomes are unbalanced between periods. Additional motivations for saving may be relevant in practice, and may contribute to the explanation of, for example, the apparently insufficient decumulation of wealth by older generations, the high correlation between income and consumption of younger agents, and the excess smoothness of consumption in reaction to income innovations. This section deals with the latter strand of literature, studying the role of a precautionary saving motive in shaping consumers' behavior.

First, we will spell out the microeconomic foundations of precautionary saving, pointing out which assumption of the basic model must be relaxed to allow for a precautionary saving motive. Then, under the new assumptions, we shall derive the dynamics of consumption and the consumption function, and compare them with the implications of the basic version of the permanent income model previously illustrated.

1.3.1. MICROECONOMIC FOUNDATIONS

Thus far, with a quadratic utility function, *uncertainty* has played only a limited role. Indeed, only the expected value of income y affects consumption choices—other characteristics of the income distribution (e.g. the variance) do not play any role.

With quadratic utility, marginal utility is linear and the expected value of the marginal utility of consumption coincides with the marginal utility of expected consumption. An increase in uncertainty on future consumption, with an unchanged expected value, does not cause any reaction by the consumer.[15] As we shall see, if marginal utility is a *convex* function of consumption, then the consumer displays a *prudent* behavior, and reacts to an increase in uncertainty by saving more: such saving is called *precautionary*, since it depends on the uncertainty about future consumption.

---

[15] In the basic version of the model, the consumer is interested only in the *certainty equivalent* value of future consumption.

Convexity of the marginal utility function $u'(c)$ implies a positive sign of its second derivative, corresponding to the third derivative of the utility function: $u'''(c) > 0$. A precautionary saving motive, which does not arise with quadratic utility ($u'''(c) = 0$), requires the use of different functional forms, such as exponential utility.[16] With risk aversion ($u''(c) < 0$) and convex marginal utility ($u'''(c) > 0$), under uncertainty about future incomes (and consumption), unfavorable events determine a loss of utility greater than the gain in utility obtained from favorable events of the same magnitude. The consumer fears low-income states and adopts a prudent behavior, saving in the current period in order to increase expected future consumption.

An example can make this point clearer. Consider a consumer living for two periods, t and $t + 1$, with no financial wealth at the beginning of period t. In the first period labor income is $\bar{y}$ with certainty, whereas in the second period it can take one of two values—y_{t+1}^A or $y_{t+1}^B < y_{t+1}^A$—with equal probability. To focus on the precautionary motive, we rule out any other motivation for saving by assuming that $E_t(y_{t+1}) = \bar{y}$ and $r = \rho = 0$. In equilibrium the following relation holds: $E_t u'(c_{t+1}) = u'(c_t)$. At time t the consumer chooses saving s_t (equal to $\bar{y} - c_t$) and his consumption at time $t + 1$ will be equal to saving s_t plus realized income. Considering actual realizations of income, we can write the budget constraint as

$$\left.\begin{array}{c} c_{t+1}^A \\ c_{t+1}^B \end{array}\right\} = \bar{y} - c_t + \left\{\begin{array}{c} y_{t+1}^A \\ y_{t+1}^B \end{array}\right.$$

$$= s_t + \left\{\begin{array}{c} y_{t+1}^A \\ y_{t+1}^B \end{array}\right..$$

Using the definition of saving, $s_t \equiv \bar{y} - c_t$, the Euler equation becomes

$$E_t(u'(y_{t+1} + s_t)) = u'(\bar{y} - s_t). \tag{1.41}$$

Now, let us see how the consumer chooses saving in two different cases, beginning with that of *linear* marginal utility ($u'''(c) = 0$). In this case we have $E_t u'(\cdot) = u'(E_t(\cdot))$. Recalling that $E_t(y_{t+1}) = \bar{y}$, condition (1.41) becomes

$$u'(\bar{y} + s_t) = u'(\bar{y} - s_t), \tag{1.42}$$

and is fulfilled by $s_t = 0$. The consumer does not save in the first period, and his second-period consumption will coincide with current income. The uncertainty on income in $t + 1$ reduces overall utility but does not induce the consumer to modify his choice: there is no precautionary saving. On the contrary, if, as in Figure 1.1, marginal utility is *convex* ($u'''(c) > 0$), then,

---

[16] A quadratic utility function has another undesirable property: it displays increasing absolute risk aversion. Formally, $-u''(c)/u'(c)$ is an increasing function of c. This implies that, to avoid uncertainty, the agent is willing to pay more the higher is his wealth, which is not plausible.

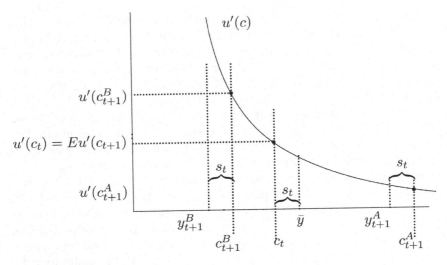

Figure 1.1. Precautionary savings

from "Jensen's inequality," $E_t u'(c_{t+1}) > u'(E_t(c_{t+1}))$.[17] If the consumer were to choose zero saving, as was optimal under a linear marginal utility, we would have (for $s_t = 0$, and using Jensen's inequality)

$$E_t(u'(c_{t+1})) > u'(c_t). \qquad (1.43)$$

The optimality condition would be violated, and expected utility would not be maximized. To re-establish equality in the problem's first-order condition, marginal utility must decrease in $t + 1$ and increase in t: as shown in the figure, this may be achieved by shifting an amount of resources s_t from the first to the second period. As the consumer saves more, decreasing current consumption c_t and increasing c_{t+1} in both states (good and bad), marginal utility in t increases and expected marginal utility in $t + 1$ decreases, until the optimality condition is satisfied. Thus, with convex marginal utility, uncertainty on future incomes (and consumption levels) entails a positive amount of saving in the first period and determines a consumption path trending upwards over time ($E_t c_{t+1} > c_t$), even though the interest rate is equal to the utility discount rate. Formally, the relation between uncertainty and the upward consumption path depends on the degree of consumer's *prudence*, which we now define rigorously. Approximating (by means of a second-order Taylor expansion) around c_t the left-hand side of the Euler equation $E_t u'(c_{t+1}) = u'(c_t)$, we get

$$E_t(c_{t+1} - c_t) = -\frac{1}{2}\frac{u'''(c_t)}{u''(c_t)} E_t(c_{t+1} - c_t)^2 \equiv \frac{1}{2}a E_t(c_{t+1} - c_t)^2, \qquad (1.44)$$

---

[17] Jensen's inequality states that, given a strictly convex function $f(x)$ of a random variable x, then $E(f(x)) > f(Ex)$.

where $a \equiv -u'''(c)/u''(c)$ is the coefficient of *absolute prudence*. Greater uncertainty, increasing $E_t((c_{t+1} - c_t)^2)$, induces a larger increase in consumption between t and $t + 1$. The definition of the coefficient measuring prudence is formally similar to that of risk-aversion coefficients: however, the latter is related to the curvature of the utility function, whereas prudence is determined by the curvature of marginal utility. It is also possible to define the coefficient of *relative prudence*, $-u'''(c)c/u''(c)$. Dividing both sides of (1.44) by c_t, we get

$$E_t\left(\frac{c_{t+1} - c_t}{c_t}\right) = -\frac{1}{2}\frac{u'''(c_t) \cdot c_t}{u''(c_t)}E_t\left(\frac{c_{t+1} - c_t}{c_t}\right)^2 = \frac{1}{2}pE_t\left(\frac{c_{t+1} - c_t}{c_t}\right)^2,$$

where $p \equiv -(u'''(c) \cdot c/u''(c))$ is the coefficient of relative prudence. Readers can check that this is constant for a CRRA function, and determine its relationship to the coefficient of relative risk aversion.

Exercise 3 *Suppose that a consumer maximizes*

$$\log(c_1) + E[\log(c_2)]$$

under the constraint $c_1 + c_2 = w_1 + w_2$ (i.e., the discount rate of period 2 utility and the rate of return on saving $w_1 - c_1$ are both zero). When c_1 is chosen, there is uncertainty about w_2: the consumer will earn $w_2 = x$ or $w_2 = y$ with equal probability. What is the optimal level of c_1?

1.3.2. IMPLICATIONS FOR THE CONSUMPTION FUNCTION

We now solve the consumer's optimization problem in the case of a non-quadratic utility function, which motivates precautionary saving. The setup of the problem is still given by (1.1) and (1.2), but the utility function in each period is now of the exponential form:

$$u(c_{t+i}) = -\frac{1}{\gamma}e^{-\gamma c_{t+i}}, \tag{1.45}$$

where $\gamma > 0$ is the coefficient of absolute prudence (and also, for such a *constant absolute risk aversion*—CARA—utility function, the coefficient of absolute risk aversion).[18] Assume that labor income follows the AR(1) stochastic process:

$$y_{t+i} = \lambda y_{t+i-1} + (1 - \lambda)\bar{y} + \varepsilon_{t+i}, \tag{1.46}$$

---

[18] Since for the exponential utility function $u'(0) = 1 < \infty$, in order to rule out negative values for consumption it would be necessary to explicitly impose a non-negativity constraint; however, a closed-form solution to the problem would not be available if that constraint were binding.

where ε_{t+i} are independent and identically distributed (i.i.d.) random variables, with zero mean and variance σ_ε^2. We keep the simplifying hypothesis that $r = \rho$.

The problem's first-order condition, for $i = 0$, is given by

$$e^{-\gamma c_t} = E_t(e^{-\gamma c_{t+1}}). \tag{1.47}$$

To proceed, we guess that the stochastic process followed by consumption over time has the form

$$c_{t+i} = c_{t+i-1} + K_{t+i-1} + v_{t+i}, \tag{1.48}$$

where K_{t+i-1} is a deterministic term (which may however depend on the period's timing within the individual's life cycle) and v_{t+i} is the innovation in consumption ($E_{t+i-1}v_{t+i} = 0$). Both the sequence of K_t terms and the features of the distribution of v must be determined so as to satisfy the Euler equation (1.47) and the intertemporal budget constraint (1.4). Using (1.48), from the Euler equation, after eliminating the terms in c_t, we get

$$e^{\gamma K_t} = E_t(e^{-\gamma v_{t+1}}) \Rightarrow K_t = \frac{1}{\gamma} \log E_t(e^{-\gamma v_{t+1}}). \tag{1.49}$$

The value of K depends on the characteristics of the distribution of v, yet to be determined. Using the fact that $\log E(\cdot) > E(\log(\cdot))$ by Jensen's inequality and the property of consumption innovations $E_t v_{t+1} = 0$, we can however already write

$$K_t = \frac{1}{\gamma} \log E_t(e^{-\gamma v_{t+1}}) > \frac{1}{\gamma} E_t(\log(e^{-\gamma v_{t+1}})) = \frac{1}{\gamma} E_t(-\gamma v_{t+1}) = 0 \Rightarrow K_t > 0.$$
$$\tag{1.50}$$

The first result is that the consumption path is *increasing* over time: the consumption change between t and $t + 1$ is expected to equal $K_t > 0$, whereas with quadratic utility (maintaining the assumption $\rho = r$) consumption changes would have zero mean. Moreover, from (1.49) we interpret $-K_t$ as the "certainty equivalent" of the consumption innovation v_{t+1}, defined as the (negative) certain change of consumption from t to $t + 1$ that the consumer would accept to avoid the uncertainty on the marginal utility of consumption in $t + 1$.

To obtain the consumption function (and then to determine the effect of the precautionary saving motive on the *level* of consumption) we use the intertemporal budget constraint (1.10) computing the expected values $E_t c_{t+i}$ from (1.48). Knowing that $E_t v_{t+i} = 0$, we have

$$\frac{1}{1+r} \sum_{i=0}^{\infty} \left(\frac{1}{1+r}\right)^i c_t + \frac{1}{1+r} \sum_{i=1}^{\infty} \left(\frac{1}{1+r}\right)^i \sum_{j=1}^{i} K_{t+j-1} = A_t + H_t. \tag{1.51}$$

Solving for c_t, we finally get

$$c_t = r(A_t + H_t) - \frac{r}{1+r} \sum_{i=1}^{\infty} \left(\frac{1}{1+r}\right)^i \sum_{j=1}^{i} K_{t+j-1}. \qquad (1.52)$$

The level of consumption is made up of a component analogous to the definition of permanent income, $r(A_t + H_t)$, less a term that depends on the constants K and captures the effect of the precautionary saving motive: since the individual behaves prudently, her consumption increases over time, but (consistently with the intertemporal budget constraint) the level of consumption in t is lower than in the case of quadratic utility.

As the final step of the solution, we derive the form of the stochastic term v_{t+i}, and its relationship to the income innovation ε_{t+i}. To this end we use the budget constraint (1.4), where c_{t+i} and y_{t+i} are realizations and not expected values, and write future realized incomes as the sum of the expected value at time t and the associated "surprise": $y_{t+i} = E_t y_{t+i} + (y_{t+i} - E_t y_{t+i})$. The budget constraint becomes

$$\frac{1}{1+r} \sum_{i=0}^{\infty} \left(\frac{1}{1+r}\right)^i c_{t+i} = A_t + H_t + \frac{1}{1+r} \sum_{i=1}^{\infty} \left(\frac{1}{1+r}\right)^i (y_{t+i} - E_t y_{t+i}).$$

Substituting for c_{t+i} (with $i > 0$) from (1.48) and for c_t from the consumption function (1.52), we get

$$\sum_{i=1}^{\infty} \left(\frac{1}{1+r}\right)^i \sum_{j=1}^{i} v_{t+j} = \sum_{i=1}^{\infty} \left(\frac{1}{1+r}\right)^i (y_{t+i} - E_t y_{t+i}).$$

Given the stochastic process for income (1.46) we can compute the income "surprises,"

$$y_{t+i} - E_t y_{t+i} = \sum_{k=0}^{i-1} \lambda^k \varepsilon_{t+i-k},$$

and insert them into the previous equation, to obtain

$$\sum_{i=1}^{\infty} \left(\frac{1}{1+r}\right)^i \sum_{j=1}^{i} v_{t+j} = \sum_{i=1}^{\infty} \left(\frac{1}{1+r}\right)^i \sum_{k=0}^{i-1} \lambda^k \varepsilon_{t+i-k}. \qquad (1.53)$$

Developing the summations, collecting terms containing v and ε with the same time subscript, and using the fact that v and ε are serially uncorrelated processes, we find the following condition that allows us to determine the form of v_{t+i}:

$$\sum_{i=1}^{\infty} \left(\frac{1}{1+r}\right)^i (v_{t+h} - \lambda^{i-1} \varepsilon_{t+h}) = 0, \qquad \forall h \geq 1. \qquad (1.54)$$

Solving the summation in (1.54), we arrive at the final form of the stochastic terms of the Euler equation guessed in (1.48): at all times $t + h$,

$$v_{t+h} = \frac{r}{1 + r - \lambda} \varepsilon_{t+h}. \tag{1.55}$$

As in the quadratic utility case (1.20), the innovation in the Euler equation can be interpreted as the *annuity value* of the revision of the consumer's human wealth arising from an innovation in income for the assumed stochastic process.

Expression (1.55) for v_{t+1} can be substituted in the equation for K_t (1.49). The fact that the innovations ε are i.i.d. random variables implies that K_t does not change over time: $K_{t+i-1} = K$ in (1.48). The evolution of consumption over time is then given by

$$c_{t+1} = c_t + K + \frac{r}{1 + r - \lambda} \varepsilon_{t+1}. \tag{1.56}$$

Substituting the constant value for K into (1.52), we get a closed-form consumption function:[19]

$$c_t = r(A_t + H_t) - \frac{r}{1 + r} \sum_{i=1}^{\infty} \left(\frac{1}{1 + r} \right)^i i \cdot K$$

$$= r(A_t + H_t) - \frac{r}{1 + r} K \frac{1 + r}{r^2}$$

$$= r(A_t + H_t) - \frac{K}{r}.$$

Finally, to determine the constant K and its relationship with the uncertainty about future labor incomes, some assumptions on the distribution of ε have to be made. If ε is *normally* distributed, $\varepsilon \sim N(0, \sigma_\varepsilon^2)$, then, letting

---

[19] To verify this result, note that

$$\sum_{i=1}^{\infty} a^i i = \sum_{i=1}^{\infty} a^i + \sum_{i=2}^{\infty} a^i + \sum_{i=3}^{\infty} a^i + \dots$$

$$= \sum_{i=1}^{\infty} a^i + a \sum_{i=1}^{\infty} a^i + a^2 \sum_{i=1}^{\infty} a^i + \dots$$

$$= (1 + a + a^2 + \dots) \sum_{i=1}^{\infty} a^i$$

$$= \sum_{i=0}^{\infty} a^i \left(\sum_{i=0}^{\infty} a^i - 1 \right),$$

which equals $\frac{1}{1-a} \frac{a}{1-a} = a/(1-a)^2$ as long as $a < 1$, which holds true in the relevant $a = 1/(1+r)$ case with $r > 0$.

$\theta \equiv r/(1 + r - \lambda)$, we have[20]

$$K_t = \frac{1}{\gamma} \log E_t(e^{-\gamma\theta\varepsilon_{t+1}}) = \frac{1}{\gamma} \log e^{\frac{\gamma^2\theta^2\sigma_\varepsilon^2}{2}} = \frac{\gamma\theta^2\sigma_\varepsilon^2}{2}. \qquad (1.57)$$

The dynamics of consumption over time and its level in each period are then given by

$$c_{t+1} = c_t + \frac{\gamma\theta^2\sigma_\varepsilon^2}{2} + \theta\varepsilon_{t+1},$$

$$c_t = r(A_t + H_t) - \frac{1}{r}\frac{\gamma\theta^2\sigma_\varepsilon^2}{2}.$$

The innovation variance σ_ε^2 has a positive effect on the change in consumption between t and $t + 1$, and a negative effect on the level of consumption in t. Increases in the uncertainty about future incomes (captured by the variance of the innovations in the process for y) generate larger changes of consumption from one period to the next and drops in the level of current consumption. Thus, allowing for a precautionary saving motive can rationalize the slow decumulation of wealth by old individuals, and can explain why (increasing) income and consumption paths are closer to each other than would be implied by the basic permanent income model. Moreover, if positive innovations in current income are associated with higher uncertainty about future income, the *excess smoothness* phenomenon may be explained, since greater uncertainty induces consumers to save more and may then reduce the response of consumption to income innovations.

Exercise 4 *Assuming $u(c) = c^{1-\gamma}/(1 - \gamma)$ and $r \neq \rho$, derive the first-order condition of the consumer's problem under uncertainty. If c_{t+1}/c_t has a lognormal distribution (i.e. if the rate of change of consumption $\Delta \log c_{t+1}$ is normally distributed with constant variance σ^2), write the Euler equation in terms of the expected rate of change of consumption $E_t(\Delta \log c_{t+1})$. How does the variance σ^2 affect the behavior of the rate of change of c over time? (Hint: make use of the fact mentioned in note 20, recall that $c_{t+1}/c_t = e^{\Delta \log c_{t+1}}$, and express the Euler equations in logarithmic terms.)*

1.4. **Consumption and Financial Returns**

In the model studied so far, the consumer uses a single financial asset with a certain return to implement the optimal consumption path. A precautionary saving motive has been introduced by abandoning the hypothesis of quadratic

---

[20] To derive (1.57) we used the following statistical fact: if $x \sim N(E(x), \sigma^2)$, then e^x is a *lognormal* random variable with mean $E(e^x) = e^{E(x)+\sigma^2/2}$.

utility. However, there is still no choice on the allocation of saving. If we assume that the consumer can invest his savings in n financial assets with uncertain returns, we generate a more complicated choice of the composition of financial wealth, which interacts with the determination of the optimal consumption path. The chosen portfolio allocation will depend on the characteristics of the consumer's utility function (in particular the degree of risk aversion) and of the distribution of asset returns. Thereby extended, the model yields testable implications on the *joint* dynamics of consumption and asset returns, and becomes the basic version of the *consumption-based capital asset pricing model* (CCAPM).

With the new hypothesis of n financial assets with uncertain returns, the consumer's budget constraint must be reformulated accordingly. The beginning-of-period stock of the jth asset, measured in units of consumption, is given by A_{t+i}^j. Therefore, total financial wealth is $A_{t+i} = \sum_{j=1}^n A_{t+i}^j \cdot r_{t+i+1}^j$ denotes the real rate of return of asset j in period $t + i$, so that $A_{t+i+1}^j = (1 + r_{t+i+1}^j) A_{t+i}^j$. This return is not known by the agent at the beginning of period $t + i$. (This explains the time subscript $t + i + 1$, whereas labor income—observed by the agent at the beginning of the period—has subscript $t + i$.) The accumulation constraint from one period to the next takes the form

$$\sum_{j=1}^n A_{t+i+1}^j = \sum_{j=1}^n (1 + r_{t+i+1}^j) A_{t+i}^j + y_{t+i} - c_{t+i}, \qquad i = 0, \dots, \infty. \quad (1.58)$$

The solution at t of the maximization problem yields the levels of consumption and of the stocks of the n assets from t to infinity. Like in the solution of the consumer's problem analyzed in Section 1.1 (but now with uncertain asset returns), we have a set of n Euler equations,

$$u'(c_t) = \frac{1}{1 + \rho} E_t \left[(1 + r_{t+1}^j) \, u'(c_{t+1}) \right] \qquad \text{for} \quad j = 1, \dots, n. \quad (1.59)$$

Since $u'(c_t)$ is not stochastic at time t, we can write the first-order conditions as

$$1 = E_t \left[(1 + r_{t+1}^j) \frac{1}{1 + \rho} \frac{u'(c_{t+1})}{u'(c_t)} \right]$$
$$\equiv E_t \left[(1 + r_{t+1}^j) \, M_{t+1} \right], \quad (1.60)$$

where M_{t+1} is the "stochastic discount factor" applied at t to consumption in the following period. Such a factor is the intertemporal marginal rate of substitution, i.e. the discounted ratio of marginal utilities of consumption in any two subsequent periods. From equation (1.60) we derive the fundamental result of the CCAPM, using the following property:

$$E_t\left[\left(1+r_{t+1}^j\right)M_{t+1}\right] = E_t(1+r_{t+1}^j)\,E_t(M_{t+1}) + \text{cov}_t(r_{t+1}^j,\,M_{t+1}). \quad (1.61)$$

Inserting (1.61) into (1.60) and rearranging terms, we get

$$E_t(1+r_{t+1}^j) = \frac{1}{E_t(M_{t+1})}\left[1 - \text{cov}_t\left(r_{t+1}^j,\,M_{t+1}\right)\right]. \quad (1.62)$$

In the case of the safe asset (with certain return r^0) considered in the previous sections,[21] (1.62) reduces to

$$1 + r_{t+1}^0 = \frac{1}{E_t(M_{t+1})}. \quad (1.63)$$

Substituting (1.63) into (1.62), we can write the expected return of each asset j in excess of the safe asset as

$$E_t(r_{t+1}^j) - r_{t+1}^0 = -(1+r_{t+1}^0)\,\text{cov}_t(r_{t+1}^j,\,M_{t+1}). \quad (1.64)$$

Equation (1.64) is the main result from the model with risky financial assets: in equilibrium, an asset j whose return has a negative covariance with the stochastic discount factor yields an expected return higher than r^0. In fact, such an asset is "risky" for the consumer, since it yields lower returns when the marginal utility of consumption is relatively high (owing to a relatively low level of consumption). The agent willingly holds the stock of this asset in equilibrium only if such risk is appropriately compensated by a "premium," given by an expected return higher than the risk-free rate r^0.

1.4.1. EMPIRICAL IMPLICATIONS OF THE CCAPM

In order to derive testable implications from the model, we consider a CRRA utility function,

$$u(c) = \frac{c^{1-\gamma} - 1}{1 - \gamma},$$

where $\gamma > 0$ is the coefficient of relative risk aversion. In this case, (1.60) becomes

$$1 = E_t\left[(1+r_{t+1}^j)\frac{1}{1+\rho}\left(\frac{c_{t+1}}{c_t}\right)^{-\gamma}\right] \qquad \text{for} \quad j = 1, \ldots, n. \quad (1.65)$$

---

[21] The following results hold also if the safe return rate r^0 is random, as long as it has zero covariance with the stochastic discount factor M.

Moreover, let us assume that the rate of growth of consumption and the rates of return of the n assets have a lognormal joint conditional distribution.[22] Taking logs of (1.65) (with the usual approximation $\log(1 + \rho) \simeq \rho$), we get

$$0 = -\rho + \log E_t \left[(1 + r_{t+1}^j) \left(\frac{c_{t+1}}{c_t} \right)^{-\gamma} \right],$$

and by the property mentioned in the preceding footnote we obtain

$$\log E_t \left[(1 + r_{t+1}^j) \left(\frac{c_{t+1}}{c_t} \right)^{-\gamma} \right] = E_t(r_{t+1}^j - \gamma \Delta \log c_{t+1}) + \frac{1}{2} \Sigma_j, \qquad (1.66)$$

where

$$\Sigma_j = E \left\{ \left[(r_{t+1}^j - \gamma \Delta \log c_{t+1}) - E_t(r_{t+1}^j - \gamma \Delta \log c_{t+1}) \right]^2 \right\}.$$

Note that the unconditional expectation $E[\cdot]$ in the definition of Σ_j may be used under the hypothesis that the innovations in the joint process for returns and the consumption growth rate have constant variance (homoskedasticity). Finally, from (1.66) we can derive the expected return on the jth asset:

$$E_t r_{t+1}^j = \gamma E_t (\Delta \log c_{t+1}) + \rho - \frac{1}{2} \Sigma_j. \qquad (1.67)$$

Several features of equation (1.67) can be noticed. In the first place, (1.67) can be immediately interpreted as the Euler equation that holds for each asset j. This interpretation can be seen more clearly if (1.67) is rewritten with the expected rate of change of consumption on the left-hand side. (See the solution to exercise 4 for the simpler case of only one safe asset.)

Second, the most important implication of (1.67) is the existence of a precise relationship between the forecastable component of (the growth rate of) consumption and asset returns. A high growth rate of consumption is associated with a high rate of return, so as to enhance saving, for a given intertemporal discount rate ρ. The degree of risk aversion γ is a measure of this effect, which is the same for all assets. At the empirical level, (1.67) suggests the following methodology to test the validity of the model.

1. A forecasting model for $\Delta \log c_{t+1}$ is specified; vector $\mathbf{x}_t$ contains only those variables, from the wider information set available to agents at time t, which are relevant for forecasting consumption growth.

---

[22] In general, when two random variables x and y have a lognormal joint conditional probability distribution, then $\log E_t(x_{t+1} y_{t+1}) = E_t(\log(x_{t+1} y_{t+1})) + \frac{1}{2} var_t(\log(x_{t+1} y_{t+1}))$, where $var_t(\log(x_{t+1} y_{t+1})) = E_t\{[\log(x_{t+1} y_{t+1}) - E_t(\log(x_{t+1} y_{t+1}))]^2\}$.

2. The following system for $\Delta \log c_{t+1}$ and r_{t+1}^j is estimated:

$$\Delta \log c_{t+1} = \delta' \mathbf{x}_t + u_{t+1},$$

$$r_{t+1}^j = \pi'_j \mathbf{x}_t + k_j + v_{t+1}^j, \qquad j = 1, \ldots, n,$$

where k_j is a constant and u and v are random errors uncorrelated with the elements of $\mathbf{x}$.

3. The following restrictions on the estimated parameters are tested:

$$\pi_j = \gamma \delta, \qquad j = 1, \ldots, n.$$

Finally, the value of Σ_j differs from one asset return to another, because of differences in the variability of return innovations and differences in the covariances between such innovations and the innovation of the consumption change. In fact, by the definition of Σ_j and the lognormality assumption, we have

$$\Sigma_j = E\left[(r_{t+1}^j - E_t(r_{t+1}^j))^2\right] + \gamma^2 E\left[(\Delta \log c_{t+1} - E_t(\Delta \log c_{t+1}))^2\right]$$

$$- 2\gamma E\left[(r_{t+1}^j - E_t(r_{t+1}^j))(\Delta \log c_{t+1} - E_t(\Delta \log c_{t+1}))\right]$$

$$\equiv \sigma_j^2 + \gamma^2 \sigma_c^2 - 2\gamma \sigma_{jc}. \tag{1.68}$$

The expected return of an asset is negatively affected by the variance of the return itself and is positively affected by its covariance with the rate of change in consumption. Thus, using (1.67) and (1.68), we obtain, for any asset j,

$$E_t r_{t+1}^j = \gamma E_t(\Delta \log c_{t+1}) + \rho - \frac{\gamma^2 \sigma_c^2}{2} - \frac{\sigma_j^2}{2} + \gamma \sigma_{jc}. \tag{1.69}$$

This equation specializes the general result given in (1.62), and it is interesting to interpret each of the terms on its right-hand side. Faster expected consumption growth implies that the rate of return should be higher than the rate of time preference ρ, to an extent that depends on intertemporal substitutability as indexed by γ. "Precaution," also indexed by γ, implies that the rate of return consistent with optimal consumption choices is lower when consumption is more volatile (a higher σ_c^2). The variance of returns has a somewhat counterintuitive negative effect on the required rate or return: however, this term appears only because of Jensen's inequality, owing to the approximation that replaced $\log E_t(1 + r_{t+1}^j)$ with $E_t r_{t+1}^j$ in equation (1.69). But it is again interesting and intuitive to see that the return's covariance with consumption growth implies a higher required rate of return. In fact, the consumer will be satisfied by a lower expected return if an asset yields more when consumption is decreasing and marginal utility is increasing; this asset provides a valuable hedge against declines in consumption to risk-averse consumers. Hence an asset with positive covariance between the own return innovations and the innovations in the rate of change of consumption is not attractive, unless (as must be the case in equilibrium) it offers a high expected return.

When there is also an asset with a safe return r^0, the model yields the following relationship between r^0 and the stochastic properties of $\Delta \log c_{t+1}$ (see again the solution of exercise 4):

$$r^0_{t+1} = \gamma \, E_t \, (\Delta \log c_{t+1}) + \rho - \frac{\gamma^2 \sigma_c^2}{2}. \tag{1.70}$$

(The return variance and covariance with consumption are both zero in this case.) Equations (1.69) and (1.70) show the determinants of the returns on different assets in equilibrium. All returns depend positively on the intertemporal rate of time preference ρ, since, for a given growth rate of consumption, a higher discount rate of future utility induces agents to borrow in order to finance current consumption: higher interest rates are then required to offset this incentive and leave the growth rate of consumption unchanged. Similarly, given ρ, a higher growth rate of consumption requires higher rates of return to offset the incentive to shift resources to the present, reducing the difference between the current and the future consumption levels. (The strength of this effect is inversely related to the intertemporal elasticity of substitution, given by $1/\gamma$ in the case of a CRRA utility function.) Finally, the uncertainty about the rate of change of consumption captured by σ_c^2 generates a precautionary saving motive, inducing the consumer to accumulate financial assets with a depressing effect on their rates of return. According to (1.69), the expected rate of return on the jth risky asset is also determined by σ_j^2 (as a result of the approximation) and by the covariance between rates of return and consumption changes. The strength of the latter effect is directly related to the degree of the consumer's risk aversion.

For any asset j, the "risk premium," i.e. the difference between the expected return $E_t \, r^j_{t+1}$ and the safe return r^0_{t+1}, is

$$E_t \, r^j_{t+1} - r^0_{t+1} = -\frac{\sigma_j^2}{2} + \gamma \sigma_{jc}. \tag{1.71}$$

An important strand of literature, originated by Mehra and Prescott (1985), has tested this implication of the model. Many studies have shown that the observed premium on stocks (amounting to around 6% per year in the USA), given the observed covariance σ_{jc}, can be explained by (1.71) only by values of γ too large to yield a plausible description of consumers' attitudes towards risk. Moreover, when the observed values of $\Delta \log c$ and σ_c^2 are plugged into (1.70), with plausible values for ρ and γ, the resulting safe rate of return is much higher than the observed rate. Only the (implausible) assumption of a negative ρ could make equation (1.70) consistent with the data.

These difficulties in the model's empirical implementation are known as the *equity premium puzzle* and the *risk-free rate puzzle*, respectively, and have motivated various extensions of the basic model. For example, a more general specification of the consumer's preferences may yield a measure of risk aversion that is independent of the intertemporal elasticity of substitution. It is therefore possible that consumers at the same time display a strong aversion toward risk, which is consistent with (1.71), and a high propensity to intertemporally substitute consumption, which solves the *risk-free rate puzzle*.

A different way of making the above model more flexible, recently put forward by Campbell and Cochrane (1999), relaxes the hypothesis of intertemporal separability of utility. The next section develops a simple version of their model.

1.4.2. EXTENSION: THE HABIT FORMATION HYPOTHESIS

As a general hypothesis on preferences, we now assume that what provides utility to the consumer in each period is not the whole level of consumption by itself, but only the amount of consumption in excess of a "habit" level. An individual's habit level changes over time, depending on the individual's own past consumption, or on the history of aggregate consumption.

In each period t, the consumer's utility function is now

$$u(c_t, x_t) = \frac{(c_t - x_t)^{1-\gamma}}{1 - \gamma} \equiv \frac{(z_t\, c_t)^{1-\gamma} - 1}{1 - \gamma},$$

where $z_t \equiv (c_t - x_t)/c_t$ is the *surplus consumption* ratio, and x_t (with $c_t > x_t$) is the level of *habit*. The evolution of x over time is here determined by aggregate (per capita) consumption and is not affected by the consumption choices of the individual consumer. Then, marginal utility is simply

$$u_c(c_t, x_t) = (c_t - x_t)^{-\gamma} \equiv (z_t\, c_t)^{-\gamma}.$$

The first-order conditions of the problem—see equation (1.65)—now have the following form:

$$1 = E_t\left[(1 + r_{t+1}^j)\frac{1}{1 + \rho}\left(\frac{z_{t+1}}{z_t}\right)^{-\gamma}\left(\frac{c_{t+1}}{c_t}\right)^{-\gamma}\right], \qquad \text{for} \quad j = 1, \ldots, n.$$

$$(1.72)$$

The evolution over time of habit and aggregate consumption, denoted by $\bar{c}$, are modeled as

$$\Delta \log z_{t+1} = \phi \varepsilon_{t+1}, \tag{1.73}$$

$$\Delta \log \bar{c}_{t+1} = g + \varepsilon_{t+1}. \tag{1.74}$$

Aggregate consumption grows at the constant average rate g, with innovations $\varepsilon \sim N(0, \sigma_\varepsilon^2)$. Such innovations affect the consumption habit,[23] with the parameter ϕ capturing the sensitivity of z to ε. Under the maintained hypothesis of lognormal joint distribution of asset returns and the consumption growth rate (and using the fact that, with identical individuals, in equilibrium $c = \bar{c}$), taking logarithms of (1.72), we get

$$0 = -\rho + E_t r_{t+1}^j - \gamma E_t(\Delta \log z_{t+1}) - \gamma E_t(\Delta \log c_{t+1})$$
$$+ \tfrac{1}{2} \operatorname{var}_t(r_{t+1}^j - \gamma \Delta \log z_{t+1} - \gamma \Delta \log c_{t+1}).$$

Using the stochastic processes specified in (1.73) and (1.74), we finally obtain the risk premium on asset j and the risk-free rate of return:

$$E_t r_{t+1}^j - r_{t+1}^0 = -\frac{\sigma_j^2}{2} + \gamma(1 + \phi)\sigma_{jc}, \qquad (1.75)$$

$$r_{t+1}^0 = \gamma g + \rho - \frac{\gamma^2(1 + \phi)^2 \sigma_c^2}{2}. \qquad (1.76)$$

Comparing (1.75) and (1.76) with the analogous equations (1.71) and (1.70), we note that the magnitude of ϕ has a twofold effect on returns. On the one hand, a high sensitivity of habit to innovations in c enhances the precautionary motive for saving, determining a stronger incentive to asset accumulation and consequently a decrease in returns, as already shown by the last term in (1.70).[24] On the other hand, a high ϕ magnifies the effect of the covariance between risky returns and consumption (σ_{jc}) on the premium required to hold risky assets in equilibrium.

Therefore, the introduction of habit formation can (at least partly) solve the two problems raised by empirical tests of the basic version of the CCAPM: for given values of other parameters, a sufficiently large value of ϕ can bring the risk-free rate implied by the model closer to the lower level observed on the markets, at the same time yielding a relatively high risk premium.

☐ APPENDIX A1: DYNAMIC PROGRAMMING

This appendix outlines the dynamic programming methods widely used in the macroeconomic literature and in particular in consumption theory. We deal first with the representative agent's intertemporal choice under certainty on future income flows; the extension to the case of uncertainty follows.

---

[23] The assumed stochastic process for the logarithm of s satisfies the condition $c > x$ ($s > 0$): consumption is never below habit.

[24] A constant ϕ is assumed here for simplicity. Campbell and Cochrane (1999) assume that ϕ decreases with s: the variability of consumption has a stronger effect on returns when the level of consumption is closer to habit.

A1.1. **Certainty**

Let's go back to the basic model of Section 1.1, assuming that future labor incomes are known to the consumer and that the safe asset has a constant return. The maximization problem then becomes

$$\max_{c_{t+i}} \left[U_t = \sum_{i=0}^{\infty} \left(\frac{1}{1+\rho} \right)^i u(c_{t+i}) \right],$$

subject to the accumulation constraint (for all $i \geq 0$),

$$A_{t+i+1} = (1+r)A_{t+i} + y_{t+i} - c_{t+i}.$$

Under certainty, we can write the constraint using the following definition of total wealth, including the stock of financial assets A and human capital H: $W_t = (1+r)(A_t + H_t)$. W_t measures the stock of total wealth at the end of period t but before consumption c_t occurs, whereas A_t and H_t measure financial and human wealth at the beginning of the period. In terms of total wealth W, the accumulation constraint for period t becomes

$$W_{t+1} = (1+r) \left[A_{t+1} + \frac{1}{1+r} \sum_{i=0}^{\infty} \left(\frac{1}{1+r} \right)^i y_{t+1+i} \right]$$

$$= (1+r) \left[(1+r)A_t + y_t - c_t + \frac{1}{1+r} \sum_{i=0}^{\infty} \left(\frac{1}{1+r} \right)^i y_{t+1+i} \right]$$

$$= (1+r) \left[(1+r)(A_t + H_t) - c_t \right]$$

$$= (1+r)(W_t - c_t).$$

The evolution over time of total wealth is then (for all $i \geq 0$)

$$W_{t+i+1} = (1+r)(W_{t+i} - c_{t+i}).$$

Formally, W_{t+i} is the *state variable*, giving, in each period $t+i$, the total amount of resources available to the consumer; and c_{t+i} is the *control variable*, whose level, optimally chosen by the utility-maximizing consumer, affects the amount of resources available in the next period, $t+i+1$. The intertemporal separability of the objective function and the accumulation constraints allow us to use dynamic programming methods to solve the above problem, which can be decomposed into a sequence of two-period optimization problems. To clarify matters, suppose that the consumer's horizon ends in period T, and impose a non-negativity constraint on final wealth: $W_{T+1} \geq 0$. Now consider the optimization problem at the beginning of the final period T, given the stock of total wealth W_T. We maximize $u(c_T)$ with respect to c_T, subject to the constraints $W_{T+1} = (1+r)(W_T - c_T)$ and $W_{T+1} \geq 0$. The solution yields the optimal level of consumption in period T as a function of wealth: $c_T = c_T(W_T)$. Also, the maximum value of utility in period $T(V)$ depends, through the optimal consumption choice, on wealth. The resulting *value function* $V_T(W_T)$ summarizes the solution of the problem for the final period T.

Now consider the consumer's problem in the previous period, $T - 1$, for a given value of W_{T-1}. Formally, the problem is

$$\max_{c_{T-1}} \left(u(c_{T-1}) + \frac{1}{1+\rho} V_T(W_T) \right),$$

subject to the constraint $W_T = (1 + r)(W_{T-1} - c_{T-1})$. As in the case above, the problem's solution has the following form: $c_{T-1} = c_{T-1}(W_{T-1})$, with an associated maximized value of utility (now over periods $T - 1$ and T) given by $V_{T-1}(W_{T-1})$. The same procedure can be applied to earlier periods recursively (*backward recursion*). In general, the problem can be written in terms of the *Bellman equation*:

$$V_t(W_t) = \max_{c_t} \left(u(c_t) + \frac{1}{1+\rho} V_{t+1}(W_{t+1}) \right), \tag{1.A1}$$

subject to $W_{t+1} = (1 + r)(W_t - c_t)$. Substituting for W_{t+1} into the objective function and differentiating with respect to c_t, we get the following first-order condition:

$$u'(c_t) = \frac{1+r}{1+\rho} V'_{t+1}(W_{t+1}). \tag{1.A2}$$

Using the Bellman equation at time t and differentiating with respect to W_t, we obtain $V'_{t+1}(W_{t+1})$:

$$\begin{aligned}
V'_t(W_t) &= u'(c_t)\frac{\partial c_t}{\partial W_t} + \frac{1+r}{1+\rho} V'_{t+1}(W_{t+1}) - \frac{1+r}{1+\rho} V'_{t+1}(W_{t+1})\frac{\partial c_t}{\partial W_t} \\
&= \left(u'(c_t) - \frac{1+r}{1+\rho} V'_{t+1}(W_{t+1}) \right)\frac{\partial c_t}{\partial W_t} + \frac{1+r}{1+\rho} V'_{t+1}(W_{t+1}) \\
&= \frac{1+r}{1+\rho} V'_{t+1}(W_{t+1}),
\end{aligned}$$

where we use the fact that the term in square brackets in the second line equals zero by (1.A2). Finally, using again the first-order condition, we find

$$V'_t(W_t) = u'(c_t). \tag{1.A3}$$

The effect on utility V_t of an increase in wealth W_t is equal to the marginal utility from immediately consuming the additional wealth. Along the optimal consumption path, the agent is indifferent between immediate consumption and saving. (The term in square brackets is zero.) The additional wealth can then be consumed in any period with the same effect on utility, measured by $u'(c_t)$ in (1.A2): this is an application of the *envelope theorem*.

Inserting condition (1.A3) in period $t + 1$ into (1.A2), we get the Euler equation,

$$u'(c_t) = \frac{1 + r}{1 + \rho} u'(c_{t+1}),$$

which is the solution of the problem (here under certainty) already discussed in Section 1.1.

The recursive structure of the problem and the backward solution procedure provide the optimal consumption path with the property of *time consistency*. Maximization of (1.A1) at time t takes into account $V_{t+1}(W_{t+1})$, which is the optimal solution of the same problem at time $t + 1$, obtained considering also $V_{t+2}(W_{t+2})$, and so forth. As time goes on, then, consumption proceeds optimally along the path originally chosen at time t. (This time consistency property of the solution is known as Bellman's *optimality principle*.)

Under regularity conditions, the iteration of Bellman equation starting from a (bounded and continuous) value function $V_T(\cdot)$ leads to a limit function $V(\cdot)$, which is unique and invariant over time. Such a function $V = \lim_{j \to \infty} V_{T-j}$ solves the consumer's problem over an infinite horizon. In this case also, the function that gives the agent's consumption $c(W)$ is invariant over time. Operationally, if the problem involves (1) a quadratic utility function, or (2) a logarithmic utility function and Cobb–Douglas constraints, it can be solved by first guessing a functional form for $V(\cdot)$ and then checking that such function satisfies Bellman equation (1.A1).

As an example, consider the case of the CRRA utility function[25]

$$u(c) = \frac{c^{1-\gamma}}{1 - \gamma}.$$

The Bellman equation is

$$V(W_t) = \max_{c_t} \left(\frac{c_t^{1-\gamma}}{1 - \gamma} + \frac{1}{1 + \rho} V(W_{t+1}) \right),$$

subject to the constraint $W_{t+1} = (1 + r)(W_t - c_t)$. Let us assume (to be proved later on) that the value function has the same functional form as utility:

$$V(W_t) = K \frac{W_t^{1-\gamma}}{1 - \gamma}, \tag{1.A4}$$

with K being a positive constant to be determined. Using (1.A4), we can write the Bellman equation as

$$K \frac{W_t^{1-\gamma}}{1 - \gamma} = \max_{c_t} \left(\frac{c_t^{1-\gamma}}{1 - \gamma} + \frac{1}{1 + \rho} K \frac{W_{t+1}^{1-\gamma}}{1 - \gamma} \right). \tag{1.A5}$$

[25] The following solution procedure can be applied also when $\gamma > 1$ and the utility function is unbounded. To guarantee this result an additional condition will be imposed below; see Stokey, Lucas, and Prescott (1989) for further details.

From this equation, using the constraint and differentiating with respect to c_t, we get the first-order condition

$$c_t^{-\gamma} = \frac{1+r}{1+\rho} K \left[(1+r)(W_t - c_t)\right]^{-\gamma},$$

and solving for c_t we obtain the consumption function $c_t(W_t)$:

$$c_t = \frac{1}{1 + (1+r)^{\frac{1-\gamma}{\gamma}}(1+\rho)^{-\frac{1}{\gamma}} K^{\frac{1}{\gamma}}} W_t, \qquad (1.A6)$$

where K is still to be determined.

To complete the solution, we combine the Bellman equation (1.A5) with the consumption function (1.A6) and define

$$B \equiv (1+r)^{1-\gamma/\gamma}(1+\rho)^{-1/\gamma}$$

to simplify notation. We can then write

$$K \frac{W_t^{1-\gamma}}{1-\gamma} = \frac{1}{1-\gamma}\left[\frac{W_t}{1 + BK^{\frac{1}{\gamma}}}\right]^{1-\gamma}$$

$$+ \frac{1}{1+\rho}\frac{K}{1-\gamma}\left[(1+r)\left(\frac{BK^{\frac{1}{\gamma}}}{1 + BK^{\frac{1}{\gamma}}}\right) W_t\right]^{1-\gamma}, \qquad (1.A7)$$

where the terms in square brackets are, respectively, C_t and W_{t+1}. The value of K that satisfies (1.A7) is found by equating the coefficient of $W_t^{1-\gamma}$ on the two sides of the equation, noting that $(1+r)^{1-\gamma}(1+\rho)^{-1} \equiv B^\gamma$, and solving for K:

$$K = \left(\frac{1}{1-B}\right)^\gamma. \qquad (1.A8)$$

Under the condition that $B < 1$, the complete solution of the problem is

$$V(W_t) = \left(\frac{1}{1 - (1+r)^{\frac{1-\gamma}{\gamma}}(1+\rho)^{-\frac{1}{\gamma}}}\right)^\gamma \frac{W_t^{1-\gamma}}{1-\gamma},$$

$$c(W_t) = \left[1 - (1+r)^{\frac{1-\gamma}{\gamma}}(1+\rho)^{-\frac{1}{\gamma}}\right] W_t.$$

A1.2. **Uncertainty**

The recursive structure of the problem ensures that, even under uncertainty, the solution procedure illustrated above is still appropriate. The consumer's objective function to be maximized now becomes

$$U_t = E_t \sum_{i=0}^{\infty} \left(\frac{1}{1+\rho}\right)^i u(c_{t+1}),$$

subject to the usual budget constraint (1.2). Now we assume that future labor incomes y_{t+i} ($i > 0$) are uncertain at time t, whereas the interest rate r is known and constant. The state variable at time t is the consumer's certain amount of resources at the end of period t: $(1 + r)A_t + y_t$. The value function is then $V_t((1 + r)A_t + y_t)$, where subscript t means that the value of available resources depends on the information set at time t. Under uncertainty, the Bellman equation becomes

$$V_t[(1 + r)A_t + y_t] = \max_{c_t} \left\{ u(c_t) + \frac{1}{1+\rho} E_t V_{t+1}[(1 + r)A_{t+1} + y_{t+1}] \right\}. \quad (1.A9)$$

The value of $V_{t+1}(\cdot)$ is stochastic, since future income are uncertain, and enters (1.A9) as an expected value.

Differentiating with respect to c_t and using the budget constraint, we get the following first-order condition:

$$u'(c_t) = \frac{1+r}{1+\rho} E_t V'_{t+1}[(1 + r)A_{t+1} + y_{t+1}].$$

As in the certainty case, by applying the envelope theorem and using the condition obtained above, we have

$$V'_t(\cdot) = \frac{1+r}{1+\rho} E_t V'_{t+1}(\cdot)$$

$$= u'(c_t).$$

Combining the last two equations, we finally get the stochastic Euler equation

$$u'(c_t) = \frac{1+r}{1+\rho} E_t u'(c_{t+1}),$$

already derived in Section 1.1 as the first-order condition of the problem.

REVIEW EXERCISES

Exercise 5 *Using the basic version of the rational expectations/permanent income model (with quadratic utility and $r = \rho$), assume that labor income is generated by the following stochastic process:*

$$y_{t+1} = \bar{y} + \varepsilon_{t+1} - \delta \varepsilon_t, \qquad \delta > 0,$$

where $\bar{y}$ is the mean value of income and ε is an innovation with $E_t \varepsilon_{t+1} = 0$.

(a) *Discuss the impact of an increase of $\bar{y}$ ($\Delta \bar{y} > 0$) on the agent's permanent income, consumption and saving.*

(b) *Now suppose that, in period $t + 1$ only, a positive innovation in income occurs: $\varepsilon_{t+1} > 0$. In all past periods income has been equal to its mean level: $y_{t-i} = \bar{y}$ for $i = 0, \ldots, \infty$. Find the change in consumption between t and $t + 1$ (Δc_{t+1}) as a function of ε_{t+1}, providing the economic intuition for your result.*

(c) *With reference to question (b), discuss what happens to saving in periods $t + 1$ and $t + 2$.*

Exercise 6 *Suppose the consumer has the following utility function:*

$$U_t = \sum_{i=0}^{\infty} \left(\frac{1}{1 + \rho} \right)^i u(c_{t+i}, S_{t+i}),$$

where S_{t+i} is the stock of durable goods at the beginning of period $t + i$. There is no uncertainty. The constraints on the optimal consumption choice are:

$$S_{t+i+1} = (1 - \delta)S_{t+i} + d_{t+i},$$

$$A_{t+i+1} = (1 + r)A_{t+i} + y_{t+i} - c_{t+i} - p_{t+i} d_{t+i},$$

where δ is the physical depreciation rate of durable goods, d is the expenditure on durable goods, p is the price of durable goods relative to non-durables, and S_t and A_t are given. Note that the durable goods purchased at time $t + i$ start to provide utility to the consumer only from the following period, as part of the stock at the beginning of period $t + i + 1$ (S_{t+i+1}). Set up the consumer's utility maximization problem and obtain the first-order conditions, providing the economic intuition for your result.

Exercise 7 *The representative consumer maximizes the following intertemporal utility function:*

$$U_t = E_t \sum_{i=0}^{\infty} \left(\frac{1}{1 + \rho} \right)^i u(c_{t+i}, c_{t+i-1}),$$

where

$$u(c_{t+i}, c_{t+i-1}) = (c_{t+i} - \gamma c_{t+i-1}) - \frac{b}{2}(c_{t+i} - \gamma c_{t+i-1})^2, \qquad \gamma > 0.$$

In each period $t + i$, utility depends not only on current consumption, but also on consumption in the preceding period, $t + i - 1$. All other assumptions made in the chapter are maintained (in particular $\rho = r$).

(a) *Give an interpretation of the above utility function in terms of habit formation.*

(b) *From the first-order condition of the maximization problem, derive the dynamic equation for c_{t+1}, and check that this formulation of utility violates the property of orthogonality of Δc_{t+1} with respect to variables dated t.*

Exercise 8 *Suppose that labor income y is generated by the following stochastic process:*

$$y_t = \lambda y_{t-1} + x_{t-1} + \varepsilon_{1t},$$

$$x_t = \varepsilon_{2t},$$

where x_t ($= \varepsilon_{2t}$) does not depend on its own past values ($x_{t-1}, x_{t-2}, \ldots$) and $E(\varepsilon_{1t} \cdot \varepsilon_{2t}) = 0$. x_{t-1} is the only additional variable (realized at time $t-1$) which affects income in period t besides past income y_{t-1}. Moreover, suppose that the information set used by agents to calculate their permanent income y_t^P is $I_{t-1} = \{y_{t-1}, x_{t-1}\}$, whereas the information set used by the econometrician to estimate the agents' permanent income is $\Omega_{t-1} = \{y_{t-1}\}$. Therefore, the additional information in x_{t-1} is used by agents in forecasting income but is ignored by the econometrician.

(a) *Using equation (1.7) in the text (lagged one period), find the changes in permanent income computed by the agents (Δy_t^P) and by the econometrician ($\Delta \tilde{y}_t^P$), considering the different information set used (I_{t-1} or Ω_{t-1}).*

(b) *Compare the variance of Δy_t^P e $\Delta \tilde{y}_t^P$, and show that the variability of permanent income according to agents' forecast is lower than the variability obtained by the econometrician with limited information. What does this imply for the interpretation of the excess smoothness phenomenon?*

Exercise 9 *Consider the consumption choice of an individual who lives for two periods only, with consumption c_1 and c_2 and incomes y_1 and y_2. Suppose that the utility function in each period is*

$$u(c) = \begin{cases} ac - (b/2)c^2 & \text{for } c < a/b; \\ (a^2/2b) & \text{for } c \geq a/b. \end{cases}$$

(Even though the above utility function is quadratic, we rule out the possibility that a higher consumption level reduces utility.)

(a) *Plot marginal utility as a function of consumption.*

(b) *Suppose that $r = \rho = 0$, $y_1 = a/b$, and y_2 is uncertain:*

$$y_2 = \begin{cases} a/b + \sigma, & \text{with probability } 0.5; \\ a/b - \sigma, & \text{with probability } 0.5. \end{cases}$$

Write the first-order condition relating c_1 to c_2 (random variable) if the consumer maximizes expected utility. Find the optimal consumption when $\sigma = 0$, and discuss the effect of a higher σ on c_1.

☐ FURTHER READING

The consumption theory based on the intertemporal smoothing of optimal consumption paths builds on the work of Friedman (1957) and Modigliani and Brumberg (1954). A critical assessment of the life-cycle theory of consumption (not explicitly mentioned in this chapter) is provided by Modigliani (1986). Abel (1990, part 1), Blanchard and Fischer (1989, para. 6.2), Hall (1989), and Romer (2001, ch. 7) present consumption theory at a technical level similar to ours. Thorough overviews of the theoretical and empirical literature on consumption can be found in Deaton (1992) and, more recently, in Browning and Lusardi (1997) and Attanasio (1999), with a particular focus on the evidence from microeconometric studies. When confronting theory and microeconomic data, it is of course very important (and far from straight-forward) to account for heterogeneous objective functions across individuals or house-holds. In particular, empirical work has found that theoretical implications are typi-cally not rejected when the marginal utility function is allowed to depend flexibly on the number of children in the household, on the household head's age, and on other observable characteristics. Information may also be heterogeneous: the information set of individual agents need not be more refined than the econometrician's (Pischke, 1995), and survey measures of expectations formed on its basis can be used to test theoretical implications (Jappelli and Pistaferri, 2000).

The seminal paper by Hall (1978) provides the formal framework for much later work on consumption, including the present chapter. Flavin (1981) tests the empirical implications of Hall's model, and finds evidence of *excess sensitivity* of consumption to expected income. Campbell (1987) and Campbell and Deaton (1989) derive theor-etical implication for saving behavior and address the problem of *excess smoothness* of consumption to income innovations. Campbell and Deaton (1989) and Flavin (1993) also provide the joint interpretation of "excess sensitivity" and "excess smoothness" outlined in Section 1.2.

Empirical tests of the role of liquidity constraints, also with a cross-country perspective, are provided by Jappelli and Pagano (1989, 1994), Campbell and Mankiw (1989, 1991) and Attanasio (1995, 1999). Blanchard and Mankiw (1988) stress the importance of the precautionary saving motive, and Caballero (1990) solves analyt-ically the optimization problem with precautionary saving assuming an exponential utility function, as in Section 1.3. Weil (1993) solves the same problem in the case of constant but unrelated intertemporal elasticity of substitution and relative risk aver-sion parameters. A precautionary saving motive arises also in the models of Deaton (1991) and Carroll (1992), where liquidity constraints force consumption to closely track current income and induce agents to accumulate a limited stock of financial assets to support consumption in the event of sharp reductions in income (*buffer-stock saving*). Carroll (1997, 2001) argues that the empirical evidence on consumers' behav-ior can be well explained by incorporating in the life-cycle model both a precautionary saving motive and a moderate degree of impatience. Sizeable responses of consump-tion to predictable income changes are also generated by models of dynamic inconsis-tent preferences arising from hyperbolic discounting of future utility; Angeletos *et al.* (2001) and Frederick, Loewenstein, and O'Donoghue (2002) provide surveys of this strand of literature.

The general setup of the CCAPM used in Section 1.4 is analyzed in detail by Campbell, Lo, and MacKinley (1997, ch. 8) and Cochrane (2001). The model's empir-ical implications with a CRRA utility function and a lognormal distribution of returns and consumption are derived by Hansen and Singleton (1983) and extended by, among others, Campbell (1996). Campbell, Lo, and MacKinley (1997) also provide a complete survey of the empirical literature. Campbell (1999) has documented the international relevance of the *equity premium* and the *risk-free rate puzzles*, originally formulated by Mehra and Prescott (1985) and Weil (1989). Aiyagari (1993), Kocherlakota (1996), and Cochrane (2001, ch. 21) survey the theoretical and empirical literature on this topic. Costantinides, Donaldson, and Mehra (2002) provide an explanation of those puzzles by combining a life-cycle perspective and borrowing constraints. Campbell and Cochrane (1999) develop the CCAPM with *habit formation* behavior outlined in Section 1.4 and test it on US data. An exhaustive survey of the theory and the empirical evidence on consumption, asset returns, and macroeconomic fluctuations is found in Campbell (1999).

Dynamic programming methods with applications to economics can be found in Dixit (1990), Sargent (1987, ch. 1) and Stokey, Lucas, and Prescott (1989), at an increasing level of difficulty and analytical rigor.

□ REFERENCES

Abel, A. (1990) "Consumption and Investment," in B. Friedman and F. Hahn (ed.), *Handbook of Monetary Economics*, Amsterdam: North-Holland.

Aiyagari, S. R. (1993) "Explaining Financial Market Facts: the Importance of Incomplete Markets and Transaction Costs," *Federal Reserve Bank of Minneapolis Quarterly Review*, 17, 17–31.

—— (1994) "Uninsured Idiosyncratic Risk and Aggregate Saving," *Quarterly Journal of Economics*, 109, 659–684.

Angeletos, G.-M., D. Laibson, A. Repetto, J. Tobacman, and S. Winberg (2001) "The Hyperbolic Consumption Model: Calibration, Simulation and Empirical Evaluation," *Journal of Economic Perspectives*, 15(3), 47–68.

Attanasio, O. P. (1995) "The Intertemporal Allocation of Consumption: Theory and Evidence," *Carnegie–Rochester Conference Series on Public Policy*, 42, 39–89.

—— (1999) "Consumption," in J. B. Taylor and M. Woodford (ed.), *Handbook of Macroeconomics*, vol. 1B, Amsterdam: North-Holland, 741–812.

Blanchard, O. J. and S. Fischer (1989) *Lectures on Macroeconomics*, Cambridge, Mass.: MIT Press.

—— and N. G. Mankiw (1988) "Consumption: Beyond Certainty Equivalence," *American Economic Review (Papers and Proceedings)*, 78, 173–177.

Browning, M. and A. Lusardi (1997) "Household Saving: Micro Theories and Micro Facts," *Journal of Economic Literature*, 34, 1797–1855.

Caballero, R. J. (1990) "Consumption Puzzles and Precautionary Savings," *Journal of Monetary Economics*, 25, 113–136.

Campbell, J. Y. (1987) "Does Saving Anticipate Labour Income? An Alternative Test of the Permanent Income Hypothesis," *Econometrica*, 55, 1249–1273.

—— (1996) "Understanding Risk and Return," *Journal of Political Economy*, 104, 298–345.

—— (1999) "Asset Prices, Consumption and the Business Cycle," in J. B. Taylor and M. Woodford (ed.), *Handbook of Macroeconomics*, vol. 1C, Amsterdam: North-Holland.

—— and J. H. Cochrane (1999) "By Force of Habit: A Consumption-Based Explanation of Aggregate Stock Market Behavior," *Journal of Political Economy*, 2, 205–251.

—— and A. Deaton (1989) "Why is Consumption So Smooth?" *Review of Economic Studies*, 56, 357–374.

—— and N. G. Mankiw (1989) "Consumption, Income and Interest Rates: Reinterpreting the Time-Series Evidence," *NBER Macroeconomics Annual*, 4, 185–216.

—— (1991) "The Response of Consumption to Income: a Cross-Country Investigation," *European Economic Review*, 35, 715–721.

—— A. W. Lo, and A. C. MacKinley (1997) *The Econometrics of Financial Markets*, Princeton: Princeton University Press.

Carroll, C. D. (1992) "The Buffer-Stock Theory of Saving: Some Macroeconomic Evidence," *Brookings Papers on Economic Activity*, 2, 61–156.

—— (1997) "Buffer-Stock Saving and the Life Cycle/Permanent Income Hypothesis," *Quarterly Journal of Economics* , 102, 1–55.

—— (2001) "A Theory of the Consumption Function, With and Without Liquidity Constraints," *Journal of Economic Perspectives*, 15 (3), 23–45.

Cochrane, J. H. (2001) *Asset Pricing*, Princeton: Princeton University Press.

Costantinides G. M., J. B. Donaldson, and R. Mehra (2002) "Junior Can't Borrow: A New Perspective on the Equity Premium Puzzle," *Quarterly Journal of Economics*, 117, 269–298.

Deaton, A. (1991) "Saving and Liquidity Constraints," *Econometrica*, 59, 1221–1248.

—— (1992) *Understanding Consumption*, Oxford: Oxford University Press.

Dixit, A. K. (1990) *Optimization in Economic Theory*, 2nd edn, Oxford: Oxford University Press.

Flavin, M. (1981) "The Adjustment of Consumption to Changing Expectations about Future Income," *Journal of Political Economy* , 89, 974–1009.

—— (1993) "The Excess Smoothness of Consumption: Identification and Interpretation," *Review of Economic Studies*, 60, 651–666.

Frederick S., G. Loewenstein, and T. O'Donoghue (2002) "Time Discounting and Time Preference: A Critical Review," *Journal of Economic Literature*, 40, 351–401.

Friedman, M. (1957) *A Theory of the Consumption Function*, Princeton: Princeton University Press.

Hall, R. E. (1978) "Stochastic Implications of the Permanent Income Hypothesis: Theory and Evidence," *Journal of Political Economy*, 96, 971–987.

—— (1989) "Consumption," in R. Barro (ed.), *Handbook of Modern Business Cycle Theory*, Oxford: Basil Blackwell.

Hansen, L. P. and K. J. Singleton (1983) "Stochastic Consumption, Risk Aversion, and the Temporal Behavior of Asset Returns," *Journal of Political Economy*, 91, 249–265.

Jappelli, T. and M. Pagano (1989) "Consumption and Capital Market Imperfections: An International Comparison," *American Economic Review*, 79, 1099–1105.

—— (1994) "Saving, Growth and Liquidity Constraints," *Quarterly Journal of Economics*, 108, 83–109.

—— and L. Pistaferri (2000), "Using Subjective Income Expectations to Test for Excess Sensitivity of Consumption to Predicted Income Growth," *European Economic Review* 44, 337–358.

Kocherlakota, N. R. (1996) "The Equity Premium: It's Still a Puzzle," *Journal of Economic Literature*, 34(1), 42–71.

Mehra, R. and E. C. Prescott (1985) "The Equity Premium: A Puzzle," *Journal of Monetary Economics* , 15(2), 145–161.

Modigliani, F. (1986) "Life Cycle, Individual Thrift, and the Wealth of Nations," *American Economic Review*, 76, 297–313.

——and R. Brumberg (1954) "Utility Analysis and the Consumption Function: An Interpretation of Cross-Section Data," in K. K. Kurihara (ed.), *Post-Keynesian Economics*, New Brunswick, NJ: Rutgers University Press.

Pischke, J.-S. (1995) "Individual Income, Incomplete Information, and Aggregate Consumption," *Econometrica*, 63, 805–840.

Romer, D. (2001) *Advanced Macroeconomics*, 2nd edn, New York: McGraw-Hill.

Sargent, T. J. (1987) *Dynamic Macroeconomic Theory*, Cambridge, Mass.: Harvard University Press.

Stokey, N., R. J. Lucas, and E. C. Prescott (1989) *Recursive Methods in Economic Dynamics*, Cambridge, Mass.: Harvard University Press.

Weil, P. (1989) "The Equity Premium Puzzle and the Risk-Free Rate Puzzle," *Journal of Monetary Economics*, 24, 401–421.

——(1993) "Precautionary Savings and the Permanent Income Hypothesis," *Review of Economic Studies*, 60, 367–383.

2 Dynamic Models of Investment

Macroeconomic IS–LM models assign a crucial role to business investment flows in linking the goods market and the money market. As in the case of consumption, however, elementary textbooks do not explicitly study investment behavior in terms of a formal dynamic optimization problem. Rather, they offer qualitatively sensible interpretations of investment behavior at a point in time. In this chapter we analyze investment decisions from an explicitly dynamic perspective. We simply aim at introducing dynamic continuous-time optimization techniques, which will also be used in the following chapters, and at offering a formal, hence more precise, interpretation of qualitative approaches to the behavior of private investment in macroeconomic models encountered in introductory textbooks. Other aspects of the subject matter are too broad and complex for exhaustive treatment here: empirical applications of the theories we analyze and the role of financial imperfections are mentioned briefly at the end of the chapter, referring readers to existing surveys of the subject.

As in Chapter 1's study of consumption, in applying dynamic optimization methods to macroeconomic investment phenomena, one can view the dynamics of aggregate variables as the solution of a "representative agent" problem. In this chapter we study the dynamic optimization problem of a firm that aims at maximizing present discounted cash flows. We focus on technical insights rather than on empirical implications, and the problem's setup may at first appear quite abstract. When characterizing its solution, however, we will emphasize analogies between the optimality conditions of the formal problem and simple qualitative approaches familiar from undergraduate textbooks. This will make it possible to apply economic intuition to mathematical formulas that would otherwise appear abstruse, and to verify the robustness of qualitative insights by deriving them from precise formal assumptions.

Section 2.1 introduces the notion of "convex" adjustment costs, i.e. technological features that penalize fast investment. The next few sections illustrate the character of investment decisions from a partial equilibrium perspective: we take as given the firm's demand and production functions, the dynamics of the price of capital and of other factors, and the discount rate applied to future cash flows. Optimal investment decisions by firms are *forward looking*, and should be based on expectations of future events. Relevant techniques and mathematical results introduced in this context are explained in detail in the

Appendix to this chapter. The technical treatment of firm-level investment decisions sets the stage for a discussion of an explicitly dynamic version of the familiar IS–LM model. The final portion of the chapter returns to the firm-level perspective and studies specifications where adjustment costs do not discourage fast investment, but do impose irreversibility constraints, and Section 2.8 briefly introduces technical tools for the analysis of this type of problem in the presence of uncertainty.

2.1. **Convex Adjustment Costs**

In what follows, $F(t)$ denotes the difference between a firm's cash receipts and outlays during period t. We suppose that such cash flows depend on the capital stock $K(t)$ available at the beginning of the period, on the flow $I(t)$ of investment during the period, and on the amount $N(t)$ employed during the period of another factor of production, dubbed "labor":

$$F(t) = R(t, K(t), N(t)) - P_k(t)G(I(t), K(t)) - w(t)N(t). \qquad (2.1)$$

The $R(\cdot)$ function represents the flow of revenues obtained from sales of the firm's production flow. This depends on the amounts employed of the two factors of production, K and N, and also on the technological efficiency of the production function and/or the strength of demand for the firm's product. In (2.1), possible variations over time of such exogenous features of the firm's technological and market environment are taken into account by including the time index t alongside K and N as arguments of the revenue function. We assume that revenue flows are increasing in both factors, i.e.

$$\frac{\partial R(\cdot)}{\partial K} > 0, \qquad \frac{\partial R(\cdot)}{\partial N} > 0, \qquad (2.2)$$

as is natural if the marginal productivity of all factors and the market price of the product are positive. To prevent the optimal size of the firm from diverging to infinity, it is necessary to assume that the revenue function $R(\cdot)$ is concave in K and N. If the price of its production is taken as given by the firm, this is ensured by non-increasing returns to scale in production. If instead physical returns to scale are increasing, the revenue function $R(\cdot)$ can still be concave if the firm has market power and its demand function's slope is sufficiently negative.

The two negative terms in the cash-flow expression (2.1) represent costs pertaining to investment, I, and employment of N. As to the latter, in this chapter we suppose that its level is directly controlled by the firm at each point in time and that utilization of a stock of labor N entails a flow cost w per unit time, just as in the static models studied in introductory microeconomic courses. As to investment costs, a formal treatment of the problem needs to be precise as to the moment when the capital stock used in production during each period is measured. If we adopt the convention that the relevant stock is measured at the beginning of the period, it is simply impossible for the firm to vary $K(t)$ at time t. When the production flow is realized, the firm cannot control the capital stock, but can only control the amount of positive or negative investment: any resulting increase or decrease of installed capital begins to affect production and revenues only in the following period. On this basis, the dynamic accumulation constraint reads

$$K(t + \Delta t) = K(t) + I(t)\Delta t - \delta K(t)\Delta t, \tag{2.3}$$

where δ denotes the depreciation rate of capital, and Δt is the length of the time period over which we measure cash flows and the investment rate per unit time $I(t)$.

By assumption, the firm cannot affect current cash flows by varying the available capital stock. The amount of gross investment $I(t)$ during period Δt does, however, affect the cash flow: in (2.1) investment costs are represented by a price $P_k(t)$ times a function $G(\cdot)$ which, as in Figure 2.1, we shall assume increasing and convex in $I(t)$:

$$\frac{\partial G(\cdot)}{\partial I} > 0, \qquad \frac{\partial^2 G(\cdot)}{\partial I^2} > 0. \tag{2.4}$$

The function $G(\cdot)$ is multiplied by a price in the definition (2.1) of cash flows. Hence it is defined in physical units, just like its arguments I and K. For example, it might measure the physical length of a production line, or the number of personal computers available in an office. The investment

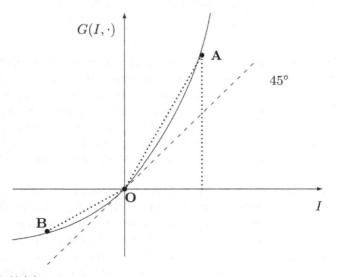

Figure 2.1. Unit investment costs

rate $I(t)$ is linearly related to the change in capital stock in equation (2.3) but, since $G(\cdot)$ is not linear, the cost of each unit of capital installed is not constant. For instance, we might imagine that a greenhouse needs to purchase $G(I, K)$ flower pots in order to increase the available stock by I units, and that the quantities purchased and effectively available for future production are different because a certain fraction (variable as a function of I and K) of pots purchased break and become useless. In the context of this example it is also easy to imagine that a fraction of pots in use also break during each period, and that the parameter δ represents this phenomenon formally in (2.3).

While such examples can help reduce the rather abstract character of the formal model we are considering, its assumptions may be more easily justified in terms of their implications than in those of their literal realism. For purposes of modeling investment dynamics, the crucial feature of the $G(I, K)$ function is the strict convexity assumed in (2.4). This implies that the average unit cost (measured, after normalization by P_k, by the slope of lines such as OA and OB in Figure 2.1) of investment flows is increasing in the total flow invested during a period. Thus, a given total amount of investment is less costly when spread out over multiple periods than when it is concentrated in a single period. For this reason, the optimal investment policy implied by convex adjustment costs is to some extent *gradual*.

The functional form of investment costs plays an important role not only when the firm intends to increase its capital stock, but also when it wishes to keep it constant, or decrease it. It is quite natural to assume that the firm should not bear costs when gross investment is zero (and capital may evolve over time only as a consequence of exogenous depreciation at rate δ). Hence, as in Figure 2.1,

$$G(0, \cdot) = 0,$$

and the positive first derivative assumed in (2.4) implies that $G(I, \cdot) < 0$ for $I < 0$: the cost function is negative (and makes positive contributions to the firm's cash flow) when gross investment is negative, and the firm is selling used equipment or structures.

In the figure, the $G(\cdot)$ function lies above a 45° line through the origin, and it is tangent to it at zero, where its slope is unitary:

$$\partial G(0, \cdot)/\partial I = 1.$$

This property makes it possible to interpret P_k as "the" unit price of capital goods, a price that would apply to all units installed if the convexity of $G(I, \cdot)$ did not deter larger than infinitesimal investments of either sign.

When negative investment rates are considered, convexity of adjustment costs similarly implies that the unit amount recouped from each unit scrapped (as measured by the slope of lines such as OB) is smaller when I is more negative, and this makes speedy reduction of the capital stock unattractive.

Comparing the slope of lines such as OA and OB, it is immediately apparent that alternating positive and negative investments is costly: even though there are no net effects on the final capital stock, the firm cannot fully recoup the original cost of positive investment from subsequent negative investment. First increasing, then decreasing the capital stock (or vice versa) entails *adjustment costs*.

In summary, the form of the function displayed in Figure 2.1 implies that investment decisions should be based not only on the contribution of capital to profits at a given moment in time, but also on their future outlook. If the relevant exogenous conditions indexed by t in $R(\cdot)$ and the dynamics of the other, equally exogenous, variables $P_k(t)$, $w(t)$, $r(t)$ suggest that the firm should vary its capital stock, the adjustment should be gradual, as will be set out below. Moreover, if large positive and negative fluctuations of exogenous variables are expected, the firm should not vary its investment rate sharply, because the cost and revenues generated by upward and downward capital stock fluctuations do not offset each other exactly. Convexity of the adjustment cost function implies that the total cost of any given capital stock variation is smaller when that variation is diluted through time, hence the firm should behave in a *forward looking* fashion when choosing the dynamics of its investment rate and should try to keep the latter stable by anticipating the dynamics of exogenous variables.

2.2. **Continuous-Time Optimization**

Neither the realism nor the implications of convex adjustment costs depend on the length Δt of the period over which revenue, cost, and investment flows are measured. The discussion above, however, was based on the idea that current investment cannot increase the capital stock available for use within each such period, implying that $K(t)$ could be taken as given when evaluating opportunities for further investment. This accounting convention, of course, is more accurate when the length of the period is shorter.

Accordingly, we consider the limit case where $\Delta t \rightarrow 0$, and suppose that the firm makes optimizing choices at every instant in continuous time. Optimization in continuous time yields analytically cleaner and often more intuitive results than qualitatively similar results from discrete time specifications, such as those encountered in this book when discussing consumption (in Chapter 1) and labor demand under costly adjustment (in Chapter 3). We also assume, for now, that the dynamics of exogenous variables is deterministic. (Only at the end of the chapter do we introduce uncertainty in a continuous-time investment problem.) This also makes the problem different from that discussed in Chapter 1: the characterization offered by continuous-time models without uncertainty is less easily applicable to empirical discrete-time observations, but is also quite insightful, and each of the modeling approaches we outline could fruitfully be applied to the various substantive problems considered. The economic intuition afforded by the next chapter's models of labor demand under uncertainty would be equally valid if applied to investment in plant and equipment investment rather than in workers, and we shall encounter consumption and investment problems in continuous time (and in the absence of uncertainty) when discussing growth models in Chapter 4.

In continuous time, the maximum present value (discounted at rate r) of cash flows generated by a production and investment program can be written as an integral:

$$V(0) \equiv \max \int_0^\infty F(t) e^{-\int_0^t r(s)ds} \, dt,$$

subject to $\dot{K}(t) = I(t) - \delta K(t)$, for all t. $\qquad$ (2.5)

The Appendix to this chapter defines the integral and offers an introduction to Hamiltonian dynamic optimization. This method suggests a simple recipe for solution of this type of problem (which will also be encountered in Chapter 4). The Hamiltonian of optimization problem (2.5) is

$$H(t) = e^{-\int_0^t r(s)ds} \left(F(t) + \lambda(t) \left(I(t) - \delta K(t) \right) \right),$$

where $\lambda(t)$ denotes the shadow price of capital at time t in current value terms (that is, in terms of resources payable at the same time t).

The first-order conditions of the dynamic optimization problem we are studying are

$$\frac{\partial H}{\partial N} = 0 \Rightarrow \frac{\partial F(\cdot)}{\partial N} = 0 \Rightarrow \frac{\partial R(\cdot)}{\partial N} = w(t),$$

$$\frac{\partial H}{\partial I} = 0 \Rightarrow \frac{\partial F(\cdot)}{\partial I} = -\lambda(t) \Rightarrow P_k \frac{\partial G}{\partial I} = \lambda(t), \qquad (2.6)$$

$$-\frac{\partial H}{\partial K} = \frac{d}{dt} \left(\lambda(t) e^{-\int_0^t r(s)ds} \right) \Rightarrow \dot{\lambda} - r\lambda = -\left(\frac{\partial F(\cdot)}{\partial K} - \delta\lambda \right).$$

The limit "transversality" condition must also be satisfied, in the form

$$\lim_{t \to \infty} e^{-\int_0^t r(s)ds} \lambda(t) K(t) = 0. \qquad (2.7)$$

The Appendix shows that these optimality conditions are formally analogous to those of more familiar static constrained optimization problems. Here, we discuss their economic interpretation. The condition

$$\frac{\partial R(\cdot)}{\partial N} = w(t) \qquad (2.8)$$

simply requires that, in flow terms, the marginal revenue yielded by employment of the flexible factor N be equal to its cost w, at every instant t. This is quite intuitive, since the level of N may be freely determined by the firm. The condition

$$P_k \frac{\partial G(\cdot)}{\partial I} = \lambda(t) \tag{2.9}$$

calls for equality, along an optimal investment path, of the marginal value of capital $\lambda(t)$ and the marginal cost of the investment flows that determine an increase (or decrease) of the capital stock at every instant. That marginal cost, in turn, is $-P_k \partial G(\cdot)/\partial I$ in the problem we are considering. Such considerations, holding at every given time t, do not suffice to represent the dynamic aspects of the firm's problem. These aspects are in fact crucial in the third condition listed in (2.6), which may be rewritten in the form

$$r\lambda = \frac{\partial F(\cdot)}{\partial K} - \delta\lambda + \dot{\lambda}$$

and interpreted in terms of financial asset valuation. For simplicity, let $\delta = 0$. From the viewpoint of time t, the marginal unit of capital adds $\partial F/\partial K$ to current cash flows, and this is a "dividend" paid by that unit to its owner at that time (the firm). The marginal unit of capital, however, also offers capital gains, in the amount $\dot{\lambda}$. If the firm attaches a (shadow) value λ to the unit of capital, then it must be the case that its total return in terms of both dividends and capital gains is financially fair. Hence it should coincide with the return $r\lambda$ that the firm could obtain from λ units of purchasing power in a financial market where, as in (2.5), cash flows are discounted at rate r. If $\delta > 0$, similar considerations hold true but should take into account that a fraction of the marginal unit of capital is lost during every instant of time. Hence its value, amounting to $\delta\lambda$ per unit time, needs to be subtracted from current "dividends."

Such considerations also offer an intuitive economic interpretation of the transversality condition (2.7), which would be violated if the "financial" value $\lambda(t)$ grew at a rate greater than or equal to the equilibrium rate of return $r(s)$ while the capital stock, and the marginal dividend afforded by the investment policy, tend to a finite limit. In such a case, $\lambda(t)$ would be influenced by a speculative "bubble": the only reason to hold the asset corresponding to the marginal value of capital is the expectation of everlasting further capital gains, not linked to profits actually earned from its use in production. Imposing condition (2.7), we acknowledge that such expectations have no economic basis, and we deny that purely speculative behavior may be optimal for the firm.

2.2.1. CHARACTERIZING OPTIMAL INVESTMENT

Consider the variable

$$q(t) \equiv \frac{\lambda(t)}{P_k(t)},$$

the ratio of the marginal capital unit's shadow value to parameter P_k, which represents the market price of capital (that is, the unit of cost of investment in the neighborhood of the zero gross investment point, where adjustment costs are negligible).

This variable, known as *marginal q*, has a crucial role in the determination of optimal investment flows. In fact, the first condition in (2.6) implies that

$$\frac{\partial G(I(t), K(t))}{\partial I(t)} = q(t), \tag{2.10}$$

and if (2.4) holds then $\partial G(\cdot)/\partial I$ is a strictly increasing function of I. Such a function has an inverse: let $\iota(\cdot)$ denote the inverse of $\partial G(\cdot)/\partial I$ as a function of I. Both $\partial G(\cdot)/\partial I$ and its inverse may depend on the capital stock K. The $\iota(q, K)$ function implicitly defined by

$$\frac{\partial G(\iota(q, K), K)}{\partial \iota} \equiv q$$

returns investment flows in such a way as to equate the marginal investment cost $\partial G(\cdot)/\partial I$ to a given q, for a given K. Condition (2.10) may then be equivalently written

$$I(t) = \iota(q(t), K(t)). \tag{2.11}$$

Since $K(t)$ is given at time t, (2.11) determines the investment rate as a function of $q(t)$.

Since, by assumption, the investment cost function $G(I, \cdot)$ has unitary slope at $I = 0$, zero gross investment is optimal when $q = 1$; positive investment is optimal when $q > 1$; and negative investment is optimal when $q < 1$. Intuitively, when $q > 1$ (hence $\lambda > P_k$) capital is worth more inside the firm than in the economy at large; hence it is a good idea to increase the capital stock installed in the firm. Symmetrically, $q < 1$ suggests that the capital stock should be reduced. In both cases, the speed at which capital is transferred towards the firm or away from it depends not only on the difference between q and unity, but also on the degree of convexity of the $G(\cdot)$ function, that is, on the relevance of capital adjustment costs. If the slope of the function in Figure 2.1 increases quickly with I, even q values very different from unity are associated with modest investment flows.

Exercise 10 *Show that, if capital has positive value, then investment would always be positive if the total investment cost were quadratic, for example if*

$G(K, I) = x \cdot I^2$ where $P_k = 1$ and $x \geq 0$ *may depend on K. Discuss the realism of more general specifications where $G(K, I) = x \cdot I^\beta$ for $\beta > 0$.*

Determining the optimal investment rate as a function of q does not yield a complete solution to the dynamic optimization problem. In fact, in order to compute q one needs to know the shadow value $\lambda(t)$ of capital, which—unlike the market price of capital, $P_k(t)$—is part of the problem's solution, rather than part of its exogenous parameterization. However, it is possible to characterize graphically and qualitatively the complete solution of the problem on the basis of the Hamiltonian conditions.

Since we expressed the shadow value of capital in current terms, calendar time t appears in the optimality conditions only as an argument of the functions, such as $\lambda(\cdot)$ and $K(\cdot)$, which determine optimal choices of I and N. Noting that

$$\dot{q}(t) = \frac{d}{dt} \frac{\lambda(t)}{P_k(t)} = \frac{\dot{\lambda}(t)}{P_k(t)} - \frac{\lambda(t)}{P_k(t)} \frac{\dot{P}_k(t)}{P_k(t)},$$

let us define $\dot{P}_k(t)/P_k(t) \equiv \pi_k$ (the rate of inflation in terms of capital), and recall that $\dot{\lambda} = (r + \delta)\lambda - \partial F(\cdot)/\partial K$ by the last optimality condition in (2.6). Thus, we may write the rate of change of q as a function of q itself, of K, and of parameters:

$$\dot{q} = (r + \delta - \pi_k)q - \frac{1}{P_k} \frac{\partial F(\cdot)}{\partial K}. \tag{2.12}$$

In this expression the calendar time t is omitted for simplicity, but all variables—particularly those, not explicitly listed, that determine the size of cash flows $F(\cdot)$ and their derivative with respect to K—are measured at a given moment in time.

Combining the constraint $\dot{K}(t) = I(t) - \delta K(t)$ with condition (2.11), we obtain a relationship between the rate of change of K, K itself, and the level of q:

$$\dot{K} = \iota(q, K) - \delta K. \tag{2.13}$$

Now, if we suppose that all exogenous variables are constant (including the price of capital P_k, to imply that $\pi_k = 0$), and recall that the investment rate and N depend on q and K through the optimality conditions in (2.6), the time-varying elements of the system formed by (2.12) and (2.13) are just $q(t)$ and $K(t)$—that is, precisely those for whose dynamics we have derived explicit expressions.

Thus, the dynamics of the two variables may be studied in the *phase diagram* of Figure 2.2. On the axes of the diagram we measure the dynamic variables of interest. On the horizontal axis of this and subsequent diagrams, one reads the level of K; on the vertical axis, a level of q. If only K and q—and variables

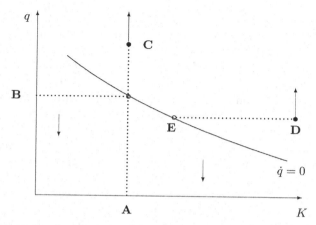

Figure 2.2. Dynamics of q (supposing that $\partial F(\cdot)/\partial K$ is decreasing in K)

uniquely determined by them, such as the investment rate $I = \iota(q, K)$—are time-varying, then each point in (K, q)-space is uniquely associated with their dynamic changes. Picking any point in the diagram, and knowing the functional form of the expressions in (2.12) and (2.13), one could in principle compute both $\dot q$ and $\dot K$. Graphically, the movement *in time* of the two variables may be represented by placing in the diagram appropriately oriented arrows.

In practice, the characterization exercise needs first to identify points where one of the variables remains constant in time. In Figure 2.2, the downward-sloping line represents combinations of K and q such that the expression on the right-hand side of (2.12) is zero. This is the case when

$$q = (r + \delta)^{-1} \frac{1}{P_k} \frac{\partial F(\cdot)}{\partial K}.$$

Given that $(r + \delta) P_k > 0$, the locus of points along which $\dot q = 0$ has a negative slope if a higher capital stock is associated with a smaller "dividend" $\partial F(\cdot)/\partial K$ from the marginal capital unit in (2.12).

This is not, in general, guaranteed by the condition $\partial^2 F(\cdot)/\partial K^2 < 0$. When drawing the phase diagram, in fact, the firm's cash flow,

$$F(\cdot) = R(t, K, N) - P_k(t) G(I, K) - w(t) N,$$

should be evaluated under the assumptions that the flexible factor N is always adjusted so as to satisfy the condition $\partial R(K, N)/\partial N = w$, and that investment satisfies the condition $\partial G(I, K)/\partial I = \lambda$. Thus, as K varies, both the optimal employment of N, which we may write as $N^* = n(K, w)$, and the optimal investment flow $\iota(K, \lambda)$ vary as well. Exercise 12 highlights certain implications of this fact for a properly drawn phase diagram. It will be convenient for now to suppose that the $\dot q = 0$ locus slopes downwards, as is the case (for example) if the adjustment cost function $G(\cdot)$ does not depend on K and revenues $R(\cdot)$ are an increasing and strictly concave function of K only.

Once we have identified the locus of points where $\dot{q} = 0$, we need to determine the sign of $\dot{q}$ for points in the diagram that are *not* on that locus. For each level of K, one and only one level of q implies that $\dot{q}$ equals zero. If for example we consider point A along the horizontal axis of the figure, q is steady only if its level is at the height of point B. If we move up to a higher value of q for the same level of K, such as that corresponding to point C in the figure, equation (2.12)—where q is multiplied by $r + \delta > 0$—implies that $\dot{q}$ is not equal to zero, as in point B, but is larger than zero. In the figure this is represented by an upward-pointing arrow: if one imagines placing a pen on the diagram at point C, and following the dynamic instructions given by (2.12), the pen should slide towards even higher values of q. The same reasoning holds for all points above the $\dot{q} = 0$ locus, for example point D, whence an upward-sloping arrow also starts. The speed of the dynamic movement represented is larger for larger values of $r + \delta$, and for greater distances from the stationary locus: the latter fact could be represented by drawing larger arrows for points farther from the $\dot{q} = 0$ locus. To convince oneself that $\dot{q} > 0$ in D, one may also consider point E on $\dot{q} = 0$ and, holding q constant, note that, if (2.12) identifies a downward-sloping locus, then a higher level of K must result in $\dot{q}$ larger than zero. Symmetrically, we have $\dot{q} < 0$ at every point below and to the left of the $\dot{q} = 0$ locus, such as those marked with downward-sloping arrows in the figure.

Applying the same reasoning to equation (2.13) enables us to draw Figure 2.3. To determine the slope of the locus along which $\dot{K} = 0$, note that the right-hand side of (2.13) is certainly increasing in q since a higher q is associated with a larger investment flow. The effect on $\dot{K}$ of a higher K is ambiguous: as long as $\delta > 0$ it is certainly negative through the second term,

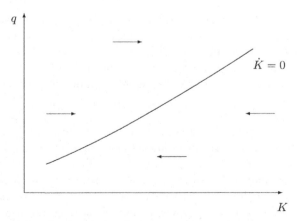

Figure 2.3. Dynamics of K (supposing that $\partial \iota(\cdot)/\partial K - \delta < 0$)

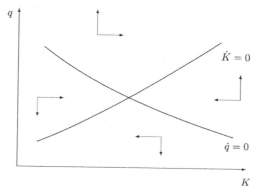

Figure 2.4. Phase diagram for the q and K system

but it may be positive through the first term. If a firm with a larger installed capital stock bears smaller unit costs for installation of a given additional investment flow I, a larger optimal investment flow is associated with a given q, and a larger K has a negative effect on $G(\cdot)$ and a positive effect on $\iota(\cdot)$. The relevance of this channel is studied in exercise 12, but the figure is drawn supposing that the negative effect dominates the positive one—for example, because the adjustment cost function $G(\cdot)$ does not depend on K, and $\delta > 0$ suffices to imply a positive slope for the $\dot{K} = 0$ locus. It is then easy to show that $\dot{K} > 0$, as indicated by arrows pointing to the right, at all points above that locus; a value of q higher than that which would maintain a steady capital stock, in fact, can only be associated with a larger investment flow and an increasing K. Symmetrically, arrows point to the left at all points below the $\dot{K} = 0$ locus.

Figure 2.4, which simply superimposes the two preceding figures, considers the joint dynamic behavior of q and K. Since arrows point up and to the right in the region above both stationary loci, from that region the system can only diverge (at the increasing speed implied by values of q and K that are increasingly far from those consistent with their stability) towards infinitely large values of q and/or K. Such dynamic behavior is quite peculiar from the economic point of view, and in fact it can be shown to violate the transversality condition (2.7) for plausible forms of the $F(\cdot)$ function. Also, starting from points in the lower quadrant of the diagram, the dynamics of the system, driven by arrows pointing left and downwards, can only lead to economically nonsensical values of q and/or K.

The system's configuration is much more sensible at the point where the $\dot{K} = 0$ and $\dot{q} = 0$ loci cross, the unique *steady state* of the dynamic system we are considering. Thus, we can focus attention on dynamic paths starting from the left and right regions of Figure 2.4, where arrows pointing towards the steady state allow the dynamic system to evolve in its general direction.

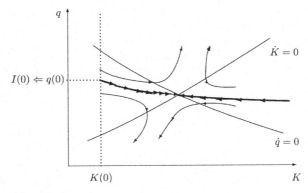

Figure 2.5. Saddlepath dynamics

As shown in Figure 2.5, however, it is quite possible for trajectories starting in those regions to cross the $\dot{K} = 0$ locus (vertically) or the $\dot{q} = 0$ locus
(horizontally) and then, instead of reaching the steady state, proceed in the
regions where arrows point *away* from it—implying that (2.7) is violated, or
that capital eventually becomes negative.

In the figure, however, a pair of dynamic paths is drawn that start from
points to the left and right of the steady state and continue towards it (at
decreasing speed) without ever meeting the system's stationarity loci. All
points along such paths are compatible with convergence towards the steady
state, and together form the *saddlepath* of the dynamic system. For any given
K, such as that labeled $K(0)$ in the figure, only one level of q (or, equivalently, only one rate of investment) puts the system on a trajectory converging
towards the steady state. If q were higher, and the $I(0)$ investment rate larger,
the firm should continue to invest at a rate faster than that leading to the
steady state in order to keep on satisfying the last optimality condition in
(2.6), and the (2.12) dynamic equation deriving from it. Sooner or later, this
would lead the firm to cross the $\dot{q} = 0$ line and, along a path of ever increasing
investment, to violate the transversality condition. Symmetrically, if the firm
invested less than what is implied by the saddlepath value of q, it would find
itself investing less and less over time, and would diverge towards excessively
small capital stocks rather than converge to the steady state.

2.3. **Steady-State and Adjustment Paths**

For a given (and supposed constant) value of exogenous variables, the firm's
investment rate should be that implied by the q level corresponding on the
saddlepath to the capital stock, which, at any point in time, is determined by
past investment decisions. The capital stock and its shadow value then move

towards their steady state (if they are not there yet). Setting $\dot{q} = \dot{K} = 0$ and $\pi_k = 0$ in (2.12) and (2.13), we can study the steady-state levels q_{ss} and K_{ss}:

$$(r + \delta)q_{ss} = \frac{1}{P_k} \left. \frac{\partial F(\cdot)}{\partial K} \right|_{K=K_{ss}}, \tag{2.14}$$

$$\iota(q_{ss}, K_{ss}) = \delta K_{ss}. \tag{2.15}$$

The second equation simply indicates that the gross investment rate $I_{ss} = \iota(q_{ss}, K_{ss})$ must be such as to compensate depreciation in the stock of capital (stock that is constant, by definition, in steady state). The first equation is less obvious. Recalling that $q_{ss} = \lambda_{ss}/P_k$, however, we may rewrite it as

$$\lambda_{ss} = (r + \delta)^{-1} \left. \frac{\partial F(\cdot)}{\partial K} \right|_{K=K_{ss}} = \int_t^\infty e^{-(r+\delta)(\tau-t)} \left. \frac{\partial F(\cdot)}{\partial K} \right|_{K=K_{ss}} d\tau.$$

Thus, in steady state the shadow value of capital is equal to the stream of future marginal contributions by capital to the firm's cash flows, discounted at rate $r + \delta > 0$ over the infinite planning horizon. If it were the case that $r + \delta = 0$, the relevant present value would be ill-defined: hence, as mentioned above and discussed in more detail below, it must be the case that $r + \delta > 0$ in a well-defined investment problem.

The steady state is readily interpreted along the lines of a simple approach to investment which should be familiar from undergraduate textbooks (see Jorgenson 1963, 1971). One may treat the capital stock as a factor of production whose user cost is $(r_k + \delta)P_k$ when P_k is the price of each stock unit, $r_k = i - \Delta P_k/P_k$ is the real rate of interest in terms of capital, and δ is the physical depreciation rate of capital. If the profit flow is an increasing concave function $F(K, \dots)$ of capital K, the first-order condition

$$\frac{\partial F(K^*(\dots), \dots)}{\partial K} = (r_k + \delta)P_k \tag{2.16}$$

identifies the K^* stock that maximizes $F(K, \dots)$ in each period, neglecting adjustment costs. If capital does not depreciate and $\delta = 0$, however, condition (2.15) implies that $q_{ss} = 1$, since $\partial G(\cdot)/\partial I = 1$ when $I = 0$, and condition (2.14) simply calls for capital's marginal productivity to coincide with its financial cost, just as in static approaches to optimal use of capital:

$$\frac{\partial F(\cdot)}{\partial K} = r P_k.$$

If instead $\delta > 0$, then steady-state investment is given by $I_{ss} = \delta K_{ss} > 0$, and therefore $q_{ss} > 1$. The unit cost of capital being installed to offset ongoing depreciation is higher than P_k, because of adjustment costs.

Phase diagrams are useful not only for characterizing adjustment paths starting from a given initial situation, but also for studying the investment effects of permanent changes in parameters. To this end, one may specify a functional form for cash flows $F(\cdot)$ in (2.1), as is done in the exercises at the end of the chapter, and study the effects of a change in its parameters on the $\dot{q} = 0$ locus, on the steady-state capital stock, and on the system's adjustment path.

Consider, for example, the effect of a smaller wage w. This event, as the following exercise verifies in a special case, may (or may not) imply an increase in the optimal capital stock in the static context of introductory economics textbooks—and, equivalently, a higher stock K_{ss} in the steady state of the dynamic problem we are studying.

Exercise 11 *Suppose that the adjustment cost function $G(\cdot)$ does not depend on the capital stock, and let $\delta = 0$. If the firm's revenue function has the Cobb–Douglas form $R(K, N, t) = K^{\alpha} N^{\beta}$, does a lower w increase or decrease the steady-state capital stock K_{ss}?*

At the time when parameters change, however, the capital stock is given. The new configuration of the system can affect only q and the investment rate, and the resulting dynamics *gradually* increase (or decrease) the capital stock. The gradual character of the optimal adjustment path derives from strictly convex adjustment costs, which, as we know, make fast investment unattractive. At any time, the speed of adjustment depends on the difference between the current and steady-state levels of q. Hence the speed of movement along the saddlepath is decreasing, and the growth rate of capital becomes infinitesimally small as the steady state is approached. In fact, it is by avoiding perpetually accelerating capital and investment trajectories that the "saddle" adjustment paths can satisfy the transversality condition.

It is also interesting to study the effects on investment of future expected events. Suppose that at time $t = 0$ it becomes known that the wage will remain constant at $w(0)$ until $t = T$, will then fall to $w(T) < w(0)$, and will remain constant at that new level. The optimal investment flow anticipates such a future exogenous event: if a lower wage and the resulting higher employment of N implies a larger marginal contribution of capital to cash flows, then the firm begins at time zero to invest more than what would be optimal if it were known that $w(t) = w(0)$ for ever. However, since between $t = 0$ and $t = T$ the wage is still $w(0)$ and there is no reason to increase N for given K, it cannot be optimal for the firm to behave as in the solution of the exercise above, where the wage decreased permanently to $w(t) = w(T)$ for all t.

In order to characterize the optimal investment policy, recall that to avoid divergent dynamics the firm should select a dynamic path that leads towards the steady state while satisfying the optimality conditions. From time T onwards, all parameters are constant and we know that the firm should be

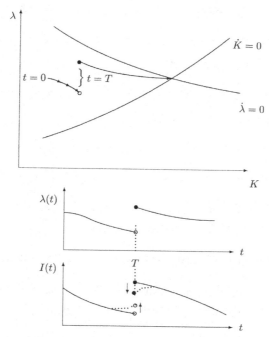

Figure 2.6. A hypothetical jump along the dynamic path, and the resulting time path of $\lambda(t)$ and investment ($\uparrow + \downarrow$) $\Rightarrow$ smaller investment costs

on the saddlepath leading to the new steady state. To figure out the dynamics of q and K during the period when the system's dynamics are still those implied by $w(0)$, note that the system should evolve so as to find itself on the new saddlepath at time T, *without experiencing discontinuous jumps*. To see why, consider the implications of a dynamic path such that a discontinuous jump of q is needed to bring the system on the saddlepath, as in Figure 2.6. Formally, it would be impossible to define $\dot{q}(T)$, hence $\dot{\lambda}(T)$, and neither equation (2.12) nor the optimality condition (2.6) could be satisfied. From the economic point of view, recall that a sudden change of q would necessarily entail a similarly abrupt variation of the investment flow, as in the figure. As we know, however, strictly convex adjustment costs imply that such an investment policy is more costly than a smoother version, such as that represented by dots in the figure. Whenever a path with foreseeable discontinuities is considered as an optimal-policy candidate, it can be ruled out by the fact that a more gradual investment policy would reduce overall investment costs. (A more gradual investment policy also affects the capital path, of course, but investment can be redistributed over time so as to make this effect relatively small on a present discounted basis.) Since such reasoning can be applied at every instant, the optimal path is necessarily free of discontinuities—other than the unavoidable

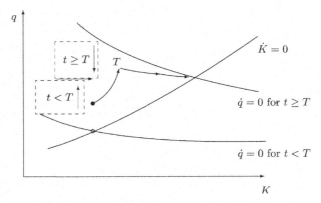

Figure 2.7. Dynamic effects of an announced future change of w

one associated with the initial re-optimization in light of new, unforeseen information arriving at time zero.

It is now easy to display graphically, as in Figure 2.7, the dynamic response of the system. Starting from the steady state, the height of q's jump at time zero (when the parameter change to be realized at time T is announced) depends on how far in the future is the expected event. In the limit case where $T = 0$ (that is, where the parameter change occurs immediately) q would jump directly on the new saddlepath. If, as in Figure 2.7, T is rather far in the future, q jumps to a point intermediate between the initial one (the old steady state, in the figure) and the saddlepath: the firm then follows the dynamics implied by the initial parameters until time T, when the dynamic path meets the new saddlepath. Intuitively, the firm finds it convenient to dilute over time the adjustment it foresees. For larger values of T the height of the initial jump would be smaller, and the apparently divergent dynamics induced by the expectation of future events would follow slower, more prolonged, dynamics.

These results offer a more precise interpretation of the investment determination assumptions made in the IS–LM model familiar from introductory macroeconomics courses, where business investment I depends on exogenous variables $\left(\text{say, } \bar{I}\right)$ and negatively on the interest rate. This relationship can be rationalized qualitatively considering that the propensity to invest should depend on (exogenous) expectations of future (hence, discounted) profits to be obtained from capital installed through current investment. From this point of view, any variable relevant to expectations of future profits influences the exogenous component $\bar{I}$ of investment flows. Since the present discounted value of profits is lower for large discount factors, for any given $\bar{I}$ the investment flow I is a decreasing function of the current interest rate i. In the context of the dynamic model we are considering, the firm's investment tends to a steady state, which, inasmuch as it depends on future events, depends in obvious and important ways on *expectations*.[26]

2.4. The Value of Capital and Future Cash Flows

As we have seen, in steady state it is possible to express $q(t)$ in terms of the present value of future marginal effects of K on the firm's cash flows. In fact, a similar expression is *always* valid along an optimal investment path. If we set $P_k(t) = 1$ for all t (and therefore $\pi_k \equiv 0$) for simplicity, then q and λ are equal. The last condition in (2.6) may be written

$$\frac{d}{d\tau}\lambda(\tau) - (r + \delta)\lambda(\tau) = -F_K(\tau), \tag{2.17}$$

where

$$F_K(\tau) = \frac{\partial F(\tau, K(\tau), N(\tau))}{\partial K} \tag{2.18}$$

denotes the marginal cash-flow effect of capital at every time τ along the firm's optimal trajectory. Multiplying by $e^{-(r+\delta)\tau}$, we can rewrite (2.17) in the form

$$\frac{d}{d\tau}\left(\lambda(\tau)e^{-(r+\delta)\tau}\right) = -F_K(\tau)e^{-(r+\delta)\tau},$$

which may be integrated between $\tau = 0$ and $\tau = T$ to obtain

$$e^{-(r+\delta)T}\lambda(T) - \lambda(0) = -\int_0^T F_K(\tau)e^{-(r+\delta)\tau}\,d\tau.$$

In the limit for $T \to \infty$, as long as $K(\infty) > 0$ condition (2.7) implies that the first term vanishes and

$$\lambda(0) = \int_0^\infty F_K(\tau)e^{-(r+\delta)\tau}\,d\tau. \tag{2.19}$$

Along an optimal investment trajectory, the marginal value of capital at time zero is the present value of cash flows generated by an additional unit of capital at time zero which, depreciating steadily over time at rate δ, adds $e^{-\delta t}$ units of capital at each time $t > 0$. *Taking as given the capital stock installed at time t,* each additional unit of capital increases cash flows according to $F_K(\cdot)$. The firm could indeed install such an additional unit and then, *keeping its investment policy unchanged,* increase discounted cash flows by the amount in (2.19).

---

[26] Keynes (1936, ch. 12) emphasizes the relevance of expectation later adopted as a key feature of Keynesian IS–LM models. Of course, his framework of analysis is quite different from that adopted here, and does not quite agree with the notion that investment should always tend to some long-run equilibrium configuration.

This reasoning does not take into account the fact that a hypothetical variation of investment (hence of capital in use in subsequent periods) should lead the firm to vary its choices of further investment. Any such variation, however, has no effect on capital's marginal value as long as its size is infinitesimally small. If at time zero a small additional amount of capital were in fact installed, the firm would indeed vary its future investment policy, but only by similarly small amounts. This would have no effect on discounted cash flows *around an optimal trajectory*, where first-order conditions are satisfied and small perturbations of endogenous variables have no first-order effect on the firm's value.

This fact, an application of the *envelope theorem*, makes it possible to compute capital's marginal value taking as given the optimal dynamic path of capital—or, equivalently, to gauge the optimality of each investment decision taking all other such decisions as given. In general, equation (2.19) does not offer an explicit solution for $\lambda(0)$, because its right-hand side depends on future levels of K whenever $\partial F_K(\cdot)/\partial K \neq 0$, that is, whenever the function linking cash flows to capital is strictly concave. Inasmuch as the marginal contribution of capital to cash flows depends on the stock of capital, one would need to know the level of $K(\tau)$ for $\tau > 0$ in order to compute the right-hand side of (2.19). But future capital stocks depend on current investment flows, which in turn depend on the very λ that one is attempting to evaluate. The obvious circularity of this reasoning generally makes it impossible to compute the optimal policy through this route. For a finite planning horizon T, one could obtain a solution starting from the given (possibly zero) value of capital at the time when the firm ceases to exist. But if $T \to \infty$ one needs to compute the optimal policy as a whole, or at least to characterize it graphically as we did above. In fact, it is easy to interpret the dynamics of q in Figure 2.7 in terms of expected cash flows: favorable exogenous events become nearer in time (and are more weakly discounted) along the first portion of the dynamic path illustrated in the figure.

It can be the case, however, that $F(\cdot)$ is only weakly concave (hence linear) in K; then $F_K(\cdot) \equiv \partial F(\cdot)/\partial K$ does not depend on exogenous variables, equation (2.19) yields an explicit value for λ, and the firm's investment policy follows immediately. For example, if

$$\frac{\partial G(\cdot)}{\partial K} = 0, \qquad R(t, K(t), N(t)) = \bar{R}(t)K(t), \qquad (2.20)$$

then (2.19) reads

$$\lambda(0) = \int_0^\infty \bar{R}(\tau)e^{-(r+\delta)\tau}\,d\tau. \qquad (2.21)$$

The first equation in (2.20) states that capital's installation costs depend only on I, not on K. Hence, unit investment costs do depend on the size of investment flows per unit time, but the cost of a given capital stock increase is independent of the firm's initial size. The second equation in (2.20) states that each unit of installed capital makes the same contribution to the firm's capital stock, again denying that the firm's size is relevant at the margin.

A relationship in the form (2.21) holds true, more generally, whenever the scale of the firm's operations is irrelevant at the margin. Consider the case of a firm using a production function $f(K, N)$ with constant returns to scale, and operating in a competitive environment (taking as given prices and wages). By the constant-returns assumption, $f(K, N) = f(K/x, N/x)x$, and, setting $x = K$, total revenues may be written

$$R(t, K, N) = P(t)f(K, N) = P(t)f(1, N/K)K.$$

The first-order condition $\partial R(\cdot)/\partial N = w$, which takes the form

$$P(t)f_N(1, N/K) = w(t),$$

determines the optimal N/K ratio as a function $v(\cdot)$ of the $w(t)/P(t)$ ratio. In the absence of adjustment costs for factor N, this condition holds at all times, and $N(t)/K(t) = v(w(t)/P(t))$ for all t. Hence,

$$F(t) = P(t)f(1, v(w(t)/P(t)))K - w(t)v(w(t)/P(t))$$

$$K - P_k(t)G(I(t), K(t)),$$

and, using the first equation in (2.20), we arrive at

$$\frac{\partial F(\cdot)}{\partial K} = P(t)f(1, v(w(t)/P(t))) - w(t)v(w(t)/P(t)). \tag{2.22}$$

This expression is independent of K, like $\tilde{R}(\cdot)$ in (2.21), and allows us to conclude that the constant-returns function $F(\cdot)$ is simply proportional to K.

This algebraic derivation introduces simple mathematical results that will be useful when characterizing the average value of capital in the next section. It also has interesting implications, however, when one allows for the possibility that future realizations of exogenous variables such as $w(t)$ and $P(t)$ may be random. A formal redefinition of the problem to allow for uncertainty in continuous time requires more advanced technical tools, introduced briefly in the last section of this chapter. Intuitively, however, if the firm's objective function is defined as the *expected value* of the integral in (2.5), an expression similar to (2.19) should also hold in expectation:

$$\lambda(0) = \int_0^\infty E_0[F_K(\tau)]e^{-(r+\delta)\tau}d\tau. \tag{2.23}$$

In discrete time, one would replace the integral with a summation and the exponential function with compound discount factors. It would still be true, of course, that along an optimal investment trajectory the marginal value of

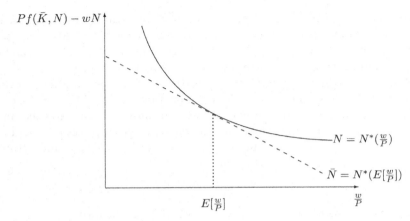

Figure 2.8. Unit profits as a function of the real wage

capital is equal to the present expected value of its contributions to future cash flows.

Now, if the firm operates in perfectly competitive markets, produces under constant returns, and chooses the flexible factor optimally at all times, so that (2.22) holds, then optimal cash flows are a *convex* function of the real product wage, $w(t)/P(t)$. It is easy to see why when we consider Figure 2.8, which displays the profit accruing to the firm from each unit of capital. (A study of unit profits is equivalent to that of total profits if, as in the present case, the latter are proportional to the former.) If the firm did not vary its employment of N in response to a change in the real wage, then, for given K, the difference between revenues and variable-factor costs would be a linear function of the real wage. By definition, the profits afforded by optimal adjustment of N must be larger for every possible real wage, and will be equal only where the supposedly constant employment level is optimal. Thus, profits are a convex function of the real wage. Flexibility in employment of N allows the firm to use each unit of capital so as to exploit favorable conditions and to limit losses in unfavorable ones.

By Jensen's inequality (already encountered when introducing precautionary savings in Chapter 1), the conditions listed above imply that

$$\text{Var}\left(\frac{w(t)}{p(t)}\right) > 0 \quad \Rightarrow E_t\left[F_K(w(t)/P(t))\right] > F_K\left(E_t[w(t)/P(t)]\right).$$

Thus, uncertainty *increases* expected profits earned by each unit of capital, and induces more intense investment by a firm that, like the one we are studying, is *risk-neutral* (that is, is concerned only with expectations of future cash flows).

2.5. **Average Value of Capital**

We now recall the expression for $F(\cdot)$ in (2.1), and consider the case where $R(\cdot)$ and $G(\cdot)$ are *linearly homogeneous* as functions of K, N, and I. A function $f(\cdot)$ is linearly homogeneous if

$$f(\lambda x, \lambda y) = \lambda f(x, y),$$

as in the case of constant-returns production functions. Then, *Euler's theorem* states that[27]

$$f(x, y) = \frac{\partial f(x, y)}{\partial x} x + \frac{\partial f(x, y)}{\partial y} y.$$

If $G(I, K)$ did not depend on K, as in the case considered above, then it could be linearly homogeneous only if adjustment costs were linear (hence not strictly convex) in the investment flow I. But in the more general case, omitting t and denoting partial derivatives by subscripts as in (2.18), we obtain

$$\begin{aligned}
F(t) &= R(t, K(t), N(t)) - P_k(t)G(I(t), K(t)) - w(t)N(t) \\
&= K R_K + N R_N - (I G_I + K G_K) P_k - wN \\
&= (R_K - G_K P_k) K - P_k G_I I,
\end{aligned} \tag{2.24}$$

where the first step applies Euler's theorem to $R(\cdot)$ and $G(\cdot)$, and the second recognizes that $R_N = w$ by the second condition in (2.6).

Noting that $R_K - G_K P_k \equiv F_K$, and that the other conditions in (2.6) and the accumulation constraint imply

$$P_k G_I = \lambda, \quad F_K = (r + \delta)\lambda - \dot{\lambda}, \quad I = \dot{K} + \delta K,$$

equation (2.24) simplifies to

$$F(t) = r\lambda(t)K(t) - \dot{\lambda}(t)K(t) - \lambda(t)\dot{K}(t) \tag{2.25}$$

along an optimal trajectory. It is immediately verified that this is equivalent to

$$e^{-rt}F(t) = \frac{d}{dt}\left[-e^{-rt}\lambda(t)K(t)\right], \tag{2.26}$$

---

[27] This implies that, if x and y are factors of production whose units are compensated according to marginal productivity, then the total compensation of the two factors exhausts production. (There are no pure profits.) This will be relevant when, in Ch. 4, we discuss income distribution in a dynamic general equilibrium.

and it is easy to evaluate the integral in the definition (2.5) of the firm's value:

$$V(0) = \int_0^\infty F(t)e^{-rt}\,dt$$

$$= \left(-e^{-rt}\lambda(t)K(t)\right)_0^\infty$$

$$= \lambda(0)K(0), \tag{2.27}$$

where the last step recognizes that $\lim_{t\to\infty} e^{-rt}\lambda(t)K(t) = 0$ if the limit condition (2.7) holds.

Thus, $\lambda(0) = V(0)/K(0)$, and since this holds true for any time zero and all steps are valid for any $P_k(t)$ (constant, or variable), we have in general

$$q(t) \equiv \frac{\lambda(t)}{P_k(t)} = \frac{V(t)}{P_k(t)K(t)}. \tag{2.28}$$

Hence marginal q, which in the models considered above determines optimal investment, is the same as the ratio of the firm's market value to the replacement cost of its capital stock.

This result offers a precise interpretation for another intuitive idea familiar from introductory textbooks, namely the Tobin (1969) notion that investment flows may be interpreted on the basis of financial considerations. In other words, it is profitable to install capital and increase the production possibilities of each firm and of the whole economy only if the cost of investment compares favorably to the value of installed capital, as measured by the value of firms in the financial market. As we have seen, the *average q* measure identified by the Tobin approach is indeed the determinant of investment decisions when firms face convex, linearly homogeneous adjustment costs, and produce under constant returns.

Exercise 12 *If the $F(\cdot)$ and $G(\cdot)$ functions are linearly homogeneous in K, I, and N (so that average and marginal q coincide), what is the shape of the $\dot{K} = 0$ and $\dot{q} = 0$ loci in the phase diagram discussed in Section 2.2.1?*

Such reasoning and results suggest an empirical approach to the study of investment. On the basis of equation (2.11), investment should be *completely* explained by q, which in turn is directly measurable from stock market and balance-sheet data under the hypotheses listed above. Investment does depend on (unobservable) expectations of future events. But, since the same expectations also affect the value of the firm in a rational financial market, one may test the proposed theoretical framework by considering empirical relationships between investment flows and measured q. Of course, both the value of the firm (and the average q it implies) and its investment are endogenous variables. Hence the empirical strategy is akin to that, based on Euler equations for aggregate consumption, encountered in Chapter 1. One does not estimate a function relating investment (or consumption) to exogenous variables, but rather verifies a property that endogenous variables should display under certain theoretical assumptions.

As regards revenues, the assumption leading to the conclusion that investment and average q should be strictly related may be interpreted supposing that the firm produces under constant returns to scale and behaves in perfectly competitive fashion. As regards adjustment costs, the assumption is that they pertain to proportional increases of the firm's size, rather than to absolute investment flows. A larger firm bears smaller costs to undertake a given amount of investment, and the whole optimal investment program may be scaled upwards or downwards if doubling the size of the firms yields the same unit investment costs for twice-as-large investment flows, that is if the adjustment cost function has constant returns to scale and $G(I, K) = g(I/K)K$. The realism of these (like any other) assumptions is debatable, of course. They do imply that different initial sizes of the firm simply yield a proportionally rescaled optimal investment program. As always under constant returns to scale and perfectly competitive conditions, the firm does not have an optimal size and, in fact, does not quite have a well-defined identity. In more general models, the value of the firm is less intimately linked to its capital stock and therefore may vary independently of optimal investment flows.

2.6. **A Dynamic IS–LM Model**

We are now ready to apply the economic insights and technical tools introduced in the previous sections to study an explicitly macroeconomic, and explicitly dynamic, modeling framework. Specifically, we discuss a simplified version of the dynamic IS–LM model of Blanchard (1981), capturing the interactions between forward-looking prices of financial assets and output and highlighting the role of expectations in determining (through investment) macroeconomic outcomes and the effects of monetary and fiscal policies. As in the static version of the IS–LM model, the level of goods prices is exogenously fixed and constant over time. However, the previous sections' positive relationship between the forward-looking q variable and investment is explicitly accounted for by the aggregate demand side of the model.

A linear equation describes the determinants of aggregate goods spending $y^D(t)$:

$$y^D(t) = a q(t) + c y(t) + g(t), \qquad a > 0, \ 0 < c < 1. \qquad (2.29)$$

Spending is determined by aggregate income y (through consumption), by the flow g of public spending (net of taxes) set exogenously by the fiscal authorities, and by q as the main determinant of private investment spending.

We shall view q as the market valuation of the capital stock of the economy incorporated in the level of stock prices: for simplicity, we disregard the distinction between average and marginal q, as well as any role of stock prices in determining aggregate consumption.

Output y evolves over time according to the following dynamic equation:

$$\dot{y}(t) = \beta\left(y^D(t) - y(t)\right), \qquad \beta > 0. \tag{2.30}$$

Output responds to the excess demand for goods: when spending is larger than current output, firms meet demand by running down inventories and by increasing production gradually over time. In our setting, output is a "predetermined" variable (like the capital stock in the investment model of the preceding sections) and cannot be instantly adjusted to fill the gap between spending and current production.

A conventional linear LM curve describes the equilibrium on the money market:

$$\frac{m(t)}{p} = h_0 + h_1\, y(t) - h_2\, r(t), \tag{2.31}$$

where the left-hand side is the real money supply (the ratio of nominal money supply m to the constant price level p), and the right-hand side is money demand. The latter depends positively on the level of output and negatively on the interest rate r on short-term bonds.[28] Conveniently, we assume that such bonds have an infinitesimal duration; then, the instantaneous rate of return from holding them coincides with the interest rate r with no possibility of capital gains or losses.

Shares and short-term bonds are assumed to be perfect substitutes in investors' portfolios (a reasonable assumption in a context of certainty); consequently, the rates of return on shares and bonds must be equal for any arbitrage possibility to be ruled out. The following equation must then hold in equilibrium:

$$\frac{\pi(t)}{q(t)} + \frac{\dot{q}(t)}{q(t)} = r(t), \tag{2.32}$$

where the left-hand side is the (instantaneous) rate of return on shares, made up of the firms' profits π (entirely paid out as dividends to shareholders) and the capital gain (or loss) $\dot{q}$. At any time this composite rate of return on shares must equal the interest rate on bonds r.[29] Finally, profits are positively related to the level of output:

$$\pi(t) = a_0 + a_1\, y(t). \tag{2.33}$$

---

[28] The assumption of a constant price level over time implies a zero expected inflation rate; there is then no need to make explicit the difference between the nominal and real rates of return.

[29] If long-term bonds were introduced as an additional financial asset, a further "no arbitrage" equation similar to (2.32) should hold between long and short-term bonds.

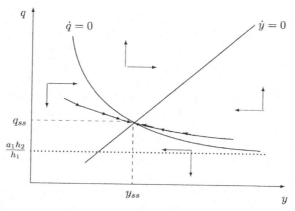

Figure 2.9. A dynamic IS–LM model

The two dynamic variables of interest are output y and the stock market valuation q. In order to study the steady-state and the dynamics of the system outside the steady-state, following the procedure adopted in the preceding sections, we first derive the two stationary loci for y and q and plot them in a (q, y)-phase diagram. Setting $\dot{y} = 0$ in (2.30) and using the specification of aggregate spending in (2.29), we get the following relationship between y and q:

$$y = \frac{a}{1-c} q + \frac{1}{1-c} g, \tag{2.34}$$

represented as an upward-sloping line in Figure 2.9. A higher value of q stimulates aggregate spending through private investment and increases output in the steady state. This line is the equivalent of the IS schedule in a more traditional IS–LM model linking the interest rate to output. For each level of output, there exists a unique value of q for which output equals spending: higher values of q determine larger investment flows and a corresponding excess demand for goods, and, according to the dynamic equation for y, output gradually increases. As shown in the diagram by the arrows pointing to the right, $\dot{y} > 0$ at all points above the $\dot{y} = 0$ locus. Symmetrically, $\dot{y} < 0$ at all points below the stationary locus for output.

The stationary locus for q is derived by setting $\dot{q} = 0$ in (2.32), which yields

$$q = \frac{\pi}{r} = \frac{a_0 + a_1 y}{h_0/h_2 + h_1/h_2\, y - 1/h_2\, m/p}, \tag{2.35}$$

where the last equality is obtained using (2.33) and (2.31). The steady-state value of q is given by the ratio of dividends to the interest rate, and both are affected by output. As y increases, profits and dividends increase, raising q; also, the interest rate (at which profits are discounted) increases, with a depressing effect on stock prices. The slope of the $\dot{q} = 0$ locus then depends on the relative strength of those two effects; in what follows we assume that the "interest rate effect" dominates, and consequently draw a downward-sloping stationary locus for q.[30] The dynamics of q out of its stationary locus are governed by the dynamic equation (2.32). For each level of output (that uniquely determines dividends and the interest rate), only the value of q on the stationary locus is such that $\dot{q} = 0$. Higher values of q reduce the dividend component of the rate of return on shares, and a capital gain, implying $\dot{q} > 0$, is needed to fulfill the "no arbitrage" condition between shares and bonds: q will then move upwards starting from all points above the $\dot{q} = 0$ line, as shown in Figure 2.9. Symmetrically, at all points below the $\dot{q} = 0$ locus, capital losses are needed to equate returns and, therefore $\dot{q} < 0$.

The unique steady state of the system is found at the point where the two stationary loci cross and output and stock prices are at y_{ss} and q_{ss} respectively. As in the dynamic model analyzed in previous sections, in the present framework too there is a unique trajectory converging to the steady-state, the *saddlepath* of the dynamic system. To rationalize its negative slope in the (q, y) space, let us consider at time t_0 a level of output $y(t_0) < y_{ss}$. The associated level $q(t_0)$ on the saddlepath is higher than the value of q on the stationary locus $\dot{y} = 0$. Therefore, there is excess demand for goods owing to a high level of investment, and output gradually increases towards its steady-state value. As y increases, the demand for money increases also and, with a given money supply m, the interest rate rises. The behavior of q is best understood if the dynamic equation (2.32) is solved forward, yielding the value of $q(t_0)$ as the present discounted value of future dividends:[31]

$$q(t_0) = \int_{t_0}^{\infty} \pi(t)\, e^{-\int_{t_0}^{t} r(s)\, ds}\, dt. \tag{2.36}$$

Over time q changes, for two reasons: on the one hand, q is positively affected by the increase in dividends (resulting from higher output); on the other, future dividends are discounted at higher interest rates, with a negative effect on q. Under our maintained assumption that the "interest rate effect" dominates, q declines over time towards its steady-state value q_{ss}.

Let us now use our dynamic IS–LM model to study the effects of a change in macroeconomic policy. Suppose that at time $t = 0$ a future fiscal restriction is announced, to be implemented at time $t = T$: public spending, which is initially constant at $g(0)$, will be decreased to $g(T) < g(0)$ at $t = T$ and will then remain permanently at this lower level. The effects of this anticipated fiscal restriction on the steady-state levels of output and the interest rate are immediately clear from a conventional IS–LM (static) model: in the new

---

[30] Formally, $dq/dy|_{\dot{q}=0} < 0 \Leftrightarrow a_1 < q(h_1/h_2)$. Moreover, as indicated in Fig. 2.9, the $\dot{q} = 0$ line has the following asymptote: $\lim_{y \to \infty} q|_{\dot{q}=0} = a_1 h_2/h_1$.

[31] In solving the equation, the terminal condition $\lim_{t \to \infty} \pi(t) e^{-\int_{t_0}^{t} r(s) ds} = 0$ is imposed.

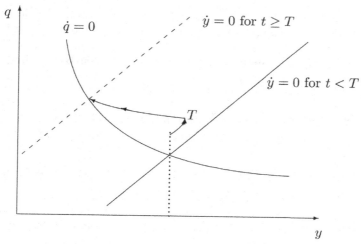

Figure 2.10. Dynamic effects of an anticipated fiscal restriction

steady state both y and r will be lower. Both changes affect the new steady-state level of q: lower output and dividends depress stock prices, whereas a lower interest rate raises q. Again, the latter effect is assumed to dominate, leading to an increase in the steady-state value of q. This is shown in Figure 2.10 by an upward shift of the stationary locus $\dot{y} = 0$, which occurs at $t = T$ along an unchanged $\dot{q} = 0$ schedule, leading to a higher q and a lower y in steady-state.

In order to characterize the dynamics of the system, we note that, from time T onwards, no further change in the exogenous variables occurs: to converge to the steady state, the economy must then be on the saddlepath portrayed in the diagram. Accordingly, from T onwards, output decreases (since the lower public spending causes aggregate demand to fall below current production) and q increases (owing to the decreasing interest rate). What happens between the time of the fiscal policy announcement and that of its delayed implementation? At $t = 0$, when the future policy becomes known, agents in the stock market anticipate lower future interest rates. (They also foresee lower dividends, but this effect is relatively weak.) Consequently, they immediately shift their portfolios towards shares, bidding up share prices. Then at the announcement date, with output and the interest rate still at their initial steady-state levels, q increases. The ensuing dynamics from $t = 0$ up to the date T of implementation follow the equations of motion in (2.30) and (2.32) on the basis of the parameters valid in the initial steady state. A higher value of q stimulates investment, causing an excess demand for goods; starting from $t = 0$, then, output gradually *increases*, and so does the interest rate. The dynamic adjustment of output and q is such that, when the fiscal policy is implemented at T (and the stationary locus $\dot{y} = 0$ shifts upwards), the economy is exactly on the saddlepath leading to the new steady-state:

aggregate demand falls and output starts decreasing along with the interest rate, whereas q and investment continue to rise. Therefore, an apparently "perverse" effect of fiscal policy (an expansion of investment and output following the announcement of a future fiscal restriction) can be explained by the forward-looking nature of stock prices, anticipating future lower interest rates.

Exercise 13 *Consider the dynamic IS–LM model proposed in this section, but suppose that (contrary to what we assumed in the text) the "interest rate effect" is dominated by the "dividend effect" in determining the slope of the stationary locus for q.*

(a) *Give a precise characterization of the $\dot{q} = 0$ schedule and of the dynamic properties of the system under the new assumption.*

(b) *Analyze the effects of an anticipated permanent fiscal restriction (announced at $t = 0$ and implemented at $t = T$), and contrast the results with those reported in the text.*

2.7. **Linear Adjustment Costs**

We now return to a typical firm's partial equilibrium optimal investment problem, questioning the realism of some of the assumptions made above and assessing the robustness of the qualitative results obtained from the simple model introduced in Section 2.1. There, we assumed that a given increase of the capital stock would be more costly when enacted over a shorter time period, but this is not necessarily realistic. It is therefore interesting to study the implications of relaxing one of the conditions in (2.4) to

$$\frac{\partial^2 G(\cdot)}{\partial I^2} = 0, \tag{2.37}$$

so that in Figure 2.1 the $G(I, \cdot)$ function would coincide with the 45° line. Its slope, $\partial G(\cdot)/\partial I$, is constant at unity, independently of the capital stock.

Since the cost of investment does not depend on its intensity or the speed of capital accumulation, the firm may choose to invest "infinitely quickly" and the capital stock is *not* given (predetermined) at each point in time. This appears to call into question all the formal apparatus discussed above. However, if we suppose that all paths of exogenous variables are continuous in time and simply proceed to insert $\partial G/\partial I = 1$ (hence $\lambda = P_k$, $\dot{\lambda} = \dot{P}_k = \pi_k P_k$) in conditions (2.6), we can obtain a simple characterization of the firm's optimal policy. As in the essentially static cost-of-capital approach outlined above, condition (2.12) is replaced by

$$\frac{\partial F(\cdot)}{\partial K} = (r + \delta - \pi_k) P_k(t). \tag{2.38}$$

Hence the firm does not need to look forward when choosing investment. Rather, it should simply invest at such a (finite, or infinite) rate as needed to equate the current marginal revenues of capital to its user cost. The latter concept is readily understood noting that, in order to use temporarily an additional unit of capital, one may borrow its purchase cost, P_k, at rate r and re-sell the undepreciated (at rate δ) portion at the new price implied by π_k. If $F_K(\cdot)$ is a decreasing function of installed capital (because the firm produces under decreasing returns and/or faces a downward-sloping demand function), then equation (2.38) identifies the desired stock of capital as a function of exogenous variables. Investment flows can then be explained in terms of the dynamics of such exogenous variables between the beginning and the end of each period. In continuous time, the investment rate per unit time is well defined if exogenous variables do not change discontinuously.

Recall that we had to rule out all changes of exogenous variables (other than completely unexpected or perfectly foreseen one-time changes) when drawing phase diagrams. In the present setting, conversely, it is easy to study the implications of ongoing exogenous dynamics. This enhances the realism and applicability of the model, but the essentially static character of the perspective encounters its limits when applied to real-life data. In reality, not only the growth rates of exogenous variable in (2.38), but also their past and future dynamics appear relevant to current investment flows.

An interesting compromise between strict convexity and linearity is offered by piecewise linear adjustment costs. In Figure 2.11, the $G(I, \cdot)$ function has unit slope when gross investment is positive, implying that P_k is the cost of

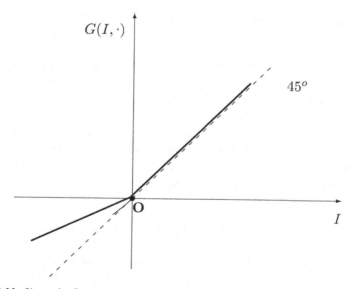

Figure 2.11. Piecewise linear unit investment costs

each unit of capital purchased and installed by the firm, regardless of how many units are purchased together. The adjustment cost function remains linear for $I < 0$, but its slope is smaller. This implies that when selling previously installed units of capital the firm receives a price that is independent of $I(t)$, but lower than the purchase price. This adjustment cost structure is realistic if investment represents purchases of equipment with given off-the-shelf price, such as personal computers, and constant unit installation cost, such as the cost of software installation. If installation costs cannot be recovered when the firm sells its equipment, each firm's capital stock has a degree of specificity, while capital would need to be perfectly transferable into and out of each firm for (2.16) to apply at all times. Linear adjustment costs do not make speedy investment or scrapping unattractive, as strictly convex adjustment costs would. The kink at the origin, however, still makes it unattractive to mix periods of positive and negative gross investment. If a positive investment were immediately followed by a negative one, the firm would pay installation costs without using the marginal units of capital for any length of time. In general, a firm whose adjustment costs have the form illustrated in Figure 2.11 should avoid investment when very temporary events call for capital stock adjustment. Installation costs put a premium on inactivity: the firm should cease to invest, even as current conditions improve, if it expects (or, in the absence of uncertainty, knows) that bad news will arrive soon.

To study the problem formally in the simplest possible setting, it is convenient to suppose that the price commanded by scrapped units of capital is so low as to imply that investment decisions are effectively *irreversible*. This is the case when the slope of $G(I, \cdot)$ for $I < 0$ is so small as to fall short of what can be earned, on a present discounted basis, from the use of capital in production. Since adjustment costs do not induce the firm to invest slowly, the investment rate may optimally jump between positive and negative values. In fact, nothing prevents optimal investment from becoming infinitely positive or negative, or the optimal capital stock path from jumping. If exogenous variables follow continuous paths, however, there is no reason for any such jump to occur along an optimal path. Hence the Hamiltonian solution method remains applicable. Among the conditions in (2.6), only the first needs to be modified: if capital has price P_k when purchased and is never sold, the first-order condition for investment reads

$$P_k \begin{cases} = \lambda(t), & \text{if } I > 0, \\ \geq \lambda(t), & \text{if } I = 0. \end{cases} \tag{2.39}$$

The optimality condition in (2.39) requires $\lambda(t)$, the marginal value of capital at time t, to be equal to the unit cost of investment *only* if the firm is indeed investing. Hence in periods when $I(t) > 0$ we have $\lambda(t) = P_k$, $\dot{\lambda}(t) = \pi_k P(t)$, and the third condition in (2.6) implies that (2.38) is valid at all t such that $I(t) > 0$. If the firm is investing, capital installed must line up with $\partial F(\cdot)/\partial K$ and with the user cost of capital at each instant.

It is not necessarily optimal, however, always to perform positive investment. It is optimal for the firm *not* to invest whenever the marginal value of capital is (weakly) lower than what it would cost to increase its stock by a unit. In fact, when the firm expects unfavorable developments in the near future of the variables determining the "desired" capital stock that satisfies condition (2.38), then if it continued to invest it would find itself with an excessive of capital stock.

To characterize periods when the firm optimally chooses zero investment, recall that the third condition in (2.6) and the limit condition (2.7) imply, as in (2.19), that

$$q(t) \equiv \frac{\lambda(t)}{P_k(t)} = \frac{1}{P_k(t)} \int_t^\infty F_K(\tau) e^{-(r+\delta)(\tau-t)} \, d\tau. \qquad (2.40)$$

In the upper panel of Figure 2.12, the curve represents a possible dynamic path of desired capital, determined by cyclical fluctuations of $F(\cdot)$ for given K. Since that curve falls faster than capital depreciation for a period, the firm ceases to invest at time t_0 and starts again at time t_1. We know from the

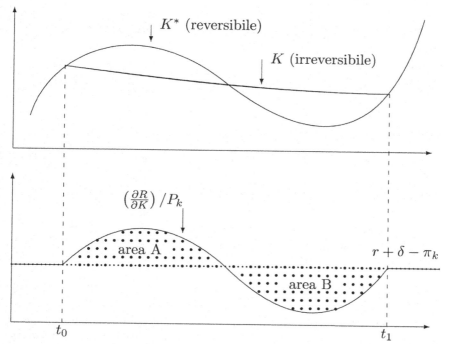

Figure 2.12. Installed capital and optimal irreversible investment

optimality condition (2.39) that the present value (2.40) of marginal revenue products of capital must be equal to the purchase price $P_k(t)$ at all t when gross investment is positive, such as t_0 and t_1. Thus, if we write

$$P_k(t_0) = \int_{t_0}^{\infty} F_K(\tau) e^{-(r+\delta)(\tau - t_0)} \, d\tau$$

$$= \int_{t_0}^{t_1} F_K(\tau) e^{-(r+\delta)(\tau - t_0)} \, d\tau + \int_{t_1}^{\infty} F_K(\tau) e^{-(r+\delta)(\tau - t_0)} \, d\tau, \qquad (2.41)$$

noting that

$$\int_{t_1}^{\infty} F_K(\tau) e^{-(r+\delta)(\tau - t_0)} \, d\tau = e^{-(r+\delta)(t_1 - t_0)} \int_{t_1}^{\infty} F_K(\tau) e^{-(r+\delta)(\tau - t_1)} \, d\tau,$$

and recognizing $\lambda(t_1) = P_k(t_1)$ in the last integral, we obtain

$$P_k(t_0) = \int_{t_0}^{t_1} F_K(\tau) e^{-(r+\delta)(\tau - t_0)} \, d\tau + e^{-(r+\delta)(t_1 - t_0)} P_k(t_1)$$

from (2.41). If the inflation rate in terms of capital is constant at π_k, then $P_k(t_1) = P_k(t_0) e^{\pi_k(t_1 - t_0)}$ and

$$P_k(t_0) = \int_{t_0}^{t_1} F_K(\tau) e^{-(r+\delta)(\tau - t_0)} d\tau + P_k(t_0) e^{-(r+\delta-\pi_k)(t_1 - t_0)}$$

$$\Rightarrow P_k(t_0) \left(1 - e^{-(r+\delta-\pi_k)(t_1 - t_0)}\right) = \int_{t_0}^{t_1} F_K(\tau) e^{-(r+\delta)(\tau - t_0)} d\tau.$$

Noting that

$$\int_{t_0}^{t_1} (r + \delta - \pi_k) e^{-(r+\delta-\pi_k)(\tau - t_0)} d\tau = 1 - e^{-(r+\delta-\pi_k)(t_1 - t_0)},$$

we obtain

$$\int_{t_0}^{t_1} F_K(\tau) e^{-(r+\delta)(\tau - t_0)} d\tau - P_k(t_0) \int_{t_0}^{t_1} (r + \delta - \pi_k) e^{-(r+\delta-\pi_k)(\tau - t_0)} d\tau = 0.$$

Again, using $P_k(t_0) e^{\pi_k(\tau - t_0)} = P_k(\tau)$ yields

$$\int_{t_0}^{t_1} F_K(\tau) e^{-(r+\delta)(\tau - t_0)} d\tau - \int_{t_0}^{t_1} (r + \delta - \pi_k) P_k(\tau) e^{-(r+\delta)(\tau - t_0)} d\tau = 0,$$

and (2.41) may be rewritten as

$$\int_{t_0}^{t_1} [F_K(\tau) - (r + \delta - \pi_k) P_k(\tau)] e^{-(r+\delta)(\tau - t_0)} \, d\tau = 0. \qquad (2.42)$$

Thus, the marginal revenue product of capital should be equal to its user cost in present discounted terms (at rate $r + \delta$) not only when the firm invests continuously, but also over periods throughout which it is optimal not to invest. In Figure 2.12, area A should have the same size as the discounted value of B. Adjustment costs, as usual, affect the dynamic aspects of the firm's behavior. As the cyclical peak nears, the firm stops investing because it knows that in the near future it would otherwise be impossible to preserve equality between marginal revenues and costs of capital.

Similar reasoning is applicable, with some slightly more complicated notation, to the case where the firm may sell installed capital at a positive price $p_k(t) < P_k(t)$ and find it optimal to do so at times. In this case, we should draw in Figure 2.12 another dynamic path, below that representing the desired capital stock when investment is positive, to represent the capital stock that satisfies condition (2.38) when the user cost of capital is computed on the basis of its resale price. The firm should follow this path whenever its desired investment is negative and optimal inaction would lead it from the former to the latter line.

Even though the speed of investment is not constrained, the existence of transaction costs implies that the firm's behavior should be forward-looking. Investment should cease before a slump reveals that it would be desirable to reduce the capital stock. This is yet another instance of the general importance of expectations in dynamic optimization problems. Symmetrically, the capital stock at any given time is not independent of past events. In the latter portion of the inaction period illustrated in the figure, the capital stock is larger than what would be optimal if it could be chosen in light of current conditions. This illustrates another general feature of dynamic optimization problems, namely the character of interaction between endogenous capital and exogenous forcing variables: the former depends on the whole dynamic path of the latter, rather than on their level at any given point in time.

2.8. **Irreversible Investment Under Uncertainty**

Throughout the previous sections, the firm was supposed to know with certainty the future dynamics of exogenous variables relevant to its optimization problem. (And, in order to make use of phase diagrams, we assumed that those variables were constant through time, or only changed discretely in perfectly foreseeable fashion.) This section briefly outlines formal modeling techniques allowing uncertainty to be introduced in explicit, if stylized, ways into the investment problem of a firm facing linear adjustment costs.

We try, as far as possible, to follow the same logical thread as in the derivations encountered above. We continue to suppose that the firm operates in continuous time. The assumption that time is indefinitely divisible is of course far from completely realistic; also less than fully realistic are the assumptions that the capital stock is made up of infinitesimally small particles, and that it may be an argument of a differentiable production function. As was the case under certainty, however, such assumptions make it possible to obtain precise and elegant quantitative results by means of analytical calculus techniques.

2.8.1. STOCHASTIC CALCULUS

First of all, we need to introduce uncertainty into the formal continuous-time optimization framework introduced above. So far, all exogenous features of the firm's problem were determined by the time index, t: knowing the position in time of the dynamic system was enough to know the product price, the cost of factors, and any other variable whose dynamics are taken as given by the firm. To prevent such dynamics from being perfectly foreseeable, one must let them depend not only on time, but also on something else: an index, denoted ω, of the unknown *state of nature*. A function $\{z(t; \omega)\}$ of a time index t and of the state of nature ω is a *stochastic process*, that is, a collection of random variables. The state of nature, by definition, is not observable. If the true ω were known, in fact, the path of the process would again depend on t only, and there would be no uncertainty. But if ω belongs to a set on which a probability distribution is defined, one may formally assign likelihood levels to different possible ω and different possible time paths of the process. This makes it possible to formulate precise answers to questions, clearly of interest to the firm, concerning the probability that processes such as revenues or costs reach a given level within a given time interval.

In order to illustrate practical uses of such concepts, it will not be necessary to deal further with the theory of stochastic processes. We shall instead introduce a type of stochastic process of special relevance in applications: *Brownian motion*. A standard *Brownian motion*, or *Wiener process*, is a basic building block for a class of stochastic process that admits a stochastic counterpart to the functional relationships studied above, such as integrals and differentials. This process, denoted $\{W(t)\}$ in what follows, can be defined by its probabilistic properties. $\{W(t)\}$ is a Wiener process if

1. $W(0; \omega) = 0$ for "almost all" all ω, in the sense that the probability is one that the process takes value zero at $t = 0$;
2. fixing ω, $\{W(t; \omega)\}$ is continuous in t with probability one;
3. fixing $t \geq 0$, probability statements about $W(t; \omega)$ can be made viewing $W(t)$ as a normally distributed random variable, with mean zero and variance t as of time zero: realizations of $W(t)$ are quite concentrated for small values of t, while more and more probability is attached to values far from zero for larger and larger values of t;

4. $W(t') - W(t)$, for every $t' > t$, is also a normally distributed random variable with mean zero and variance $(t' - t)$; and $W(T') - W(T)$ is uncorrelated with—and independent of—$W(t') - W(t)$ for all $T' > T > t' > t$.

Assumption 1 is a simple normalization, and assumption 2 rules out jumps of $W(t)$ to imply that large changes of $W(t)$ become impossible as smaller and smaller time intervals are considered. Indeed, property 3 states that the variance of changes is proportional to time lapsed, hence very small over short periods of time. The process, however, has normally distributed increments over any finite interval of time. Since the normal distribution assigns positive probability to any finite interval of the real line, arbitrarily large variations have positive probability on arbitrarily short (but finite) intervals of time.

Normality of the process's increments is useful in applications, because linear transformations of $W(t)$ can also be normal random variables with arbitrary mean and variance. And the independence over time of such increments stated as property 4 (which implies their normality, by an application of the Central Limit Theorem) makes it possible to make probabilistic statements on all future values of $W(t)$ on the basis of its current level only. It is particularly important to note that, if $\{W(t); 0 \leq t \leq t_1\}$ is known with certainty, or equivalently if observation of the process's trajectory has made it possible to rule out all states of the world ω that would not be consistent with the observed realization of the process up to time t_1, then the probability distribution of the process's behavior in subsequent periods is completely characterized. Since increments are independent over non-overlapping periods, $W(t) - W(t_1)$ is a normal random variable with mean zero and variance $t - t_1$. Hence the process enjoys the Markov property in levels, in that its realization at any time τ contains all information relevant to formulating probabilistic statements as to its realizations at all $t > \tau$.

Independence of the process's increments has an important and somewhat awkward implication: for a fixed ω, the path $\{W(t)\}$ is continuous but (with probability one) *not* differentiable at any point t. Intuitively, a process with differentiable sample paths would have locally predictable increments, because extrapolation of its behavior over the last dt would eliminate all uncertainty about the behavior of the process in the immediate future. This, of course, would deny independence of the process's increments (property 4 above). For increments to be independent over any t interval, including arbitrarily short ones, the direction of movement must be random at arbitrarily close t points. A typical sample path then turns so frequently that it fails to be differentiable at any t point, and has *infinite variation*: the absolute value of its increments over infinitesimally small subdivisions of an arbitrarily short time interval is infinite.

Non-existence of the derivative makes it impossible to apply familiar calculus tools to functions when one of their arguments is a Brownian process $\{W\}$. Such functions—which, like their argument, depend on t, ω and are themselves stochastic process—may however be manipulated by *stochastic calculus* tools, developed half a century ago by Japanese mathematician T. Itô along the lines of classical calculus. Given a process $\{A(t)\}$ with finite variation, a process $\{y(t)\}$ which satisfies certain regularity conditions, and a Wiener process $\{W(t)\}$, the integral

$$z(T; \omega) = z(t; \omega) + \int_t^T y(\tau; \omega) \, d W(\tau; \omega) + \int_t^T d A(t; \omega) \qquad (2.43)$$

defines an *Itô process* $\{z(t)\}$. The expression $\int y \, dW$ denotes a *stochastic* or Itô integral. Its exact definition need not concern us here: we may simply note that it is akin to a weighted sum of the Wiener process's increments $dW(t)$, where the weight function $\{y(t)\}$ is itself a stochastic process in general. The properties of Itô integrals are similar to those of more familiar integrals (or summations). Stochastic integrals of linear combinations can be written as linear combinations of stochastic integrals, and the *integration by parts* formula

$$z(t)x(t) = z(0)x(0) + \int_0^t z(\tau)dx(\tau) + \int_0^t x(\tau)dz(\tau). \qquad (2.44)$$

holds when z and x are processes in the class defined by (2.43) and one of them has finite variation. The stochastic integral has one additional important property. By the unpredictable character of the Wiener process's increments,

$$E_t \left(\int_t^T y(\tau) \, d W(\tau) \right) = 0,$$

for any $\{y(t)\}$ such that the expression is well defined, where $E_t[\cdot]$ denotes the *conditional expectation at time t* (that is, an integral weighting possible realizations with the probability distribution reflecting all available information on the state of nature as of that time).

Recall that, if function $x(t)$ has first derivative $x'(t) = dx(t)/dt = \dot{x}$, and function $f(\cdot)$ has first derivative $f'(x) = df(x)/dx$, then the following relationships are true:

$$dx = \dot{x} \, dt, \quad df(x) = f'(x) \, dx, \quad df(x) = f'(x) \dot{x} \, dt. \qquad (2.45)$$

The integral (2.43) has differential form

$$dz(t) = y(t) \, d W(t) + d A(t), \qquad (2.46)$$

and it is natural to formulate a stochastic version of the "chain rule" relationships in (2.45), used in integration "by substitution." The rule is as follows: if a function $f(\cdot)$ is endowed with first *and second* derivatives, and $\{z(t)\}$

is an Itô process with differential as in (2.46), then

$$df(z(t)) = f'(z(t))y(t)\,dW(t) + f'(z(t))\,dA(t) + \tfrac{1}{2}f''(z(t))(y(t))^2\,dt.$$

$$(2.47)$$

Comparing (2.46–2.47) with (2.45), note that, when applied to an Itô process, variable substitution must take into account not only the first, but also the second, derivative of the transformation. Heuristically, the order of magnitude of $dW(t)$ increments is higher than that of dt if uncertainty is present in every dt interval, no matter how small. Independent increments also imply that the sign of $dW(t)$ is just as likely to be positive as to be negative, and by Jensen's inequality the curvature of $f(z)$ influences locally non-random behavior even in the infinitesimal limit. Taking conditional expectations in (2.47), where $E_t[dW(t)] = 0$ by unpredictability of the Wiener process, we have

$$E_t[df(z(t))] = f'(z(t))\,dA(t) + \tfrac{1}{2}f''(z(t))(y(t)^2)\,dt.$$

Hence $E_t[df(z(t))] \lesseqqgtr f'(z(t))\,E_t[dz(t)]$ depending on whether $f''(z(t)) \lesseqqgtr 0$.

2.8.2. OPTIMIZATION UNDER UNCERTAINTY AND IRREVERSIBILITY

We are now ready to employ these formal tools in the study of a firm that, in partial equilibrium, maximizes the present discounted value at rate r of its cash flows. In the presence of uncertainty, exogenous variables relevant to profits are represented by the realization of a stochastic process, $Z(t)$, rather than by the time index t. As seen above, the optimal profit flow may be a convex function of exogenous variables (but it may also, under different assumptions, be concave). In such cases Jensen's inequality introduces a link between the expected value and variability of capital's marginal revenue product. For simplicity, we will disregard such effects, supposing that the profit flow is linear in Z. Like in the previous section, let $K(t)$ be the capital stock installed at time t. For simplicity, let this be the only factor of production, so that the firm's cash flow gross of investment-related expenditures is $F(K)Z$. We suppose further that units of capital may be purchased at a constant price P_k and have no scrap value. As long as capital is useful—that is, as long as $F'(K) > 0$—this implies that all investment is irreversible.

The exogenous variable Z, which multiplies a function of installed capital, could be interpreted as the product's price. Let its dynamics be described by a stochastic process with differential

$$dZ(t) = \theta Z(t)\,dt + \sigma Z(t)\,dW(t).$$

This is a simple special case of the general expression in (2.46), with $A(t) = \theta Z(t) dt$ and $y(t) = \sigma Z(t)$ for θ and σ constant parameters. This process is a *geometric Brownian motion*, and it is well suited to economic applications because $Z(t)$ is positive (as a price should be) for all $t > 0$ if $Z(0) > 0$; as it gets closer to zero, in fact, this process's increments become increasingly smaller in absolute value, and it can never reach zero. If σ is equal to zero, the proportional growth rate of Z, $dZ/Z = \theta$, is constant and known with certainty, implying that $Z(T)$ is known for all $T > 0$ if $Z(0)$ is. But if σ is larger than zero, that deterministic proportional growth rate is added, during each time interval $(t' - t)$, to the realization of a normally distributed random variable with mean zero and variance $(t' - t)\sigma^2$. This implies that the logarithm of Z is normally distributed (that is, $Z(t)$ is a lognormal random variable), and that the dispersion of future possible levels of Z is increasingly wide over longer forecasting horizons.

As we shall see, the firm's optimal investment policy implies that one may not generally write an expression for $\dot{K} = dK(t)/dt$. If capital depreciates at rate δ, the accumulation constraint is better written in differential form,

$$dK(t) = dX(t) - \delta K(t) dt,$$

for a process $X(t)$ that would correspond to the integral $\int_0^t I(\tau)d\tau$ of gross investment $I(t)$ per unit time if such concepts were well defined.

Apart from such formal peculiarities, the firm's problem is substantially similar to those studied above. We can define, also in the presence of uncertainty, the shadow value of capital at time t, which still satisfies the relationship

$$\lambda(t) = \int_t^T E_t[F'(K(\tau))Z(\tau)]e^{-(r+\delta)(\tau-t)} d\tau. \tag{2.48}$$

As in the previous sections, and quite intuitively, the optimal investment policy must be such as to equate $\lambda(t)$—the marginal contribution of capital to the firm's value—to the marginal cost of investment. If the second derivative of $F(\cdot)$ is not zero, however, the marginal revenue products on the right-hand side of (2.48) depend on the (optimal) investment policy, which therefore must be determined simultaneously with the shadow value of capital.

If investment is irreversible and has constant unit cost P_k, then the firm, as we saw in (2.39), must behave so as to obtain $\lambda(t) = P_k$ when gross investment is positive, that is when $dX(t) > 0$ in the notation introduced here; and to ensure that $\lambda(t) \leq P_k$ at all times. The shadow value of capital is smaller than its cost when a binding irreversibility constraint prevents the firm from keeping them equal to one another, as would be possible (and optimal) if, as in the first few sections of this chapter, investment costs were uniformly convex and smoothly differentiable at the origin.

Now, if the firm only acts when $\lambda(t)/P_k \equiv q$ equals unity, and since the future path of the $\{Z(\tau)\}$ process depends only on its current level $Z(t)$, the expected value in (2.48) and the level of q must be functions of $K(t)$ and $Z(t)$. Thus, we may write $\lambda(t)/P_k \equiv q\,(K(t), Z(t))$, noting that (2.48) implies

$$(r + \delta)\frac{\lambda(t)}{P_k}\,dt = \frac{F'(K(t))Z(t)}{P_k}\,dt + \frac{E_t[d\lambda(t)]}{P_k}, \qquad (2.49)$$

and we use a multivariate version of the differentiation rule (2.47) to expand the expectation in (2.49) to

$$(r + \delta)q(K, Z) = \frac{F'(K)Z}{P_k} + \frac{\partial q(K, Z)}{\partial K}K(-\delta)$$

$$+ \frac{\partial q(K, Z)}{\partial Z}\theta Z + \frac{\partial^2 q(K, Z)}{\partial Z^2}\frac{\sigma^2}{2}Z^2, \qquad (2.50)$$

an equation satisfied by q at all times when the firm is not investing (and therefore when capital is depreciating at a rate δ).

This is a relatively simple differential equation, which may be further simplified supposing that $\delta = 0$. A particular solution of

$$rq(K, Z) = \frac{F'(K)Z}{P_k} + \frac{\partial q(K, Z)}{\partial Z}\theta Z + \frac{\partial^2(K, Z)}{\partial Z^2}\frac{\sigma^2}{2}Z^2 \qquad (2.51)$$

is linear in Z and reads

$$q_0(K, Z) = \frac{F'(K)Z}{(r - \theta)P_k}.$$

The "homogeneous" part of the equation,

$$rq_i(K, Z) = \frac{\partial q_i(K, Z)}{\partial Z}\theta Z + \frac{\partial^2 q_i(K, Z)}{\partial Z^2}\frac{\sigma^2}{2}Z^2,$$

is solved by functions in the form

$$q_i(K, Z) = A_i Z^\beta \qquad (2.52)$$

if β is a solution of the quadratic equation

$$r = \beta\theta + (\beta - 1)\beta\frac{\sigma^2}{2}, \qquad (2.53)$$

for any constant A_i, as is easily checked inserting its derivatives

$$\frac{\partial q_i(K, Z)}{\partial Z} = A_i Z^{\beta-1}\beta, \qquad \frac{\partial^2 q_i(K, Z)}{\partial Z^2} = (\beta - 1)\beta A_i Z^{\beta-2}$$

in the differential equation and simplifying the resulting expression.

The quadratic equation has two distinct roots if $\sigma^2 > 0$:

$$\beta_1 = \frac{1}{\sigma^2}\left[-(\theta - \tfrac{1}{2}\sigma^2) + \sqrt{(\theta - \tfrac{1}{2}\sigma^2)^2 + 2\sigma^2 r}\,\right] > 0,$$

$$\beta_2 = \frac{1}{\sigma^2}\left[-(\theta - \tfrac{1}{2}\sigma^2) - \sqrt{(\theta - \tfrac{1}{2}\sigma^2)^2 + 2\sigma^2 r}\,\right] < 0.$$

Thus, there exist two groups of solutions in the form (2.52), $q_1(K, Z) = A_1 Z^{\beta_1}$ and $q_2(K, Z) = A_2 Z^{\beta_2}$. Hence, all solutions to (2.51) may be written

$$q(K, Z) = \frac{F'(K)Z}{(r - \theta)P_k} + A_1 Z^{\beta_1} + A_2 Z^{\beta_2}.$$

(Recall that we have set $\delta = 0$.)

To determine the constants A_1 and A_2, we recall that this expression represents the ratio of capital's marginal value to its purchase price. From this economic point of view, it is easy to argue that A_2, the constant associated with the negative root of (2.53), must be zero. Otherwise, as Z tends to zero the shadow value of capital would diverge towards infinity (or negative infinity), which would be quite difficult to interpret since capital's contribution to profits tends to vanish in that situation.

We also know that the firm's investment policy prevents $q(K, Z)$ from exceeding unity. The other constant, A_1, and the firm's investment policy should therefore satisfy the equation

$$\frac{F'(K^*(Z))Z}{(r - \theta)P_k} + A_1 Z^{\beta_1} = 1, \tag{2.54}$$

where $K^*(Z)$ denotes the capital stock chosen by the firm when exogenous conditions are indexed by Z and the irreversibility constraint is not binding, so that it is possible to equate capital's shadow value and cost ($\lambda = P_k$, and $q = 1$).

The single equation (2.54) does not suffice to determine both $K^*(Z)$ and A_1. But the structure of the problem implies that another condition should also be satisfied by these two variables: this is the *smooth pasting* or *high-contact* condition that

$$\frac{\partial q(\cdot)}{\partial Z} = 0$$

whenever $q = 1$, $K = K^*(Z)$ and, therefore, gross investment dX may be positive. To see why, consider the character of the firm's optimal investment policy. When following the proposed optimal policy, the firm invests if and only if an infinitesimal stochastic increment of the Z process would otherwise lead q to exceed unity. Since the stochastic process that describes Z's dynamics has "infinite variation," each instant when investment is positive is followed immediately by an instant (at least) when Z declines and there is no investment. (It is for this reason that the time path of the capital stock, while of finite variation, is not differentiable and the notation could not feature the usual rate of investment per unit time, $I(t) = dK(t)/dt$.) When $K = K^*(Z)$, a relationship in the form (2.50) should be satisfied:

$$(r + \delta)q(K^*(Z), Z)dt = \frac{F'(K^*(Z))Z}{P_k}dt + \frac{\partial q(K^*(Z), Z)}{\partial K}dK$$
$$+ \frac{\partial q(K^*(Z), Z)}{\partial Z}\theta Z dt + \frac{\partial^2(K^*(Z), Z)}{\partial Z^2}\frac{\sigma^2}{2}Z^2 dt,$$
$$(2.55)$$

where the variation of both arguments of the $q(\cdot)$ function is taken into account, and $dK(t)$ may be positive when $dX > 0$.

Along the $K = K^*(Z)$ locus the relationship $q(K^*(Z), Z) = 1$ is also satisfied. As long as the function is differentiable (as it is in this model), total differentiation yields

$$\frac{\partial q(K^*(Z), Z)}{\partial K}dK = -\frac{\partial q(K^*(Z), Z)}{\partial Z}dZ.$$

Inserting this in (2.55) yields

$$(r + \delta)q(K^*(Z), Z)dt = \frac{F'(K^*(Z))Z}{P_k}dt + \frac{\partial q(K^*(Z), Z)}{\partial Z}(\theta Z dt - dZ)$$
$$+ \frac{\partial^2(K^*(Z), Z)}{\partial Z^2}\frac{\sigma^2}{2}Z^2 dt. \qquad (2.56)$$

Since the path of all variables is continuous, the $q(\cdot)$ function must also satisfy the differential equation (2.51) that holds during zero-investment periods. Thus, it must be the case that

$$rq(K, Z) = \frac{F'(K)Z}{P_k} + \frac{\partial q(K, Z)}{\partial Z}\theta Z + \frac{\partial^2(K, Z)}{\partial Z^2}\frac{\sigma^2}{2}Z^2 \qquad (2.57)$$

for K and Z values arbitrarily close to those that induce the firm to invest. By continuity, in the limit where investment becomes positive (for an instant) and $(\theta Z dt - dZ) \neq \theta Z dt$, equations (2.56) and (2.57) can hold simultaneously only if

$$\frac{\partial q(K^*(Z), Z)}{\partial Z} = 0,$$

the smooth-pasting condition.

In the case we are studying,

$$\frac{\partial q(K, Z)}{\partial Z}\bigg|_{K=K^*(Z)} = \frac{F'(K^*(Z))}{(r - \theta)P_k} + A_1\beta_1 Z^{\beta_1 - 1}.$$

Setting this expression to zero we have

$$A_1 = -\frac{F'(K^*(Z))Z^{1-\beta_1}}{\beta_1(r - \theta)P_k},$$

and inserting this in (2.54) we obtain a characterization of the firm's optimal investment policy:

$$F'(K^*(Z))Z = \frac{\beta_1}{\beta_1 - 1}(r - \theta)P_k,$$

or, recalling that β_1 is the positive solution of equation (2.53) and rearranging it to read $\beta/(\beta - 1) = \left(r + \frac{1}{2}\beta\sigma^2\right)/(r - \theta)$,

$$F'(K^*(Z))Z = \left(r + \frac{1}{2}\beta_1\sigma^2\right)P_k.$$

It is instructive to compare this equation with that which would hold if the firm could sell as well as purchase capital at the constant price P_k. In that case, since $\delta = 0$, it should be true that $F'(K)Z = rP_k$ at all times. Since $\beta_1 > 0$, at times of positive investment the marginal revenue product of capital is higher—and, with $F''(\cdot) < 0$, the capital stock is lower—than in the case of reversible investment. Intuitively, the irreversibility constraint makes it suboptimal to invest so as to equate the *current* marginal revenue product of capital to its user cost rP_k: the firm knows that it will be impossible to reduce the capital stock in response to future negative developments, and aims at avoiding large excessive capacity in such instances by restraining investment in good times. The β_1 root is a function of σ, and it is possible to show that $\beta_1\sigma^2$ is increasing in σ—or that, quite intuitively, a larger wedge between the current marginal profitability of capital and its user cost is needed to trigger investment when the wedge may very quickly be erased by more highly volatile fluctuations.

Substantially similar, but more complex, derivations can be performed for cases where capital depreciates and/or the firm employs perfectly flexible factors (such as N in the previous sections' models). To obtain closed-form solutions in such cases, it is necessary to assume that the firm's demand and production functions have constant-elasticity forms. (Further details are in the references at the end of the chapter.)

Irreversible investment models are more complex and realistic than the models introduced above. They do not, however, deny their fundamental assumption that optimal investment policies rule out arbitrage opportunities, and similarly support simple present-value financial considerations. Intuitively, if investment is irreversible future decisions to install capital may only increase its stock and—under decreasing returns—reduce its marginal revenue product. Just like in the certainty model of Section 2.6, it is precisely the expectation of future excess capacity (and low marginal revenue products) that makes the firm reluctant to invest. In present expected value terms, in fact, capital's marginal revenue product fluctuates around the same user-cost level that would determine it in the absence of adjustment costs.

A model with long periods of inaction, of course, cannot represent well the dynamics of aggregate investment, which is empirically much smoother than would be implied by the dynamics illustrated in Figure 2.12, or by similar pictures one might draw tracing the dynamics of a stochastic desired capital stock and of the irreversibly installed stock associated with it. This suggests that aggregate dynamics should not be interpreted as the optimal choices of a single, "representative" firm—as is assumed by most micro-founded macro-economic models. If one allows part of uncertainty to be "idiosyncratic," that is relevant only to individual firms but completely offset in the aggregate, then aggregation of intermittent and heterogeneous firm-level investment poli-cies yields smoother macroeconomic dynamics. Inaction by individual firms implies some degree of inertia in the aggregate series' response to aggregate shocks. Such inertia could be interpreted in terms of convex adjustment costs for a hypothetical representative firm, but reflects heterogeneity of micro-economic dynamics if one maintains that adjustment costs do not necessar-ily imply higher unit costs for faster investment. This interpretation allows aggregate variables to react quickly to unusual large events and, in particular, to drastic changes of future expectations. Co-existence of firms with very different dynamic experiences is perhaps most obvious from a labor-market perspective, since employment typically increases in some sectors and firms at the same time as it declines in others. Employment changes can in fact be interpreted as "investment" if, as is often the case, hiring and firing workers entails costs for employers. The next chapter discusses dynamic labor demand issues from this perspective.

☐ APPENDIX A2: HAMILTONIAN OPTIMIZATION METHODS

The chapter's main text makes use of Hamiltonian methods for the solution of dynamic optimization problems in continuous time, emphasizing economic inter-pretations of optimality conditions which, as usual, impose equality at the margin between (actual or opportunity) costs and revenues. The more technical treatment in this appendix illustrates the formal meaning of the same conditions. More detailed expositions of the relevant continuous-time optimization techniques may be found in Dixit (1990) or Barro and Sala-i-Martin (1995).

In continuous time, any optimization problem must be posed in terms of relationships among *functions*, more complex mathematical objects than ordinary real numbers. As we shall see, however, the appropriate methods may still be interpreted in light of the simple notions that are familiar from the solution of static constrained optimization problems. Dynamic optimization problems under uncertainty may be formulated in substantially similar ways, taking into account that optimality con-ditions introduce links among yet more complex mathematical objects: *stochastic processes* which, like those introduced in the final section of the chapter, are functions not only of time, but also of the state of nature.

It is important, first of all, to recall what precisely is meant by posing a problem *in continuous time*. Investment is a flow variable, measured *during* a time period; capital is a stock variable, measured at a point in time, for example at the beginning of each period. In continuous time, stock and flow variables are measured at extremely small time intervals. If in discrete time the obvious accounting relationship (2.3) holds, that is if

$$K(t + \Delta t) = K(t) + I(t)\Delta t - \delta K(t)\Delta t,$$

where $I(t)$ denotes the average rate of investment between t and $t + \Delta t$, then when going to continuous time we need to consider the limit for $\Delta t \to 0$ in that relationship. Recalling the definition of a derivative, we obtain

$$\lim_{\Delta t \to 0} \frac{K(t + \Delta t) - K(t)}{\Delta t} \equiv \frac{dK(t)}{dt} \equiv \dot{K}(t) = I(t) - \delta K(t).$$

This expression is a particular case of more general dynamic constraints encountered in economic applications. The level and rate of change of $y(t)$, a stock variable, are linked to one or more flow variables z and to exogenous variables by an *accumulation constraint* in the form of

$$\dot{y}(t) = g(t, z(t), y(t)). \tag{2.A1}$$

The presence of t as an argument of this function represents exogenous variables which, in the absence of uncertainty, may all be simply indexed by calendar time. The flow variable, $z(t)$, is directly controlled by an economic agent, hence it is *endogenous* to the problem under study. It is important to realize, however, that the stock variable $y(t)$ is also under *dynamic* control by the agent. In (2.A1), the rate of change of the stock $\dot{y}$ depends, at every point in time, on the levels of $y(t)$ and $z(t)$. Since (2.A1) states that the stock $y(t)$ has a first derivative with respect to time, its level is given by past history at every t. Hence, $y(t)$ cannot be an instrument of optimization at time t; however, $z(t)$ may be chosen, and since in turn this affects $\dot{y}(t)$, it is possible to change future levels of the y stock variable.

Working in continuous time, it will be necessary to make use of simple integrals. Recall that the accumulation relationship

$$K(t + n\Delta t) = K(t) + \sum_{j=1}^{n} [I(t + j\Delta t) - \delta K(t + j\Delta t)]\Delta t$$

has a continuous time counterpart: fixing $t + n\Delta t = T$ and letting $n \to \infty$ as $\Delta t \to 0$,

$$K(T) = K(t) + \int_{t}^{T} [I(\tau) - \delta K(\tau)] \, d\tau.$$

Given a function of time $I(\tau)$ and a starting point $K(t) = \bar{\kappa}$, the integral determining $K(T)$ is solved by a function $K(\cdot)$ such that

$$\frac{d}{d\tau}K(\tau) = I(\tau) - \delta K(\tau), \quad K(t) = \bar{\kappa}.$$

For example, let $I(\tau) = \vartheta K(\tau)$. A function in the form $K(\tau) = Ce^{(\vartheta-\delta)\tau}$ with $C = e^{-(\vartheta-\delta)t}\bar{\kappa}$ satisfies the conditions, and capital grows exponentially at rate $\vartheta - \delta$:

$$K(T) = K(t)e^{(\vartheta-\delta)(T-t)}.$$

A2.1. Objective function

In order to characterize the economic agent's optimal choices, we need to know not only the form of the accumulation constraint,

$$\dot{K}(t) = I(t) - \delta K(t), \tag{2.A2}$$

but also that of an objective function which also explicitly recognizes the time dimension.

If flows of benefits (utility, profits,...) are given by some function $f(t, I(t), K(t))$, the total value as of time zero of a dynamic optimization program may be measured by the integral

$$\int_0^\infty f(t, I(t), K(t))e^{-\rho t}\, dt, \tag{2.A3}$$

where $\rho \geq 0$ (supposed constant for simplicity) is the intertemporal rate of discount of the relevant benefits.

One could of course express in integral (rather than summation) form the objective function of consumption problems, such as those encountered in Chapter 1: we shall deal with such expressions in Chapter 4. Here, we will interpret the optimization problem in terms of capital and investment. It is sensible to suppose that

$$\frac{\partial f(t, I, K)}{\partial K} > 0,$$

i.e., a larger stock of capital must increase the cash flow;

$$\frac{\partial f(t, I, K)}{\partial I} < 0,$$

i.e., investment expenditures reduce current cash flows; and

$$\frac{\partial^2 f(t, I, K)}{\partial K^2} \leq 0, \qquad \frac{\partial^2 f(t, I, K)}{\partial I^2} \leq 0,$$

with at least one strict inequality; i.e., returns to capital must be decreasing, and/or marginal investment costs are increasing. As usual, such concavity of the objective function ensures that, subject to the linear constraint (2.A2), the optimization problem has a unique internal solution, identified by first-order conditions, where the second-order condition is surely satisfied.

A2.2. Constrained optimization

The problem is that of maximizing the objective function in (2.A3), while satisfying the constraint (2.A2). The instruments of optimization are two functions, $I(t)$ and $K(t)$. Hence an infinitely large set of choices are available: one needs to choose the flow variable $I(t)$ for each of uncountably many time intervals $[t, t + dt)$, taking into account its direct (negative) effects on $f(\cdot)$ and thus on the integral in (2.A3); its (positive) effects on the $K(\cdot)$ accumulation path; and the (positive) effects of $K(\cdot)$ on $f(\cdot)$ and on the integral. "The" constraint (2.A2) is a *functional* constraint, that is, a set of infinitely many constraints in the form

$$I(t) - \delta K(t) - \dot{K}(t) = 0,$$

each valid at an instant t.

From the economic point of view, the agent is faced by a clear trade-off: investment is costly, but it makes it possible to increase the capital stock and enjoy additional benefits in the future.

We recall at this point that, in order to maximize a function subject to one or more constraints, one forms a Lagrangian as a linear combination of the objective functions and the constraints. To each constraint, the Lagrangian assigns a coefficient (a Lagrange multiplier, or shadow price) measuring the variation of the optimized objective function in response to a marginal loosening of the constraint. In the case we are considering, loosening the accumulation constraint (2.A2) at time t means granting additional capital at the margin without requiring the costs entailed by additional investment. Thus, the shadow price is the marginal value of capital at time t evaluated—like all of (2.A3)—at time zero.

In the case we are considering, a continuum of constraints is indexed by t, and the Lagrange multipliers define a function of t, denoted $\mu(t)$ in what follows. In practice, the Lagrangian linear combination has uncountably many terms and adds them up giving infinitesimal weight "dt" to each; we may write it in integral form:

$$L = \int_0^\infty f(t, I(t), K(t))e^{-\rho t}\, dt + \int_0^\infty \mu(t)(I(t) - \delta K(t) - \dot{K}(t))\, dt.$$

Using the integration by parts rule,

$$\int_a^b f'(x)g(x)\, dx = f(b)g(b) - f(a)g(a) - \int_a^b f(x)g'(x)\, dx,$$

we obtain

$$-\int_0^\infty \mu(t)\dot{K}(t)\,dt = -\left(\lim_{t\to\infty}\mu(t)K(t) - \mu(0)K(0)\right) + \int_0^\infty \dot{\mu}(t)K(t)\,dt.$$

The optimization problem is ill defined if the limit does not exist. If it exists, it must be zero (as we shall see). Setting

$$\lim_{t\to\infty}\mu(t)K(t) = 0, \tag{2.A4}$$

we can rewrite the "Lagrangian" as

$$\tilde{L} = \int_0^\infty [\, f(t, I(t), K(t))e^{-\rho t} + \mu(t)(I(t) - \delta K(t)) + \dot{\mu}(t)K(t)]\,dt + \mu(0)K(0).$$

Given the (2.A4), this form is completely equivalent to the previous one, and, conveniently, it does not feature $\dot{K}$.

The necessary conditions for a constrained maximization problem are that all derivatives of the Lagrangian with respect to instruments (here, $I(t)$ and $K(t)$) and shadow prices (here, $\mu(t)$) be zero. If we were dealing with summations rather than integrals of expressions, which depend on the various instruments and shadow prices, we would equate to zero the derivative of each expression. By analogy, we can differentiate the function being integrated with respect to $\mu(t)$ for each t in L: comfortingly, this procedure retrieves the functional accumulation constraint

$$(I(t) - \delta K(t) - \dot{K}(t)) = 0;$$

and we can differentiate the function being integrated in the equivalent expression $\tilde{L}$ with respect to $I(t)$ and $K(t)$ for each t, obtaining

$$\frac{\partial f(t, I(t), K(t))}{\partial I(t)}e^{-\rho t} + \mu(t) = 0, \tag{2.A5}$$

$$\frac{\partial f(t, I(t), K(t))}{\partial K(t)}e^{-\rho t} - \mu(t)\delta + \dot{\mu}(t) = 0. \tag{2.A6}$$

Note that we have disregarded the term $\mu(0)K(0)$ in $\tilde{L}$ when differentiating (2.A6) at $t = 0$. In fact, the initial stock of capital is a parameter rather than an endogenous variable in the optimization problem: it would be nonsensical to impose a first-order condition in the form $\mu(0) = 0$. Similar considerations also rationalize the assumption made in (2.A4). Intuitively, if the limit of $K(t)\mu(t)$ were finite but different from zero, then $\mu(\infty)K(\infty)$ should satisfy first-order conditions: differentiating with respect to $\mu(\infty)$, we would need $K(\infty) = 0$, and differentiating with respect to $K(\infty)$, we would need $\mu(\infty) = 0$. Either one of these conditions implies (2.A4). (Of course, this is a very heuristic argument: it is not really rigorous to take such derivatives directly at the limit. A more rigorous approach would consider a similar problem with a finite planning horizon T, and take the limit for $T \to \infty$ of first-order conditions at T.)

A2.3. **The Hamiltonian recipe**

Conditions (2.A5) and (2.A6) can be derived directly from the *Hamiltonian* (rather than Lagrangian) of the problem, defined as follows:

$$H(t) = [\, f(t, I(t), K(t)) + \lambda(t)(I(t) - \delta K(t))]e^{-\rho t}.$$

In this definition the shadow price $\mu(t)$ (which measures values "at time zero") is replaced by $\lambda(t) \equiv \mu(t)e^{\rho t}$ (which measures values "at time t," without discounting them back to zero). In all other respects, the Hamiltonian expression is similar to the function integrated in the Lagrangians introduced above, and therefore measures the flow of benefits offered by a dynamic policy.[32] The expression proposed, in fact, multiplies the accumulation constraint's shadow price by $I(t) - \delta K(t)$, which is the same as $\dot{K}(t)$, along any possible dynamic path. Thus, the benefit flow includes the value (in terms of the objective function) of the increase in the stock variable $K(t)$. This term makes it possible to take into account properly the problem's intertemporal linkages when maximizing the Hamiltonian expression.

In current-value terms, the optimality conditions encountered above read

$$\frac{\partial H}{\partial I} = 0, \tag{2.A7}$$

$$-\frac{\partial H}{\partial K} = \frac{d(\lambda(t)e^{-\rho t})}{dt}, \tag{2.A8}$$

$$\lim_{t \to \infty} \lambda(t)e^{-\rho t} K(t) = 0. \tag{2.A9}$$

The constraint, which in a static problem would be equivalent to the first-order condition with respect to the shadow price, is imposed by the condition

$$\frac{\partial H(\cdot)}{\partial [\lambda e^{-\rho t}]} = \dot{K}.$$

A2.4. **The general case**

All the above derivations took the accumulation constraint to be linear, as in (2.A2), and the rate of discount per unit time to be constant at ρ. More general specifications can be treated similarly. If the problem given is

$$\max \left[\int_0^\infty f(t, z(t), y(t))e^{-\int_0^t r(s)ds}\, dt \right] \tag{2.A10}$$

---

[32] Note that the benefit flow is discounted back to zero in the expression proposed. Since the discount factor is always strictly positive, one may equivalently define a *current value Hamiltonian*, a similar expression without the discount factor. The interpretation of the shadow value and the relevant dynamic optimality conditions will be different, but jointly equivalent to those outlined here.

subject to

$$\dot{y}(t) = g(t, z(t), y(t)), \qquad \text{for all } t \geq 0, \tag{2.A11}$$

then one forms the Hamiltonian

$$H(t) = [f(t, z(t), y(t)) + \lambda(t)(g(t, z(t), y(t)))]e^{-\int_0^t r(s)ds},$$

and imposes first-order conditions in the form

$$\frac{\partial H}{\partial z} = 0, \tag{2.A12}$$

$$-\frac{\partial H}{\partial y} = \frac{d(\lambda(t)e^{-\int_0^t r(s)ds})}{dt}, \tag{2.A13}$$

$$\lim_{t \to \infty} \lambda(t)e^{-\int_0^t r(s)ds} y(t) = 0. \tag{2.A14}$$

If the constraint is not linear, then these conditions can identify an optimum even when $f(\cdot)$ is not strictly concave. For example, one may have $\partial f/\partial z < 0$ constant (a constant unit investment cost) if $g(\cdot)$ is increasing and convex in z.

REVIEW EXERCISES

Exercise 14 *Consider a firm with capital as the only factor of production. Its revenues at time t are $R(K(t))$ if installed capital is $K(t)$. The accumulation constraint has the usual form, $\dot{K}(t) = I(t) - \delta K(t)$, and the cost of investing $I(t)$ is a function $G(I(t))$ that does not depend on installed capital (for simplicity, $P_k \equiv 1$).*

(a) *Suppose the firm aims at maximizing the present discounted value at rate r of its cash flows, $F(t)$. Express cash flows, in terms of the functions $R(\cdot)$ and $G(\cdot)$, derive the relevant first-order conditions, and characterize the solution graphically making specific assumptions as to the derivatives of $R(\cdot)$ and $G(\cdot)$.*

(b) *Characterize the solution under more specific assumptions: suppose revenues are a linear function of installed capital, $R(K) = \alpha K$, and let the investment cost function be quadratic, $G(I) = I + bI^2$. Derive and interpret an expression for the steady-state capital stock. What happens if $\delta = 0$?*

Exercise 15 *A firm's cash flows are*

$$K^\alpha N^\beta - P_k G(\dot{K}, K) - wN,$$

where K is the capital stock, $\dot{K}$ its rate of change, and N is a perfectly flexible factor. Let r be the rate of discount applied to future cash flows, over an infinite planning horizon.

(a) *What needs to be assumed about α, β, $G(\cdot, \cdot)$ to ensure that the Hamiltonian first-order conditions identify the optimal solution?*

(b) *Let $\alpha + \beta < 1$. Draw a saddlepath diagram for given P_k, w, and r; be specific as to what you assume about the form of $G(\cdot, \cdot)$. Show the effects of an unexpected, permanent change of P_k, starting from the steady state.*

(c) *What does P_k represent in the problem? Would it be a good idea to let*

$$G(\dot{K}_t, K_t) = \left(\frac{\dot{K}_t}{K_t}\right)^2 ?$$

Or would it be preferable to let $G(x, y) = (x/y)^3$? What about $G(x, y) = (x)^3$?

(d) *Suppose that $\alpha + \beta = 1$, and let $P_k G(\dot{K}, K) = g(\dot{K})$. (Adjustment costs do not depend on K.) The wage is constant at $w(t) = 1$ only for $0 \leq t < T$: thereafter, its level is random, and for $t \geq T$*

$$w(t) = \begin{cases} 1 + \xi, & \text{with prob. } 1/2 \\ 1 - \xi, & \text{with prob. } 1/2. \end{cases}$$

Write the first-order condition for investment at $t = 0$. How does the investment flow depend on ξ for $t < 1$?

Exercise 16 *A firm's production function is*

$$Y(t) = a\sqrt{K(t)} + \beta\sqrt{L(t)},$$

and its product is sold at a given price, normalized to unity. Factor L is not subject to adjustment costs, and is paid w per unit time. Factor K obeys the accumulation constraint

$$\dot{K}(t) = I(t) - \delta K(t),$$

and the cost of investing I is

$$G(I) = I + \frac{\gamma}{2}I^2$$

per unit time (letting $P_k = 1$). The firm maximizes the present discounted value at rate r of its cash flows.

(a) *Write the Hamiltonian for this problem, derive and discuss briefly the first-order conditions, and draw a diagram to illustrate the solution.*

(b) *Analyze graphically the effects of an increase in δ (faster depreciation of installed capital) and give an economic interpretation of the adjustment trajectory.*

(c) *If, instead of being constant, the cost of factor L were a random variable, would this matter for the firm's investment policy? Explain.*

Exercise 17 *As a function of installed capital K, a firm's revenues are given by*

$$R(K) = K - \tfrac{1}{2}K^2.$$

The usual accumulation constraint has $\delta = 0.25$, *so* $\dot{K} = I - 0.25K$. *Investing I costs* $P_k G(I) = P_k \left(I + \frac{1}{2}I^2\right)$.

The firm maximizes the present discounted value at rate $r = 0.25$ *of its cash flows.*

(a) Write the first-order conditions of the dynamic optimization problem, and characterize the solution graphically supposing that $P_k = 1$ (constant).

(b) Starting from the steady state of the $P_k = 1$ case, show the effects of a 50% subsidy of investment (so that P_k is halved).

(c) Discuss the dynamics of optimal investment if at time $t = 0$, when P_k is halved, it is also announced that at some future time $T > 0$ the interest rate will be tripled, so that $r(t) = 0.75$ for $t \geq T$.

Exercise 18 *The revenue flow of a firm is given by*

$$R(K, N) = 2K^{1/2}N^{1/2},$$

where N is a freely adjustable factor, paid a wage $w(t)$ *at time t; K is accumulated according to*

$$\dot{K} = I - \delta K,$$

and an investment flow I costs

$$G(I) = \left(I + \frac{1}{2}I^2\right).$$

(Note that $P_k = 1$, *hence* $q = \lambda$.)

(a) Write the first-order conditions for maximization of present discounted (at rate r) value of cash flows over an infinite planning horizon.

(b) Taking r and δ to be constant, write an expression for $\lambda(0)$ in terms of $w(t)$, the function describing the time path of wages.

(c) Evaluate that expression in the case where $w(t) = \bar{w}$ is constant, and characterize the solution graphically.

(d) How could the problem be modified so that investment is a function of the average value of capital (that is, of Tobin's average q)?

☐ FURTHER READING

Nickell (1978) offers an early, very clear treatment of many issues dealt with in this chapter. Section 2.5 follows Hayashi (1982). For a detailed and clear treatment of saddlepath dynamics generated by anticipated and non-anticipated parameter changes, see Abel (1982). The effects of uncertainty on optimal investment flows under convex adjustment costs, sketched in Section 2.4, were originally studied by Hartman (1972). A more detailed treatment of optimal inaction in a certainty setting may be found in Bertola (1992).

Dixit (1993) offers a very clear treatment of optimization problems under uncertainty in continuous time, introduced briefly in the last section of the chapter. Dixit and Pindyck (1994) propose a more detailed and very accessible discussion of the relevant issues. Bertola (1998) contains a more complete version of the irreversible investment problem solved here. For a very complex model of irreversible investment and dynamic aggregation, and for further references, see Bertola and Caballero (1994).

When discussing consumption in Chapter 1, we emphasized the empirical implications of optimization-based theory, and outlined how theoretical refinements were driven by the imperfect fit of optimality conditions and data. Of course, theoretical relationships have also been tested and estimated on macroeconomic and microeconomic investment data. These attempts have met with considerably less success than in the case of consumption. While aggregate consumption changes are remarkably close to the theory's unpredictability implication, aggregate investment's relationship to empirical measures of q is weak and leaves much to be explained by output and by distributed lags of investment, and its relationship to empirical measures of Jorgenson's user cost are also empirically elusive. (For surveys, see Chirinko, 1993, and Hubbard, 1998.) The evidence does not necessarily deny the validity of theoretical insights, but it certainly calls for more complex modeling efforts. Even more than in the case of consumption, financial constraints and expectation formation mechanisms play a crucial role in determining investment in an imperfect world.

Together with monetary and fiscal policy reactions, financial and expectational mechanisms are relevant to more realistic models of macroeconomic dynamics of the type studied in Section 2.5. As in the case of consumption, however, attention to microeconomic detail (as regards heterogeneity of individual agents' dynamic environment, and adjustment-cost specifications leading to infrequent bursts of investment) has proven empirically useful: aggregate cost-of-capital measures are statistically significant in the long run, and short-run dynamics can be explained by fluctuations of the distribution of individual firms within their inaction range (Bertola and Caballero, 1994).

▯ REFERENCES

Abel, A. B. (1982) "Dynamic Effects of Temporary and Permanent Tax Policies in a q model of Investment," *Journal of Monetary Economics*, 9, 353–373.

Barro, R. J., and X. Sala-i-Martin (1995) "Appendix on Mathematical Methods," in *Economic Growth*, New York: McGraw-Hill.

Bertola, G. (1992) "Labor Turnover Costs and Average Labor Demand," *Journal of Labor Economics*, 10, 389–411.

——(1998) "Irreversible Investment (1989)," *Ricerche Economiche/Research in Economics*, 52, 3–37.

——and R. J. Caballero (1994) "Irreversibility and Aggregate Investment," *Review of Economic Studies*, 61, 223–246.

Blanchard, O. J. (1981) "Output, the Stock Market and the Interest Rate," *American Economic Review*, 711, 132–143.

Chirinko, R. S. (1993) "Business Fixed Investment Spending: A Critical Survey of Modelling Strategies, Empirical Results, and Policy Implications," *Journal of Economic Literature*, 31, 1875–1911.

Dixit, A. K. (1990) *Optimization in Economic Theory*, Oxford: Oxford University Press.

—— (1993) *The Art of Smooth Pasting*, London: Harcourt.

—— and R. S. Pindyck (1994) *Investment under Uncertainty*, Princeton: Princeton University Press.

Hartman, R. (1972) "The Effect of Price and Cost Uncertainty on Investment," *Journal of Economic Theory*, 5, 258–266.

Hayashi, F. (1982) "Tobin's Marginal q and Average q: A Neoclassical Interpretation," *Econometrica*, 50, 213–224.

Hubbard, R. G. (1998) "Capital-Market Imperfections and Investment," *Journal of Economic Literature* 36, 193–225.

Jorgenson, D. W. (1963) "Capital Theory and Investment Behavior," *American Economic Review (Papers and Proceedings)*, 53, 247–259.

—— (1971) "Econometric Studies of Investment Behavior," *Journal of Economic Literature*, 9, 1111–1147.

Keynes, J. M. (1936) *General Theory of Employment, Interest, and Money*, London: Macmillan.

Nickell, S. J. (1978) *The Investment Decisions of Firms*, Cambridge: Cambridge University Press.

Tobin, J. (1969) "A General Equilibrium Approach to Monetary Theory," *Journal of Money, Credit, and Banking*, 1, 15–29.

3 Adjustment Costs in the Labor Market

In this chapter we use dynamic methods to study labor demand by a single firm and the equilibrium dynamics of wages and employment. As in previous chapters, we aim at familiarizing readers with methodological insights. Here we focus on how uncertainty may be treated simply in an environment that allows economic circumstances to change, with given probabilities, across a well-defined and stable set of possible states (a Markov chain). We derive some generally useful technical results from first principles and, again as in previous chapters, we discuss their economic significance intuitively, with reference to their empirical and practical relevance in a labor market context. In reality, adjustment costs imposed on firms by job security legislation are widely different across countries, sectors, and occupations, and the literature has given them a prominent role when comparing European and American labor market dynamics. (See Bertola, 1999, for a survey of theory and evidence.) In most European countries, legislation imposes administrative and legal costs on employers wishing to shed redundant workers. Together with other institutional differences (reviewed briefly in the suggestions for further reading at the end of the chapter), this has been found to be an important factor in shaping the European experience of high unemployment in the last three decades of the twentieth century.

Section 3.1 derives the optimal hiring and firing decisions of a firm that is subject to adjustment costs of labor. The next two sections characterize the implications of these optimal policies for the dynamics and the average level of employment. Finally, in Section 3.4 we study the interactions between the decisions of firms and workers when workers are subject to mobility costs, focusing in particular on equilibrium wage differentials. The entire analysis of this chapter is based on a simple model of uncertainty, characterized formally in the appendix to the chapter.

Remember that in Chapter 2 we viewed the factor N, which was not subject to adjustment costs, as labor. Hence we called its remuneration per unit of time, w, the "wage rate." In the absence of adjustment costs, the optimal labor input had a simple and essentially static solution: that is, the optimal employment level needed to satisfy the condition

$$\frac{\partial R(t, K(t), N)}{\partial N} = w(t). \tag{3.1}$$

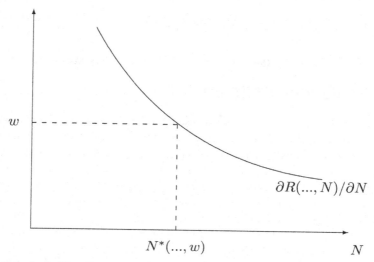

Figure 3.1. Static labor demand

This first-order condition is necessary and sufficient if the total revenues $R(\cdot)$ are an increasing and concave function of N. Under this condition, $\partial R(\cdot)/\partial N$ is a decreasing function of N and (3.1) implicitly defines the demand function for labor $N^*(t, K(t), w(t))$.

If the above condition holds, the employment level depends only on the levels of K, of wages, and of the exogenous variables that, in the absence of uncertainty, are denoted by t. This relationship between employment, wages, and the value of the marginal product of labor is illustrated in Figure 3.1, which is familiar from any elementary textbook. In fact, the same relation can be obtained assuming that firms simply maximize the flow of profits in a given period, rather than the discounted flow of profits over the entire time horizon.

The fact that the static optimality condition remains valid in the potentially more complex dynamic environment illustrates a general principle. In order for the dynamic aspects of an economic problem to be relevant, the effects of decisions taken today need to extend into the future; likewise, decisions taken in the past must condition current decisions. Adjustments costs (linear or strictly convex) introduced for investment in Chapter 2 make it costly for firms to undo previous choices. As a result, when firms decide how much to invest, they need to anticipate their future input of capital. But if labor is simply compensated on the basis of its effective use, and if variations in $N(t)$ do not entail any cost, then forward-looking considerations are irrelevant. Firms do not need to form expectations about the future because they know that it will always be possible for them to react immediately, and without any cost, to future events.[33]

3.1. Hiring and Firing Costs

In Chapter 2, on investment, the presence of more than one state variable would have complicated the analysis of the dynamic aspects of optimal investment behavior. In particular, we would not have been able to use the simple two-dimensional phase diagram. It was therefore helpful to assume that no factors other than capital were subject to adjustment costs. Since in this chapter we aim to analyze the dynamic behavior of employment, it would not be very useful or realistic to retain the assumption that variations in employment do not entail any costs for the firm. For example, as a result of the technological and organizational specificity of labor, firms incur *hiring costs* because they need to inform and instruct newly hired workers before they are as productive as the incumbent workers. The creation and destruction of jobs (*turnover*) often entails costs for the workers too, not only because they may need to learn to perform new tasks, but also in terms of the opportunity cost of unemployment and the costs of moving. The fact that mobility is costly for workers affects the equilibrium dynamics of wages and employment, as we will see below. In fact, it is in order to protect workers against these costs of mobility that labor contracts and laws often impose *firing costs*, so that firms incur costs both when they expand and when they reduce their labor demand.

We start this chapter by considering the optimal hiring and firing policies of a single firm that is subject to hiring and firing costs. As in the case of investment, the solution described by (3.1), in which the marginal productivity and the marginal costs of labor are equated in every period, is no longer efficient with adjustment costs. Like the installation costs for machinery and equipment, the costs of hiring and firing require a firm to adopt a forward-looking employment policy.

The economic implications of such behavior could well be studied using the continuous time optimization methods introduced in the previous chapter, and some of the exercises below explore analogies with the methods used in the study of investment there. We adopt a different approach, however, in order to explore new aspects of the dynamic problems that we are dealing with and to learn new techniques. As in Chapter 1, we assume that the decisions

---

[33] Even in the absence of adjustment costs, the consumption and savings decisions studied in Chapter 1 have dynamic implications via the budget constraint of agents, since current consumption affects the resources available for future consumption. Adjustment costs may also be relevant for the consumption of non-durable goods if the utility of agents depends directly on variations (and not just levels) of consumption. This could occur for instance as a result of habits or addiction.

are taken in discrete time and under uncertainty about the future. Since we also want to take adjustment costs and equilibrium features into account, it is useful to simplify the model.

In what follows, we assume that firms operate in an environment in which one or more exogenous variables (like the retail price of the output, the productive efficiency, or the costs of inputs other than labor) fluctuate so that a firm is sometimes more and sometimes less inclined to hire workers. In (3.1), the capital stock of a firm $K(t)$ (which we do not analyze explicitly in this chapter) and the time index t could represent these exogenous factors. To simplify the analysis as much as possible, we assume that the complex of factors that are relevant for the intensity of labor demand has only two states: a strong state indexed by g, and a weak state indexed by b. If the alternation between these two states were unambiguously determined by t, the firm would be able to determine the evolution of the exogenous variables. Here we shall assume that the evolution of demand is uncertain. In each period the demand conditions change with probability p from weak to strong or vice versa. Hence, in each period the firm takes its decisions on how many workers to hire or fire knowing that the prevailing demand conditions remain unchanged with probability $(1 - p)$.

As in the analysis of investment, we assume that the firm maximizes the current discounted value of future cash flows. Given that the variations of Z are stochastic, the objective of the firm needs to be expressed in terms of the expected value of future cash flows. To simplify the interpretation of the transition probability p, it is convenient to adopt a discrete-time setup. Assuming that firms are risk-neutral, we can then write

$$V_t = E_t \left[\sum_{i=0}^{\infty} \left(\frac{1}{1+r} \right)^i (R(Z_{t+i}, N_{t+i}) - w N_{t+i} - G(\Delta N_{t+i})) \right], \quad (3.2)$$

where:

- $E_t[\cdot]$ denotes the expected value conditional on the information available at date t (this concept is defined formally in the chapter's appendix within the context of the simple model studied here);

- r is the discount rate of future cash flow, which we assume constant for simplicity; likewise, w denotes the constant wage that a worker receives in any given period;

- the total revenues $R(\cdot)$ depend on employment N and a variety of exogenous factors indexed by Z_{t+i}: if the demand for labor is strong in period $t + i$, then $Z_{t+i} = Z_g$, while if labor demand is weak, then $Z_{t+i} = Z_b$;

- the function $G(\cdot)$ represents the costs of hiring and firing, or *turnover*, which in any given period $t + i$ depends on the net variation $\Delta N_{t+i} \equiv$

$N_{t+i} - N_{t+i-1}$ of the employment level with respect to the preceding period; this net variation of employment plays the same role as the investment level $I(t)$ in the analysis of capital in the preceding chapter.

Exercise 19 *To explore the analogy with the investment problem of the previous chapter, rewrite the objective function of the firm assuming that the turnover costs depend on the gross variations of employment, and that this does not coincide with ΔN because a fraction δ of the workers employed in each period resign, for personal reasons or because they reach retirement age, without costs for the firm. Note also that (3.2) does not feature the price of capital, P_k: what could such a parameter mean in the context of the problems we study in this chapter?*

In order to solve the model, we need to specify the functional form of $G(\cdot)$. As in the case of investment, the adjustment costs may be strictly convex. In that case, the unit costs of *turnover* would be an increasing function of the actual variation in the employment level. This would slow down the optimal response to changes in the exogenous variables. However, there are also good reasons to suppose that adjustment costs are concave. For instance, a single instructor can train more than one recruit, and the administrative costs of a firing procedure may well be at least partially independent of the number of workers involved.

The case of linear adjustment costs that we consider here lies in between these extremes. The simple proportionality between the cost and the amount of *turnover* simplifies the characterization of the optimal labor demand policies. We therefore assume that

$$G(\Delta N) = \begin{cases} (\Delta N)H & \text{if } \Delta N \geq 0, \\ -(\Delta N)F & \text{if } \Delta N < 0, \end{cases} \tag{3.3}$$

where the minus sign that appears in the $\Delta N < 0$ case ensures that any variation in employment is costly for positive values of parameters H and F. By (3.3), the firm incurs a cost H for each unit of labor hired, while any unit of labor that is laid off entails a cost F. Both unit costs are independent of the size of ΔN, and, since H is not necessarily equal to F, the model allows for a separate analysis of hiring and firing costs.

As in the analysis of investment, firms' optimal actions are based on the *shadow value* of labor, defined as the marginal increase in the discounted cash flow of the firm if it hires one additional unit of labor. When a firm increases the employment level by hiring an infinitesimally small unit of labor while keeping the hiring and firing decisions unchanged, the objective function defined in (3.2) varies by an amount of

$$\lambda_t = E_t \left[\sum_{i=0}^{\infty} \left(\frac{1}{1+r} \right)^i \left(\frac{\partial R(Z_{t+i}, N_{t+i})}{\partial N_{t+i}} - w \right) \right] \tag{3.4}$$

per unit of additional employment. If the employment levels N_{t+i} on the right-hand side of this equation are the optimal ones, (3.4) measures the marginal contribution of an infinitesimally small labor input variation around the optimally chosen one. This follows from the envelope theorem, which implies that infinitesimally small variations in the employment level do not have first-order effects on the value of the firm.

3.1.1. OPTIMAL HIRING AND FIRING

To characterize the optimal policies of the firm, we assume that the realization of Z_t is revealed at the beginning of period t, before a firm chooses the employment level N_t that remains valid for the entire time period.[34] Hence,

$$E_t \left[\frac{\partial R(Z_t, N_t)}{\partial N_t} - w \right] = \frac{\partial R(Z_t, N_t)}{\partial N_t} - w.$$

We can separate the first term of the summation in (3.4), whose discount factor is equal to one, from the remaining terms. To simplify notation, we define

$$\mu(Z_{t+i}, N_{t+i}) \equiv \frac{\partial R(Z_{t+i}, N_{t+i})}{\partial N_{t+i}},$$

and write

$$\lambda_t = \mu(Z_t, N_t) - w + E_t \left[\sum_{i=1}^{\infty} \left(\frac{1}{1+r} \right)^i (\mu(Z_{t+i}, N_{t+i}) - w) \right]$$

$$= \mu(Z_t, N_t) - w + \left(\frac{1}{1+r} \right) E_t \left[\sum_{i=0}^{\infty} \left(\frac{1}{1+r} \right)^i (\mu(Z_{t+1+i}, N_{t+1+i}) - w) \right].$$

At date $t + 1$ agents know the realization of Z_{t+1}, while at t they know only the probability distribution of Z_{t+1}. The conditional expectation at date $E_{t+1}[\cdot]$ is therefore based on a broader information set than that at $E_t[\cdot]$.

---

[34] We could have adopted other conventions for the timing of the exogenous and endogenous stock variables. For example, retaining the assumption that N_t is determined at the *start* of period t, we could assume that the value of Z_t is not yet observed when firms take their hiring and firing decisions; it would be a useful exercise to repeat the preceding analysis under this alternative hypothesis. Such timing conditions would be redundant in a continuous-time setting, but the elegance of a reformulation in continuous time would come at the cost of additional analytical complexity in the presence of uncertainty.

Applying the *law of iterative expectations*, which is discussed in detail in the Appendix, we can then write

$$E_t \left[\sum_{i=0}^{\infty} \left(\frac{1}{1+r} \right)^i (\mu(Z_{t+1+i}, N_{t+1+i}) - w) \right]$$

$$= E_t \left[E_{t+1} \left[\sum_{i=0}^{\infty} \left(\frac{1}{1+r} \right)^i (\mu(Z_{t+1+i}, N_{t+1+i}) - w) \right] \right].$$

Recognizing the definition of λ_{t+1} in the above expression, we obtain a recursive relation between the shadow value of labor in successive periods:

$$\lambda_t = \mu(Z_t, N_t) - w + \frac{1}{1+r} E_t[\lambda_{t+1}]. \tag{3.5}$$

This relationship is similar to the expression that was obtained by differentiating the Bellman equation in the appendix to Chapter 1, and is thus equivalent to the Euler equation that we have already encountered on various occasions in the preceding chapters.

Exercise 20 *Rewrite this equation in a way that highlights the analogy between this expression and the condition $r\lambda = \partial R(\cdot)/\partial K + \dot{\lambda}$, which was derived when we solved the investment problem using the Hamiltonian method.*

The optimal choices of the firm are obvious if we express them in terms of the shadow value of labor. First of all, the marginal value of labor cannot exceed the costs of hiring an additional unit of labor. Otherwise the firm could increase profits by choosing a higher employment level, contradicting the hypothesis that employment maximizes profits. Hence, given that the costs of a unit increase in employment are equal to H, while the marginal value of this additional unit is λ_t, we must have $\lambda_t \leq H$.

Similarly, if $\lambda_t < -F$, the firm could increase profits immediately by firing workers at the margin: the immediate cost of firing one unit of labor, $-F$, would be more than compensated by an increase in the cash flow of the firm. Again, this contradicts the assumption that firms maximize profits. Hence, if the dynamic labor demand of a firm is such that it maximizes (3.2), we must have

$$-F \leq \lambda_t \leq H \tag{3.6}$$

for each t. Moreover, either the first or the second inequality turns into an equality sign if $\Delta N_t \neq 0$: formally, at an interior optimum for the hiring and firing policies of a firm, we have $dG(\Delta N_t)/d(\Delta N_t) = \lambda_t$.

Whenever the firm prefers to adjust the employment level rather than wait for better or worse circumstances, the marginal cost and benefit of that action need to equal each other. If the firm hires a worker we have $\lambda_t = H$, which implies that the marginal benefit of an additional worker is equal to the hiring costs. Similarly, if a firm fires workers, it must be true that $\lambda = -g$; that is, the negative marginal value of a redundant worker needs to be compensated exactly by the cost of firing this worker g. Notice also that the shadow value of the marginal worker can be negative only if the wage exceeds the value of marginal productivity.

As in the case of investment, the conditions based on the shadow value defined in (3.4) are not in themselves sufficient to formulate a solution for the dynamic optimization problem. In particular, if $\partial R(\cdot)/\partial N$ depends on N, then in order to calculate λ_t as in (3.4) we need to know the distribution of $\{N_{t+i},\ i = 0, 1, 2, \dots\}$, and thus we need to have already solved the optimal demand for labor. It would be useful if we could study the case in which the revenues of the firm are linear in N. This would be analogous to the model we used to show that optimal investment (with convex adjustment costs) could be based on the average q. However, in this case static labor demand is not well defined. In Figure 3.1 the value of marginal productivity would give rise to a horizontal line at the height of w and the optimality conditions would be satisfied for a continuum of employment levels. In fact, in the case of investment we saw that the value of capital stock and the size of firms were ill defined when the average value of q was the only determinant of investment; to characterize optimal investment decisions, we needed convex adjustment costs.

These difficulties are familiar from the study of dynamic investment problems in an environment without uncertainty. In the presence of uncertainty, even after solving the dynamic optimization problem, we could not assume that firms know their future employment levels: the evolution of employment $\{N_{t+i},\ \text{for } i = 0, 1, 2, \dots\}$ depends not only on the passing of time i, but also on the stochastic realizations of $\{Z_{t+i}\}$. To tackle this difficulty, we can use the fact that a profit-maximizing firm will react optimally to each realization of this random variable. Hence we can deduce the probability distribution of the endogenous variable N_{t+i} from the probability distribution of $\{Z_{t+i}\}$.

At this point, the advantage of restricting the state space to two realizations becomes clear. In what follows we guess that the endogenous variables take on only two different values depending on the realization of Z_t. If $Z_t = Z_g$, then $N_t = N_g$ and $\lambda_t = \lambda_g$; on the contrary, if $Z_t = Z_b$, then the employment level is given by $N_t = N_b$, and its shadow value is equal to $\lambda_t = \lambda_b$. When labor demand is strong, equation (3.5) can therefore be written in the form

$$\lambda_g = \mu(Z_g, N_g) - w + \frac{1}{1+r}[(1-p)\lambda_g + p\lambda_b]. \tag{3.7}$$

The shadow value λ_g is given by the expected discounted shadow value in the next period plus the "dividend" in the current period, which is equal to the difference between the value of marginal productivity $\mu(\cdot)$ and the wage w.

Given that λ_{t+1} has only two possible values, the expected value in (3.7) is simply the product of λ_g and the probability $(1 - p)$ that the state remains unchanged, plus λ_b times the probability p that the state changes from good to bad. Similarly, when labor demand is weak, we can write

$$\lambda_b = \mu(N_b, Z_b) - w + \frac{1}{1 + r}[\, p\lambda_g + (1 - p)\lambda_b]. \tag{3.8}$$

If each transition from the "strong" to the "weak" state induces a firm to fire workers, then in order to satisfy (3.6) we need to have $\lambda_b = -F$ in bad states, and $\lambda_g = H$ in good states. Given that H and F are constants, λ_t indeed takes only two values, as was guessed in order to derive (3.7) and (3.8). Substituting $\lambda_b = -F$ and $\lambda_g = H$ in these expressions, we can solve the resulting system of linear equations to obtain

$$\mu(N_g, Z_g) = w + p\frac{F}{1 + r} + (r + p)\frac{H}{1 + r},$$

$$\mu(N_b, Z_b) = w - (r + p)\frac{F}{1 + r} - p\frac{H}{1 + r}. \tag{3.9}$$

3.2. **The Dynamics of Employment**

The character of the optimal labor demand policy is illustrated in Figure 3.2. The weak case is associated with a demand curve that lies below the demand curve in the strong case. Without hiring and firing costs, firms would equalize the value of marginal productivity to the wage rate w in each of the two states. Hence, with $H = F = 0$, the costs of labor are simply equal to w and employment oscillates between the levels identified by vertical dashed lines in the figure. If the cost of hiring H and/or the cost of firing F are positive, this equality no longer holds. If labor demand $(Z = Z_g)$ is strong, the marginal productivity of labor exceeds the wage rate. Symmetrically, when labor demand is weak $(Z = Z_b)$, the value of marginal productivity is less than the wage. Hence, it looks as if the optimal hiring decisions are based on a wage that is higher than w, while the firing decisions seem to be based on one that is lower. The dashed lines in Figure 3.2 illustrate a pair of "shadow wages" and employment levels that may be compatible with this. The vertical arrows indicate how these "shadow wages" differ from the actual wage, while the horizontal arrows indicate the differences between the static and dynamic employment levels in both states.

Exercise 21 *In Figure 3.2 both demand curves for labor are decreasing functions of employment. That is, we have assumed that $\partial^2 R(\cdot)/\partial N^2 < 0$. How would the problem of optimal labor demand change if $\partial^2 R(Z^i, N)/\partial N^2 = 0$ for $i = b, g$? And if this were true only for $i = b$?*

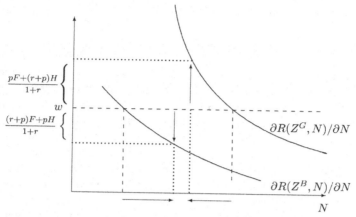

Figure 3.2. Adjustment costs and dynamic labor demand

Hiring and firing costs reduce the size of fluctuations in the employment level between good and bad states. As mentioned in the introduction to this chapter, this very intuitive insight can be brought to bear on empirical evidence from markets characterized by differently stringent employment protection legislation. In fact, the evidence unsurprisingly indicates that countries with more stringent labor market regulations feature less pronounced cyclical variations in employment. This is consistent with the simple model considered here (which takes wages to be exogenously given and constant) if the "firm" represents all employers in the economy, since wages in all countries are quite insensitive to cyclical fluctuations at the aggregate level (see Bertola, 1990, 1999, and references therein).

It is certainly not surprising to find that turnover costs imply employment stability. If a negative cash flow is associated with each variation in the employment level, firms optimally prefer to respond less than fully to fluctuations in labor demand. As indicated by the term *labor hoarding*, the firm values its labor force when considering the future as well as the current marginal revenue product of labor.

Exercise 22 *Show that it is optimal for the firm not to hire or fire any worker if both H and F are large relatively to the fluctuations in Z.*

To illustrate the role of the various parameters and of the functional form of $R(\cdot)$, it is useful to examine some limit cases. First of all, we consider the case in which $F = 0$ and $H > 0$: firms can fire workers at no cost, but hiring workers entails a cost over and above the wage. In order to evaluate how these costs affect firms' propensity to create jobs, we rewrite the first-order condition for the strong labor demand case as

$$\mu(N_g, Z_g) - w = r\frac{H}{1+r} + p\frac{H}{1+r}. \tag{3.10}$$

The first term on the right-hand side of this expression can be interpreted as a pure financial opportunity cost. If invested in an alternative asset with interest rate r, the hiring cost would yield a perpetual flow of dividends equal to rH from next period onwards, or, equivalently, a flow return of $rH/(1+r)$ starting this period. Hence, if the good state lasts for ever and $p = 0$, the presence of hiring costs simply corresponds to a higher wage rate. If, on the contrary, the future evolution of labor demand is uncertain and $p > 0$, the hiring costs also influence the employment level via the second term on the right of (3.10). The higher is p, the less inclined are firms to hire workers. The explanation is that firms might lose the resources invested in hiring a worker if this worker is laid off when labor demand switches from the good to the bad state. In the limit case with $p = 1$, labor demand oscillates permanently between the two states and (3.10) simplifies to $\mu(N_g, Z_g) = w + H$: since the marginal unit of labor that is hired in a good state is fired with probability one in the next period, we need to add the entire hiring cost to the salary.

In periods with weak labor demand, the firm does not hire and hence does not incur any hiring cost. Nonetheless, the firm's choices are still influenced by H: the employment level in the bad state needs to satisfy the following condition:

$$\mu(N_b, Z_b) = w - p\frac{H}{1+r}. \tag{3.11}$$

In this equation a higher value of H is equivalent to a *lower* wage flow. This may seem surprising, but is easily explained. Retaining one additional unit of labor in the bad state costs the firm w, but the firm saves the cost of hiring an additional unit of labor in the next period if the demand conditions improve, which occurs with probability p.

The reasoning for the case $H = 0$ and $F > 0$ is similar. In periods with weak labor demand,

$$\mu(N_b, Z_b) = w - (r + p)\frac{F}{1+r}. \tag{3.12}$$

The firing cost F—which is saved if the firm decides *not* to fire a marginal worker—is equivalent to a *lower* wage in periods with weak labor demand. Conversely, in periods of strong labor demand we have

$$\mu(N_g, Z_g) = w + p\frac{F}{1+r}, \tag{3.13}$$

and in this case the firing costs have the same effect as a wage increase: the fear that the firm may have to pay the firing cost if (with probability p) labor demand weakens in the next period deters the firm from hiring. Like hiring costs, firing costs therefore induce labor hoarding on the part of firms. In the case of firing costs, the firm values the units of labor it decides *not* to fire: moreover, the fear that the firm may not be able to reduce employment levels enough in periods with weak labor demand deters firms from hiring workers in good states.

Before turning to further implications and applications of these simple results, it is worth mentioning that qualitatively similar insights would of course be valid in more formally sophisticated continuous-time models, such as those introduced in Chapter 2's treatment of investment. Convex adjustment costs are not a particularly realistic representation of real-life employment protection legislation, but it is conceptually simple to let downward adjustment be costly (rather than impossible, or never profitable) in the irreversible investment models introduced in Sections 2.6 and 2.7.

Readers familiar with that material may wish to try the following exercises, which propose relatively simple versions of the models solved in the references given. Such readers, however, should be warned that both settings only yield a set of equations whose solutions have to be sought numerically, thus illustrating the advantages in terms of tractability of the Markov chain methods discussed in this chapter.

Exercise 23 (*Bertola, 1992*) *Let time be continuous. Suppose labor's revenue is given by*

$$R(L, Z) = Z \frac{L^{1-\beta}}{1-\beta}, \qquad 0 < \beta < 1,$$

and let the cyclical index Z be the following trigonometric function of time:

$$Z(\tau) = K_1 + K_2 \sin\left(\frac{2\pi}{p}\tau\right), \qquad K_1 > K_2 > 0.$$

Discuss the possible realism of such perfectly predictable cycles, and outline the optimality conditions that must be obeyed over each cycle by the optimal employment path if the wage is given at w and the employer faces adjustment costs $C(\dot{L}(\tau))\dot{L}(\tau)$ for $C(x) = h$ if $\dot{X} > 0$, $C(x) = -f$ if $\dot{X} < 0$.

Exercise 24 (*Bentolila and Bertola, 1990*). *Let the dynamics of the exogenous variables relevant for labor demand be given by*

$$dZ(t) = \theta Z(t) dt + \sigma Z(t) dW(t),$$

and let the marginal revenue product of labor be written in the form $ZL^{-\beta}$. The wage is given at w, hiring is costless, firing costs f per unit of labor, and workers quit costlessly at rate δ so that $dL(t) = -\delta L(t)$ if the firm neither hires nor fires at time t. Write the optimality conditions for the firm's employment policy and discuss how a solution may be found.

3.3. **Average Long-Run Effects**

We have seen that positive values of H and F reduce a firm's propensity to hire and fire workers. Adjustment costs therefore reduce fluctuations in the employment level. Their effect on the average employment level is less clear-cut. This depends essentially on the magnitude of the increase in employment in periods with strong labor demand, relative to the decrease in employment in periods with a weak labor demand. In general, either of the two effects may dominate. The net effect on average employment is therefore *a priori* ambiguous and depends, as we will see, on two specific elements of the model: on the one hand, that firms discount future cash flows at a positive rate, and on the other hand, that optimal static labor demand is often a non-linear function of the wage and of aggregate labor market conditions denoted by Z.

Since transitions between strong and weak states are symmetric, the ergodic distribution is very simple: as shown in the appendix to this chapter, the probability that we observe weak labor demand in a period indefinitely far away in the future is independent of the current state. Hence, in the long run, both states have equal probability. Assigning a probability of one-half to each of the two first-order conditions in (3.9), we can calculate the average value of the marginal productivity of labor:

$$\frac{\mu(N_g, Z_g) + \mu(N_b, Z_b)}{2} = w + \frac{r}{2}\frac{H - F}{1 + r}. \tag{3.14}$$

If $r > 0$, then the costs of hiring tend to increase the value of marginal productivity in the long run: intuitively, the quantity $\frac{1}{2}rH/(1 + r)$ is added to the wage w, because in half of the periods the firm pays a cost H to hire the marginal unit of labor. In doing so, the firm forgoes the flow proceed rH that would accrue from next period onwards if it had invested H in a financial asset. The effects of firing costs F are similar, but perhaps less intuitive. If $F > 0$ and discount r is positive, then average marginal productivity is reduced by an amount equal to $\frac{1}{2}rF/(1 + r)$. To understand how a higher-cost F may *reduce* marginal productivity despite the increase in labor costs, it is useful to note that this effect is absent if $r = 0$. Hence, the reduction in marginal productivity is a dynamic feature. Because the firm discounts future revenues, the cash flow in different periods is not equivalent: firing costs increase the willingness of a firm to pay any given wage level by more than they reduce this willingness in periods with a strong labor demand when only in the smaller discounted value is taken into consideration.

Graphically, with a positive value of r, firing costs are more important than hiring costs in the determination of the length of the arrow that points downwards in Figure 3.2. Conversely, hiring costs are more important in the determination of the length of the arrows that point upwards. Considering the employment levels associated with each level of the (shadow) wage, we can conclude that the positive impact of firing costs on low levels of employment are more pronounced than their negative impact on the employment level in the good state.

3.3.1. AVERAGE EMPLOYMENT

Figure 3.2 shows that variations in employment levels depend not only on differences between marginal products in the two cases and the wage, but also on the slope of the demand curve. If, as is the case in the figure, the slope of the demand curve is much steeper in the good state than in the bad state, the relative length of the two horizontal arrows can be such as to imply net employment effects that differ from what is suggested by the shadow wages in the two states. To isolate this effect, it is useful to set $r = 0$. In that case optimal demand maximizes the average rather than the actual value of the cash flow, and (3.14) then simplifies to

$$\frac{\mu(N_g, Z_g) + \mu(N_b, Z_b)}{2} = w. \tag{3.15}$$

The *turnover costs* no longer appear in this expression. This indicates that a firm can maximize average profits by setting the average value of marginal productivity equal to wages. The average equality does not imply that both terms are necessarily the same. In fact, rewriting the conditions in (3.9) for the case in which $r = 0$ gives

$$\mu(N_g, Z_g) = w + p(F + H),$$
$$\mu(N_b, Z_b) = w - p(F + H). \tag{3.16}$$

Hence the firm imputes a share p of the total turnover costs that it incurs along a completed cycle to the marginal unit on the hiring and the firing margin.

Exercise 25 *Discuss the case in which the firm receives a payment each time it hires a worker, for example because the state subsidizes employment creation, and $H = -F$. What would happen if the cost of hiring were so strongly negative that $H + F < 0$ even in the case of firing costs $F \geq 0$?*

Even in the case when $r = 0$ and hiring and firing costs do not affect the expected marginal productivity of labor, the effect of adjustment costs on average employment is zero only when the slope of the labor demand curve is constant. In fact, if

$$\mu(N, Z_g) = f(Z_g) - \beta N, \qquad \mu(N, Z_b) = g(Z_b) - \beta N,$$

then, for any pair of functions $f(\cdot)$ and $g(\cdot)$, the relationships in (3.16) imply

$$N_g = \frac{f(Z_g) - w - p(F + H)}{\beta}, \qquad N_b = \frac{g(Z_b) - w + p(F + H)}{\beta}.$$

Hence, in this case average employment,

$$\frac{N_g + N_b}{2} = \frac{1}{2} \frac{f(Z_g) + g(Z_b) - w}{\beta},$$

coincides with the employment level that would be generated by the (wider) fluctuations that would keep the marginal productivity of labor always equal to the wage rate.

Conversely, if the slope of the labor demand curve depends on the employment level and/or on Z, then the average of N_g and N_b that satisfies (3.16) for $H + F > 0$, and thus (3.15), is not equal to the average of the employment levels that satisfy the same relationships for $H = F = 0$. The mechanism by which nonlinearities with respect to N generate mean effects, even in the case where $r = 0$, is similar to the one encountered in the discussion of the effects of uncertainty on investment in Chapter 2. If $y = \mu(N; Z)$ is a convex function in its first argument, then the inverse $\mu^{-1}(y; Z)$ is also convex, so that $N = \mu(y; Z)$. For each given value of Z, therefore, Jensen's inequality implies that

$$\frac{\mu(x; Z) + \mu(y; Z)}{2} > \mu\left(\frac{x + y}{2}; Z\right).$$

As illustrated in Figure 3.3, this means that, if deviations from the wage in (3.16) occurred around a stable marginal revenue product of labor function, that function's convexity would imply that employment fluctuations average to a lower level, because the lower N associated with a given productivity increase is larger in absolute value than the employment increase associated with a symmetric productivity decline.

Exercise 26 *Suppose that $r = 0$, so that (3.15) holds, and that $\mu(N, Z_g) = f(Z_g) + \beta(N)$ and $\mu(N, Z_b) = g(Z_b) + \beta(N)$ for a decreasing function $\beta(\cdot)$ which does not depend on Z. Discuss the relationship between variations of employment and its average level.*

In general, the functional form of the labor demand function need not be constant and may depend on the average conditions of the labor market. The shape of labor demand may depend not only on N, but also on Z. Hence, Jensen's inequality does not suffice to pin down an unambiguous relationship between the convexity of the demand function in each of the states and the average level of employment. State dependency of the functional form of labor demand is therefore an additional (and ambiguous) element in the determination of average employment.

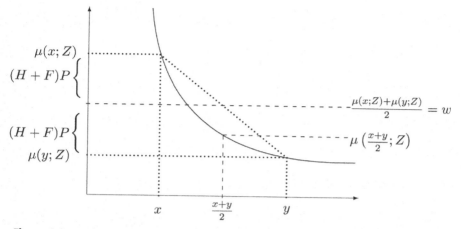

Figure 3.3. Nonlinearity of labor demand and the effect of turnover costs on average employment, with $r = 0$

Exercise 27 *Consider the case where $\mu(N, Z_g) = Z_g - \beta N$ and $\mu(N, Z_b) = Z_b - \gamma N$, and where β and γ satisfy $\beta > \gamma > 0$. What is the general effect of firing costs on the average employment level? And what is its effect in the limit case with $r = 0$? Why can't we analyze this effect in the limit case with $\gamma = 0$ as in exercise 21?*

3.3.2. AVERAGE PROFITS

In summary, average employment is very mildly and ambiguously related to turnover costs and, in particular, to firing costs. This is consistent with empirical evidence across countries characterized by differently stringent employment protection legislation, in that it is hard to find convincing effects of such legislation on average long-run unemployment when other relevant factors (such as the upward pressure on wages exercised by unions) are appropriately taken into account (see Bertola 1990, 1999, and references therein).

If not for employment levels, one can obtain unambiguous results for the average profits of the firm, or, more precisely, the average of the objective function in (3.2). Defined in this chapter as the surplus of the revenues of the firm over the total cost of labor, that function could obviously also include costs that are not related to labor, like the compensation of other factors of production. The negative slope of the demand curve for labor implies that a firm's revenues would exceed the costs of labor in a static environment if all units of labor were paid according to marginal productivity (the striped area in Figure 3.4). Since total revenues correspond to the area below the marginal revenue curve, this surplus is given by the dotted area in Figure 3.4.

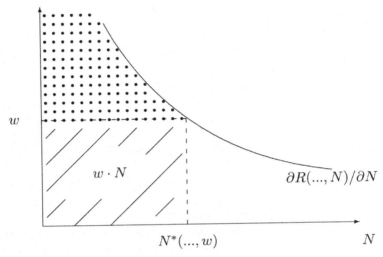

Figure 3.4. The employer's surplus when marginal productivity is equal to the wage

The same negative slope guarantees that the dynamic optimization problem studied above has a well defined solution, and that the firm's surplus is smaller when turnover costs are larger—not only when these costs are associated with a lower average employment level, but also when the adjustment costs induce an increase in the average employment level of the firm.

To illustrate these (general) results, we shall consider the simple case of a linear demand curve for labor: with $\mu(N, Z) = Z - \beta N$, the total revenues associated with given values of Z and N are simply given by $\pi(N, Z) = ZN - \frac{1}{2}\beta N^2$. Since the surplus $\pi(N, Z) - wN$ is maximized when $N = N^* = (Z - w)/\beta$ and the marginal return from labor coincides with the wage, the first-order term is zero in a Taylor expansion of the surplus around the optimum. In the case considered here, all terms of order three and above are also zero, and from

$$\pi(N, Z) - wN = \pi(N^*, Z) - wN^* + \frac{1}{2} \frac{\partial^2 [\pi(N, Z) - wN]}{\partial N^2}\bigg|_{N^*} (N - N^*)^2,$$

we can conclude that the choice of employment level $N \neq N^*$ implies a loss of surplus equal to $\frac{1}{2}\beta(N - N^*)^2$.

As a result of hiring and firing costs, firms choose employment levels that differ from those that maximize the static optimality conditions and thus accept lower flow returns. In the case examined here, the marginal productivity of labor is a linear function and optimal employment levels can easily be derived from (3.9):

$$N_g = \left(Z_g - w - \frac{pF + (r + p)H}{1 + r} \right) \frac{1}{\beta},$$

$$N_b = \left(Z_b - w + \frac{(r + p)F + pH}{1 + r} \right) \frac{1}{\beta}.$$

Hence, the surplus is inferior to the static optimum by a quantity equal to

$$\left(\frac{pF + (r + p)H}{1 + r} \right)^2 \frac{1}{2}$$

in the strong case, and by

$$\left(\frac{(r + p)F + pH}{1 + r} \right)^2 \frac{1}{2}$$

in the weak case.

Given the presence of *turnover costs*, it is rational for the firm to accept these static losses, because the smaller variations in employment permit the firm to save expenses on hiring and firing costs. But even though firms correctly weigh the marginal loss of revenues and the costs of turnover, the firm does experience the lower revenues and adjustment costs. Hence, both average profits and the optimized value of the firm are necessarily lower in the presence of turnover costs, and this can have adverse implications for the employers' investment decisions.

3.4. **Adjustment Costs and Labor Allocation**

In this section we shift attention from the firms to workers, and we analyze the factors that determine the equilibrium value of wages in this dynamic environment. If the entire aggregate demand for labor came from a single firm, then wages and aggregate employment should fluctuate along a curve that is equally "representative" of the supply side of the labor market. Looking at the implications of hiring and firing restrictions from this aggregate perspective suggests that the increased stability of wages and employment around a more or less stable average may or may not be desirable for workers. Moreover, these costs reduce the surplus of firms, which in turn may have a negative impact on investment and growth. Here readers should remember the results of Chapter 2, which showed that a higher degree of uncertainty increased firms' willingness to invest as long as labor was flexible. Conversely, the rigidity of employment due to turnover costs can therefore be expected to reduce investment.

Obviously, however, it is not very realistic to interpret variations in aggregate employment in terms of a more or less intense use of labor by a representative agent. In fact, real wages are more or less constant along the business cycle, making it very difficult to interpret the dynamics of employment in terms of the aggregate supply of labor. Moreover, unemployment is typically concentrated within some subgroups of the population. Higher firing costs are associated with a smaller risk of employment loss and therefore have important implications when, as is realistic, losing one's job is painful (because real wages do not make agents indifferent to employment). In order to concentrate on these disaggregate aspects, it is instructive to consider the implications of adjustment costs for the flow of employment between firms subject to the type of demand shocks analyzed above. To abstract from purely macroeconomic phenomena, it is useful to assume that there is such a large number of firms that the law of large numbers holds, so that exactly half of the firms are in the good state in any period. The same arguments used to compute the ergodic distribution of a single firm imply that, if the transition probability is the same for all firms, and if transitions are independent events, then the aggregate distribution of firms is stable over time. In fact, if we denote the share of firms with a strong demand by P_t, then a fraction pP_t of these firms will move to the state with a low demand. Hence, if the transitions of firms are independent events, the effective share of firms that is hit by a decline in demand approaches the expected value if the number of firms is higher.[35] Symmetrically, we can expect that a share p of the $1 - P_t$ firms in the bad state receive a positive *shock*. The inflow of firms into ranks of the firms with strong product demand is thus equal to a share $p - pP_t$ of the total number of firms if the latter is infinitely large. Since P_t diminishes in proportion to pP_t and increases in proportion to $p(1 - P_t)$, the variation in the fraction P_t of firms with strong product demand is given by

$$P_{t+1} - P_t = p - pP_t - pP_t = p(1 - 2P_t). \qquad (3.17)$$

This expression is positive if $P_t < 0.5$, negative if $P_t > 0.5$, and equal to zero if $P_t = P_\infty = 0.5$. Hence, the frequency distribution of a large number of firms tends to stabilize at $P = 0.5$, as does the probability distribution of a single firm (discussed in the chapter's appendix).

Exercise 28 *What is the role of p in (3.17)? Discuss the case $p = 0.5$.*

---

[35] Imagine that the "relevant states of nature" are represented by the outcome of a series of coin tosses. Associate the value one with the outcome "heads" and zero with "tails," so that the resulting random variable X has expected value $\frac{1}{2}$ and variance $\frac{1}{4}$. The fraction of $X_i = 1$ with n tosses, $P_n = \sum_{i=1}^{n} X_i / n$, has expected value $\frac{1}{2}$, and, if the realizations are independent, its variance $(1/n^2)(n/4) = (1/4n)$ decreases with n. Hence, in the limit with $n \to \infty$, the variation is zero and $P_\infty = 0.5$ with certainty.

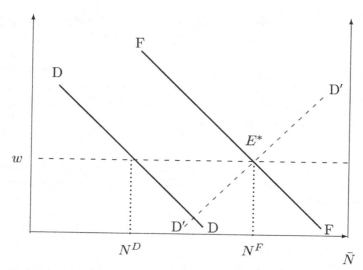

Figure 3.5. Dynamic supply of labor from downsizing firms to expanding firms, without adjustment costs

This analogy between the probability and frequency distributions is valid whenever a large population of agents faces "idiosyncratic uncertainty," and not just in the simple case described above. The "idiosyncratic" character of uncertainty means that individual agents are hit by independent events. With a large enough number of agents, the flows into and out of a certain state will then cancel each other out and the frequency distribution of these states will tend to converge to a stable distribution.

Exercise 29 *Assume that the probability of a transition from b to g is still given by p, while the probability of a transition in the opposite direction is now allowed to be q ≠ p. What is the steady-state proportion of firms in state g?*

In the steady state with idiosyncratic uncertainty, in which $P_{t+1} = P_t = 0.5$, each time a firm incurs a negative shock, another firm will incur a positive shock to labor productivity. Notice that this does not rely on a causal relationship between these events. That is, given that the demand shocks are assumed to be idiosyncratic, the above simultaneity does not refer to a particular other firm. We do not know which particular firm is hit by a symmetric shock, but we do know that there are as many firms with strong and weak product demand. It is therefore the relative size of these two groups that is constant over time, while the identity of individual firms belonging to each group changes over time.

As before, the downward-sloping curves in Figure 3.5 correspond to the two possible positions of the demand curve for labor. Owing to the linearity of these curves, we can directly translate predictions in terms of wages into predictions about employment, abstracting from relatively unimportant effects deriving from Jensen's inequality. The length of the horizontal axis represents the total labor force that is available to firms. The workers who are available for employment within a hiring firm are those who cannot find employment elsewhere—and, in particular, those who decided to leave their jobs in firms that are hit by a negative shock and are firing workers. The dotted line in the figure represents the labor demand by one such firm which is *measured from right to left*, that is in terms of residual employment after accounting for employment generated by firms with a strong demand.

The workers who move from a shrinking firm to an expanding firm lose their employment in the first firm. The *alternative wage* of workers who are hired by expanding firms is therefore given by the demand curve for labor of downsizing firms, which essentially plays the role of an aggregate supply curve of labor. Hence, in the absence of firing costs, the equilibrium will be located at point E^* in Figure 3.5, at which the marginal productivity is the same in all firms and is equal to the common wage rate w.

3.4.1. DYNAMIC WAGE DIFFERENTIALS

As noted in the introduction to this chapter, it is certainly not very realistic to assume that labor mobility is costless for workers. Therefore we shall assume here that workers need to pay a cost κ each time they move to a new job. In reality, these costs could correspond at least partly to the loss of income (unemployment); however, for simplicity we shall assume that labor mobility is instantaneous. The objective in the dynamic optimization program of workers is to maximize the net expected income from work—given by the wage w_t in periods in which the worker remains with her current employer, and by $w_t - \kappa$ in the other periods. Denoting the net expected value of labor income (or "human capital") of individual j by W_t^j implies the following relation:

$$
W_t^j = \begin{cases} w_t^j + \frac{1}{1+r} E_t(W_{t+1}^j) & \text{if she does not move,} \\ w_t^j - \kappa + \frac{1}{1+r} E_t(W_{t+1}^j) & \text{if she moves to a new job.} \end{cases} \tag{3.18}
$$

Notice that each individual worker can be in two states only. At the beginning of a period a worker may be employed by a firm with a strong demand for labor, in which case the worker can earn w_g without having to incur mobility costs. Since a firm in state g may receive a negative shock with probability p, the human capital W_g of each of its workers satisfies the following recursive relationship:

$$
W_g = w_g + \frac{1}{1+r}[pW_b + (1-p)W_g], \tag{3.19}
$$

where W_b denotes the human capital of a worker employed by a firm with weak demand. The human capital of these workers satisfies the relationship

$$W_b = w_b + \frac{1}{1+r}[pW_g + (1-p)W_b] \qquad (3.20)$$

if the worker chooses to remain with the same firm. In this case the worker earns a wage w_b, which, as we will see, is generally lower than w_g. Because a transition to the bad state is accompanied by a wage reduction, it pays the worker to consider a move to a firm in the good state. In the long-run equilibrium there is a constant fraction of these firms in the economy. Hence, each time a firm incurs a negative shock, there is another firm that incurs a positive shock and will be willing to hire the workers who choose to leave their old firm. For these workers, (3.18) implies that

$$W_b = w_g - \kappa + \frac{1}{1+r}[(1-p)W_g + pW_b]. \qquad (3.21)$$

The mobility to a good firm g entails a cost κ, but, since the move is instantaneous, it immediately entitles the worker to a wage w_g and to consider the future from the perspective of a firm with strong demand—which is different from the firms considered in (3.20), since the probability is $1-p$ rather than p that state g will be realized next period. Since the option to move is available to all workers, the two alternatives considered in (3.20) and (3.21) need to be equivalent; otherwise there would be an arbitrage opportunity inducing all or none of the workers to move. Both of these outcomes would be inconsistent with equilibrium. From the equality between (3.20) and (3.21), we can immediately obtain

$$w_g - w_b = k - \frac{1-2p}{1+r}(W_g - W_b). \qquad (3.22)$$

If $p = 0.5$, the wage differential between expanding and shrinking firms is exactly equal to κ, the cost for a worker of moving between any two firms in a period. But if $p < 0.5$, that is if shocks to demand are persistent, then (3.22) takes into account the capital gains $W_g - W_b$ from mobility. Subtracting (3.20) from (3.19) and using (3.22), we obtain

$$W_g - W_b = \kappa. \qquad (3.23)$$

In equilibrium, the cost of mobility needs to be equal to the gain in terms of higher future income. Substituting (3.23) into (3.22), we obtain an explicit expression for the difference between the flow salaries in the two states:

$$w_g - w_b = \frac{2p+r}{1+r}\kappa. \qquad (3.24)$$

As mentioned above, firms in the good state pay a higher wage if mobility is voluntary and costly for workers. Equilibrium is illustrated in Figure 3.6:

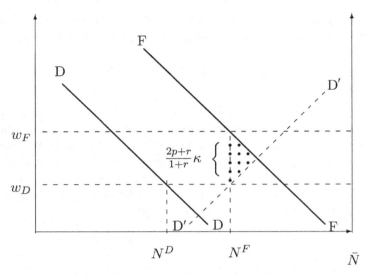

Figure 3.6. Dynamic supply of labor from downsizing firms to expanding firms, without employers' adjustment costs, if mobility costs κ per unit of labor

in order to offer a higher salary, firms in state g employ fewer workers than in Figure 3.5, where we assumed that labor mobility was costless. Intuitively, workers are willing to bear the cost κ only if there are advantages associated with mobility, and the market can offer this advantage in terms of a higher wage. As in the case of the hiring and firing costs for firms, workers face a trade-off between the maximization of the static flow income—which would be obtained at point E^* in Figure 3.5—and minimizing the costs of mobility— which obviously would be zero if employment at each firm were completely stable, and if we would consider a uniform allocation of labor across firms without taking into account the differences in idiosyncratic productivity. The equilibrium allocation illustrated in Figure 3.6, in which (3.24) is satisfied, balances two requirements: the shaded area represents the loss of flow output in each period, which is such that it exactly offsets the mobility costs that would have to be incurred to move the economy closer to E^*.

This modeling perspective has interesting empirical implications. Wage dispersion should be more pronounced in situations of higher uncertainty for given workers' mobility costs, and when workers bear larger mobility costs. Bertola and Ichino (1995) and Bertola and Rogerson (1997) find that these implications offer useful insights when comparing disaggregate wage and employment dispersion statistics from different countries and different periods. From a methodological point of view, it is important to note that the relationships between the various endogenous variables that are implied by the optimal dynamic mobility choices of workers satisfy non-arbitrage conditions of a financial nature. If a single worker intends to maximize the net expected value of her future income, then the labor market needs to offer workers who decide to move the appropriate increase in wages to make this "investment" profitable.

☐ APPENDIX A3: (TWO-STATE) MARKOV PROCESSES

We now illustrate some of the techniques that are applicable to stochastic processes in the form

$$
x_{t+1} = \begin{cases} x_b & \text{with prob. } p \text{ if } x_t = x_g, \text{ with prob. } 1 - p \text{ if } x_t = x_b \\ x_g & \text{with prob. } p \text{ if } x_t = x_b, \text{ with prob. } 1 - p \text{ if } x_t = x_g, \end{cases} \tag{3.A1}
$$

the simple Markov chain that describes the evolution of all of the endogenous and exogenous variables in this chapter.

A3.1. **Conditional probabilities**

Let $P_{t,\,t+i} = \text{Prob}_t(x_{t+i} = x_g | \mathcal{I}_t)$ denote the probability, *based on all the information available at time t*, of the realization (or 'the actual level') of the process at $t + i$ equals x_g. From (3.A1) it is clear that

$$
P_{t,\,t+1} = \begin{cases} p & \text{if } x_t = x_b \\ 1 - p & \text{if } x_t = x_g \end{cases} \tag{3.A2}
$$

Figure A3.1 illustrates how we can compute this probability for $i > 1$. If the process starts from x_g at $t = 1$, probability $P_{1,3}$ is given by the sum of the two paths that are consistent with $x_3 = x_g$: the first one, which is constant, has probability $(1 - p)^2$; the second one, in which we observe two consecutive variations of opposite sign, has p^2. Hence, $P_{1,3} = (1 - p^2) + p^2 = 1 - 2p(1 - p)$ if $x_1 = x_g$. Similar reasoning implies that $P_{1,3} = 2p(1 - p)$ if $x_1 = x_b$.

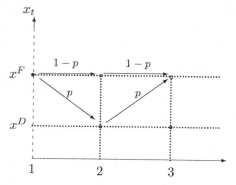

Figure A3.1. Possible time paths of a two-state Markov chain

Using similar techniques, we could calculate the probability of observing x_g at each date $i > 2$, starting from x_b or x_g. However, it is not necessary to do so in order to understand that all conditional probabilities from the point of view of period t are functions of x_t. In fact,

$$P_{t,t+1} \equiv \text{Prob}_t(x_{t+1} = x_g | \mathcal{I}_t) = p \qquad \text{if } x_t = x_b,$$

$$P_{t,t+1} = 1 - p \qquad \text{if } x_t = x_g,$$

and the two possible values of $P_{t,t+1}$ are different if $p \neq 1 - p$, that is if $p \neq 0.5$. Conversely, any other information available at t is irrelevant for the evaluation of both $\text{Prob}_t(x_{t+1} = x_g)$ and $P_{t,t+i}$ for $i > 1$. Since the transition probabilities in (3.A1) are valid between $t + 1$ and $t + 2$,

$$P_{t,t+2} = (1 - p)P_{t,t+1} + p(1 - P_{t,t+1}) = (1 - 2p)P_{t,t+1} + p \qquad \text{(3.A3)}$$

depends only on $P_{t,t+1}$, which in turn depends only on x_t (or is constant, and equal to 0.5, if $p = 0.5$). Equation (3.A3) can be generalized to any pair of dates, in the form

$$P_{t,t+i+1} = (1 - p)P_{t,t+i} + p(1 - P_{t,t+i}) = (1 - 2p)P_{t,t+i} + p. \qquad \text{(3.A4)}$$

Even if we extend the length of the chain beyond time $t + 2$, all probabilities $P_{t,t+i}$ are still functions of x_t only. (Thus, the process is Markovian process in levels.)

A3.2. **The ergodic distribution**

Using equation (3.A4), we can characterize the dynamics of the conditional probabilities for any future period. We write

$$P_{t,t+i+1} - P_{t,t+i} = (1 - 2P_{t,t+i})p \begin{cases} > 0 & \text{if } P_{t,t+i} < 0.5, \\ < 0 & \text{if } P_{t,t+i} > 0.5. \end{cases} \qquad \text{(3.A5)}$$

Evaluating the probability that the process is in state g for ever increasing values of i, that is for periods increasingly further away in the future, we find that this probability decreases if it is above 0.5, and increases if it is below 0.5. Hence, with time the probability $P_{t,t+i}$ converges monotonically to its "ergodic" value $P_{t,\infty} = 0.5$.

A3.3. **Iterated expectations**

The *conditional expectation* of x_{t+i} at date t for each $i \geq 0$ is given by

$$E_t[x_{t+i}] = x_g P_{t,t+i} + x_b(1 - P_{t,t+i}) = x_b + (x_g - x_b)P_{t,t+i}, \qquad \text{(3.A6)}$$

which depends only on the current value of the process if (3.A1) is satisfied.

We can use (3.A1) again to obtain the relationship between $P_{t,t+i}$ and $P_{t+1,t+i}$, that is between the probabilities that are assigned at different moments in time to realizations of x_{t+i} within the same future period. As we saw above, the realization of x_{t+1} is in general not relevant for the probability of $x_{t+i} = x_g$ from the viewpoint of $t + 1$. From the viewpoint of period t, the probabilities of the same event can be written as

$$P_{t,t+i} = (P_{t+1,t+i}|x_{t+1} = x_b) \cdot P(x_{t+1} = x_b|\mathcal{I}_t)$$
$$+ (P_{t+1,t+i}|x_{t+1} = x_g) \cdot P(x_{t+1} = x_g|\mathcal{I}_t) \tag{3.A7}$$

(where $P(x_{t+1} = x_g|\mathcal{I}_t) = 1 - p$ if $x_t = x_g$, and so forth). This allows us to verify the validity of the *law of iterative expectations* in this context. For $i \geq 2$, we write

$$E_{t+1}[x_{t+i}] = x_b + (x_g - x_b)P_{t+1,t+i}. \tag{3.A8}$$

At date $t + 1$, the probability on the right-hand side of (3.A8) is given, while at time t it is not possible to evaluate this probability with certainty: it could be $(P_{t+1,t+i}|x_{t+1} = x_b)$, or $(P_{t+1,t+i}|x_{t+1} = x_g)$, depending on the realization of x_{t+1}. Given the uncertainty associated with this realization, from the point of view of time t the conditional expectation $E_{t+1}[x_{t+1+i}]$ is itself a *random variable*, and we can therefore calculate its expected value:

$$E_t[E_{t+1}[x_{t+i}]] = P(x_{t+1} = x_b|\mathcal{I}_t)E_{t+1}[x_{t+i}|x_{t+1} = x_b]$$
$$+ P(x_{t+1} = x_g|\mathcal{I}_t)E_{t+1}[x_{t+i}|x_{t+1} = x_g].$$

Inserting (3.A8), using (3.A7), and recalling (3.A6), it follows that

$$E_t[x_{t+i}] = x_b + (x_g - x_b)P_{t,t+1} = E_t[E_{t+1}[x_{t+i}]].$$

EXERCISES

Exercise 30 *Consider the production function*

$$F(k, l; a) = (k + l)a - \frac{\beta}{2}l^2 - \frac{\gamma}{2}k^2.$$

(a) *Suppose a firm with that production function has given capital $k = 1$, can hire l costlessly, pays given wage $w = 1$, and must pay $F = 1$ for each unit of l fired. If a_t takes the values 4 or 2 with equal probability $p = 0.5$, and future cash flows are discounted at rate $r = 1$, what is the optimal dynamic employment policy?*

(b) *Suppose capital depreciates at rate $\delta = 1$ and can be costlessly adjusted to ensure that its marginal product is equal to the cost of funds $r + \delta$. Does capital adjustment change the optimal employment pattern? What are the optimal levels of capital when $a_t = 4$ and when $a_t = 2$?*

Exercise 31 *Consider a labor market in which firms have a linear demand curve for labor subject to parallel oscillations, $\mu(N, Z) = Z - \beta N$. As in the main text, Z can take two values, Z_b and $Z_g > Z_b$, and oscillates between these values with transition probability p. Also, the wage oscillates between two values, w_b and $w_g > w_b$, and the oscillations of the wage are synchronized with those of Z.*

(a) Calculate the levels of employment N_b and N_g that maximize the expected discounted value of the revenues of the firm if the discount rate is equal to r and if the unit hiring and firing costs are given by H and F respectively.

(b) Compute the mobility cost k at which the optimal mobility decisions are consistent with a wage differential $\Delta w = w_g - w_b$ when workers discount their future expected income at rate r.

(c) Assume that the labor market is populated by 1,000 workers and 100 firms of which exactly half are in a good state in each period. What levels of the wage w_b are compatible with full employment (with $w_g = w_b + \Delta w$ as above), under the hypothesis that labor mobility is instantaneous?

Exercise 32 Suppose that the marginal productivity of labor is given by $\mu(Z, N) = Z - \beta N$, and that the indicator Z_t can assume three rather than two values $\{Z_b, Z_M, Z_g\}$, with $Z_b < Z_M < Z_g$, where the realizations of Z_t are independent, while the wage rate is constant and equal to $\bar{w}$ in each period. Finally, hiring and firing costs are given by H and F respectively. What form does the recursive relationship

$$\lambda(Z_t, N_t) = \mu(Z_t, N_t) - \bar{w} + E_t[\lambda(Z_{t+1}, N_{t+1})]$$

take if the parameters are such that only fluctuations from Z_b to Z_g or vice versa induce the firm to adjust its labor force, while the employment level is unaffected for fluctuations from and to the average level of labor demand (from Z_b to Z_M or vice versa, or from Z_M to Z_g or vice versa)? Which are the two employment levels chosen by the firm?

☐ FURTHER READING

Theoretical implications of employment protection legislation and firing costs are potentially much wider than those illustrated in this chapter. For example, Bertola (1994) discusses the implications of increased rigidity (and less efficiency) in models of growth like the ones that will be discussed in the next chapter, using a two-state Markov process similar to the one introduced in this chapter but specified in a continuous-time setting where state transitions are described as Poisson events of the type to be introduced in Chapter 5.

Economic theory can also explain why employment protection legislation is imposed despite its apparently detrimental effects. Using models similar to those discussed here, Saint-Paul (2000) considers how politico-economic interactions can rationalize labor market regulation and resistance to reforms, and Bertola (2004) shows that, if workers are risk-averse, then firing costs may have beneficial effects: redundancy payments not only can remedy a lack of insurance but also can foster efficiency if they allow forward-looking mobility decisions to be taken on a more appropriate basis.

Of course, job security provisions are only one of the many institutional features that help explain why European labor markets generate lower employment than American ones. Union behavior and taxation play important roles in determining high-wage, low-employment outcomes. And macroeconomic shocks interact in interesting

ways with wage and employment rigidities in determining the dynamics of employment and unemployment across the Atlantic and within Europe. For economic and
empirical analyses of the European unemployment problem from an international
comparative perspective, see Bean (1994), Alogoskoufis *et al.* (1995), Nickell (1997),
Nickell and Layard (1999), Blanchard and Wolfers (2000), and Bertola, Blau, and Kahn
(2002), which all include extensive references.

☐ REFERENCES

Alogoskoufis, G., C. Bean, G. Bertola, D. Cohen, J. Dolado, G. Saint-Paul (1995) *Unemployment:
Choices for Europe*, London: CEPR.

Bean, C. (1994) "European Unemployment: A Survey," *Journal of Economic Literature*, 32,
573–619.

Bentolila, S., and G. Bertola (1990) "Firing Costs and Labor Demand: How Bad is Eurosclerosis?"
Review of Economic Studies, 57, 381–402.

Bertola, G. (1990) "Job Security, Employment and Wages," *European Economic Review*, 34,
851–886.

—— (1992) "Labor Turnover Costs and Average Labor Demand," *Journal of Labor Economics*,
10, 389–411.

—— (1994) "Flexibility, Investment, and Growth," *Journal of Monetary Economics*, 34, 215–238.

—— (1999) "Microeconomic Perspectives on Aggregate Labor Markets," in O. Ashenfelter
and D. Card (eds.), *Handbook of Labor Economics*, vol. 3B, 2985–3028, Amsterdam: North-
Holland.

Bertola, G. (2003) "A Pure Theory of Job Security and Labor Income Risk," *Review of Economic
Studies*, 71(1): 43–61.

—— F. D. Blau, and L. M. Kahn (2002) "Comparative Analysis of Labor Market Outcomes:
Lessons for the US from International Long-Run Evidence," in A. Krueger and R. Solow (eds.),
The Roaring Nineties: Can Full Employment Be Sustained? New York: Russell Sage, pp. 159–218.

—— and A. Ichino (1995) "Wage Inequality and Unemployment: US vs Europe," in B. Bernanke
and J. Rotemberg (eds.), *NBER Macroeconomics Annual 1995*, 13–54, Cambridge, Mass.: MIT
Press.

—— and R. Rogerson (1997) "Institutions and Labor Reallocation," *European Economic Review*,
41, 1147–1171.

Blanchard, O. J., and J. Wolfers (2000) "The Role of Shocks and Institutions in the Rise of
European Unemployment: The Aggregate Evidence," *Economic Journal*, 110: C1–C33.

Nickell, S. (1997) "Unemployment and Labor Market Rigidities: Europe versus North America,"
Journal of Economic Perspectives, 11(3): 55–74.

—— and R. Layard (1999) "Labor Market Institutions and Economic Performance," in
O. Ashenfelter and D. Card (eds.), *Handbook of Labor Economics*, vol. 3C, 3029–3084, Amsterdam: North-Holland.

Saint-Paul, G. (2000) *The Political Economy of Labour Market Institutions*, Oxford: Oxford
University Press.

4 Growth in Dynamic General Equilibrium

The previous chapters analyzed the optimal dynamic behavior of single consumers, firms, and workers. The interactions between the decisions of these agents were studied using a simple partial equilibrium model (for the labor market). In this chapter, we consider general equilibrium in a dynamic environment.

Specifically, we discuss how savings and investment decisions by individual agents, mediated by more or less perfect markets as well as by institutions and collective policies, determine the aggregate growth rate of an economy from a long-run perspective. As in the previous chapters, we cannot review all aspects of a very extensive theoretical and empirical literature. Rather, we aim at familiarizing readers with technical approaches and economic insights about the interplay of technology, preferences, market structure, and institutional features in determining dynamic equilibrium outcomes. We review the relevant aspects in the context of long-run growth models, and a brief concluding section discusses how the mechanisms we focus on are relevant in the context of recent theoretical and empirical contributions in the field of economic growth.

Section 4.1 introduces the basic structure of the model, and Section 4.2 applies the techniques of dynamic optimization to this base model. The next two sections discuss how decentralized decisions may result in an optimal growth path, and how one may assess the relevance of exogenous technological progress in this case. Finally, in Section 4.5 we consider recent models of endogenous growth. In these models the growth rate is determined endogenously and need not coincide with the optimal growth rate.

The problem at hand is more interesting, but also more complex, than those we have considered so far. To facilitate analysis we will therefore emphasize the economic intuition that underlies the formal mathematical expressions, and aim to keep the structure of the model as simple as possible. In what follows we consider a closed economy. The national accounting relationship

$$Y(t) = C(t) + I(t) \tag{4.1}$$

between the flows of production (Y), consumption (C), and investment therefore holds at the aggregate level. Furthermore, for simplicity, we do not distinguish between flows that originate in the private and the public sectors.

The distinction between consumption and investment is based on the concept of capital. Broadly speaking, this concept encompasses all durable factors of production that can be reproduced. The supply of capital grows in proportion with investments. At the same time, however, existing capital stock is subject to depreciation, which tends to lower the supply of capital. As in Chapter 2, we formalize the problem in continuous time. We can therefore define the stock of capital, $K(t)$ at time t, without having to specify whether it is measured at the beginning or the end of a period. In addition, we assume that capital depreciates at a constant rate δ. The evolution of the supply of capital is therefore given by

$$\lim_{\Delta t \to 0} \frac{K(t + \Delta t) - K(t)}{\Delta t} \equiv \frac{dK(t)}{dt} \equiv \dot{K}(t) = I(t) - \delta K(t).$$

The demand for capital stems from its role as an input in the productive process, which we represent by an aggregate production function,

$$Y(t) = F(K(t), \ldots).$$

This expression relates the flow of aggregate output between t and $t + \Delta t$ to the stocks of production factors that are available during this period. In principle, these stocks can be measured for any infinitesimally small time period Δt. However, a formal representation of the aggregate production process in a single equation is normally not feasible. In reality, the capital stock consists of many different durable goods, both public and private. At the end of this chapter we will briefly discuss some simple models that make this disaggregate structure explicit, but for the moment we shall assume that investment and consumption can be expressed in terms of a single good as in (4.1). Furthermore, for simplicity we assume that "capital" is combined with only one non-accumulated factor of production, denoted $L(t)$.

In what follows, we will characterize the long-run behavior of the economy. More precisely, we will consider the time period in which *per capita* income grows at a non-decreasing rate and in which the ratio between aggregate capital K and the flow of output Y tends to stabilize. The amount of capital per worker therefore tends to increase steadily. The case in which the growth rate of output and capital exceeds the growth rate of the population represents an extremely important phenomenon: the steady increase in living standards. But in this chapter our interest in this type of growth pattern stems more from its simplicity than from reality. Even though simple models cannot capture all features of world history, analyzing the economic mechanisms of a growing economy may help us understand the role of capital accumulation in the real world and, more generally, characterize the economic structure of growth processes.

4.1. **Production, Savings, and Growth**

The dynamic models that we consider here aim to explain, in the simplest possible way, on the one hand the relationship between investments and growth, and on the other hand the determinants of investments. The production process is defined by

$$Y(t) = F(K(t), L(t)) = F(K(t), A(t)N(t)), \qquad (4.2)$$

where $N(t)$ is the number of workers that participate in production in period t and $A(t)$ denotes labor productivity; at time t each of the $N(t)$ workers supplies $A(t)$ units of labor. Clearly, there are various ways to specify the concept of productive efficiency in more detail. The amount of work of an individual may depend on her physical strength, on the time and energy invested in production, on the climate, and on a range of other factors. However, modeling these aspects not only complicates the analysis, but also forces us to consider economic phenomena other than the ones that most interest us.

To distinguish the role of capital accumulation (which by definition depends endogenously on savings and investment decisions) from these other factors, it is useful to assume that the latter are exogenous. The starting point of our analysis is the Solow (1956) growth model. This model is familiar from basic macroeconomics textbooks, but the analysis of this section is relatively formal. We assume that $L(t)$ grows at a constant rate g,

$$\dot{L}(t) = gL(t), \qquad L(t) = L(0)e^{gt},$$

and for the moment we abstract from any economic determinant for the level or the growth rate of this factor of production. Furthermore, we assume that the production function exhibits constant returns to scale, so that

$$F(\lambda K, \lambda L) = \lambda F(K, L)$$

for any λ. The validity of this assumption will be discussed below in the light of its economic implications. Formally, the assumption of constant returns to scale implies a direct relationship between the level of output and capital per unit of the non-accumulated factor,

$$y(t) \equiv Y(t)/L(t) \quad \text{and} \quad k(t) \equiv K(t)/L(t).$$

Omitting the time index t, we can write

$$y = \frac{F(K, L)}{L} = \frac{LF(K/L, 1)}{L} = f(k),$$

which shows that the per capita production depends only on the capital/labor ratio. The accumulation of the stock of capital per worker is given by

$$k(t) = \frac{d}{dt}\left(\frac{K(t)}{L(t)}\right) = \frac{\dot{K}(t)L(t) - \dot{L}(t)K(t)}{L(t)^2} = \frac{\dot{K}(t)}{L(t)} - \frac{\dot{L}(t)}{L(t)}\frac{K(t)}{L(t)}.$$

Since $\dot{K}(t) = I(t) - \delta K(t)$ and $\dot{L}(t) = gL(t)$, we thus get

$$k(t) = \frac{I(t)}{L(t)} - (g + \delta)k(t).$$

Assuming that the economy as a whole devotes a constant proportion s of output to the accumulation of capital,

$$C(t) = (1 - s)Y(t), \qquad I(t) = sY(t),$$

then $I(t)/L(t) = sY(t)/L(t) = sy(t) = sf(k(t))$, and thus

$$k(t) = sf(k(t)) - (g + \delta)k(t).$$

The main advantage of this expression, which is valid only under the simplifying assumptions above, is that it refers to a single variable. For any value of $k(t)$, the model predicts whether the capital stock per worker tends to increase or decrease, and using the intermediate steps described above one can fully characterize the ensuing dynamics of the aggregate and per capita income.

The amount of capital per worker tends to increase when

$$sf(k(t)) > (g + \delta)k(t), \tag{4.3}$$

and to decrease when

$$sf(k(t)) < (g + \delta)k(t). \tag{4.4}$$

Having reduced the dynamics of the entire economy to the dynamics of a single variable, we can illustrate the evolution of the economy in a simple graph as shown in Figure 4.1. Clearly, the function $sf(k)$ plays a crucial role in these relationships. Since $f(k) = F(k, 1)$ and $F(\cdot)$ has constant returns to scale, we have

$$f(\lambda k) = F(\lambda k, 1) \le F(\lambda k, \lambda) = \lambda F(k, 1) = \lambda f(k) \qquad \text{for} \quad \lambda > 1, \tag{4.5}$$

where the inequality is valid under the hypothesis that increasing L, the second argument of $F(\cdot, \cdot)$, cannot decrease production. Note, however, that the inequality is weak, allowing for the possibility that using more L may leave production unchanged for some values of λ and k.

If the inequality in (4.5) is strict, then income per capita tends to increase with k, but at a decreasing rate, and $f(k)$ takes the form illustrated in the figure. If a steady state k_{ss} exists, it must satisfy

$$sf(k_{ss}) = (g + \delta)k_{ss}. \tag{4.6}$$

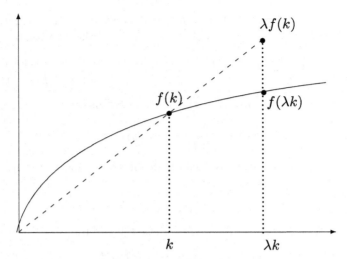

Figure 4.1. Decreasing marginal returns to capital

4.1.1. BALANCED GROWTH

The expression on the right in (4.3) defines a straight line with slope $(g + \delta)$. In Figure 4.2, this straight line meets the function $sf(k)$ at k_{ss}: for $k < k_{ss}$, $\dot{k} = sf(k) - (g + \delta)k > 0$, and the stock of capital tends to increase towards k_{ss}; for $k > k_{ss}$, on the contrary, $\dot{k} < 0$, and in this case k tends to decrease towards its steady state value k_{ss}.

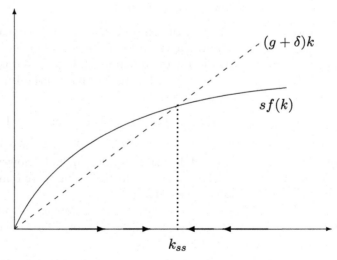

Figure 4.2. Steady state of the Solow model

The speed of convergence is proportional to the vertical distance between the two functions, and thus decreases in absolute value while k approaches its steady-state value. In the long-run the economy will be very close to the steady state. If $k \approx k_{ss} \neq 0$, then $k = K/L$ is approximately constant; given that

$$\frac{d}{dt}\frac{K(t)}{L(t)} = \left(\frac{\dot{K}(t)}{K(t)} - \frac{\dot{L}(t)}{L(t)}\right)\frac{K(t)}{L(t)} \approx 0 \Rightarrow \frac{\dot{K}(t)}{K(t)} \approx \frac{\dot{L}(t)}{L(t)},$$

the long-run growth rate of K is close to the growth rate of L. Moreover, since $F(K, L)$ has constant returns to scale, $Y(t)$ will grow in the same proportion. Hence, in steady state the model follows a "balanced growth" path, in which the ratio between production and capital is constant. For the *per capita* capital stock and output, we can use the definition that $L(t) = A(t)N(t)$. This yields

$$\frac{Y(t)}{N(t)} = \frac{Y(t)}{L(t)}\frac{L(t)}{N(t)} = f(k_t)A(t), \qquad \frac{K(t)}{N(t)} = k_t A(t).$$

In terms of growth rates, therefore, we get the expression

$$\frac{(d/dt)[Y(t)/N(t)]}{Y(t)/N(t)} = \frac{(d/dt)f(k_t)}{f(k_t)} + \frac{\dot{A}(t)}{A(t)}.$$

When k_t tends to a constant k_{ss}, as in the above figure, then $df(k_t)/dt = f'(k_t)\dot{k}$ tends to zero; only a positive growth rate $\dot{A}(t)/A(t)$ can allow a long-run growth in the levels of *per capita* income and capital. In other words, the model predicts a long-run growth of *per capita* income only when L grows over time and whenever this growth is at least partly due to an increase in A rather than an increase in the number of workers N.

If we assume that the effective productivity of labor $A(t)$ grows at a positive rate g_A, and that

$$g \equiv \frac{\dot{L}}{L} = \frac{\dot{A}}{A} + \frac{\dot{N}}{N} = g_A + g_N,$$

then the economy tends to settle in a balanced growth path with exogenous growth rate g_A: the only endogenous mechanism of the model, the accumulation of capital, tends to accompany rather than determine the growth rate of the economy. A once and for all increase in the savings ratio shifts the curve $sf(k)$ upwards, as in Figure 4.3. As a result, the economy will converge to a steady state with a higher capital intensity, but the higher saving rate will have no effect on the long-run growth rate.

In particular, the accumulation of capital cannot sustain a constant growth of income (whatever the value of s) if $g = 0$ and $f''(k) < 0$. For simplicity, consider the case in which L is constant and $\delta = 0$. In that case,

$$\frac{\dot{Y}}{Y} = \frac{f'(k)\dot{k}}{f(k)} = s\,f'(k), \tag{4.7}$$

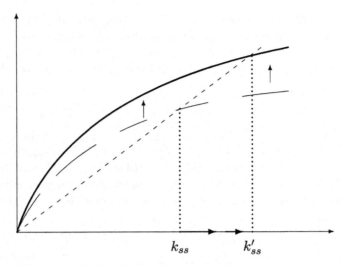

Figure 4.3. Effects of an increase in the savings rate

and an increase in k clearly reduces the growth rate of per capita income. Asymptotically, the growth rate of the economy is zero if $\lim_{k\to\infty} f'(k) = 0$, or it reaches a positive limit if for $k \to \infty$ the limit of $f'(k) = \partial F(\cdot)/\partial K$ is strictly positive.

Exercise 33 *Retaining the assumption that s is constant, let $\delta > 0$. How does the asymptotic behavior of $\dot{Y}/Y$ depend on the value of $\lim_{k\to\infty} f'(k)$?*

4.1.2. UNLIMITED ACCUMULATION

Even if $f'(k)$ is decreasing in k, nothing prevents the expression on the left of (4.3) from remaining above the line $(g + \delta)k$ for *all* values of k, implying that no finite steady state exists ($k_{ss} \to \infty$). For this to occur the following condition needs to be satisfied:

$$\lim_{k\to\infty} f'(k) \equiv f'(\infty) \geq \frac{g + \delta}{s}, \qquad (4.8)$$

so that the distance between the functions does not diminish any further when k increases from a value that is already close to infinity.

Consider, for example, the case in which $g = \delta = 0$: in this case the steady-state capital stock k is infinite even if $\lim_{k\to\infty} f'(k) = 0$. This does not imply that the growth rate remains high, but only that the growth rate slows down so much that it takes an infinite time period before the economy approaches something like a steady state in which the ratio between capital and output remains constant. In fact, given that the speed of convergence is determined by the distance between the two curves in (4.2), which tends to zero in the neighborhood of a steady state, the economy *always* takes an infinite time period to attain the steady state. The steady state is therefore more like a theoretical reference point than an exact description of the final configuration for an economy that departs from a different starting position.

Nevertheless, in the long-run a positive growth rate is sustainable if the inequality in (4.8) holds strictly:

$$\lim_{k \to \infty} f'(k) \equiv f'(\infty) > \frac{g + \delta}{s}.$$

If L is constant, and if there is no depreciation ($\delta = 0$), the long-run growth rate is

$$\frac{\dot{Y}}{Y} = s \, f'(\infty) > 0,$$

and it is dependent on the savings ratio s and the form of the production function.

Consider, for example, the case of a constant elasticity of substitution (CES) production function:

$$F(K, L) = [aK^\lambda + (1 - a)L^\lambda]^{1/\lambda}, \qquad \lambda \le 1. \qquad (4.9)$$

In this case we have

$$f(k) = [ak^\lambda + (1 - a)]^{1/\lambda}$$

and thus

$$f'(k) = [ak^\lambda + (1 - a)]^{(1/\lambda)-1}ak^{\lambda-1} = a[a + (1 - a)k^{-\lambda}]^{(1-\lambda)/\lambda}.$$

If λ is positive, the term $k^{-\lambda}$ tends to zero if k approaches infinity, and $\lim_{k \to \infty} f'(k) = a(a)^{(1/\lambda)-1} = a^{1/\lambda} > 0$: hence, this production function satisfies $f'(\infty) > 0$ when $0 \le \lambda < 1$.

The production function (4.9) is also well defined for $\lambda < 0$. In this case, the term in parentheses tends to infinity and, since its exponent $(1 - \lambda)/\lambda$ is negative, $\lim_{k \to \infty} f'(k) = 0$. For $\lambda = 0$ the functional form (4.9) raises unity to an infinitely large exponent, but is well defined. Taking logarithms, we get

$$\ln(f(k)) = \frac{1}{\lambda} \ln \left(ak^\lambda + (1 - a)\right).$$

The limit of this expression can be evaluated using l'Hôpital's rule, and is equal to the ratio of the limit of the derivatives with respect to λ of the numerator and the denominator. Using the differentiation rules $d \ln(x)/dx = 1/x$ and $dy^x/dx = y^x \ln y$, the derivative of the numerator can be written as

$$\left(ak^\lambda + (1 - a)\right)^{-1} (ak^\lambda \ln k),$$

while the derivative of the denominator is equal to one. Since $\lim_{\lambda \to 0} k^\lambda = 1$, the limit of the logarithm of $f(k)$ is thus equal to $\alpha \ln k$, which corresponds to the logarithm of the Cobb–Douglas function k^α.

Exercise 34 *Interpret the limit condition in terms of the substitutability between K and L. Assuming $\delta = g = 0$, analyze the growth rate of capital and production in the case where $\lambda = 1$, and in the case where $\alpha = 1$.*

4.2. **Dynamic Optimization**

The model that we discussed in the previous section treated the savings ratio s as an exogenous variable. We therefore could not discuss the economic motivation of agents to save (and invest) rather than to consume, nor could we determine the optimality of the growth path of the economy. To introduce these aspects into the analysis, we will now consider the welfare of a representative agent who consumes an amount $C(t)/N(t) \equiv c(t)$ in each period t. Suppose that the welfare of this agent at date zero can be measured by the following integral

$$U = \int_0^\infty u(c(t))e^{-\rho t}\, dt. \tag{4.10}$$

The parameter ρ is the discount rate of future consumption; given $\rho > 0$, the agent prefers immediate consumption over future consumption. The function $u(\cdot)$ is identical to the one introduced in Chapter 1: the positive first derivative $u'(\cdot) > 0$ implies that consumption is desirable in each period; however, the marginal utility of consumption is decreasing in consumption, $u''(\cdot) < 0$, which gives agents an incentive to smooth consumption over time.

The decision to invest rather than to consume now has a precise economic interpretation. For simplicity, we assume that $g = 0$, so that normalizing by population as in (4.10) is equivalent to normalizing by the labor force. Assuming that $\delta = 0$ too, the accumulation constraint,

$$f(k(t)) - c(t) - \dot{k}(t) = 0, \tag{4.11}$$

implies that higher consumption (for a given $k(t)$) slows down the accumulation of capital and reduces future consumption opportunities. At each date t, agents thus have to decide whether to consume immediately, obtaining utility $u(c(t))$, or to save, obtaining higher (discounted) utility in the future.

This problem is equivalent to the maximization of objective function (4.10) given the feasibility constraint (4.11). Consider the associated Hamiltonian,

$$H(t) = [u(c(t)) + \lambda(t)(\, f(k(t)) - c(t))]\, e^{-\rho t},$$

where the shadow price is defined in current values. This shadow price measures the value of capital at date t and satisfies $\lambda(t) = \mu(t)e^{\rho t}$ where $\mu(t)$ measures the value at date zero. The optimality conditions are given by

$$\frac{\partial H}{\partial c} = 0, \tag{4.12}$$

$$-\frac{\partial H}{\partial k} = \frac{d\left(\lambda(t)e^{-\rho t}\right)}{dt}, \tag{4.13}$$

$$\lim_{t \to \infty} \lambda(t)e^{-\rho t}k(t) = 0. \tag{4.14}$$

4.2.1. ECONOMIC INTERPRETATION AND OPTIMAL GROWTH

Equations (4.12) and (4.13) are the first-order conditions for the optimal path of growth and accumulation. In this section we provide the economic intuition for these conditions, which we shall use to characterize the dynamics of the economy. The advantage of using the present-value shadow price $\lambda(t)$ is that we can draw a phase diagram in terms of λ (or c) and k, leaving the time dependence of these variables implicit.

From (4.12), we have

$$u'(c) = \lambda. \tag{4.15}$$

$\lambda(t)$ measures the value in terms of utility (valued at time t) of an infinitesimal increase in $k(t)$. Such an increase in capital can be obtained only by a reduction of current consumption. The loss of utility resulting from lower current consumption is measured by $u'(c)$. For optimality, the two must be the same.

In addition, we also have the condition that

$$\dot{\lambda} = (\rho - f'(k))\lambda, \tag{4.16}$$

which has an interpretation in terms of the evaluation of a financial asset: the marginal unit of capital provides a "dividend" $f'(k)\lambda$, in terms of utility, and a capital gain $\dot{\lambda}$. Expression (4.16) implies that the sum of the "dividend" and the capital gain are equal to the rate of return ρ multiplied by λ. This relationship guarantees the equivalence of the flow utilities at different dates, and we can interpret λ as the value of a financial activity (the marginal unit of capital).

An economic interpretation is also available for the "transversality" condition in (4.14): it imposes that either the stock of capital, or its present value $\lambda(t)e^{-\rho t}$ (or both) need to be equal to zero in the limit as the time horizon extends to infinity.

Combining the relationships in (4.15) and (4.16), we derive the following condition:

$$\frac{d}{dt}u'(c) = (\rho - f'(k))\, u'(c).$$

Along the optimal path of growth and accumulation, the proportional growth rate of marginal utility is equal to $\rho - f'(k)$, the difference between the exponential discount rate of utility and the growth rate of the available resources arising from the accumulation of capital. This condition is a *Euler equation*, like that encountered in Chapter 1. (Exercise 36 asks you to show that it is indeed the same condition, expressed in continuous rather than discrete time.)

Making the time dependence explicit and differentiating the function on the left of this equation with respect to t yields

$$du'(c(t))/dt = u''(c(t))dc(t)/dt.$$

Thus, we can write (omitting the time argument)

$$\dot{c} = \left(\frac{u'(c)}{-u''(c)}\right)(f'(k) - \rho). \tag{4.17}$$

Since the law of motion for capital is given by

$$\dot{k} = f(k) - c, \tag{4.18}$$

we can therefore study the dynamics of the system in c, k-space.

4.2.2. STEADY STATE AND CONVERGENCE

The steady state of the system of equations (4.17) and (4.18) satisfies

$$f'(k_{ss}) = \rho, \qquad c_{ss} = f(k_{ss}),$$

if it exists. For the dynamics we make use of a phase diagram as in Chapter 2. On the horizontal axis we measure the stock of capital k (which now refers to the economy-wide capital stock rather than the capital stock of a single firm). On the vertical axis we measure consumption, c, rather than the shadow price of capital. (The two quantities are univocally related, as was the case for q and investment in Chapter 2.) If $f(\cdot)$ has decreasing marginal returns and in addition there exists a $k_{ss} < \infty$ such that $f'(k_{ss}) = \rho$, then we have the situation illustrated in Figure 4.4.

Clearly, more than one initial consumption level $c(0)$ can be associated with a given initial capital stock $k(0)$. However, only one of these consumption levels leads the economy to the steady state: the dynamics are therefore of the *saddlepath* type which we already encountered in Chapter 2. Any other path

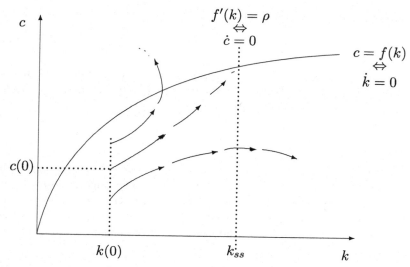

Figure 4.4. Convergence and steady state with optimal savings

leads the economy towards points where $c = 0$, or where $k = 0$ (which in turn implies that $c = 0$ if $f(0) = 0$ and if capital cannot become negative). Under reasonable functional form restrictions the solution is unique, and one can show that only the saddlepath satisfies (4.14).

Exercise 35 *Repeat the derivation, supposing that $g_A = 0$ but $\delta > 0$, $g_N > 0$. Show that the system does not converge to the capital stock associated with maximum per capita consumption in steady state.*

4.2.3. UNLIMITED OPTIMAL ACCUMULATION

In the above diagram the accumulation of capital cannot sustain an indefinite increase of labor productivity and of per capita consumption. However, as in the Solow model, the hypothesis that $F(\cdot)$ has constant returns to scale in capital and labor does not necessarily imply that $k_{ss} < \infty$. In these cases one cannot speak about a steady state in terms of the level of capital, consumption, and production. However, it is still possible that there exists a steady state in terms of the growth rates of these variables—that is, a situation in which the economy has a positive and non-decreasing long-run growth rate even in the absence of exogenous technological change. Suppose for instance that $f'(k) = b$, which is constant and independent of k for all the relevant values of the capital stock. If the elasticity of marginal utility is constant, so that

$$u''(c)\frac{c}{u'(c)} = -\sigma$$

for all values of c, then we can rewrite (4.17) as

$$\frac{\dot{c}(t)}{c(t)} = \frac{b - \rho}{\sigma}, \tag{4.19}$$

and consumption increases (or decreases, if $b < \rho$ and agents can disinvest) at a constant exponential rate. The utility function considered here is of the *constant relative risk aversion* (CRRA) type, given by

$$u(c) = \frac{c^{1-\sigma}}{1 - \sigma}, \qquad u'(c) = c^{-\sigma}, \qquad u''(c) = -\sigma c^{-\sigma-1}. \tag{4.20}$$

The conditions $u'(\cdot) > 0$, $u''(\cdot) < 0$ are satisfied if $\sigma > 0$. If $\sigma = 1$, the functional form (4.20) is not well defined, but the marginal utility function $u'(x) = x^{-1}$ (which completely characterizes preferences) coincides with the derivative of $\log(x)$: hence, for $\sigma = 1$ we can write $u(c) = \log(c)$. Given $f'(k) = b$, we can write $f(k) = bk + \xi$ with ξ a constant of integration. From the law of motion for capital,

$$\dot{k}(t) = f(k(t)) - c(t) = \xi + bk(t) - c(t),$$

we can derive

$$\frac{\dot{k}(t)}{k(t)} = \frac{\xi}{k(t)} + b - \frac{c(t)}{k(t)}.$$

If we focus on the case in which $k(t)$ tends to infinity and $\xi/k(t)$ to zero, we have

$$\lim_{t \to \infty} \frac{\dot{k}(t)}{k(t)} = b - \lim_{t \to \infty} \frac{c(t)}{k(t)}. \tag{4.21}$$

The proportional growth rate of k then tends to a constant if $k(t)$ tends to grow at the same (exponential) rate as $c(t)$.

One can show that this condition is necessarily true if the economy satisfies the transversality condition (4.14). With equation (4.20) for $u(\cdot)$, we get

$$\lambda(t) = u'(c(t)) = (c(t))^{-\sigma}.$$

Given that $c(t)$ grows at a constant exponential rate, $\mu(t) = \lambda(t)e^{-\rho t}$ has exponential dynamics.

Now, consider (4.21). If $c(t)/k(t)$ diminishes over time, then $k(t)$ grows at a more than exponential rate and the limit in (4.14) does not exist. If, on the contrary, $c(t)/k(t)$ is growing, $\dot{k}(t)/k(t)$ becomes increasingly negative. As a result, $k(t)$ will eventually equal zero, and production, consumption, and accumulation will come to a halt—which is certainly not optimal, since for the case of (4.20) we have $u'(0) = \infty$.

The first case corresponds to paths that hit or approach the vertical axis in Figure 4.4; the second corresponds to paths that hit or approach the horizontal axis. Hence, as in the case of the phase diagram, there is only one initial level of consumption that satisfies the transversality condition. (In fact, the phase diagram remains valid in a certain sense; however, the economy is always arbitrarily far from the steady state.) The consumption/capital ratio is therefore constant over time under our assumptions. Imposing

$$\frac{\dot{k}}{k} = \frac{\dot{c}}{c}$$

in (4.19) and in (4.21), we get

$$c(t) = \frac{(\sigma - 1)b + \rho}{\sigma} k(t). \tag{4.22}$$

Equation (4.22) implies that the initial consumption is an increasing function of b, the intertemporal rate of transformation, if $\sigma > 1$. In this case the income effect of a higher b dominates the substitution effect, which induces capital accumulation and hence tends to reduce the level of consumption. For $\sigma = 1$, equation (4.20) is replaced by $u(c) = \ln(c)$, and the ratio c/k is equal to ρ and does not depend on b.

Since $y(t) = bk(t)$, savings are a constant fraction of income as in the Solow model:

$$s = 1 - \frac{(\sigma - 1)b + \rho}{b\sigma}.$$

Nonetheless, in the model with optimization, the savings ratio s is constant only if $u(\cdot)$ is given by (4.20) and if $f(\cdot) = bk$, and not in more general cases. Moreover, s is not a given constant as in the Solow model. The savings ratio depends on the parameters that characterize utility (σ and ρ) and technology (b).

Having shown that capital grows at an exponential rate, we now return to (4.14). In order to satisfy this transversality condition, the growth rate of capital needs to be smaller than the rate at which the discounted marginal utility diminishes along the growth path. We thus have

$$\frac{d}{dt} \left(\ln(c(t)^{-\sigma} e^{-\rho t}) \right) = -\sigma \frac{b - \rho}{\sigma} - \rho = -b.$$

Since in the case considered here $\mu(t) = e^{-\rho t} c(t)^{-\sigma}$ and $f'(k) = b$, this is a reformulation of condition (4.13).

In addition, we have $\dot{k} = sy = sbk$ where s is the savings ratio. The transversality condition is therefore satisfied if

$$\frac{\dot{k}}{k} = sb < \frac{d}{dt} | \left(\ln(c(t)^{-\sigma} e^{-\rho t}) \right) | = b,$$

or equivalently if $s < 1$. Hence, the propensity to save $s = 1 - C/Y$, which is implied by (4.22), must be smaller than one: this leads to the condition that

$$0 < 1 - s = \frac{c(t)}{y(t)} = \frac{c(t)}{bk(t)} = \frac{(\sigma - 1)b + \rho}{b\sigma},$$

which is equivalent to

$$(1 - \sigma)b < \rho. \tag{4.23}$$

If the parameters of the model violated (4.23), the steady state growth path that we identified would not satisfy (4.14). But in that case the optimal solution would not be well defined since the objective function (4.10) could take an infinite value: although technically speaking consumption could grow at rate b, the integral in (4.10) does not converge when $(1 - \sigma)b - \rho > 0$. The steady-state growth path describes the optimal dynamics of the economy without any transitional dynamics if $f(k) = bk$ for each $0 \le k \le \infty$. We should note, however, that the constant b is not allowed to be a function of L if $F(\lambda K, \lambda L) = \lambda F(K, L)$. Hence, $F(K, L) = bK = \tilde{F}(K)$, and the non-accumulated factor L cannot be productive for the economy considered, that grows at a constant rate in the absence of any (exogenous) growth in L, if the production function has constant returns to scale in K and L together. Alternatively, the economy may converge asymptotically to the steady-state growth path if $\lim_{k \to \infty} f'(k) = b > 0$ even though $f''(k) < 0$ for any $0 \le k < \infty$. In this case the marginal productivity of L can be positive for each value of K and L, but the productive role of the non-accumulated factor becomes asymptotically negligible (in a sense that we will make more precise in Section 4.4). In both cases we have or are approaching a steady-state growth path: the economy grows at a positive rate if $b > \rho$, and (less realistically) at a negative rate if $b < \rho$. With $\delta > 0$, it is not difficult to prove that the economy can grow indefinitely if $\lim_{k \to \infty} f'(k) > \delta$.

4.3. **Decentralized Production and Investment Decisions**

The analysis of the preceding section proceeded directly from the maximization of the objective function of a representative agent (4.10), subject to technological constraint represented by the production function. Under certain conditions, the optimal solution coincides with the growth of an economy in which the decisions to save and invest are decentralized to households and firms. In order to study this decentralized economy, we need to define the economic nature and the productive role of capital in greater detail. Let us assume for now that K is a *private* factor of production. The property rights of this factor are owned by individual agents who in the past saved part of their disposable income.

The economy is populated by infinitely lived agents, or "households," which for the moment we assume to be identical. The typical household, indexed by i, owns one unit of labor. For simplicity, we assume that the growth rate of the population is zero. In addition, each household owns $a_i(t)$ units of financial wealth (measured in terms of output, consumption, or capital) at date t. Moreover, individual agents or households take the wage rate $w(t)$ and the interest rate $r(t)$ at which labor and capital are compensated as given. (In other words, agents behave competitively on all markets.)

Family i maximizes

$$U = \int_0^\infty u(c_i(t))e^{-\rho t}\, dt, \qquad (4.24)$$

subject to the budget constraint

$$w(t) + r(t)a_i(t) = c(t) + \dot{a}_i(t).$$

The flow income earned by capital and labor is either consumed, or added to (subtracted from, when negative) the family's financial wealth.

Production is organized in *firms*. Firms hire the production factors from households and offer their goods on a competitive market. At each date t, the firm indexed by j produces $F(K_j(t), L_j(t))$ using quantities $K_j(t)$ and $L_j(t)$ of the two factors, in order to maximize the difference between its revenues and costs. Since all prices are expressed in terms of the final good, firms solve the following static problem:

$$\max_{K_j, L_j}(F(K_j, L_j) - rK_j - wL_j).$$

Given that $F(\cdot, \cdot)$ has constant returns to scale, we can write

$$\max_{K_j, L_j}\left[L_j\, f\left(\frac{K_j}{L_j}\right) - rK_j - wL_j \right],$$

where $f(\cdot)$ corresponds to the output per worker defined in the previous section. The first-order conditions of the firm are therefore given by

$$f'\left(\frac{K_j(t)}{L_j(t)}\right) = r(t),$$

$$f\left(\frac{K_j(t)}{L_j(t)}\right) - \frac{K_j(t)}{L_j(t)} f'(K_j(t)/L_j(t)) = w(t),$$

which are valid for each t and each j.

Since all firms face the same unit costs of capital and labor, every firm will choose the same capital/labor ratio, $K_j/L_j \equiv k$. In equilibrium firms therefore can differ only as regards the scale of their operation: if L is the aggregate stock of labor (or the number of households), we can index the scale of individual firms by ξ_j so that $\sum_j \xi_j = 1$, and denote $L_j = \xi_j L$. Thanks to the assumption of constant returns to scale, we can assume that $F(\cdot, \cdot)$ has the same functional form as at the aggregate level. We can then immediately derive a simple expression for the aggregate output of the economy:

$$Y \equiv \sum_j F(K_j, L_j) = \sum_j L_j f(K_j/L_j) = \left(\sum_j \xi_j\right) L f(k) = F(K, L).$$

Hence if the production function has constant returns to scale and if all markets are competitive, the number of active firms and the scale of their operation is irrelevant.[36]

At this point we note that $\sum_j L_j = L = AN = A\left(\sum_{j=1}^N 1\right)$. Hence, the same factor of labor efficiency A is applied to each individual unit of labor that is offered on the labor market. Moreover, we notice that in equilibrium the profits of each firm are equal to zero. It is therefore irrelevant to know which family owns a particular firm and at which scale this firm operates.

Let us now return to the household. The dynamic optimization problem of the household is expressed by the following Hamiltonian:

$$H(t) = e^{-\rho t}[u(c_i(t)) + \lambda_i(t)(w(t) + r(t)a_i(t) - c_i(t))].$$

The first-order conditions are analogous to (4.12)–(4.14), and can be rewritten as

$$\frac{d}{dt}c_i(t) = \frac{-u'(c_i(t))}{u''(c_i(t))}\left(r(t) - \rho\right),$$

$$\lim_{t \to \infty} e^{-\rho t} u'(c_i(t))a_i(t) = 0.$$

Exercise 36 *Compare this optimality condition with*

$$u'(c_t) = \frac{1+r}{1+\rho}u'(c_{t+1}),$$

also known as a Euler equation, *which holds in a deterministic environment with discrete time. Complete the parallel between the consumption problems studied here and in Chapter 1 by deriving a version of the cumulated budget restriction in continuous time.*

---

[36] For simplicity, we suppose that the stock of capital may vary without adjustment costs. The following derivations would remain valid if, as in some of the models studied in Chapter 2, returns to scale were constant in adjustment as well as in production, implying that—at least in the long run—the size of firms is irrelevant.

4.3.1. OPTIMAL GROWTH

We close the model by imposing the restriction that the total wealth of house-holds must equal the aggregate stock of capital. Inter-family loans and debts cancel out on aggregate, and in any case there is no reason why such loans and debts should exist if households are identical and start with the same initial wealth: $a_i(t) = a(t)$. From

$$\sum_{i=1}^{L} a_i(t) = La(t) = K(t),$$

we get

$$a_i(t) = a(t) = k(t).$$

Furthermore given that

$$r = f'(k),$$

it is easy to verify that optimality conditions for the accumulation of financial wealth coincide with those for the accumulation of capital along the path of aggregate growth that maximizes (4.10). (This also remains true if $g > 0$, if $\delta > 0$, and even if $n > 0$ — where we should note that, in the presence of population growth, the *per capita* rate of return on capital a is given by $r - n$, and that if capital depreciates we have $r = f'(k) - \delta$.)

Hence, the growth path of a market economy will coincide with the optimal growth path if the following conditions are satisfied.

(A) Production has constant returns to scale.

(B) Markets are competitive.

(C) Savings and consumption decisions are taken by agents who independently solve identical problems.

Conditions (A) and (B) guarantee that $r(t) = f'(k)$. The savings of an individual household are compensated according to the *aggregate* marginal productivity of capital. Moreover, given conditions (A) and (B), the market structure is very simple and the entire economy behaves as a "representative" firm.

Hypothesis (C) allows us to represent the savings decisions in terms of the optimization of a single "representative agent." Most differences between individual agents on the market are made irrelevant by the presence of a perfectly competitive capital market (as implicitly assumed above). For example, the supply of labor may follow different dynamics across households, but access to a perfectly competitive capital market may prevent this from having any effect at the aggregate level: individuals or households whose labor income is temporarily low can borrow from households that are in the opposite position, with no aggregate effects as long as total labor supply in the economy is fixed. This is an application of the permanent income hypothesis discussed in Chapter 1.

It is also useful to note that differences in individual consumption have no impact at the aggregate level if agents have a common utility function with a constant elasticity of substitution as in (4.20). In this case the *growth rate* of consumption is the same for all households, so that

$$\frac{\dot{C}}{C} = \frac{\sum_i \dot{c}_i}{\sum_i c_i} = \frac{\sum_i \frac{r(t)-\rho}{\sigma} c_i}{\sum_i c_i} = \frac{r(t)-\rho}{\sigma}.$$

Functional form (4.20) thus has *two* advantages. On the one hand, this functional form is compatible with a steady-state growth path (as we saw above). On the other hand, it allows us to aggregate the individual investment decisions, even in the case in which agents consume different amounts, because the interest rate $r(t)$ is the same for all agents.

4.4. **Measurement of "Progress": The Solow Residual**

The hypotheses of constant returns to scale and perfectly competitive markets (realistic or not) not only are crucial for the equivalence between the optimization at the aggregate and decentralized levels, but also make it possible to measure the technological progress that may allow unlimited growth of labor productivity when $k_{ss} < \infty$.

Differentiating the production function $Y(t) = F(K(t), L(t))$, we get

$$\dot{Y}(t) = F_K(\cdot)\dot{K}(t) + F_L(\cdot)\dot{L}(t) = F_K(\cdot)\dot{K}(t) + F_L(\cdot)\left[\dot{N}(t)A(t) + N(t)\dot{A}(t)\right],$$

where $F_L(\cdot)$ and $F_K(\cdot)$ denote the partial derivatives with respect to the production factors, which are measured in current values. The second equality exploits our definition of labor supply $L(t) \equiv N(t)A(t)$. Rewriting the above expression in terms of proportional growth yields

$$\frac{\dot{Y}}{Y} = \frac{F_K(\cdot)K}{Y}\frac{\dot{K}}{K} + \frac{F_L(\cdot)AN}{Y}\frac{\dot{N}}{N} + \frac{F_L(\cdot)N}{Y}\dot{A}, \qquad (4.25)$$

where we have omitted the time dependence. Now, if labor markets are perfectly competitive, we have $w = \partial F(\cdot)/\partial N = AF_L(\cdot)$. We can thus write

$$\frac{F_L(\cdot)AN}{Y} = \frac{wN}{Y} \equiv \gamma,$$

which expresses labor's share of national income, which is in general observable, in terms of a derivative of the aggregate production function. Moreover, given that the production technology has constant returns to scale in K and L, the entire value of output will be paid to the production factors if these are paid according to their marginal productivity. In fact, for each $F(\cdot, \cdot)$ with constant returns to scale,

$$F\left(\frac{K}{Y}, \frac{L}{Y}\right) = 1 \quad \text{with } Y = F(K, L).$$

Using Euler's Theorem, we therefore have

$$1 = F\left(\frac{K}{Y}, \frac{L}{Y}\right) = \frac{\partial F(K, L)}{\partial K}\frac{K}{Y} + \frac{\partial F(K, L)}{\partial L}\frac{L}{Y}. \tag{4.26}$$

Hence,

$$\frac{F_K(\cdot)K}{Y} = 1 - \frac{AF_L(\cdot)N}{Y} = 1 - \gamma,$$

and (4.25) implies

$$\gamma\frac{\dot{A}}{A} = \frac{\dot{Y}}{Y} - (1 - \gamma)\frac{\dot{K}}{K} - \gamma\frac{\dot{N}}{N}. \tag{4.27}$$

If accurate measures of γ (the income share of the non-accumulated factor N) and the proportional growth rate of Y, K, and N are available, then (4.27) provides a measure known as "Solow's residual," which indicates how much of the growth in income is accounted for by an increase in the measure of efficiency $A(t)$ (which as such is not measurable) rather than by an increase in the supply of productive inputs.

If the production function has the Cobb–Douglas form,

$$Y = F(K, L) = F(K, AN) = K^{\alpha}(AN)^{1-\alpha}, \tag{4.28}$$

or, equivalently, if

$$Y = \tilde{A}\tilde{F}(K, N) = \tilde{A}K^{\alpha}N^{1-\alpha}, \qquad \text{where } \tilde{A} = A^{1-\alpha}, \tag{4.29}$$

then γ is constant and equal to $1 - \alpha$. The Cobb–Douglas function is therefore convenient from an analytic point of view, and also because it does not attach any practical relevance to the difference between a labor-augmenting technical change as in (4.28) and a *neutral* technological change as in (4.29). In fact, the Solow residual defined in (4.27) corresponds to the rate of growth of $\tilde{A}$.

Exercise 37 *Verify that, if $\dot{K}/K = \dot{A}/A + \dot{N}/N$, the income shares of capital and labor are constant as long as the production function has constant returns to scale, even if it does not have the Cobb–Douglas form.*

Unfortunately, the functional form (4.28) implies that

$$\lim_{k\to\infty} f'(k) = \lim_{k\to\infty} \tilde{A}\alpha k^{\alpha-1} = 0$$

if $\alpha < 1$, that is if $\gamma > 0$ and labor realistically receives a positive share of national income. Given that the labor share is approximately constant (around

60% in the long-run), the empirical evidence does not seem supportive of unlimited growth with constant returns to scale.

More generally, for each case in which the aggregate production function $F(\cdot, \cdot)$ has constant returns to scale and

$$\lim_{k \to \infty} f'(k) = \lim_{k \to \infty} \frac{\partial F(K, L)}{\partial K} = b > 0,$$

then $F_L(\cdot) L / F(\cdot)$ tends to zero when K and k approach infinity for a constant L. It suffices to take the limit of expression (4.26) with $K \to \infty$ (and thus $L/Y = L/F(K, L) \to 0$), which yields

$$1 = F\left(\lim_{K \to \infty} \frac{K}{Y}, 0\right)$$

$$= b \lim_{K \to \infty} \frac{K}{F(K, L)} + \lim_{K \to \infty} \left(\frac{\partial F(K, L)}{\partial L} \frac{L}{F(K, L)}\right), \qquad (4.30)$$

l'Hôpital's rule then implies (as in exercise 33 above) that

$$\lim_{K \to \infty} \frac{K}{F(K, L)} = 1 \bigg/ \left(\lim_{K \to \infty} \frac{\partial F(K, L)}{\partial K}\right) = \frac{1}{b}.$$

Hence, the first term on the right-hand side of (4.30) tends to one, and the second term (the income share of the non-accumulated factor) therefore has to tend to zero.

In sum, the income share of the non-accumulated factor γ needs to decline to zero with the accumulation of an infinite amount of capital if

(i) the accumulation of capital allows the economy to grow indefinitely, and

(ii) the production function has constant returns to scale.

This conclusion is intuitive in light of the reasoning that led us to draw a convex production function in Figure 4.1, and to identify a steady state in Figure 4.2; if we have equality rather than a strict inequality in (4.5), that is if

$$f(\lambda k) = F(\lambda k, 1) = F(\lambda k, \lambda) = \lambda F(k, 1) = \lambda f(k)$$

for $\lambda \neq 1$, then output is proportional to K and increasing L will not have any effect on output. If the increase in the stock of capital tends to have proportional effects on output, then both marginal productivity and the income share of the non-accumulated factor must steadily decrease.

Exercise 38 *Verify this result for the case of a function in the form (4.9).*

Naturally, equation (4.27) and its implications are valid only under the twin assumptions that the production technology exhibits constant returns to scale and that production factors are paid according to their marginal productivity.

From a formal point of view, nothing would prevent us from considering models in which either assumption is violated. As illustrated in the exercise below, in that case it does not make much sense to measure $\dot{A}/A$ by inserting labor's income share γ in (4.27).

Exercise 39 *Consider a Cobb–Douglas production function with increasing returns to scale,*

$$Y = AN^\alpha K^\beta, \qquad \alpha + \beta > 1.$$

Suppose, in addition, that wages are below the marginal productivity of labor,

$$AF_N(\cdot) = \frac{w}{1 - \mu},$$

where $\mu > 0$ can be interpreted as a monopolistic mark-up. What does the Solow residual measured by (4.27) correspond to in this case?

The above hypotheses correspond to conditions (A) and (B) in the previous section, which allowed us to connect the macroeconomic dynamics to the savings and consumption decisions of individual agents. Constant returns to scale allowed us simply to aggregate the production functions of the individual firms. And the remuneration of production factors equal to their marginal product (which in turn followed from the assumption that all markets are characterized by free entry and perfect competition) ensured that the dynamic path of the economy maximized the welfare of a hypothetical representative agent. In the rest of this chapter we consider models for which the macroeconomic dynamics are well-defined (but not necessarily optimal from the aggregate point of view) in the absence of perfectly competitive markets and in the presence of increasing returns to scale.

4.5. Endogenous Growth and Market Imperfections

To obtain an income share for the non-accumulated factor that is not reduced to zero in the long-run and at the same time allow for an endogenous growth rate that is determined by the investment decisions of individual agents, we need to reconsider the assumption of constant returns to scale. Henceforth we will consider steady-state growth paths only in the absence of exogenous technological change. We know that, in order to sustain long-run (proportional) growth, the economy needs to exhibit constant returns to capital: from now on we therefore assume that $f'(k) = b$, with b independent of k. If that condition is satisfied, and if the productivity of the non-accumulated factor L is positive, aggregate production is characterized by increasing returns to scale.

Multiplying K and L by the same constant increases aggregate production more than proportionally.

As shown above, constant returns to scale are a crucial condition for the decentralization of the socially optimal savings and investment decisions. Allowing for increasing returns to scale means (in general) that we lose this result. It becomes important therefore to confront the optimal growth path of the economy with the growth path that results from decentralized investment decisions. In addition, we need to pay attention to the criteria for the distribution of income: with increasing returns to scale, it is no longer possible to remunerate all factors of production on the basis of their marginal product because the sum of these payments would exceed the value of production. Some factor of production needs to receive less than the value of its marginal product, and it is obviously of interest to know how that may result.

4.5.1. PRODUCTION AND NON-RIVAL FACTORS

To understand the economic mechanisms behind the division of the value of output within each productive unit and in the economy as a whole, it is useful briefly to reconsider the hypothesis of constant returns to scale.

One possible microeconomic foundation for this assumption is based on the idea that production processes can be *replicated*. If a firm or productive unit j produces Y_j using quantities K_j and L_j (and these are the only necessary factors of production), then one can obviously obtain double the amount of production by doubling the input of both factors, simply by organizing these additional factors in an identical production unit. The same reasoning applies to different factors of proportionality as long as the factors of production are perfectly divisible, as is implicit in the concept of marginal productivity.

A model with constant returns to scale in production implies not only that a doubling of inputs may lead to a doubling of output, but also that such a doubling of inputs is *necessary* to obtain twice the amount of output. In reality, however, there are factors of production whose input need not be doubled in order to double output; for instance, to build a house one needs a blueprint, a piece of land, and a certain quantity of materials, manual labor, and energy (all inputs that can be expressed in units of labor and other primary inputs). To build a second house one probably needs the same amounts of materials, labor, and energy and an identical piece of land. However, nothing prevents the use of the same plan. The same input can therefore be used to build several houses. This is an example of a more general phenomenon: certain factors of production (like the architectural plan) may be used contemporaneously by one or more production processes, and their use in a production process need not reduce its productivity in other processes. These factors are normally referred to as *non-rival* inputs. It is not difficult to find other examples: every factor that provides intangible (but necessary) input of know-how (or software) is non-rival.

The presence of non-rival factors makes the assumption of increasing returns plausible. It is still possible to build a second house using double the amount of all inputs including a completely new plan. But this is no longer necessary: since the product can be doubled without any work on the plan, doubling all inputs makes it possible to improve its quality, or perhaps to build a larger house.

As we know, the assumption of constant returns was useful to decentralize production and to distribute its revenues. On the contrary, with non-rival factors and increasing returns to scale, it is no longer possible to pay all factors according to their marginal productivity. The total productivity of the factors used in design depends on the number of houses that are built with one and the same design. This number can in principle be very high. Moreover, if each additional house requires a constant amount of labor and material, then the production technology has constant returns to these variable inputs, and if these factors were paid according to their true marginal productivity, there would be nothing left to pay the architect.

How can one decentralize production decisions under these circumstances? Non-rival factors are mostly identified with intangible resources (know-how, software) which, by their nature, are often non-rival, *non-excludable*. When a productive input is non-rival it is often difficult to prevent other agents from making an economic use of this factor. The regulation of property rights and licenses is meant to resolve this type of problem. Nonetheless, the theft of intellectual property remains difficult to prove and is also hard to punish, because the knowledge (the stolen "object") remains in the hands of the thief. In the example of the house, the private property in the physical sense (calculations and designs) can be guaranteed, and unauthorized duplication of the plan can be punished legally. However, certain innovative aspects of the project may be evident by simply observing the final product, and it is not easy to prevent or punish reproduction of these aspects by third parties.

Many recent growth models allow for increasing rather than constant returns to scale, and are therefore naturally forced to study markets and productive structures characterized by non-rivalry and non-excludability of certain factors.

4.5.2. INVOLUNTARY TECHNOLOGICAL PROGRESS

In the model outlined below the level of technology, A is treated as an entirely non-rival and non-excludable productive input in Solow's model of exogenous growth. The production function therefore has three arguments, K, N, and A:

$$Y = F(K, L) = F(K, AN) \equiv \tilde{F}(K, N, A).$$

If $F(\cdot, \cdot)$ has constant returns to scale in K and L (both of which have strictly positive marginal productivity), then $\tilde{F}(\cdot, \cdot, \cdot)$ has increasing returns to scale in K, N, and A. In fact, doubling K, N, and A doubles K but quadruples L, so aggregate production more than doubles if $F_L(\cdot) > 0$. Since firms hire capital and labor from households, we can interpret the situation in terms of the non-rivalry and non-excludability of A: each unit of labor has free access to the current level of A, which is the same for all.

As we know, growth in the Solow model is exogenous. More precisely, the dynamics of the level of technological change or efficiency $A(t)$ is not influenced by economic decisions: if one interprets A as a production factor in the decentralized model, then this factor

(A1) is completely non-excludable from the viewpoint of production and receives no remuneration;

(A2) is reproduced over time without any interaction with the production system; in fact, if we have exponential technological change at a constant rate g_A, the expression $\dot{A}(t) = g_A A(t)$ can be interpreted as an expression of accumulation in which $A(t)$ is used in the production of further technological progress (besides its use in the production of final goods).

To integrate technological change in the economic structure of the model, we can preserve aspect (A1) (no remuneration for the "factor" technology) and relax aspect (A2), assuming that the growth in efficiency is linked to economic activity (and remunerated).

For example, one can specify a model in which technological change is a by-product of production (*learning by doing*). One can for instance assume that

$$A(t) = A\left(\frac{K(t)}{N}\right), \qquad A'(\cdot) > 0,$$

so that the effective productivity of labor is a function of the amount of capital per worker. To interpret this assumption, one could assume that experience makes workers more efficient. That is, while doing, workers learn from their mistakes, and their additional experience thereby increases the productive efficiency of the non-accumulated factor N.

The proposed functional form assumes that labor efficiency is a function of the capital stock and thus of the total amount of past investments. It may be more realistic to assume that total accumulated production, rather than investments, determines the efficiency of N. However, such an extension would complicate the analysis without providing substantially different results.

Much more important is the implicit assumption that the efficiency of each unit of labor does not depend on its own productive activity, but rather on aggregate economic activity. Agents in this economy learn not only from their own mistakes, so to speak, but also from the mistakes of others. When deciding how much to invest, agents do not consider the fact that their actions affect the productivity of the other agents in the economy; the economic interactions are thus affected by externalities. These externalities are similar (albeit with an opposite sign) to the externalities that one encounters in any basic textbook treatment of pollution, or to those that we will discuss in Chapter 5 when we consider coordination problems.

If we retain the assumptions that firms produce homogeneous goods with the constant-returns-to-scale production technology $F(K_j, AN_j)$, that A is non-rival and non-excludable, and that all markets are perfectly competitive, then output decisions can be decentralized as in Section 4.3. In particular, the marginal productivity of capital needs to coincide with $r(t)$, the rate at which it is remunerated in the market,

$$r(t) = \frac{\partial F(\cdot)}{\partial K} \equiv F_1(\cdot) = f'(K/L),$$

and the dynamic optimization problem of households implies a proportional growth rate of consumption equal to $(r(t) - \rho)/\sigma$ if the function of marginal utility has constant elasticity. Hence, recalling that $L = AN$, it follows that both individual and aggregate consumption grow at a rate

$$\frac{\dot{C}(t)}{C(t)} = \left[f'\left(\frac{K(t)}{NA(t)}\right) - \rho \right] \bigg/ \sigma.$$

If, as in the case of a Cobb–Douglas function, the economy distributes a constant (or non-vanishing) share of national income to the non-accumulated factor, then $\lim_{k\to\infty} f'(k) = 0 < \rho$ and consumption growth can remain positive only if A and L grow together with K, which would prevent the marginal productivity of capital from approaching zero. However, since A is a function of k in the model of this section, the growth of A itself depends on the accumulation of capital. If

$$\lim_{k\to\infty} \frac{A(k)}{k} = \frac{1}{a} > 0,$$

we have

$$\lim_{K/N\to\infty} f'\left(\frac{K}{A(K/N)N}\right) = \lim_{K/N\to\infty} F_1\left(\frac{K}{A(K/N)N}, 1\right) = F_1(a, 1),$$

which may well be above ρ.

Exercise 40 *Let* $F(K, L) = K^a L^{1-a}$, *and* $A(\cdot) = aK/N$: *what is the growth rate of the economy?*

Hence, in the presence of *learning by doing*, the economy can continue to grow endogenously even if the non-accumulated factor receives a non-vanishing share of national income. There is however an obvious problem. From the aggregate viewpoint, true marginal productivity is given by

$$\frac{d}{dK} F(K, A(K/N)N) = F_1(\cdot) + F_2(\cdot)A'(k) > F_1(\cdot), \quad \text{for } F_2(\cdot) \equiv \frac{\partial F(\cdot)}{\partial L}.$$

Hence, growth that is induced by the optimal savings decisions of individuals does not correspond to the growth rate that results if one optimizes (4.10) directly. In fact, the decentralized growth rate is below the efficient growth rate because individuals do not take the external effects of their actions into account, and they disregard the share of investment benefits that accrues to the economy as a whole rather than to their own private resources.

4.5.3. SCIENTIFIC RESEARCH

It may well be the case that innovative activity has an economic character and that it requires specific productive efforts rather than being an unintentional by-product. For example, we may have

$$Y(t) = C(t) + \dot{K}(t) = F(K_y(t), L_y(t)), \tag{4.31}$$

$$\dot{A}(t) = F(K_A(t), L_A(t)), \tag{4.32}$$

with $K_y(t) + K_A(t) = K(t)$, $L_y(t) + L_A(t) = L(t) = A(t)N(t)$. In other words, new and more efficient modes of production may be "produced" by dedicating factors of production to research and development rather than to the production of final goods.

If, as suggested by the notation, the production function is the same in both sectors and has constant returns to scale, then we can write

$$\dot{A} = F(K_A, L_A) = \frac{\partial F(K_A, L_A)}{\partial K} K_A + \frac{\partial F(K_A, L_A)}{\partial L} L_A.$$

Assuming that the rewards r and w of the factors employed in research are the same as the earnings in the production sector, then

$$\dot{A} = rK_A + wL_A \tag{4.33}$$

is a measure of research output in terms of goods. If A is (non-rival and) non-excludable, then this output has no market value. Since it is impossible to prevent others from using knowledge, private firms operating in the research sector would not be able to pay any salary to the factors of production that they employ.

Nonetheless, the increase in productive efficiency has value for society as a whole, if not for single individuals. Like other non-rival and non-excludable goods, such as national defense or justice, research may therefore be financed by the government or other public bodies if the latter have the authority to impose taxes on final output that has a market value. One could for example tax the income of all private factors at rate τ, and use the revenue to finance "firms" which (like universities or national research institutes, or like monasteries in the Middle Ages) produce only research which is of no market value. Thanks to constant returns to scale, one can calculate national income in both sectors by evaluating the output of the research sector at the cost of production factors, as in (4.33). Moreover, the accumulation of tangible and intangible assets obeys the following laws of motion:

$$\dot{K} = (1 - \tau)F(K, AN) - C,$$

$$\dot{A} = \tau F(K, AN).$$

The return on private investments is given by

$$r(t) = (1 - \tau)f'(k),$$

and if $f(\cdot)$ has decreasing returns the economy possesses a steady-state growth path in which A, K, Y, and C all grow at the same rate. It is not difficult to see that there is no unambiguous relation between this growth rate and the tax τ (or the size of the public research sector). In fact, in the long-run there is no growth if $\tau = 0$, since in that case $\dot{A}(t) = 0$; but neither is there growth if τ is so high that $r(t) = (1 - \tau)f'(k)$ tends toward values below the discount rate of utility, and prevents growth of private consumption and capital. For intermediate values, however, growth can certainly be positive. (We shall return to this issue in Section 4.5.5.)

4.5.4. HUMAN CAPITAL

Retaining assumptions (4.32) and (4.31), one can reconsider property (A1), and allow A to be a *private* and excludable factor of production. In this case, the problem of how to distribute income to the three factors A, K, and L if there are increasing returns to scale can be resolved if one assumes that a person (a unit of N) does not have productive value unless she owns a certain amount of the measure of efficiency A. Reverting to the hypothesis implicit in the Solow model, in which N is remunerated but not A, the presence of N is thus completely irrelevant from a productive point of view.

The factor A, if remunerated, is not very different from K, and may be dubbed *human capital*. In fact, for A to be excludable it should be embodied in individuals, who have to be employed and paid in order to make productive use of knowledge. One example of this is the case of privately funded professional education.

In the situation that we consider here, all the factors are accumulated. Given constant returns to scale, we can therefore easily decentralize the decisions to devote resources to any of these uses. If as in (4.31) and (4.32) the two factors of production are produced with the same technology, and if one assumes that all markets are competitive so that A and K are compensated at rates $F_A(\cdot)$ and $F_K(\cdot)$ respectively, then the following laws of motion hold:

$$\dot{K} = F((1-\tau)K, (1-\tau)A) - C = (1-\tau)F(K, A) - C$$

$$\dot{A} = \tau F(K, A).$$

In these equations τ no longer denotes the tax on private income, but rather more generally the overall share of income that is devoted to the accumulation of human capital instead of physical capital (or consumption).

If technological change does indeed take the form suggested here, then we need to reinterpret the empirical evidence that was advanced when we discussed the Solow residual. Given that the worker's income includes the return on human capital, we need to refine the definition of labor stock, which is no longer identical to the number of workers in any given period. The accumulation of this factor may for example depend on the enrolment rates of the youngest age cohorts in education more than on demographic changes as such. However, the fact that agents have a finite life, and that they dedicate only the first part of their life to education, implies that it is difficult to claim that education is the only exclusive source of technological progress. Each process of learning and transmission of knowledge uses knowledge that is generated in the past and is not necessarily compensated. Hence also the accumulation of human capital is subject to the type of externalities that we encountered in the discussion of *learning by doing*.[37]

4.5.5. GOVERNMENT EXPENDITURE AND GROWTH

Besides the capacity to finance the accumulation of non-excludable technological change, government spending may provide the economy with those (non-rival and non-excludable) factors that make the assumption of increasing returns plausible. Non-rivalry and non-excludability are in fact main features

---

[37] Drafting and studying the present chapter, for example, would have been much more difficult if Robert Solow, Paul Romer, and many others had not worked on growth issues. Yet, no royalty is paid to them by the authors and readers of this book.

of pure public goods like defense or police, and of quasi-public goods like roads, telecommunications, etc. To analyze these aspects, we assume that

$$Y(t) = \tilde{F}(K(t), L(t), G(t)),$$

where, besides the standard factors K and L (the latter constant in the absence of exogenous technological change), the amount of public goods G appears as a separate input. Since L and K are private factors of production, the competitive equilibrium of the private sector requires that the production function $\tilde{F}(\cdot, \cdot, \cdot)$ has constant returns to its first two arguments:

$$\tilde{F}(\lambda K, \lambda L, G) = \lambda \tilde{F}(K, L, G).$$

Hence, given $\partial \tilde{F}(\cdot)/\partial G > 0$, a proportional change of G and of the private factors L and K results in a more than proportional increase in production. The function $\tilde{F}(\cdot, \cdot, \cdot)$ therefore has increasing returns to scale, but this does not prevent the existence of a competitive equilibrium as long as G is a non-rival and non-excludable factor which is made available to all productive units without any cost. If the provision of public goods is constant over time ($G(t) = \bar{G}$ for each t) then, as in the preceding section, constant returns to K and L would imply decreasing returns to K. With an increase in the stock of capital, the growth rate that is implied by the optimization of (4.10) and (4.20), i.e.

$$\frac{\dot{C}(t)}{C(t)} = \left(\frac{\partial \tilde{F}(K(t), L(t), \bar{G})}{\partial K} - \rho \right) \Big/ \sigma,$$

can only decrease, and will fall to zero in the limit if L continues to receive a positive share of aggregate income.

To allow indefinite growth, the provision of public goods needs to increase exponentially. If, as seems realistic, a higher $G(t)$ has a positive effect on the marginal productivity of capital, then $\dot{G}(t) > 0$ has a similar effect to the (exogenous) growth of $A(t)$ in the preceding sections. Hence, an ever increasing supply of public goods may allow the return on savings to remain above the discount rate ρ so that the economy as a whole can grow indefinitely.

As we saw in Section 4.5.2, the development of $A(t)$ could be made endogenous by assuming that the accumulation of this index of efficiency depended on the capital stock. Similarly, and even more obviously, the provision of public goods is a function of private economic activity if one assumes that their provision is financed by the taxation of private income. If

$$G(t) = \tau \tilde{F}(K(t), L(t), G(t)), \tag{4.34}$$

then each increase in production will be shared in proportion between consumption, investments and the increase of $G(t)$, which can offset the secular decrease in the marginal productivity of capital.

To obtain a balanced growth path, the production function needs to have constant returns to K and G for any constant L. In fact, if

$$\tilde{F}(\lambda K, L, \lambda G) = \lambda \tilde{F}(K, L, G),$$

a constant increase of capital will imply proportional growth of income if G grows at the same rate as K—this is in turn implied by the proportionality of income, tax revenues, and the provision of public goods in (4.34). To calculate the growth rate that is compatible with a balanced government budget and with the resulting savings and investment decisions, we must to take into account the fact that we have to subtract the tax rate τ from the private return on savings; hence, consumption grows at the rate

$$\frac{\dot{C}(t)}{C(t)} = \left((1 - \tau) \frac{\partial \tilde{F}(K(t), L(t), G(t))}{\partial K} - \rho \right) \Big/ \sigma, \qquad (4.35)$$

and the growth path of the economy will satisfy the above equation and (4.34).

Exercise 41 *Consider the production function*

$$\tilde{F}(K, L, G) = K^\alpha L^\beta G^\gamma.$$

Determine what relation α, β, and γ need to satisfy so that the economy has a balanced growth path. What is the growth rate along this balanced growth path?

4.5.6. MONOPOLY POWER AND PRIVATE INNOVATIONS

An important aspect of the models described above is the fact that the decentralized growth path need not be optimal in the absence of a complete set of competitive markets. The formal analysis of economic interactions that are less than fully efficient plays an important role in modern macroeconomics, and in this concluding section we briefly discuss how imperfectly competitive markets may imply inefficient outcomes.

In order to decentralize production decisions, we have so far assumed that markets are perfectly competitive (allowing only for the possibility of *missing* markets in the case of non-excludable factors). However, it is realistic to assume that there are firms that have monopoly power and that do not take prices as given. From the viewpoint of the preceding sections, it is interesting to note the relationship between monopoly power and increasing returns to scale *within* firms. Returning to the example of a house, we assume that the project is in fact *excludable*. That is, a given productive entity (a firm) can legally prevent unauthorized use of the project by third parties. However, within the firm the project is still non-rival, and the firm can use the same blueprint to build any arbitrary number of houses. If we assume that the firm is competitive, it will be willing to supply houses as long as the price of each is above marginal cost. Hence for a price above marginal cost supply tends to infinity, while for any price below marginal cost supply is zero. But if the price is exactly equal to marginal cost, then revenues are just enough to recover the variable cost (materials, labor, land)—and the fixed cost (the project) would need to be paid by the firm, which should rationally refuse to enter the market.

A firm that bears a fixed cost but does not have increasing marginal costs (or more generally has increasing returns) has to be able to charge a price above marginal cost in order to exist. Formally, we assume that firm j needs to pay a fixed cost κ_0 to be able to produce, and a variable cost (per unit of output) equal to κ_1. In addition, we assume that the demand function has constant elasticity, with $p_j = x_j^{a-1}$ where x_j is the number of units produced and offered on the market. The total revenues are thus $p_j x_j = x_j^a$, and to maximize profits,

$$\max_{x_j} x_j^a - \kappa_0 - \kappa_1 x_j,$$

the firm chooses output level

$$x_j = \left(\frac{\kappa_1}{a}\right)^{1/(a-1)}$$

and charges price

$$p_j = \frac{\kappa_1}{a}.$$

With free entry of firms (that is any firm that pays κ_0 can start production of this item), profits will be zero in equilibrium:

$$(p_j - \kappa_1)x_j = \kappa_0 \Rightarrow x_j = \frac{\kappa_0}{\kappa_1}\frac{a}{1-a}, \qquad (4.36)$$

and the resulting price is equal to the *average* cost of production, rather than the marginal cost, as in the case of perfect competition. The costs of each firm are thus given by

$$\kappa_0 + \kappa_1 x_j = \kappa_0 + \kappa_1 \frac{\kappa_0}{\kappa_1}\frac{a}{1-a} = \frac{\kappa_0}{1-a}. \qquad (4.37)$$

This condition determines the scale of production, or in our example the number of houses that are produced with each project.

To incorporate this monopolistic behavior in a dynamic general equilibrium model, we consider the aggregate production (valued at market prices) of N identical firms:

$$X = \sum_{j=1}^{N} p_j x_j = \sum_{j=1}^{N} x^a = N x^a.$$

If κ_0 and κ_1 are given and if N is an integer, then this measure of output can only be a multiple of the scale of production calculated in (4.36). However, nothing constrains us from indexing firms with a continuous variable and replacing the summation sign by an integral.[38] Writing

$$X = \int_0^N x_j^a \, dj = x^a \int_0^N dj = N x^a,$$

and treating N as a continuous variable, the zero profit condition can be exactly satisfied for any value of aggregate production. Given that profits are zero, the value of production equals the cost of production, which in turn is given by N times the quantity in (4.37). Assume for a moment that the costs of a firm (both fixed and variable) are given by the quantity of K multiplied by $r(t)$. For a given supply of productive factors, we can then determine the number of production processes that can be activated as well as the remuneration of the production factors. The scale of production of each of the N identical firms is proportional to K/N, and the constant of proportionality is given by $\kappa_0/(1-a)$.

We thus have

$$X = \int_0^N \left(\frac{\kappa_0}{1-a} \frac{K}{N} \right)^a dj = \left(\frac{\kappa_0}{1-a} \right)^a N^{1-a} K^a. \qquad (4.38)$$

Because the goods are imperfect substitutes, the value of output increases with the number of varieties N for any given value of K. In other words, for a given value of income it is more satisfying to consume a wider variety of goods.

Suppose that the value of aggregate output is defined by

$$Y = L^{1-a} \left(\int_0^N x_j^a \, dj \right) = L^{1-a} X.$$

That is, output (which can be consumed or invested in the form of capital) is obtained by combining the market value X of the intermediate goods x_j with factor L which, as usual, is assumed to be exogenous and fixed.

Let us assume in addition that utility has the constant-elasticity form (4.20), so that the optimal rate of growth of consumption is constant if the rate of return on savings is constant. Given that, in equilibrium,

$$Y = L^{1-a} X = L^{1-a} \xi^{1-a} K,$$

---

[38] Approximating N by a continuous variable is substantially appropriate if the number of firms is large. Formally, one would let the economic size of each firm go to zero as their number increases, and keep the product of the number of firms by the distance between their indexes constant at N.

so that $\partial Y/\partial K$ is constant (non decreasing), we find that equilibrium has a growth path with a constant growth rate if

$$\frac{\partial Y}{\partial K} = L^{1-a}\xi^{1-a} > \rho.$$

In the decentralized equilibrium, the rate of growth is $(r - \rho)/\sigma$ where r denotes the remuneration of capital in terms of the final good. To determine r, we notice that each factor is paid according to its marginal productivity in the final goods sector provided that this sector is competitive. Hence, the total value of income that accrues to capital is equal to

$$rK = a(Y/K)K = aL^{1-a}\xi^{1-a}K$$

and

$$r = aL^{1-a}\xi^{1-a} < L^{1-a}\xi^{1-a} = \frac{\partial Y}{\partial K}.$$

The private accumulation of capital is rewarded at a rate that is below its productivity at the aggregate level. As before, the economy therefore grows below the optimum growth rate. Intuitively, given that the production technology is characterized by increasing returns at the level of an individual firm, firms can make positive profits only if prices exceed marginal costs. The rate r which determines marginal costs is therefore below the true aggregate return on capital. The difference between private and social returns on capital is given by the mark-up, which distorts savings decisions and implies that growth is slower than optimal.

Admitting that prices may be above marginal cost, one can add further realism to the model by assuming that monopolistic market power is of a long-run nature. This requires that fixed flow costs be incurred once the firm is created. Over time firms can therefore gradually recover fixed costs, thanks to monopolistic rents. Obviously, this is the right way to formalize the above house example: the fixed cost of designing the house is paid once, but the resulting project can be used many times. We refer readers to the bibliographical references at the end of this chapter for a complete treatment of the resulting dynamic optimization problem and its implications for the aggregate growth rate.

REVIEW EXERCISES

Exercise 42 *Consider the production function*

$$Y = F(K) = \begin{cases} aK - \frac{1}{2}K^2 & \text{if } K < a, \\ \frac{1}{2}a^2 & \text{otherwise.} \end{cases}$$

(a) *Determine the optimality conditions for the problem*

$$\max \int_0^\infty u(C(t))e^{-\rho t}\,dt$$

s.t. $C(t) = F(K(t)) - \dot{K}(t), \qquad K(0) < a\ given$

with utility function

$$u(x) = \begin{cases} v + \beta x - \frac{1}{2}x^2 & \text{if } x < \beta \\ v + \frac{1}{2}\beta^2 & \text{otherwise.} \end{cases}$$

(b) *Calculate the steady-state value of capital, production, and consumption. Draw the phase diagram in the capital–consumption space. (The formal derivations can be limited to the region $K < a$, $C < \beta$ assuming that the parameters a, β, ρ satisfy appropriate conditions. You may also provide an (informal) discussion of the optimal choices outside this region in which the usual assumptions of convexity are not satisfied.)*

(c) *To draw the phase diagram, one needs to keep in mind the role of parameters a and ρ. But what is the role of β?*

(d) *The production function does not have constant returns to scale. This is a problem (why?) if one wants to interpret the solution as a dynamic equilibrium of a market economy. Show that for a certain $g(L)$ the production function*

$$Y = F(K, L) = aK - g(L)K^2$$

has constant returns to K and L in the relevant region. Also show that the solution characterized above corresponds to the dynamic equilibrium of an economy endowed with an amount $L = 2$ of a non-accumulated factor.

Exercise 43 *Consider an economy in which output and accumulation satisfy*

$$Y(t) = \ln(L + K(t)),$$
$$\dot{K}(t) = sY(t),$$

with L and s constant.

(a) *Can this economy experience unlimited growth of consumption $C(t) = (1 - s)\,Y(t)$? Explain why this may or may not be the case.*

(b) *Can the productive structure of this economy be decentralized to competitive firms?*

Exercise 44 *Consider an economy with a production function and a law of motion for capital given by*

$$Y(t) = L + L^{1-a}K(t)^a, \qquad \dot{K}(t) = Y(t) - C(t).$$

(a) *Let $0 \le a \le 1$. How are L and $K(t)$ compensated if markets are competitive?*

(b) *Determine the growth rate of aggregate consumption $C(t)$ if there is a fixed number of identical consumers that maximize the same objective function,*

$$U = \int_0^\infty \frac{c(t)^{1-\sigma} - 1}{1 - \sigma} e^{-\rho t} \, dt,$$

where $r(t)$ denotes the real interest rate on savings. Provide a brief discussion.

(c) *Given the above assumptions, characterize graphically the dynamics of the economy in the space (C, K) if $a < 1$, and calculate the steady state.*

(d) *How are the dynamics if $a = 1$? How do the income shares of the two factors evolve? Discuss the realism of this model with reference to the empirical plausibility of the balanced growth path.*

Exercise 45 *An economic system is endowed with a fixed amount of a production factor L. Of this, L_Y units are employed in the production of final goods destined for consumption and accumulation,*

$$Y(t) = A(t)K^a L_Y^{1-a}, \qquad \dot{K}(t) = Y(t) - C(t).$$

The remaining units of L are used to increase $A(t)$ according to the following technology:

$$\dot{A}(t) = (L - L_Y)A(t).$$

(a) *Consider the case in which the propensity to save is equal to s. Characterize the balanced growth path of this economy.*

(b) *What feature allows this economy to grow endogenously? What economic interpretation can we give for the difference between K and A?*

(c) *Discuss the possibility of decentralizing production with the above technology if A, K, and L are "rival" and "excludable" factors.*

Exercise 46 *Consider an economy in which output Y, capital K, and consumption C are related as follows:*

$$Y(t) = F(K(t), L) = (K(t)^\gamma + L^\gamma)^{1/\gamma}, \qquad \dot{K}(t) = Y(t) - C(t) - \delta K(t),$$

where $L > 0, \delta > 0$, and $\gamma \le 1$ are fixed parameters.

(a) *Show that the production function has constant returns to scale.*

(b) *Write the production function in the form* $y = f(k)$ *for* $y \equiv Y/L$ *and* $k \equiv K/L$.

(c) *Calculate the net rate of return on capital,* $r = f'(k) - \delta$, *and show that in the limit with* k *approaching infinity this rate tends to* $-\delta$ *if* $\gamma \leq 0$, *and to* $1 - \delta$ *if* $\gamma > 0$.

(d) *Denote the net production by* $\tilde{Y} \equiv Y - \delta K = F(K, L) - \delta K$, *and assume that* $C(t) = 0.5\tilde{Y}(t)$ *(aggregate consumption is equal to half the net income). What happens to consumption if the economy approaches a steady state?*

(e) *If on the contrary consumption is chosen to maximize*

$$U = \int_0^\infty \log(c(t)) e^{-\rho t}\, dt,$$

for which values of γ *and* ρ *will there be endogenous growth?*

Exercise 47 *Consider an economy in which*

$$Y(t) = K(t)^\alpha \bar{L}^\beta, \qquad \dot{K}(t) = P(t)s\, Y(t),$$

and in which the labor force is constant, and a fraction s *of* $P(t)Y(t)$ *is dedicated to the accumulation of capital.*

(a) *Consider* $P(t) = \bar{P}$ *(constant). For which values of* α *and* β *does there exist a steady state in levels or in growth rates? For which values can we decentralize the production decisions to competitive firms?*

(b) *Let* $P(t) = e^{ht}$, *where* $h > 0$ *is a constant. With* $\alpha < 1$, *at which rate can* $Y(t)$ *grow?*

(c) *How does the economy grow if on the contrary* $P(t) = K(t)^{1-\alpha}$?

(d) *What does* $P(t)$ *represent in this economy? How can we interpret the assumption made in (b) and (c)?*

Exercise 48 *Consider an economy in which all individuals maximize*

$$U = \int_0^\infty U(c(t)) e^{-\rho t}\, dt, \qquad \text{with } U(c) = 1 - \frac{1}{c} \text{ and } \rho = 1.$$

(a) *Let* r *denote the return in private savings and determine the rate of growth of consumption.*

(b) *Suppose that production utilizes private capital and labor according to*

$$Y(t) = F(K, L, t) = B(t)L + 3K.$$

Determine the per-unit income of L *and* K, *denoted by* $w(t)$ *and* $r(t)$ *respectively, if capital and labor are paid their marginal productivity.*

(c) *Suppose that* L *is constant, that* $\dot{K}(t) = Y(t) - C(t)$, *and that* $\dot{B}(t) = B(t)$. *Can capital and production grow for ever at the same rate as the* *optimal consumption? Determine the relation between $C(t)$, $K(t)$, and $B(t)$ along the balanced growth path.*

(d) *Suppose that at the aggregate level $B(t) = K(t)$, but that factors are compensated on the basis of their marginal productivity taking as given $B(t)$. Show that the resulting decentralized growth rate is below the socially efficient growth rate.*

☐ FURTHER READING

This chapter offers a concise introduction to key notions within a subject treated much more exhaustively by Grossman and Helpman (1991), Barro and Sala-i-Martin (1995), and Aghion and Howitt (1998). Models of endogenous growth were originally formulated in Romer (1986, 1990), Rebelo (1991), and other contributions that may be fruitfully read once familiar with the technical aspects discussed here. Blanchard and Fisher (1989, section 2.2) offers a concise discussion of how optimal growth paths may be decentralized in competitive markets. For a discussion of general equilibrium in more complex growth environments, readers are referred to Jones and Manuelli (1990) and Rebelo (1991). These papers consider production technologies that enable endogenous growth, and the optimal growth paths of these economies can be decentralized as in the models of Sections 4.2.3 and 4.5.4. The model of Rebelo allows for a distinction between investment goods and consumption goods. As a result, the optimal production decisions may be decentralized even in the presence of non-accumulated factors like L in this chapter. However, this requires that non-accumulated factors be employed in the production of consumption goods only, and not in the production of investment goods. An extensive recent literature lets non-accumulated factors be employed in a (labor-intensive) research and development sector, where endogenous growth is sustained by learning by doing or informational spillover mechanisms of the type discussed in Sections 4.2 and 4.3 above. McGrattan and Schmidtz (1999) offer a nice macro-oriented introduction to the relevant insights. Romer (1990) and Grossman and Helpman (1991) are key references in this literature. Grossman and Helpman (1991) offer fully dynamic versions of the model with monopolistic competition, introduced in the last section of this chapter. The role of research and development is also treated in Barro and Sala-i-Martin (1995), who discuss the role of government spending in the growth process, an issue that was originally dealt with in Barro (1990).

As to empirical aspects, there is an extensive literature on the measurement of the growth rate of the Solow residual; for a discussion of this issue see e.g. Maddison (1987) or Barro and Sala-i-Martin (1995), chapter 10. Barro and Sala-i-Martin (1995) and McGrattan and Schmidtz (1999) offer extensive reviews of recent empirical findings regarding long-run economic growth phenomena. Briefly, the treatment of human capital as an accumulated factor (as in Section 5.4 above) and careful measurement of government interference with market interactions (as in Section 5.5 above) have both proven crucial in interpreting cross-country income dynamics. More detailed and realistic theoretical models than those offered by this chapter's stylized treatment have of course proved empirically useful, especially as regards the government's role in protecting investors' legal rights to the fruits of their efforts, and open-economy aspects. Theoretical and empirical contributions have also paid well-deserved attention to politico-economic tensions regarding all relevant policies' implications for growth and distribution (see Bertola, 2000, and references therein), as well as to the role of finite lifetimes in determining aggregate saving rates (see Blanchard and Fischer, 1989, and Heijdra and van der Ploeg, 2002).

More generally, treatment of policy influences and market imperfections along the lines of this chapter's argument is becoming more prominent in macroeconomic equilibrium models. As noted by Solow (1999), much of the recent methodological progress on such aspects was prompted by the need to allow for increasing returns to scale in endogenous growth models, but the relevant insights have much wider applicability, and need not play a particularly crucial role in explaining long-run growth phenomena.

☐ REFERENCES

Aghion, P., and P. Howitt (1998) *Macroeconomic Growth Theory*, Cambridge, Mass.: MIT Press.

Barro, R. J. (1990) "Government Spending in a Simple Model of Endogenous Growth," *Journal of Political Economy*, 98, S103–S125.

—— and X. Sala-i-Martin (1995) *Economic Growth*, New York: McGraw-Hill.

Bertola, G. (2000) "Macroeconomics of Income Distribution and Growth," in A. B. Atkinson and F. Bourguignon (eds.), *Handbook of Income Distribution*, vol. 1, 477–540, Amsterdam: North-Holland.

Blanchard, O. J., and S. Fischer (1989) *Lectures on Macroeconomics*, Cambridge, Mass.: MIT Press.

Grossman, G. M., and E. Helpman (1991) *Innovation and Growth in the Global Economy*, Cambridge, Mass.: MIT Press.

Heijdra, B. J., and F. van der Ploeg (2002) *Foundations of Modern Macroeconomics*, Oxford: Oxford University Press.

Jones, L. E., and R. Manuelli (1990) "A Model of Optimal Equilibrium Growth," *Journal of Political Economy*, 98, 1008–1038.

Maddison, A. (1987) "Growth and Slowdown in Advanced Capitalist Economies," *Journal of Economic Literature*, 25, 649–698.

McGrattan, E. R., and J. A. Schmidtz, Jr (1999) "Explaining Cross-Country Income Differences," in J. B.Taylor and M. Woodford (eds.), *Handbook of Macroeconomics*, vol. 1A, 669–736, Amsterdam: North-Holland.

Rebelo, S. (1991) "Long-Run Policy Analysis and Long-Run Growth," *Journal of Political Economy*, 99, 500–521.

Romer, P. M. (1986) "Increasing Returns and Long-Run Growth," *Journal of Political Economy*, 94, 1002–1037.

—— (1990) "Endogenous Technological Change," *Journal of Political Economy*, 98, S71–S102.

—— (1987) "Growth Based on Increasing Returns Due to Specialization," *American Economic Review (Papers and Proceedings)*, 77, 56–72.

Solow, R. M. (1956) "A Contribution to the Theory of Economic Growth," *Quarterly Journal of Economics*, 70, 65–94.

—— (1999) "Neoclassical Growth Theory," in J. B. Taylor and M. Woodford (eds.), *Handbook of Macroeconomics*, vol. 1A, 637–667, Amsterdam: North-Holland.

5 Coordination and Externalities in Macroeconomics

As we saw in Chapter 4, externalities play an important role in endogenous growth theory. Many recent contributions have explored the relevance of similar phenomena in other macroeconomic contexts. In general, aggregate equilibria based on microeconomic interactions may differ from those mediated by the equilibrium of a perfectly competitive market in which agents take prices as given. If every agent correctly solves her own individual problem, taking into consideration the actions of all other agents rather than the equilibrium price, then nothing guarantees that the resulting equilibrium is efficient at the aggregate level. Uncoordinated "strategic" interactions may thus play a crucial role in many modern macroeconomic models with micro foundations.

In this chapter we begin by considering the relationship between the externalities that each agent imposes on other individuals in the same market and the potential multiplicity of equilibria, first in an abstract trade setting (Section 5.1) and then in a simple monetary economy (Section 5.2). (The appendix to this chapter describes a general framework for the analysis of the relationship between externalities, strategic interactions, and the properties of multiplicity and efficiency of the aggregate equilibria.) Then we study a labor market characterized by a (costly) process of search on the part of firms and workers. This setting extends the analysis of the dynamic aspects of labor markets of Chapter 3, focusing on the flows into and out of unemployment. Attention to labor market flows is motivated by their empirical relevance: even in the absence of changes in the unemployment rate, job creation and job destruction occur continuously, and the reallocation of workers often involves periods of frictional unemployment. The stylized "search and matching" modeling framework introduced below is realistic enough to offer empirically sensible insights, reviewed briefly in the "Further Readings" section at the end of the chapter. We formally analyze determination of the steady state equilibrium in Section 5.3 and the dynamic adjustment process in Section 5.4. Finally, Section 5.5 characterizes the efficiency implications of externalities in labor market search activity.

5.1. **Trading Externalities and Multiple Equilibria**

This section analyzes a basic model where the nature of interactions among individuals creates a potential for multiple equilibria. These equilibria are characterized by different levels of "activity" (employment, production) in the economy. The model presented here is based on Diamond (1982a) and features a particular type of *externality* among agents operating in a given market: the larger the number of potential trading partners, the higher the probability that an agent will make a profitable trade (*trading externality*). Markets with a high number of participants thus attract even more agents, which reinforces their characteristic as a "thick" market, while "thin" markets with a low number of participants remain locked in an inferior equilibrium.

5.1.1. STRUCTURE OF THE MODEL

The economy is populated by a high number of identical and infinitely lived individuals, who engage in *production, trade*, and *consumption* activities.

Production opportunities are created stochastically according to a Poisson distribution, whose parameter a defines the instantaneous probability of the creation of a production opportunity. At each date t_0, the probability that no production opportunity is created before date t is given by $e^{-a(t-t_0)}$ (and the probability that at least one production opportunity is created within this time interval is thus given by $1 - e^{-a(t-t_0)}$). This probability depends only on the length of the time interval $t - t_0$ and not on the specific date t_0 chosen. The probability that a given agent receives a production opportunity between t_0 and t is therefore independent of the distribution of production prior to t_0.[39]

All production opportunities yield the same quantity of output y, but they differ according to the associated cost of production. This cost is defined by a random variable c, with distribution function $G(c)$ defined on $c \geq \underline{c} > 0$, where $\underline{c}$ represents the minimum cost of production. *Trade* is essential in the model, because goods obtained from exploiting a production opportunity cannot be consumed directly by the producer. This assumption captures in a stylized way the high degree of specialization of actual production processes, and it implies that agents need to engage in trade before they can consume. At each moment in time, there are thus two types of agent in the market:

1. There are agents who have exploited a production opportunity and wish to exchange its output for a consumption good: the fraction of agents in this state is denoted by e, which can be interpreted as a "rate of

---

[39] The stochastic process therefore has the Markov property and is completely memoryless. In a more general model, a may be assumed to be variable. The function $a(t)$ is known as the *hazard function*.

employment," or equivalently as an index of the intensity of production effort.

2. There are agents who are still searching for a production opportunity: the corresponding fraction $1 - e$ can be interpreted as the "unemployment rate."

Like production opportunities, trade opportunities also occur stochastically, but their frequency depends on the share of "employed" agents: the probability intensity of arrivals per unit of time is not a constant, like the a parameter introduced above, but a function $b(e)$, with $b(0) = 0$ and $b'(e) > 0$. The presence of a larger number of employed agents in the market increases the probability that each individual agent will find a trading opportunity. This property of the *trading technology* is crucial for the results of the model and its role will be highlighted below.

Consumption takes place immediately after agents exchange their goods. The instantaneous utility of an agent is linear in consumption (y) and in the cost of production $(-c)$, and the objective of maximizing behavior is

$$V = E\left[\sum_{i=1}^{\infty}\left(-e^{-rt_i}c + e^{-r(t_i+\tau_i)}y\right)\right],$$

where r is the subjective discount rate of future consumption, the sequence of times $\{t_i\}$ denotes dates when production takes place, and $\{\tau_i\}$ denotes the interval between such dates and those when consumption and trade take place. Since production and trade opportunities are random, both $\{t_i\}$ and $\{\tau_i\}$ are uncertain, and the agent maximizes the expected value of discounted utility flows.

To maximize V, the agent needs to adopt an optimal rule to decide whether or not to exploit a production opportunity. This decision is based on the cost that is associated with each production opportunity or, equivalently, on the effort that a producer needs to exert to exploit the production opportunity. The agent chooses a critical level for the cost c^*, such that all opportunities with a cost level equal to $c \leq c^*$ are exploited, while those with a cost level $c > c^*$ are refused.

To solve the model, we need to determine this critical value c^* and the dynamic path of the level of activity or "employment" e.

5.1.2. SOLUTION AND CHARACTERIZATION

To study the behavior of the economy outlined above, we first derive the equations that describe the dynamics of the level of activity (employment) e and the critical value of the costs c^* (the only choice variable of the model).

The evolution of *employment* is determined by the difference between the flow into and out of employment. The first is equal to the fraction of the unemployed agents that receive and exploit a production opportunity: this fraction is equal to $(1 - e)aG(c^*)$. The flow out of employment is equal to the fraction of employed agents who find a trading opportunity and who thus, after consumption, return to the pool of unemployed. This fraction is equal to $eb(e)$. The assumption $b'(e) > 0$ that was introduced above now has a clear interpretation in terms of the increasing returns to scale in the process of trade. Calculating the elasticity of the flow out of employment $eb(e)$ with respect to the rate of employment e, we get

$$\varepsilon = 1 + \frac{eb'(e)}{b(e)},$$

which is larger than one if $b'(e) > 0$ (implying increasing returns in the trading technology). In other words, a higher rate of activity increases the probability that an employed agent will meet a potential trading partner.

Given the expressions for the flows into and out of employment, we can write the following law of motion for the employment rate:

$$\dot{e} = (1 - e)aG(c^*) - eb(e). \tag{5.1}$$

In a steady state of the system the two flows exactly compensate each other, leaving e constant. The following relation between the steady-state value of employment and the critical cost level c^* therefore holds:

$$(1 - e)aG(c^*) = eb(e)$$

$$\Rightarrow \left. \frac{de}{dc^*} \right|_{\dot{e}=0} = \frac{(1 - e)aG'(c^*)}{b(e) + eb'(e) + aG(c^*)} > 0. \tag{5.2}$$

A rise in c^* increases the flow into employment, since it raises the share of production opportunities that agents find attractive, and thus determines a higher steady-state value for e, as depicted in the left-hand panel of Figure 5.1. For points that are not located on the locus of stationarity, the dynamics of employment are determined by the effect of e on $\dot{e}$: according to (5.1), a higher value for e reduces $\dot{e}$, as is also indicated by the direction of the arrows in the figure.

In order to determine the production cost below which it is optimal to exploit the production opportunity, agents compare the expected discounted value of utility in the two states: employment (the agent has produced the good and is searching for a trading partner) and unemployment (the agent is looking for a production opportunity with sufficiently low cost). The value of the objective function in the two states is denoted by E and U, respectively. These values depend on the path of employment e and thus vary over time;

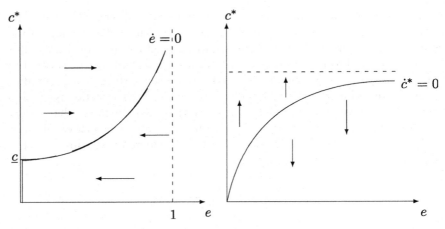

Figure 5.1. Stationarity loci for e and c^*

however, if we limit attention to steady states for a moment, then E and U are constant over time ($\dot{E} = 0$ and $\dot{U} = 0$). The relationships that tie the values of E and U can be derived by observing that the flow utility from employment ($r E$) needs to be equal to utility of consumption y, which occurs with probability $b(e)$, plus the expected value of the ensuing change from employment to unemployment:

$$r E = b(e)y + b(e)(U - E). \tag{5.3}$$

There is a clear analogy with the pricing of financial assets (which yield periodic dividends and whose value may change over time), if we interpret the left-hand side of (5.3) as the flow return (opportunity cost) that a risk-neutral investor demands if she invests an amount E in a risk-free asset with return r. The right-hand side of the equation contains the two components of the flow return on the alternative activity "employment": the expected dividend derived from consumption, and the expected change in the asset value resulting from the change from employment to unemployment. This interpretation justifies the term "asset equations" for expressions like (5.3) and (5.4).

Similarly, the flow utility from unemployment comprises the expected value from a change in the state (from unemployment to employment) which occurs with probability $a G(c^*)$ whenever the agent decides to produce; and the expected cost of production, equal to the rate of occurrence of a production opportunity a times the average cost (with a negative sign) of the production opportunities that have a cost below c^* and are thus realized.

The corresponding asset equation is therefore given by

$$rU = aG(c^*)(E - U) - a \int_{\underline{c}}^{c^*} c \, dG(c)$$

$$= a \int_{\underline{c}}^{c^*} (E - U - c) \, dG(c), \tag{5.4}$$

where $G(c^*) \equiv \int_{\underline{c}}^{c^*} dG(c)$.

Equations (5.3) and (5.4) can be derived more rigorously using the principle of dynamic programming which was introduced in Chapter 1. In the following we consider a discrete time interval Δt, from $t = 0$ to $t = t_1$, and we keep e constant. Moreover, we assume that an agent who finds a production opportunity and returns to the pool of unemployed does not find a new production opportunity in the remaining part of the interval Δt. Given these assumptions, we can express the value of employment at the start of the interval as follows:

$$E = \int_0^{t_1} be^{-bt} e^{-rt} y \, dt + e^{-r\Delta t}[e^{-b\Delta t} E + (1 - e^{-b\Delta t})U], \tag{5.5}$$

where the dependence of b on e is suppressed to simplify notation. The first term on the right-hand side of (5.5) is the expected utility from consumption during the interval, which is discounted to $t = 0$. (Remember that e^{-bt} defines the probability that no trading opportunity arrives before date t.) The second term defines the expected (discounted) utility that is obtained at the end of the interval at $t = t_1$. At this date, the agent may be either still "employed," having not had a chance to exchange the produced good (which occurs with probability $e^{-b\Delta t}$), or "unemployed," after having traded the good (which occurs with complementary probability $1 - e^{-b\Delta t}$).[40] Solving the integral in (5.5) yields

$$E = \frac{b}{b+r}(1 - e^{-(r+b)\Delta t})y + e^{-r\Delta t}[e^{-b\Delta t} E + (1 - e^{-b\Delta t})U]$$

$$= \frac{b}{r+b} y + \frac{e^{-r\Delta t}(1 - e^{-b\Delta t})}{1 - e^{-(r+b)\Delta t}} U. \tag{5.6}$$

Taking the limit of (5.6) for $\Delta t \to 0$ and applying l'Hôpital's rule to the second term, so that

$$\lim_{\Delta t \to 0} \frac{-re^{-r\Delta t}(1 - e^{-b\Delta t}) + be^{-r\Delta t}e^{-b\Delta t}}{(r+b)e^{-(r+b)\Delta t}} = \frac{b}{r+b},$$

[40] Since we limit attention to steady-state outcomes in which e is constant, E and U are also constant over time. As a result, there is no difference between the values at the beginning and at the end of the time interval.

we get the asset equation for E which was already formulated in (5.3):

$$E = \frac{b}{r+b}y + \frac{b}{r+b}U$$
$$\Rightarrow rE = by + b(U - E).$$

Similar arguments can be used to derive the second asset equation in (5.4). The critical value c^* is set in order to maximize E and U.

In the optimum, therefore, the following first-order conditions hold:

$$\frac{\partial E}{\partial c^*} = \frac{\partial U}{\partial c^*} = 0.$$

The derivative of the value of "unemployment" with respect to the threshold cost level c^* can be obtained from (5.4) using Leibnitz's rule,[41]

$$\frac{d}{db}\int_a^b f(z)dz = f(b).$$

In our case, $f(z) = (E - U - z)(dG/dz)$. Differentiating (5.4) with respect to c^* and equating the resulting expression to zero yields

$$r\frac{\partial U}{\partial c^*} = a(E - U - c^*)G'(c^*) = 0$$
$$\Rightarrow c^* = E - U. \tag{5.7}$$

In words, whoever is unemployed (searching for a production opportunity) is willing to bear a cost of production that is at most equal to the gain, in terms of expected utility, from exploiting a production opportunity to move from unemployment to "employment." Now, subtracting (5.4) from (5.3), we get

$$r(E - U) = b(e)y - b(e)(E - U) - aG(c^*)(E - U) + a\int_{\underline{c}}^{c^*} cdG(c). \tag{5.8}$$

Using (5.8) we can now derive the equation for the stationary value of c^*, which expresses c^* as a function of e. Writing

$$E - U = c^* = \frac{b(e)y + a\int_{\underline{c}}^{c^*} cdG(c)}{r + b(e) + aG(c^*)}, \tag{5.9}$$

---

[41] In general, the definition of an integral implies

$$\frac{d}{dx}\int_{a(x)}^{b(x)} f(z; x)dz = \int_{a(x)}^{b(x)} \frac{\partial f(z; x)}{\partial x}dz + b'(x)f(b(x)) - a'(x)f(a(x))$$

(*Leibnitz's rule*). Intuitively, the area below the curve of $f(\cdot)$ and between the points $a(\cdot)$ and $b(\cdot)$ is equal to the integral of the derivative of $f(\cdot)$ over the interval. Moreover, an increase in the upper limit increases this area in proportion to $f(b(x))$, while an increase in the lower limit decreases it in proportion to $f(a(x))$.

rearranging to

$$b(e)y + a \int_{\underline{c}}^{c^*} c\,dG(c) = (r + b(e) + aG(c^*))c^*,$$

and differentiating, we find that the slope of the locus of stationarity (5.9) is

$$\frac{dc^*}{de}\bigg|_{\dot{c}^*=0} = \frac{b'(e)(y - c^*)}{r + b(e) + aG(c^*)}. \tag{5.10}$$

The sign of this derivative is positive since $y > c^*$ (agents accept only those production possibilities with a cost below the value of output) and $b'(e) > 0$. Notice also that if $e = 0$ no trade ever takes place. (There are no agents with goods to offer.) In this case, agents are indifferent between employment and unemployment and there is no incentive to produce: $c^* = E - U = 0$. Finally, if we assume that $b''(e) < 0$, one can show that $d^2c^*/de^2 < 0$. Hence, the function that represents the locus of stationarity is strictly concave, and the locus of stationarity, which is drawn in the right-hand panel of Figure 5.1, starts in the origin and increases at a decreasing rate. The positive sign of $dc^*/de|_{\dot{c}^*=0}$ implies that there exists a strategic complementarity between the actions of individual agents. The concept of strategic complementarity is formally introduced in the appendix to this chapter. Intuitively, it implies that the actions of one agent increase the payoffs from action for all other agents; expressed in terms of the model studied here, the higher the fraction of employed agents, the more likely each individual agent will find a trading partner. This induces agents to increase the threshold for acceptance of production opportunities. At the aggregate level, therefore, the optimal individual response implies a more than proportional increase in the level of activity. To determine the dynamics of c^*, we need to remember that the equilibrium relations (5.3) and (5.4) are obtained on the basis of the assumption that E and U are constant over time. In general, however, these values will depend on the path of employment e. In that case, we need to add the terms $\dot{E} = \dot{e}\partial E(\cdot)/\partial e$ and $\dot{U} = \dot{e}\partial U(\cdot)/\partial e$ to the right-hand sides of (5.3) and (5.4), respectively, yielding:

$$rE(\cdot) = \frac{\partial E(\cdot)}{\partial e}\dot{e} + b(e)(y - E(\cdot) + U(\cdot)) \tag{5.11}$$

$$rU(\cdot) = \frac{\partial U(\cdot)}{\partial e}\dot{e} + a\int_{\underline{c}}^{c^*}(E(\cdot) - U(\cdot) - c)\,dG(c). \tag{5.12}$$

In terms of asset equations, $\dot{E}$ and $\dot{U}$ represent the "capital gains" that, together with the flow utility, give the "total returns" rE and rU.

Now, subtracting (5.12) from (5.11), and noting from (5.7) that

$$\dot{c}^* = \dot{E} - \dot{U} = \left(\frac{\partial E(\cdot)}{\partial e} - \frac{\partial U(\cdot)}{\partial e} \right) \dot{e},$$

we can derive the expression for the dynamics of c^*:

$$\dot{c}^* = rc^* - b(e)(y - c^*) + a \int_{\underline{c}}^{c^*} (c^* - c)dG(c). \qquad (5.13)$$

Moreover, if we assume that $\dot{c}^* = 0$, we obtain exactly (5.9). Since

$$\frac{\partial \dot{c}^*}{\partial c^*} = r + b(e) + aG(c^*) > 0,$$

the response of $\dot{c}^*$ to c^* is positive, as shown by the direction of the arrows in Figure 5.1. We are now in a position to analyze the possible equilibria of the economy, and we can make the interpretation of individual behavior in terms of the strategic complementarity more explicit.

First of all, given the shape of the two loci of stationarity, there may be *multiple equilibria*. The origin ($c^* = e = 0$) is always an equilibrium of the system. In this case the economy has zero activity (*shut-down equilibrium*). If there are more equilibria, then we may have the situation depicted in Figure 5.2. In this case there are two additional equilibria: E_1, in which the economy has a low level of activity, and E_2, with a high level of activity.

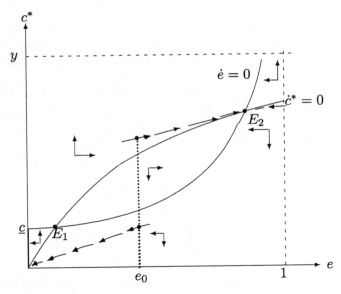

Figure 5.2. Equilibria of the economy

Graphically, the direction of the arrows in Figure 5.2 implies that the system can settle in the equilibrium with a high level of activity only if it starts from the regions to the north-east or the south-west of E_2. As in the continuous-time models analyzed in Chapters 2 and 4, the dynamics are therefore characterized by a saddlepath. Also drawn in the figure is a saddlepath that leads to equilibrium in the origin; finally, there is an equilibrium with low (but non-zero) activity. For a formal analysis of the dynamics we linearize the system of dynamic equations (5.1) and (5.13) around a generic equilibrium $(\bar{e}, \bar{c}^*)$.

In matrix notation, this linearized system can be expressed as follows:

$$\begin{pmatrix} \dot{e} \\ \dot{c}^* \end{pmatrix} = \begin{pmatrix} -(a\,G(\bar{c}^*) + b(\bar{e}) + \bar{e}b'(\bar{e})) & (1 - \bar{e})a\,G'(\bar{c}^*) \\ -b'(\bar{e})(y - \bar{c}^*) & r + b(\bar{e}) + a\,G(\bar{c}^*) \end{pmatrix} \begin{pmatrix} e - \bar{e} \\ c^* - \bar{c}^* \end{pmatrix}$$

$$\equiv \begin{pmatrix} \alpha & \beta \\ \gamma & \delta \end{pmatrix} \begin{pmatrix} e - \bar{e} \\ c^* - \bar{c}^* \end{pmatrix}, \qquad \text{where } \alpha, \gamma < 0; \ \beta, \delta > 0. \tag{5.14}$$

If in a given equilibrium the curve $\dot{e} = 0$ is steeper than $\dot{c}^* = 0$, then this equilibrium is a *saddlepoint*, as in the case of E_2. Formally, we need to verify the following condition:

$$\det \begin{pmatrix} \alpha & \beta \\ \gamma & \delta \end{pmatrix} = \alpha\delta - \beta\gamma < 0.$$

This can be rewritten as

$$-\frac{\alpha}{\beta} > -\frac{\gamma}{\delta},$$

where $-\alpha/\beta$ is the slope of the curve $\dot{e} = 0$ and $-\gamma/\delta$ is the slope of the curve $\dot{c}^* = 0$. In contrast, at E_1 the relationship between the steepness of the two curves is reversed and the determinant of the matrix is positive. Such an equilibrium is called a *node*. The trace of the matrix is $\alpha + \delta = r - \bar{e}b'(\bar{e})$: whether its node is negative or positive depends on its sign. This in turn depends on the specific values of r and $\bar{e}$ and on the properties of the function $b(\cdot)$. The existence of a strategic complementarity, arising from the trading externality implied by the assumption that $b'(e) > 0$, has thus resulted in multiple equilibria.

A low level of employment induces agents to accept only few production opportunities (c^* is low) and in equilibrium the economy is characterized by a low level of activity. If, on the contrary, employment is high, each agent will accept many production opportunities and this allows the economy to maintain an equilibrium with a high level of activity. Finally, it is important to note that agents' expectations play a crucial role in the selection of the equilibrium. Looking at point e_0 in Figure 5.2, it is clear that there exist values of e for which the economy can either jump to the saddlepath that leads to the "inferior" equilibrium (the origin), or to the one that leads to the equilibrium with a high level of activity. Which of these two possibilities is actually realized depends on the beliefs of agents. If agents are "optimistic" (i.e. if they expect a high level of activity and thus a convergence to the equilibrium at E_2), then they choose a value of c^* on the higher saddlepath, while if they are "pessimistic" (and anticipate convergence to the origin), they choose a point on the lower saddlepath.

5.2. A Search Model of Money

The stylized Diamond model of the previous section represents a situation where heterogeneous tastes and specialization in production force agents to trade in order to consume. Unlike Robinson Crusoe, the economic agents of the model cannot consume their own production: in the original article, Diamond (1982a) outlines how the economic decisions and interactions of his model could be applicable to a tropical island where a religious taboo prevents each of the natives from eating fruit he has picked. And, since trade occurs on a bilateral basis, rather than in a competitive auctioneered market, the economy's general equilibrium cannot be viewed as a representative-agent welfare maximization problem of the type that is sometimes discussed in terms of Robinson Crusoe's activities in undergraduate microeconomics textbooks.

The insights are qualitatively relevant in many realistic settings. In particular, whenever trade does not occur simultaneously in a frictionless centralized market, a potential role arises for a "medium of exchange"—an object that is accepted in a trade not to be directly consumed or used in production, but only to be exchanged in future trades. It would certainly be inconvenient for the authors of this book to carry copies of it into stores selling groceries they wish to consume, hoping that the owner might be interested in learning advanced macroeconomic techniques. In reality, of course, authors and publishers exchange books for money, and money for groceries. So, money's medium-of-exchange role facilitates exchanges of goods and, ultimately, consumption. The model presented in this section, a simplified version of that in Kiyotaki and Wright (1993), formalizes the use of money as a medium of exchange. As in the Diamond model of the previous section, strategic interaction among individuals is crucial in determining the equilibrium outcome. Moreover, different equilibria (characterized by different degrees of acceptability of money in the exchange process) may arise, depending on the particular traders' beliefs: again, agents' expectations are self-fulfilling.

5.2.1. THE STRUCTURE OF THE ECONOMY

Consider an economy populated by a large number of infinitely lived agents. There is also a large number of differentiated and costlessly storable consumption goods, called *commodities*, coming in indivisible units. Agents differ as to their preferences for commodities: each individual "likes" (and can consume) only a fraction $0 < x < 1$ of the available commodities. The same exogenous parameter x denotes the fraction of agents that like any given commodity. Production occurs only jointly with consumption: when an agent consumes one unit of a commodity in period t, he immediately produces one unit of a different good, which becomes his endowment for the next period $t + 1$. The utility obtained from consumption, net of any production cost, is $U > 0$. As in Diamond's model of Section 5.1, we assume that commodities cannot be consumed directly by the producer: this motivates the need for agents to engage in a trading activity before being able to consume.

In the economy, besides commodities, there is also a certain amount of costlessly storable *fiat money*, coming in indivisible units as well as the commodities. Fiat money has two distinguishing features: it has *no intrinsic value* (it does not yield any utility in consumption and cannot be used as a production input), and it is *inconvertible* into commodities having intrinsic worth. Initially, an exogenously given fraction $0 < M < 1$ of the agents are each endowed with one unit of money, whereas $1 - M$ are each endowed with one unit of a commodity.

We can now describe how agents in the economy behave during any given period t, in which a fraction M of them are money holders and a fraction $1 - M$ are commodity holders.

- A *money holder* will try to exchange money for a consumable commodity. For this to happen, two conditions must jointly be fulfilled: (i) she must meet an agent holding a commodity she "likes" (since only a fraction x of all commodities can be consumed by each agent), and (ii) the commodity holder must be willing to accept money in exchange for the consumption good. Only when these two conditions are met does trade take place: the money holder exchanges her unit of money for a commodity that she consumes enjoying utility U; she then immediately produces one unit of a different commodity (that she "dislikes"), and will start the next period as a commodity holder. If, on the contrary, trade does not occur, she will carry money over to the next period.

- A *commodity holder* will also try to exchange his endowment for a commodity he "likes." For this to happen, he must meet another commodity holder and both must be willing to trade (i.e. each agent must "like" the commodity he would receive in the exchange). Exchanges of commodities for commodities occur only if they are mutually agreeable, and therefore both goods are consumed after trade.[42] It is also possible that a commodity holder meets a money holder who "likes" his particular commodity; if trade takes place, then the agent starts the next period as a money holder.

---

[42] The introduction of an arbitrarily small transaction cost paid by the receiver can rule out the possibility that an agent agrees to receive in a trade a commodity he cannot consume.

The artificial economy here described highlights the different degree of *acceptability* of commodities and fiat money. Each consumption good will always be accepted in exchange by *some* agents, whereas money will be accepted only if agents expect to trade it in the future in exchange for consumable goods.

A final assumption concerns the meeting technology generating the agents' trading opportunities. Agents meet pairwise and at random; in each period an agent meets another with a constant probability $0 < \beta \leq 1$.

5.2.2. OPTIMAL STRATEGIES AND EQUILIBRIA

Each agent chooses a trading strategy in order to maximize the expected discounted utility from consumption. A *trading strategy* is a rule allowing the agent to decide whether to accept a commodity or money in exchange for what he is offering (either a commodity or money). The optimal trading strategy is obtained by solving the utility maximization problem, taking as given the strategies of other traders: this is the agent's *optimal response* to other traders' strategies. When all optimal strategies are mutually consistent, a *Nash equilibrium* configuration arises. We focus attention on symmetric and stationary equilibria, that is, on situations where all agents follow the same time-invariant strategies. In equilibrium, agents exchange commodities for other commodities only when both traders can consume the good they receive, whereas fiat money is used only if it has a "value." Such a value depends on its acceptability, which is not an intrinsic property of money but is determined endogenously in equilibrium.

The agent's strategy is defined by the following rule of behavior: when a meeting occurs, the agent accepts a commodity only if he or she "likes" it (then with probability x), and he or she accepts money in exchange with probability π when other agents accept money with probability Π. The agent must choose π as the best response to the common strategy of other agents, Π. To this end, at the beginning of period t he or she compares the payoffs (in terms of expected utility) from holding money and from holding a commodity, which we call $V_M(t)$ and $V_C(t)$ respectively.

For a *money* holder, the payoff is equal to

$$V_M(t) = \frac{1}{1+r} \{(1-\beta) V_M(t+1) + \beta[(1-M) x \Pi (U + V_C(t+1))$$

$$+ (1 - (1-M) x \Pi) V_M(t+1)]\}, \tag{5.15}$$

where r is the rate of time preference. If a meeting does not occur (with probability $1 - \beta$) the agent will end period t holding money with a value $V_M(t+1)$, whereas if a meeting does occur (with probability β) she will end the period with an expected payoff given by the term in square brackets on the right-hand side of (5.15). If the agent meets a commodity holder who is offering a good that she "likes" and is willing to accept money, the exchange can take place and the payoff is the sum of the utility from consumption U and the value of the newly produced commodity $V_C(t + 1)$. This event occurs with probability $(1 - M)x\Pi$. With the remaining probability, $1 - (1 - M)x\Pi$, trade does not take place and the agent's payoff is simply $V_M(t + 1)$.

For a *commodity* holder, the payoff is

$$V_C(t) = \frac{1}{1 + r} \{(1 - \beta) V_C(t + 1) + \beta [(1 - M) x^2 U + + M \pi x V_M(t + 1)$$
$$+ (1 - M\pi x) V_C(t + 1)]\}. \tag{5.16}$$

Again, the term in square brackets gives the expected payoff if a meeting occurs and is the sum of three terms. The first is utility from consumption U, which is enjoyed only if the agent meets a commodity holder and both like each other's commodity (a "double coincidence of wants" situation), so that a barter can take place; the probability of this event is $(1 - M)x^2$. The second term is the payoff from accepting money in exchange for the commodity, yielding a value $V_M(t + 1)$: this trade occurs only if the agent is willing to accept money (with probability π) and meets a money holder who is willing to receive the commodity he offers (with probability Mx). The third term is the payoff from ending the period with a commodity, which happens in all cases except for trade with a money holder, so occurs with probability $1 - M\pi x$.

To derive the agent's best response, we focus on equilibria in which all agents choose the same strategy, whereby $\pi = \Pi$, and payoffs are stationary, so that $V_M(t) = V_M(t + 1) \equiv V_M$ and $V_C(t) = V_C(t + 1) \equiv V_C$. Using these properties in (5.15) and (5.16), multiplying by $1/(1 + r)$, and rearranging terms we get

$$r V_M = \beta \{(1 - M) x \Pi U + (1 - M) x \Pi (V_C - V_M)\}, \tag{5.17}$$

$$r V_C = \beta \{(1 - M) x^2 U + M x \Pi (V_M - V_C)\}. \tag{5.18}$$

Expressed in this form, (5.17) and (5.18) are readily interpreted as asset valuation equations. The left-hand side represents the flow return from investing in a risk-free asset. The right-hand side is the flow return from holding either money or a commodity and includes the expected utility from consumption (the "dividend" component) as well as the expected change in the value of the asset held (the "capital gains" component). Finally, subtracting (5.17) from (5.18), we obtain

$$V_C - V_M = \beta \frac{(1 - M)xU}{r + \beta x \Pi} (x - \Pi). \tag{5.19}$$

The sign of $V_C - V_M$ depends on the sign of the difference between the degree of acceptability of commodities (parameterized by the fraction of agents that "like" any given commodity x) and that of money (Π). Consequently, the agents' optimal strategy in accepting money in a trade depends solely on Π.

- If $\Pi < x$, money is being accepted with lower probability than commodities. Then $V_C > V_M$, and the best response is never to accept money in exchange for a commodity: $\pi = 0$.

- If $\Pi > x$, money is being accepted with higher probability than commodities. In this case $V_C < V_M$, and the best response is to accept money whenever possible: $\pi = 1$.

- Finally, if $\Pi = x$, money and commodities have the same degree of acceptability. With $V_C = V_M$, agents are indifferent between holding money and commodities: the best response then is any value of π between 0 and 1.

The optimal strategy $\pi = \pi(\Pi)$ is shown in Figure 5.3. Three (stationary and symmetric) *Nash equilibria*, represented in the figure along the 45° line where $\pi = \Pi$, are associated with the three best responses illustrated above:

(i) A *non-monetary* equilibrium ($\Pi = 0$): agents expect that money will never be accepted in trade, so they never accept it. Money is valueless ($V_M = 0$) and barter is the only form of exchange (point A).

(ii) A *pure monetary* equilibrium ($\Pi = 1$): agents expect that money will be universally acceptable, so they always accept it in exchange for goods (point C).

(iii) A *mixed monetary* equilibrium ($\Pi = x$): agents are indifferent between accepting and rejecting money, as long as other agents are expected

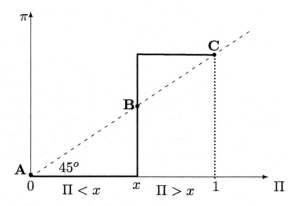

Figure 5.3. Optimal $\pi(\Pi)$ response function

to accept it with probability x. In this equilibrium money is only partially acceptable in exchanges (point B).

The main insight of the Kiyotaki–Wright search model of money is that *acceptability* is not an intrinsic property of money, which is indeed worthless. Rather, it can emerge endogenously as a property of the equilibrium. Moreover, as in Diamond's model, multiple equilibria can arise. Which of the possible equilibria is actually realized depends on the agents' beliefs: if they expect a certain degree of acceptability of money (zero, partial or universal) and choose their optimal trading strategy accordingly, money will display the expected acceptability in equilibrium. Again, as in Diamond's model, expectations are self-fulfilling.

5.2.3. IMPLICATIONS

The above search model can be used to derive some implications concerning the agents' *welfare* and the *optimal quantity of money*.

Welfare

We can now compare the values of expected utility for a commodity holder and a money holder in the three possible equilibria. Solving (5.17) and (5.18) with $\Pi = 0$, x, and 1 in turn, we find the values of V_C^i and V_M^i, where the superscript $i = n, m, p$ denotes the non-monetary, the mixed monetary, and the pure monetary equilibria associated with $\Pi = 0, x, 1$ respectively. The resulting expected utilities are reported in Table 5.1, where $K \equiv (\beta(1 - M)xU/r) > 0$.

Some welfare implications can be easily drawn from the table. First of all, the welfare of a money holder intuitively increases with the degree of acceptability of money. In fact, comparing the expected utilities in column (3), we find that $V_M^n < V_M^m < V_M^p$.

Further, in the pure monetary equilibrium (third row of the table) money holders are better off than commodity holders: $V_C^p < V_M^p$. Holding universally acceptable money guarantees consumption when the money holder meets a

Table 5.1.

Π (1)	V_C^i (2)	V_M^i (3)
0	Kx	0
x	Kx	Kx
1	$Kx\dfrac{r + \beta((1 - M)x + M)}{r+\beta x} > Kx$	$K\dfrac{r + \beta x((1 - M)x + M)}{r+\beta x} > Kx$

commodity holder with a good that she "likes": trade increases the welfare of both agents and occurs with certainty. On the contrary, a commodity holder can consume only if another commodity holder is met and both like each other's commodity: a "double coincidence of wants" is necessary, and this reduces the probability of consumption with respect to a money holder.

Exercise 49 *Check that, in a pure monetary equilibrium, when a money holder meets a commodity holder with a good she "likes" both agents are willing to trade.*

Finally, looking at column (2) of the table, we note that a commodity holder is indifferent between a non-monetary and a mixed monetary equilibrium, but is better off if money is universally acceptable, as in the pure monetary equilibrium:

$$V_C^n = V_C^m < V_C^p.$$

Summarizing, the existence of universally accepted fiat money makes all agents better off. Moreover, moving from a non-monetary to a mixed monetary equilibrium increases the welfare of money holders without harming commodity holders. Thus, in general, an increase in the acceptability of money (Π) makes at least some agents better off and none worse off (a Pareto improvement).

Optimal quantity of money

We now address the issue of the optimal quantity of money from the social welfare perspective. The amount of money in circulation is directly related to the fraction of agents endowed with money M; we therefore consider the possibility of choosing M so as to maximize some measure of social welfare. A reasonable such measure is an agent's *ex ante* expected utility, that is the expected utility of each agent before the initial endowment of money and commodities is randomly distributed among them. The social welfare criterion is then

$$W = (1 - M)V_C + MV_M. \tag{5.20}$$

The fraction of agents endowed with money can be optimally chosen in the three possible equilibria of the economy. First, we note that, in both the non-monetary and the mixed monetary equilibria, money does not facilitate the exchange process (thus making consumption more likely); it is then optimal to endow all agents with commodities, thereby setting $M = 0$. In the pure monetary equilibrium, social welfare W^p can be expressed as

$$W^p = (1 - M)V_C^p + MV_M^p$$
$$= K \cdot [M + x(1 - M)]$$
$$= \beta \frac{U}{r}(1 - M)[Mx + (1 - M)x^2], \qquad (5.21)$$

where we used the definition of K given above. Maximization of W^p with respect to M yields the optimal quantity of money M^*:

$$\frac{\partial W^p}{\partial M} = \beta \frac{U}{r}x[(1 - 2x) - 2M^*(1 - x)] = 0$$
$$\Rightarrow 1 - 2x = 2M^*(1 - x)$$
$$\Rightarrow M^* = \frac{1 - 2x}{2 - 2x}. \qquad (5.22)$$

Since $0 \le M^* \le 1$, for $x \ge \frac{1}{2}$ we get $M^* = 0$. When each agent is willing to consume at least half of the commodities, exchanges are not very difficult and money does not play a crucial role in facilitating trade: in this case it is optimal to endow all agents with consumable commodities. Instead, if $x < \frac{1}{2}$, fiat money plays a useful role in facilitating trade and consumption, and the introduction of some amount of money improves social welfare (even though fewer consumable commodities will be circulating in the economy). From (5.22) we see that, as $x \to 0$, $M^* \to \frac{1}{2}$, as shown in the left-hand panel of Figure 5.4.

To further develop the intuition for this result, we can rewrite the last expression in (5.21) as follows:

$$r W^p = U \cdot \beta(1 - M)[Mx + (1 - M)x^2], \qquad (5.23)$$

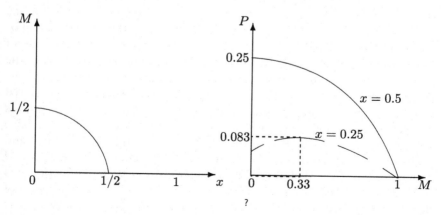

Figure 5.4. Optimal quantity of money M^* and *ex ante* probability of consumption P

where the left-hand side is the "flow" of social welfare per period and the right-hand side is the utility from consumption U multiplied by the agent's *ex ante* consumption probability. The latter is given by the probability of meeting an agent endowed with a commodity, $\beta(1 - M)$, times the probability that a trade will occur, given by the term in square brackets. Trade occurs in two cases: either the agent is a money holder and the potential counterpart in the trade offers a desirable commodity (which happens with probability Mx), or the agent is endowed with a commodity and a "double coincidence of wants" occurs (which happens with probability $(1 - M)x^2$). The sum of these two probabilities yields the probability that, after a meeting with a commodity holder, trade will take place. The optimal quantity of money is the value of M that maximizes the agent's *ex ante* consumption probability in (5.23). As M increases, there is a trade-off between a lower probability of encountering a commodity holder and a higher probability that, should a meeting occur, trade takes place. The amount of money M^* optimally weights these two opposite effects. The behavior of the consumption probability (P) as a function of M is shown in the right-hand panel of Figure 5.4 for two values of x (0.5 and 0.25) in the case where $\beta = 1$. The corresponding optimal quantities of money M^* are 0 and 0.33 respectively.

5.3. **Search Externalities in the Labor Market**

We now proceed to apply some of the insights discussed in this chapter to labor market phenomena. While introducing the models of Chapter 3, we already noted that the simultaneous processes of job creation and job destruction are typically very intense, even in the absence of marked changes in overall employment. In that chapter we assumed that workers' relocation was costly, but we did not analyze the level or the dynamics of the unemployment rate. Here, we review the modeling approach of an important strand of labor economics focused exactly on the determinants of the flows into and out of (frictional) unemployment. The agents of these models, unlike those of the models discussed in the previous sections, are not *ex ante* symmetric: workers do not trade with each other, but need to be employed by firms. Unemployed workers and firms willing to employ them are inputs in a "productive" process that generates employment, a process that is given a stylized and very tractable representation by the model we study below. Unlike the abstract trade and monetary exchange frameworks of the previous sections, the "search and matching" framework below is qualitatively realistic enough to offer practical implications for the dynamics of labor market flows, for the steady state of the economy, and for the dynamic adjustment process towards the steady state.

5.3.1. FRICTIONAL UNEMPLOYMENT

The importance of gross flows justifies the fundamental economic mechanism on which the model is based: the matching process between firms and workers. Firms create job openings (*vacancies*) and unemployed workers search for jobs, and the outcome of a match between a vacant job and an unemployed worker is a productive job. Moreover, the matching process does not take place in a coordinated manner, as in the traditional neoclassical model. In the neoclassical model the labor market is perfectly competitive and supply and demand of labor are balanced instantaneously through an adjustment of the wage. On the contrary, in the model considered here firms and workers operate in a decentralized and uncoordinated manner, dedicating time and resources to the search for a partner. The probability that a firm or a worker will meets a partner depends on the relative number of vacant jobs and unemployed workers: for example, a scarcity of unemployed workers relative to vacancies will make it difficult for a firm to fill its vacancy, while workers will find jobs easily. Hence there exists an externality between agents in the same market which is of the same "trading" type as the one encountered in the previous section. Since this externality is generated by the search activity of the agents on the market, it is normally referred to as a *search externality*. Formally, we define the labor force as the sum of the "employed" workers plus the "unemployed" workers which we assume to be constant and equal to L units. Similarly, the total demand for labor is equal to the number of filled jobs plus the number of vacancies. The total number of unemployed workers and vacancies can therefore be expressed as uL e vL, respectively, where u denotes the unemployment rate and v denotes the ratio between the number of vacancies and the total labor force. In each unit of time, the total number of matches between an unemployed worker and a vacant firm is equal to mL (where m denotes the ratio between the newly filled jobs and the total labor force). The process of matching is summarized by a *matching function*, which expresses the number of newly created jobs (mL) as a function of the number of unemployed workers (uL) and vacancies (vL):

$$mL = m(uL, vL). \tag{5.24}$$

The function $m(\cdot)$, supposed increasing in both arguments, is conceptually similar to the aggregate production function that we encountered, for example, in Chapter 4. The creation of employment is seen as the outcome of a "productive process" and the unemployed workers and vacant jobs are the "productive inputs." Obviously, both the number of unemployed workers and the number of vacancies have a positive effect on the number of matches within each time period ($m_u > 0$, $m_v > 0$). Moreover, the creation of employment requires the presence of agents on both sides of the labor market ($m(0, 0) = m(0, vL) = m(uL, 0) = 0$). Additional properties of the function

$m(\cdot)$ are needed to determine the character of the unemployment rate in a steady-state equilibrium. In particular, for the unemployment rate to be constant in a growing economy, $m(\cdot)$ needs to have *constant returns to scale*.[43] In that case, we can write

$$m = \frac{m(uL, vL)}{L} = m(u, v). \qquad (5.25)$$

The function $m(\cdot)$ determines the flow of workers who find a job and who exit the unemployment pool within each time interval. Consider the case of an unemployed worker: at each moment in time, the worker will find a job with probability $p = m(\cdot)/u$. With constant returns to scale for $m(\cdot)$, we may thus write

$$\frac{m(u, v)}{u} = m\left(1, \frac{v}{u}\right) \equiv p(\theta), \qquad \text{an increasing function of } \theta \equiv \frac{v}{u}. \quad (5.26)$$

The instantaneous probability p that a worker finds a job is thus positively related to the *tightness* of the labor market, which is measured by θ, the ratio of the number of vacancies to unemployed workers.[44] An increase in θ, reflecting a relative abundance of vacant jobs relative to unemployed workers, leads to an increase in p. (Moreover, given the properties of m, $p''(\theta) < 0$.) Finally, the average length of an unemployment spell is given by $1/p(\theta)$, and thus is inversely related to θ. Similarly, the rate at which a vacant job is matched to a worker may be expressed as

$$\frac{m(u, v)}{v} = m\left(1, \frac{v}{u}\right)\frac{u}{v} = \frac{p(\theta)}{\theta} \equiv q(\theta), \qquad (5.27)$$

a decreasing function of the vacancy/unemployment ratio. An increase in θ reduces the probability that a vacancy is filled, and $1/q(\theta)$ measures the average time that elapses before a vacancy is filled.[45] The dependence of p and q on θ captures the dual externality between agents in the labor market: an increase in the number of vacancies relative to unemployed workers increases the probability that a worker finds a job ($\partial p(\cdot)/\partial v > 0$), but at the same time it reduces the probability that a vacancy is filled ($\partial q(\cdot)/\partial v < 0$).

---

[43] Empirical studies of the *matching* technology confirm that the assumption of constant returns to scale is realistic (see Blanchard and Diamond, 1989, 1990, for estimates for the USA).

[44] As in the previous section, the matching process is modeled as a Poisson process. The probability that an unemployed worker does *not* find employment within a time interval dt is thus given by $e^{-p(\theta)\,dt}$. For a small time interval, this probability can be approximated by $1 - p(\theta)\,dt$. Similarly, the probability that the worker does find employment is $1 - e^{-p(\theta)\,dt}$, which can be approximated by $p(\theta)\,dt$.

[45] To complete the description of the functions p and q, we define the elasticity of p with respect to θ as $\eta(\theta)$. We thus have: $\eta(\theta) = p'(\theta)\theta/p(\theta)$. From the assumption of constant returns to scale, we know that $0 \leq \eta(\theta) \leq 1$. Moreover, the elasticity of q with respect to θ is equal to $\eta(\theta) - 1$.

5.3.2. THE DYNAMICS OF UNEMPLOYMENT

Changes in unemployment result from a difference between the flow of workers who lose their job and become unemployed, and the flow of workers who find a job. The inflow into unemployment is determined by the "separation rate" which we take as given for simplicity: at each moment in time a fraction s of jobs (corresponding to a fraction $1 - u$ of the labor force) is hit by a shock that reduces the productivity of the match to zero: in this case the worker loses her job and returns to the pool of unemployed, while the firm is free to open up a vacancy in order to bring employment back to its original level. Given the match destruction rate s, jobs therefore remain productive for an average period $1/s$. Given these assumptions, we can now describe the dynamics of the number of unemployed workers. Since L is constant, $d(uL)/dt = \dot{u}L$ and hence

$$\dot{u}L = s(1 - u)L - p(\theta)uL$$
$$\Rightarrow \dot{u} = s(1 - u) - p(\theta)u, \qquad (5.28)$$

which is similar to the difference equation for employment (5.1) derived in the previous section. The dynamics of the unemployment rate depend on the tightness of the labor market θ: at a high ratio of vacancies to unemployed workers, workers easily find jobs, leading to a large flow out of unemployment.[46] From equation (5.28) we can immediately derive the steady-state relationship between the unemployment rate and θ:

$$u = \frac{s}{s + p(\theta)}. \qquad (5.29)$$

Since $p'(\cdot) > 0$, the properties of the matching function determine a negative relation between θ and u: a higher value of θ corresponds to a larger flow of newly created jobs. In order to keep unemployment constant, the unemployment rate must therefore increase to generate an offsetting increase in the flow of destroyed jobs. The steady-state relationship (5.29) is illustrated graphically in the left-hand panel of Figure 5.5: to each value of θ corresponds a unique value for the unemployment rate. Moreover, the same properties of $m(\cdot)$ ensure that this curve is convex. For points above or below $\dot{u} = 0$, the unemployment rate tends to move towards the stationary relationship: keeping θ constant at θ_0, a value $u > u_0$ causes an increase in the flow out of unemployment and a decrease in the flow into unemployment, bringing u back to u_0. Moreover, given u and θ, the number of vacancies is uniquely determined by $v = \theta u$, where v denotes the number of vacancies as a proportion of the labor force. The picture on the right-hand side of the figure shows the curve

---

[46] To obtain job creation and destruction "rates," we may divide the flows into and out of employment by the total number of employed workers, $(1 - u)L$. The rate of destruction is simply equal to s, while the rate of job creation is given by $p(\theta)[u/(1 - u)]$.

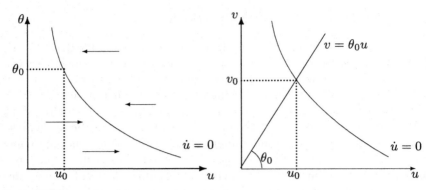

Figure 5.5. Dynamics of the unemployment rate

$\dot{u} = 0$ in (v, u)-space. This locus is known as the *Beveridge curve*, and identifies the level of vacancies v_0 that corresponds to the pair (θ_0, u_0) in the left-hand panel. In the sequel we will use both graphs to illustrate the dynamics and the comparative statics of the model. At this stage it is important to note that variations in the labor market tightness are associated with a movement along the curve $\dot{u} = 0$, while changes in the separation rate s or the efficiency of the matching process (captured by the properties of the matching function) correspond to movements of the curve $\dot{u} = 0$. For example, an increase in s or a decrease in the matching efficiency causes an upward shift of $\dot{u} = 0$. Equation (5.29) describes a first steady-state relationship between u and θ. To find the actual equilibrium values, we need to specify a second relationship between these variables. This second relationship can be derived from the behavior of firms and workers on the labor market.

5.3.3. JOB AVAILABILITY

The crucial decision of firms concerns the supply of jobs on the labor market. The decision of a firm about whether to create a vacancy depends on the expected future profits over the entire time horizon of the firm, which we assume is infinite. Formally, each individual firm solves an intertemporal optimization problem taking as given the aggregate labor market conditions which are summarized by θ, the labor market tightness. Individual firms therefore disregard the effect of their decisions on θ, and consequently on the matching rates $p(\theta)$ and $q(\theta)$ (the external effects referred to above). To simplify the analysis, we assume that each firm can offer at most one job. If the job is filled, the firm receives a constant flow of output equal to y. Moreover, it pays a wage w to the worker and it takes this wage as given. The determination of this wage is described below. On the other hand, if the job is not filled the firm incurs a flow cost c, which reflects the time and resources invested in the search for suitable workers. Firms therefore find it attractive to create a vacancy as long as its value, measured in terms of expected profits, is positive; if it is not, the firm will not find it attractive to offer a vacancy and will exit the labor market. The value that a firm attributes to a vacancy (denoted by V) and to a filled job (J) can be expressed using the asset equations encountered above. Given a constant real interest rate r, we can express these values as

$$r\,V(t) = -c + q(\theta(t))\,(J(t) - V(t)) + \dot{V}(t), \qquad (5.30)$$

$$r\,J(t) = (y - w(t)) + s\,(V(t) - J(t)) + \dot{J}(t), \qquad (5.31)$$

which are explicit functions of time. The flow return of a vacancy is equal to a negative cost component $(-c)$, plus the capital gain in case the job is filled with a worker ($J - V$), which occurs with probability $q(\theta)$, plus the change in the value of the vacancy itself ($\dot{V}$). Similarly, (5.31) defines the flow return of a filled job as the value of the flow output minus the wage ($y - w$), plus the capital loss ($V - J$) in case the job is destroyed, which occurs with probability s, plus the change in the value of the job ($\dot{J}$).

Exercise 50 *Derive equation (5.31) with dynamic programming arguments, supposing that $\dot{J} = 0$ and following the argument outlined in Section 5.1 to obtain equations (5.3) and (5.4).*

Subtracting (5.30) from (5.31) yields the following expression for the difference in value between a filled job and a vacancy:

$$r(J(t) - V(t)) = (y - w(t) + c)$$
$$- [s + q(\theta(t))](J(t) - V(t))$$
$$+ (\dot{J}(t) - \dot{V}(t)). \qquad (5.32)$$

Solving equation (5.32) at date t_0 for the entire infinite planning horizon of the firm, we get

$$J(t_0) - V(t_0) = \int_{t_0}^{\infty} (y - w(t) + c)\,e^{-\int_{t_0}^{t} [r+s+q(\theta(\tau))]\,d\tau}\,dt, \qquad (5.33)$$

where we need to impose the following transversality condition:

$$\lim_{T \to \infty} [J(T) - V(T)]\,e^{-\int_{t_0}^{T}(r+s+q(\theta(\tau)))d\tau} = 0.$$

Equation (5.33) expresses the difference between the value of a job and the value of a vacancy as the value of the difference between the flow return of a job ($y - w$) and that of a vacancy ($-c$) over the entire time horizon, which is discounted to t_0 using the appropriate "discount rate." Besides on the real interest rate, this discount rate also depends on the separation rate s and on the tightness of the labor market via $q(\theta)$. Intuitively, a higher number of vacancies relative to unemployed workers decreases the probability that a vacant firm will meet a worker. This reduces the effective discount rate and leads to an increase in the difference between the value of a filled job and a vacancy. Moreover, θ may also have an indirect effect on the flow return of a filled job via its impact on the wage w, as we will see in the next section.

Now, if we focus on steady-state equilibria, we can impose $\dot{V} = \dot{J} = 0$ in equations (5.30) and (5.31). Moreover, we assume free entry of firms and as a result $V = 0$: new firms continue to offer vacant jobs until the value of the marginal vacancy is reduced to zero. Substituting $V = 0$ in (5.30) and (5.31) and combining the resulting expressions for J, we get

$$\left.\begin{array}{l} J = c/q(\theta) \\ J = (y - w)/(r + s) \end{array}\right\} \Rightarrow y - w = (r + s)\frac{c}{q(\theta)}. \tag{5.34}$$

Equation (5.30) gives us the first expression for J. According to this condition, the equilibrium value of a filled job is equal to the expected costs of a vacancy, that is the flow cost of a vacancy c times the average duration of a vacancy $1/q(\theta)$. The second condition for J can be derived from (5.31): the value of a filled job is equal to the value of the constant profit flow $y - w$. These flow returns are discounted at rate $r + s$ to account for both impatience and the risk that the match breaks down. Equating these two expressions yields the final solution (5.34), which gives the marginal condition for employment in a steady-state equilibrium: the marginal productivity of the worker (y) needs to compensate the firm for the wage w paid to the worker and for the flow cost of opening a vacancy. The latter is equal to the product of the discount rate $r + s$ and the expected costs of a vacancy $c/q(\theta)$.

This last term is just like an adjustment cost for the firm's employment level. It introduces a wedge between the marginal productivity of labor and the wage rate, which is similar to the effect of the hiring costs studied in Chapter 3. However, in the model of this section the size of the adjustment cost is endogenous and depends on the aggregate conditions on the labor market. In equilibrium, the size of the adjustment costs depends on the unemployment rate and on the number of vacancies, which are summarized at the aggregate level by the value of θ. If, for example, the value of output minus wages ($y - w$) increases, then vacancy creation will become profitable ($V > 0$) and more firms will offer jobs. As a result, θ will increase, leading to a reduction in the matching rate for firms and an increase in the average cost of a vacancy, and both these effects tend to bring the value of a vacancy back to zero.

Finally, notice that equation (5.34) still contains the wage rate w. This is an endogenous variable. Hence the "*job creation condition*" (5.34) is not yet the steady-state condition which together with (5.29) would allow us to solve for the equilibrium values of u and θ. To complete the model, we need to analyze the process of wage determination.

5.3.4. WAGE DETERMINATION AND THE STEADY STATE

The process of wage determination that we adopt here is based on the fact that the successful creation of a match generates a surplus. That is, the value of a pair of agents that have agreed to match (the value of a filled job and an employed worker) is larger than the value of these agents before the match (the value of a vacancy and an unemployed worker). This surplus has the nature of a monopolistic rent and needs to be shared between the firm and the worker during the wage negotiations. Here we shall assume that wages are negotiated at a decentralized level between each individual worker and her employer. Since workers and firms are identical, all jobs will therefore pay the same wage.

Let E and U denote the value that a worker attributes to employment and unemployment, respectively. The joint value of a match (given by the value of a filled job for the firm and the value of employment for the worker) can then be expressed as $J + E$, while the joint value in case the match opportunity is not exploited (given by the value of a vacancy for a firm and the value of unemployment for a worker) is equal to $V + U$. The total surplus of the match is thus equal to the sum of the firm's surplus, $J - V$, and the worker's surplus, $E - U$:

$$(J + E) - (V + U) \equiv (J - V) + (E - U). \qquad (5.35)$$

The match surplus is divided between the firm and the worker through a wage bargaining process. We take their relative bargaining strength to be exogenously given. Formally, we adopt the assumption of *Nash bargaining*. This assumption is common in models of bilateral negotiations. It implies that the bargained wage maximizes a geometric average of the surplus of the firm and the worker, each weighted by a measure of their relative bargaining strength. In our case the assumption of Nash bargaining gives rise to the following optimization problem:

$$\max_{w} (J - V)^{1-\beta}(E - U)^{\beta}, \qquad (5.36)$$

where $0 \leq \beta \leq 1$ denotes the relative bargaining strength of the worker. Given that the objective function is a Cobb–Douglas one, we can immediately express the solution (the first-order conditions) of the problem as:

$$E - U = \frac{\beta}{1 - \beta}(J - V) \Rightarrow E - U = \beta[(J - V) + (E - U)]. \qquad (5.37)$$

The surplus that the worker appropriates in the wage negotiations ($E - U$) is thus equal to a fraction β of the total surplus of the job.

Similar to what is done for V and J in (5.30) and (5.31), we can express the values E and U using the relevant asset equations (reintroducing the dependence on time t):

$$r E(t) = w(t) + s(U(t) - E(t)) + \dot{E}(t) \tag{5.38}$$

$$r U(t) = z + p(\theta)(E(t) - U(t)) + \dot{U}(t). \tag{5.39}$$

For the worker, the flow return on employment is equal to the wage plus the loss in value if the worker and the firm separate, which occurs with probability s, plus any change in the value of E itself; while the return on unemployment is given by the imputed value of the time that a worker does not spend working, denoted by z, plus the gain if she finds a job plus the change in the value of U. Parameter z includes the value of leisure and/or the value of alternative sources of income including possible unemployment benefits. This parameter is assumed to be exogenous and fixed. Subtracting (5.39) from (5.38), and solving the resulting expression for the entire future time horizon, we can express the difference between the value of employment and unemployment at date t_0 as

$$E(t_0) - U(t_0) = \int_{t_0}^{\infty} (w(t) - z) e^{-\int_{t_0}^{t} [r+s+p(\theta(\tau))] d\tau} dt. \tag{5.40}$$

As in the case of firms, apart from the real interest rate r and the rate of separation s, the discount rate for the flow return of workers depends on the degree of labor market tightness via its effect on $p(\theta)$. A relative abundance of vacant jobs implies a high matching rate for workers, and this tends to reduce the difference between the value of employment and unemployment for a given wage value.

There are two ways to obtain the effect of variations θ on the wage. Restricting attention to steady-state equilibria, so that $\dot{E} = \dot{U} = 0$, we can either derive the surplus of the worker $E - U$ directly from (5.38) and (5.39), or we can solve equation (5.40) keeping w and θ constant over time:

$$E - U = \frac{w - z}{r + s + p(\theta)}. \tag{5.41}$$

According to (5.41), the surplus of a worker depends positively on the difference between the flow return during employment and unemployment $(w - z)$ and negatively on the separation rate s and on θ: an increase in the ratio of vacancies to unemployed workers increases the exit rate out of unemployment and reduces the average length of an unemployment spell. Using (5.41), and noting that in steady-state equilibrium

$$J - V = J = \frac{y - w}{r + s},$$

we can solve the expression for the outcome of the wage negotiations given by (5.37) as

$$\frac{w - z}{r + s + p(\theta)} = \frac{\beta}{1 - \beta} \frac{y - w}{r + s}.$$

Rearranging terms, and using (5.34), we obtain the following equivalent expressions for the wage:

$$w - z = \beta[(y + c\theta - w) + (w - z)] \tag{5.42}$$

$$\Rightarrow \quad w = z + \beta(y + c\theta - z). \tag{5.43}$$

Equation (5.42) is the version in terms of flows of equation (5.37): the flow value of the worker's surplus, i.e. the difference between the wage and alternative income z, is a fraction β of the total flow surplus. The term $y - w + c\theta$ represents the flow surplus of the firm, where $c\theta$ denotes the expected cost savings if the firm fills a job. Moreover, the wage is a pure redistribution from the firm to the worker. If we eliminate the wage payments in (5.42), we obtain the flow value of the total surplus of a filled job $y + c\theta - z$, which is equal to the sum of the value of output and the cost saving of the firm minus the alternative costs of the worker. Finally, equation (5.43) expresses the wage as the sum of the alternative income and the fraction of the surplus that accrues to the worker.

It can easily be verified that the only influence of aggregate labor market conditions on the wage occur via θ, the ratio of vacancies to unemployed workers. The unemployment rate u does not have any independent effect on wages. The explanation is that wages are negotiated after a firm and a worker meet. In this situation the match surplus depends on θ, as we saw above. This variable determines the average duration of a vacancy, and hence the expected costs for the firm if it continued to search.

The determination of the equilibrium wage completes the description of the steady-state equilibrium. The equilibrium can be summarized by equations (5.29), (5.34), and (5.43) which we shall refer to as BC (Beveridge curve), JC (job creation condition), and W (wage equation):

$$u = \frac{s}{s + p(\theta)} \qquad (BC) \tag{5.44}$$

$$y - w = (r + s)\frac{c}{q(\theta)} \qquad (JC) \tag{5.45}$$

$$w = (1 - \beta)z + \beta(y + c\theta) \quad (W) \tag{5.46}$$

For a given value of θ, the wage is independent of the unemployment rate. The system can therefore be solved recursively for the endogenous variables u, θ, and w. Using the definition for θ, we can then solve for v. The last two equations jointly determine the equilibrium wage w and the ratio of

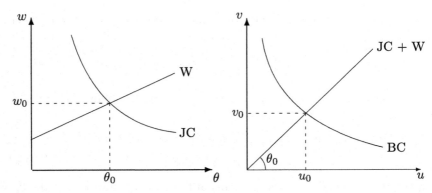

Figure 5.6. Equilibrium of the labor market with frictional unemployment

vacancies/unemployed θ, as is shown in the left-hand panel of Figure 5.6. Given θ, we can then determine the unemployment rate u, and consequently also v, which equates the flows into and out of unemployment (the right-hand panel of the figure).

This dual representation facilitates the comparative static analysis, which is intended to analyze the effect of changes in the parameters on the steady-state equilibrium. (Analysis of transitional dynamics is the subject of the next section.) In some cases, parameter changes have an unambiguous effect on all of the endogenous variables. This is true for instance in the case of an increase in unemployment benefits, a component of z, or an increase in the relative bargaining strength of workers β: the only effect of these changes is an upward shift of W which causes an increase in the wage and a reduction in θ. This reduction, along the curve BC, is accompanied by an increase in u and a reduction in v.

In other cases the effects are more complex and not always of unambiguous sign. Consider, for example, the effects of the following two types of shock which may be at the root of cyclical variations in overall unemployment. The first is an "aggregate" disturbance. This is represented by a variation in the productivity of labor y which affects all firms at the same time and with the same intensity. The second shock is a "reallocative" disturbance, represented by a change in the separation rate s. This shock hits individual firms independently of the aggregate state of the economy (captured by labor productivity y).

A reduction in y moves both JC and W downwards. This results in a reduction of the wage but has an ambiguous effect on θ. However, formal analysis (which is required in the exercise below) shows that in a stationary equilibrium θ also decreases; since the curve BC does not shift, the unemployment rate must increase while the number of vacancies v is reduced. In the case of a reallocative shock, we observe an inward shift of JC along W. This results in a joint decrease of the wage and the labor market tightness θ, as in the case of the aggregate shock. At the same time, however, the curve BC shifts to the right. Hence, while the unemployment rate increases unambiguously, it is in general not possible to determine the effect on the number of vacancies. In reality, however, v appears to be procyclical, and this suggests that aggregate shocks are a more important source of cyclical movements in the labor market than allocative shocks.

Exercise 51 *Derive formally, using the system of equations formed by (5.44), (5.45), and (5.46), the effects on the steady-state levels of w, θ, u, and v of a smaller labor productivity (Δy < 0) and of a higher separation rate (Δs > 0).*

5.4. **Dynamics**

Until now, all the relationships we derived referred to the steady-state equilibrium of the system. In this section we will analyze the evolution of unemployment, vacancies, and the wage rate along the adjustment path toward the steady-state equilibrium.

The discussion of the flows into and out of unemployment in the previous section has already delivered the law of motion for unemployment. This equation is repeated here (stressing the time dependence of the endogenous variables):

$$\dot{u}(t) = s\left(1 - u(t)\right) - p(\theta(t))\,u(t). \tag{5.47}$$

The dynamics of u are due to the flow of separations and the flow of newly created jobs resulting from the matches between firms and workers. The magnitude of the flow out of unemployment depends on aggregate labor market conditions, captured by θ, via its effect on $p(\cdot)$. Outside a steady-state equilibrium, the path of θ will influence unemployment dynamics in the economy. Moreover, given the definition of θ as the ratio of vacancies to unemployed workers, this will also affect the value of the labor market tightness. In order to give a complete description of the adjustment process toward a steady-state equilibrium, we therefore need to study the dynamics of θ. This requires an analysis of the job creation decisions of firms.

5.4.1. MARKET TIGHTNESS

At each moment in time firms exploit all opportunities for the profitable creation of jobs. Hence in a steady-state equilibrium, as well as along the adjustment path, $V(t) = 0 \forall t$, and outside a steady-state equilibrium $\dot{V}(t) = 0$,

∀t. The value of a filled job for the firm can be derived from (5.30) and (5.31). From the first equation, setting $V(t) = \dot{V}(t) = 0$, we get

$$J(t) = \frac{c}{q(\theta(t))}. \tag{5.48}$$

Equation (5.48) is identical to the steady-state expression derived before. Firms continue to create new vacancies, thereby influencing θ, until the value of a filled job equals the expected cost of a vacancy. Since entry into the labor market is costless for firms (the resources are used to maintain open vacancies), equation (5.48) will hold at each instant during the adjustment process. Outside the steady-state, the dynamics of J needs to satisfy difference equation (5.31), with $V(t) = 0$:

$$\dot{J}(t) = (r + s)J(t) - (y - w(t)). \tag{5.49}$$

The solution of (5.49) shows that the value $J(t)$ depends on the future path of (expected) wages. Besides that, $J(t)$ also depends on labor productivity, the real interest rate, and the rate of separation, but all these variables are assumed to be constant:

$$J(t) = \int_{t}^{\infty} (y - w(t)) e^{-(r+s)\tau} d\tau. \tag{5.50}$$

Wages are continuously renegotiated. Outside steady-state equilibrium the surplus sharing rule (5.37) with $V(t) = 0$ therefore remains valid:

$$E(t) - U(t) = \frac{\beta}{1 - \beta} J(t). \tag{5.51}$$

Outside the steady-state E, U, and J may vary over time, but these variations need to ensure that (5.51) is satisfied. Hence, we have

$$\dot{E}(t) - \dot{U}(t) = \frac{\beta}{1 - \beta} \dot{J}(t). \tag{5.52}$$

The dynamics of J are given by (5.49), while the dynamics of E and U can be derived by subtracting (5.39) from (5.38):

$$\dot{E}(t) - \dot{U}(t) = [r + s + p(\theta(t))](E(t) - U(t)) - (w(t) - z). \tag{5.53}$$

Equating (5.52) to (5.53), and using (5.49) and (5.48) to replace $\dot{J}$ and J, we can solve for the level of wages outside steady-state equilibrium as:

$$w(t) = z + \beta(y + c\theta(t) - z). \tag{5.54}$$

The wage is thus determined in the same way both in a steady-state equilibrium and during the adjustment process. Moreover, given the values for the exogenous variables, the wage dynamics depends exclusively on changes in the degree of labor market tightness, which affects the joint value of a productive match.

We are now in possession of all the elements that are needed to determine the dynamics of θ. Differentiating (5.48) with respect to time, where by definition $q(\theta) \equiv p(\theta)/\theta$, we have

$$\dot{J}(t) = \frac{cp(\theta(t)) - c\theta(t)p'(\theta(t))}{p(\theta(t))^2} \; \dot{\theta}(t) = \frac{c}{p(\theta(t))}[1 - \eta(\theta(t))] \, \dot{\theta}(t), \quad (5.55)$$

where $0 < \eta(\theta) < 1$ (defined above) denotes the elasticity of $p(\theta)$ with respect to θ. To simplify the derivations, we henceforth assume that $\eta(\theta) = \eta$ is constant (which is true if the matching function $m(\cdot)$ is of the Cobb–Douglas type). Substituting (5.49) for $\dot{J}$ and using the expression $J = c(\theta/p(\theta))$, we can rewrite equation (5.55) as

$$\dot{\theta}(t) \, \frac{c}{p(\theta(t))} \, (1 - \eta) = (r + s) \frac{c \, \theta(t)}{p(\theta(t))} - (y - w(t)). \quad (5.56)$$

Finally, substituting the expression for the wage as a function of θ from (5.54), the above law of motion for θ can be written as

$$\dot{\theta}(t) = \frac{r + s}{1 - \eta} \theta(t) - \frac{p(\theta(t))}{c \, (1 - \eta)} \, [(1 - \beta) \, (y - z) - \beta c \, \theta(t)]. \quad (5.57)$$

Changes in θ depend on (in addition to all the parameters of the model) only the value of θ itself. The labor market tightness does not in any independent way depend on the unemployment rate u. In (θ, u)-space the curve $\dot{\theta} = 0$ can thus be represented by a horizontal line at $\bar{\theta}$, which defines the unique steady-state equilibrium value for the ratio between vacancies and unemployed. This is illustrated in the left-hand panel of Figure 5.7. Once we have determined $\bar{\theta}$, we can determine, for each value of the unemployment rate, the level of v that is compatible with a stationary equilibrium. For instance, in the case of u_0 this is equal to v_0.

Besides that, equation (5.57) also indicates that, for points above or below the curve $\dot{\theta} = 0$, θ tends to move away from its equilibrium value. Formally,

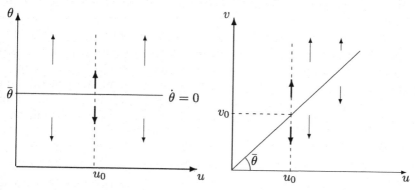

Figure 5.7. Dynamics of the supply of jobs

one can show this by calculating[47]

$$\frac{\partial \dot{\theta}}{\partial \theta}\bigg|_{\dot{\theta}=0} = (r+s) + \frac{p(\theta)}{1-\eta}\beta > 0$$

from (5.57). The apparently "unstable" behavior of θ is due to the nature of the job creation decision of firms. Looking at the future, firms' decisions on whether to open a vacancy today are based on expected future values of θ. For example, if firms expect a future increase in θ resulting from an increase in the number of vacant jobs, they will anticipate an increase in future costs to fill a vacancy. As a result, firms have an incentive to open vacancies immediately in anticipation of this increase in cost. At the aggregate level, this induces an immediate increase in v (and in θ) in anticipation of further increases in the future. Hence, there is an obvious analogy between the variations of v and the movement of asset prices which we already alluded to when we interpreted (5.30) and (5.31) as asset equations: expectations of a future increase in price cause an increase in current prices.

As a result of forward-looking behavior on the part of firms, both v and θ are "jump" variables. Their value is not predetermined: in response to changes in the exogenous parameters (even if these changes are expected in the future and have not yet materialized), v and θ may exhibit discrete changes. The unemployment rate, on the other hand, is a "predetermined" or state variable. The dynamics of the unemployment rate are governed by (5.47), and u adjusts gradually to changes in θ, even in case of a discrete change in the labor market tightness. An unanticipated increase in v and θ leads to an increase in the flow out of unemployment, resulting in a reduction of u. However, the positive effect of the number of vacancies on unemployment is mediated via the stochastic matching process on the labor market. The immediate effect of an increase in θ is an increase in the matching rate for workers $p(\theta)$, and this translates only gradually in an increase in the number of filled jobs. The unemployment rate therefore will start to decrease only after some time.

The aggregate effect of the decentralized decisions of firms (each of which disregards the externalities of its own decision on aggregate variables) consists of changes in the degree of labor market tightness θ and, as a result, in changes in the speed of adjustment of the unemployment rate. The dynamics of u are therefore intimately linked to the presence of the externalities that characterize the functioning of the labor market in the search and matching literature.

---

[47] Note that this derivative is computed at a steady-state equilibrium point (on the $\dot{\theta}=0$ locus). Hence, we may use (5.34), and replace $y-w$ with $(r+s)(c\theta/p(\theta))$ to obtain the expression in the text.

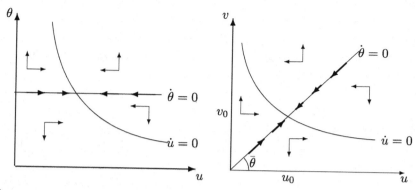

Figure 5.8. Dynamics of unemployment and vacancies

5.4.2. THE STEADY STATE AND DYNAMICS

We are now in a position to characterize the system graphically, using the differential equations (5.47) and (5.57) for u and θ. In both panels of Figure 5.8 we have drawn the curves for $\dot{\theta} = 0$ and $\dot{u} = 0$. Moreover, for each point outside the unique steady-state equilibrium we have indicated the movement of θ and u.

As we have seen in the analysis of dynamic models of investment and growth theory, the combination of a single-state variable (u) and a single jump variable (θ) implies that there is only one *saddlepath* that converges to the steady-state equilibrium (*saddlepoint*).[48] Since the expression for $\dot{\theta} = 0$ does not depend on u, the saddlepath coincides with the curve for $\dot{\theta} = 0$: all the other points are located on paths that diverge from the curve $\dot{\theta} = 0$ and never reach the steady-state, violating the transversality conditions. Hence, as a result of the forward-looking nature of the vacancy creation decisions of firms, the labor market tightness θ will jump immediately to its long-run value and remain there during the entire adjustment process.

Let us now analyze the adjustment process in response first to a reduction in labor productivity y (an aggregate shock) and then to an increase in the rate of separation s (a reallocative shock). Figure 5.9 illustrates the dynamics following an unanticipated *permanent reduction* in productivity ($\Delta y < 0$) at date

---

[48] Formally, we can determine the saddlepoint nature of the equilibrium by evaluating the linearized system (5.47) and (5.57) around the steady-state equilibrium point ($\bar{u}, \bar{\theta}$), yielding

$$\begin{pmatrix} \dot{u} \\ \dot{\theta} \end{pmatrix} = \begin{pmatrix} -(s + p(\bar{\theta})) & -\bar{u}p'(\bar{\theta}) \\ 0 & (r + s) + \frac{p(\bar{\theta})}{1-\eta}\beta \end{pmatrix} \begin{pmatrix} u - \bar{u} \\ \theta - \bar{\theta} \end{pmatrix}.$$

The pattern of signs in the matrix is $\begin{bmatrix} - & - \\ 0 & + \end{bmatrix}$. Thus, the determinant is negative, confirming that the equilibrium is a *saddlepoint*.

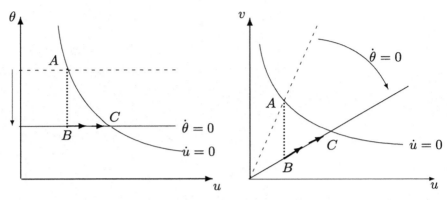

Figure 5.9. Permanent reduction in productivity

t_0. In the left-hand graph, the curve $\dot\theta = 0$ shifts downward while $\dot u = 0$ does not change. In the new steady-state equilibrium (point C) the unemployment rate is higher and labor market tightness is lower. Moreover, from the right-hand graph, it follows that the number of vacancies has also decreased. The figure also illustrates the dynamics of the variables: at date t_0 the economy jumps to the new saddlepath which coincides with the new curve $\dot\theta = 0$. Given the predetermined nature of the unemployment rate, the whole adjustment is performed by v and θ, which make a discrete jump downwards as shown by B in the two graphs. From t_0 onwards both unemployment and the number of vacancies increase gradually, keeping θ fixed until the new steady-state equilibrium is reached.

The permanent reduction in labor productivity reduces the expected profits of a filled job. Hence, from t_0 onwards firms have an incentive to create fewer vacancies. Moreover, initially the number of vacancies v falls below its new equilibrium level because firms anticipate that the unemployment rate will rise. In future it will therefore be easier to fill a vacancy. As a result, firms prefer to reduce the number of vacancies at the beginning of the adjustment process, increasing their number gradually as the unemployment rate starts to rise.

Finally, the reduction in labor productivity also reduces wages, but this reduction is smaller than the decrease in y. Since the labor market immediately jumps to a saddlepath along which $\theta(t)$ is constant, equation (5.54) implies that the wage $w(t)$ is constant along the whole adjustment process. The short-run response of the wage is thus equal to the long-run response, which is governed by (5.34). According to this equation, the difference $y - w$ is proportional to the expected cost of a vacancy for the firm. This cost depends on the average time that is needed to fill a vacancy, which diminishes when v and θ fall in response to a productivity shock. Hence, in this version of the model

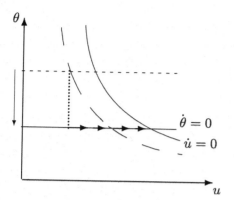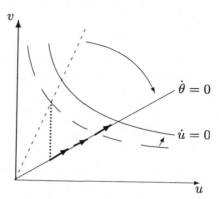

Figure 5.10. Increase in the separation rate

productivity changes do not imply proportional wage changes. (On this point see exercise 51 at the end of the chapter.)

A similar adjustment process takes place in the case of a (unanticipated and permanent) *reallocative shock* $\Delta s > 0$, as shown in Figure 5.10. However, in this case $\dot{u} = 0$ is also affected. This curve shifts to the right, which reinforces the increase in the unemployment rate, but has an ambiguous effect on the number of vacancies. (The figure illustrates the case of a reduction in v.) Finally, let us consider the case of a *temporary* reduction of productivity: agents now anticipate at t_0 that productivity will return to its higher initial value at some future date t_1. Given the temporary nature of the shock, the new steady-state equilibrium coincides with the initial equilibrium (point A in the graphs of Figure 5.11). At the time of the change in productivity, t_0, the immediate effect is a reduction in the number of vacancies which causes a discrete fall in θ. However, this reduction is smaller than the one that resulted from a permanent change, and it moves the equilibrium from the previous equilibrium A to a new point B'. From t_0 onwards, the unemployment rate and the number of vacancies increase gradually but not at the same rate: as a result, their ratio θ increases, following the diverging dynamics that leads towards the new and lower stationary curve $\dot{\theta} = 0$. To obtain convergence of the steady-state equilibrium at A, the dynamics of the adjustment need to bring θ to its equilibrium level at t_1 when the shock ceases and productivity returns to its previous level (point B''). In fact, convergence to the final equilibrium can occur only if the system is located on the saddlepath, which coincides with the stationary curve for θ, at date t_1. After t_1 the dynamics concerns only the unemployment rate u and the number of vacancies v, which decrease in the same proportion until the system reaches its initial starting point A.

The graph on the right-hand side of Figure 5.11 also illustrates that cyclical variations in productivity give rise to a counter-clockwise movement of

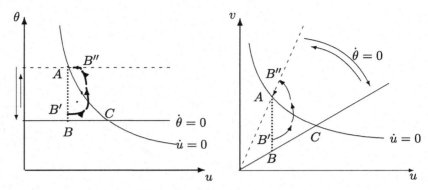

Figure 5.11. A temporary reduction in productivity

employment and vacancies around the Beveridge curve. This is consistent with empirical data for changes in unemployment and vacancies during recessions, which are approximated here by a temporary reduction in productivity.

5.5. **Externalities and efficiency**

The presence of externalities immediately poses the question of whether the decentralized equilibrium allocation is efficient. In particular, in the previous sections it was shown that firms disregard the effect of their private decisions on the aggregate labor market conditions when they are deciding whether or not to create a vacancy. In this section we analyze the implications of these external effects for the efficiency of the market equilibrium and compare the decentralized equilibrium allocation with the socially efficient allocation.

To simplify the comparison between individual and socially optimal choices, we reformulate the problem of the firm so far identified with a single job, allowing firms to open many vacancies and employ many workers. Moreover, we also modify the production technology and replace the previous linear production technology with a standard production function with decreasing marginal returns of labor. Let N_i denote the number of workers of firm i. The production function is then given by $F(N_i)$, with $F'(\cdot) > 0$ and $F''(\cdot) < 0$. The case $F''(\cdot) = 0$ corresponds to the analysis in the previous sections, while the case of decreasing marginal returns to labor corresponds to our analysis in Chapter 3.

The employment level of a firm varies over time as a result of vacancies that are filled and because of shocks that hit the firm and destroy jobs at rate s. The evolution of N_i is described by the following equation, where we have suppressed the time dependence of the variables to simplify the notation:

$$\dot{N_i} = q(\theta) X_i - s N_i, \tag{5.58}$$

where X_i represents the number of vacancies of a firm and is the control variable of the firm. Each vacancy is transformed into a filled job with instantaneous probability $q(\theta)$, which is a function of the aggregate tightness of the labor market. In deciding X_i firms take θ as given, disregarding the effect of their decisions on the aggregate ratio of vacancies to unemployed. More specifically, we assume that the number of firms is sufficiently high to justify the assumption that a single firm takes the level of θ as an exogenous variable.

The problem of the representative firm is therefore

$$\max_{X_i} \int_0^\infty [F(N_i) - w N_i - c X_i] e^{-rt} dt, \tag{5.59}$$

subject to the law of motion for employment given by (5.58). Moreover, we assume that the firm takes the wage w as given and independent of the number of workers that it employs.

The solution can be found by writing the associated Hamiltonian,

$$H(t) = [F(N_i) - w N_i - c X_i + \lambda(q(\theta) X_i - s N_i)] e^{-rt} \tag{5.60}$$

(where λ is the Lagrange multiplier associated with the law of motion for N), and by deriving the first-order conditions:

$$\frac{\partial H}{\partial X_i} = 0 \Rightarrow \lambda = \frac{c}{q(\theta)}, \tag{5.61}$$

$$-\frac{\partial H}{\partial N_i} = \frac{d(\lambda(t)e^{-rt})}{dt} \Rightarrow F'(N_i) - w = (r + s)\lambda - \dot{\lambda}, \tag{5.62}$$

$$\lim_{t\to\infty} e^{-rt} \lambda N_i = 0. \tag{5.63}$$

Equation (5.61) implies that firms continue to create vacancies until the marginal profits of a job equal the marginal cost of a vacancy $(c/q(\theta))$. This condition holds at any moment in time and is similar to the condition for job creation (5.48) derived in Section **??**. The Lagrange multiplier λ can therefore be interpreted as the marginal value of a filled job for the firm, which we denoted by J in the previous sections. The dynamics of λ are given by (5.62), which in turn corresponds to equation (5.49) for $\dot{J}$. Finally, equation (5.63) defines the appropriate transversality condition for the firm's problem.

In what follows we consider only steady-state equilibria. Combining (5.61) and (5.62) and imposing $\dot{\lambda} = 0$, we get

$$F'(N_i^*) - w = (r + s) \frac{c}{q(\theta)} \tag{5.64}$$

where N_i^* denotes the steady-state equilibrium employment level of the firm. The optimal number of vacancies, X_i^*, can be derived from constraint (5.58), with $\dot{N} = 0$:

$$q(\theta)X_i^* = s N_i^* \Rightarrow X_i^* = \frac{s}{q(\theta)} N_i^*. \tag{5.65}$$

Hence, if all firms have the same production function and start from the same initial conditions, then each firm will choose the same optimal solution and the ratio of filled jobs to vacancies for each firm will be equal to the aggregate ratio:

$$\frac{X_i^*}{N_i^*} = \frac{v}{1 - u}. \tag{5.66}$$

This completes the characterization of the decentralized equilibrium.

We now proceed with a characterization of the *socially efficient solution*. For simplicity we normalize the mass of firms to one. X and N therefore denote the stock of vacancies and of filled jobs, at both the aggregate level and the level of an individual firm. Since the relations

$$\theta \equiv \frac{v}{u} = \frac{vL}{L - N} = \frac{X}{L - N}$$

hold true, aggregate labor market conditions as captured by θ are *endogenous* in the determination of the socially efficient allocation. The efficient allocation can be found by solving the following maximization problem:

$$\max_X \int_0^\infty [F(N) - zN - cX] e^{-rt} dt, \tag{5.67}$$

subject to the condition

$$\dot{N} = q\left(\frac{X}{L - N}\right) X - s N. \tag{5.68}$$

The bracketed expression in (5.67) denotes aggregate *net output*. The first term ($F(N)$) is equal to the output of employed workers. From this we have to subtract the flow utility of employed workers (zN), and the costs of maintaining the vacancies (cX). The wage rate does not appear in this expression because it is a pure redistribution from firms to workers: in the model considered here, distributional issues are irrelevant for social efficiency. The important point to note is that the effect of the choice of X on the aggregate conditions on the labor market is explicitly taken into account: the ratio θ is expressed as $X/(L - N)$ and is *not* taken as given in the maximization of social welfare.

The problem is solved using similar methods as for the case of the problem of individual firms. Constructing the associated Hamiltonian and deriving the first-order conditions for X and N (with μ as the Lagrange multiplier for the dynamic constraint) yields

$$\frac{\partial H}{\partial X} = 0 \Rightarrow \mu = \frac{c}{q'(\theta)\theta + q(\theta)}, \tag{5.69}$$

$$-\frac{\partial H}{\partial N} = \frac{d(\mu(t)e^{-rt})}{dt} \Rightarrow F'(N) - z = \left(r + s - q'(\theta)\theta^2\right)\mu - \dot{\mu}. \tag{5.70}$$

Explicit consideration of the effects on θ introduces various differences between the above optimality conditions and the first-order conditions of the individual firm, (5.61) and (5.62). First of all, comparing (5.69) with the corresponding condition (5.61) shows that individual firms tend to offer an *excessive* number of vacant jobs compared with what is socially efficient (recall that $q' < 0$). The reason for this discrepancy is that firms disregard the effect of their decisions on the aggregate labor market conditions.

Moreover, from the marginal condition for N (5.70), it follows that the "social" discount rate associated with the marginal value of a filled job μ contains an additional term, $-q'(\theta)\theta^2 > 0$, which does not appear in the analogous condition for the individual firm (5.62). That is, an increase in the number of employed workers diminishes the probability that the firm will hire additional workers in the future. Equation (5.70) correctly reflects this dynamic aspect of labor demand, which tends to reduce the marginal value of a filled job in a steady-state equilibrium (in which $\dot{\mu} = 0$). Hence, also from this perspective the decentralized decisions of firms result in an *excessive* number of vacancies compared with the social optimum. Finally, comparing the left-hand side of equations (5.62) and (5.70) reveals that the individual conditions contain the value of productivity net of the wage w, while in the condition for social efficiency the value of productivity is net of the opportunity cost z. Hence, for the same value of θ, individual firms attribute a lower "dividend" to filled jobs since $w \geq z$, and firms thus tend to generate an *insufficient* number of vacancies. This last effect runs in the opposite direction to the two effects discussed above, and this makes a comparison between the two solutions—the individual and the social—interesting. The socially optimal solution may coincide with the corresponding decentralized equilibrium if the wage determination mechanism "internalizes" the externalities that private agents ignore. However, in the model that we have constructed, wages are determined *after* a firm and a worker meet. Hence, although the wage is perfectly flexible, it cannot perform any allocative function.

Nonetheless, we can determine the conditions that the wage determination mechanism needs to satisfy for the decentralized equilibrium to coincide with the efficient solution. For this to occur, the marginal value of a filled job in the social optimum, which is given by (5.69), needs to be equal to the marginal value that the firm and the worker attribute to this job in the decentralized equilibrium. The latter is equal to the value that a firm and a worker attribute to the joint surplus that is created by a match. Since firms continue to offer vacancies until their marginal value is reduced to zero ($V = 0$), the condition for efficiency of a decentralized equilibrium is

$$\mu = J + E - U, \tag{5.71}$$

where E and U, introduced in Section 5.3, denote the value that a worker attributes to the state of employment and unemployment, respectively.

Using (5.69), (5.48), and (5.51) we can rewrite (5.71) as:

$$\frac{c}{q'(\theta)\theta + q(\theta)} = \frac{1}{1 - \beta} \frac{c}{q(\theta)}, \tag{5.72}$$

where β denotes the relative bargaining strength of the worker. From (5.72), we obtain

$$\beta = -\frac{q'(\theta)\theta}{q(\theta)} \equiv -\big[\eta(\theta) - 1\big],$$
$$\Rightarrow \beta = 1 - \eta(\theta), \tag{5.73}$$

where $\eta(\theta)$ and $1 - \eta(\theta)$ denote the elasticity of the matching probability of a worker $p(\theta)$ and the average duration of a vacancy $1/q(\theta)$ with respect to θ. Since β is constant, condition (5.73) can be satisfied only if the matching function has constant returns to scale with respect to its arguments v and u. This condition is satisfied for a matching function of the Cobb–Douglas type:

$$m = m_0 v^\eta u^{1-\eta}, \qquad 0 < \eta < 1. \tag{5.74}$$

It is easy to verify that (5.74) has the following properties:

$$p(\theta) = m_0 \theta^\eta, \qquad q(\theta) = m_0 \theta^{\eta-1}, \qquad \frac{1}{q(\theta)} = \frac{1}{m_0} \theta^{1-\eta}. \tag{5.75}$$

The constant parameter η represents both the elasticity of the number of matches m with respect to the number of vacancies v, and the elasticity of $p(\theta)$ with respect to θ, while $1 - \eta$ denotes the elasticity of m with respect to u and also the elasticity of the medium duration of a vacancy, $1/q(\theta)$, with respect to θ.

Returning to efficiency condition (5.73), we can thus deduce that, if the average duration of a vacancy strongly increases with an increase in the number of vacancies (i.e. if $1 - \eta$ is relatively high), there is a strong tendency for firms to exceed the efficient number of vacancies. Only a relatively high value of β, which implies high wage levels, can counterbalance this effect and induce firms to reduce the number of vacancies. When $\beta = 1 - \eta$, these two opposing tendencies exactly offset each other and the decentralized equilibrium allocation is efficient. For cases in which $\beta \neq 1 - \eta$, there are two types of inefficiency:

1. if $\beta < 1 - \eta$ firms offer an excessive number of vacancies and the equilibrium unemployment rate is below the socially optimal level;
2. if $\beta > 1 - \eta$ wages are excessively high because of the strong bargaining power of workers and this results in an unemployment rate that is above the socially efficient level.

In sum, in the model of the labor market that we have described here we cannot make *a priori* conclusions about the efficiency of the equilibrium unemployment rate. Given the complex externalities between the actions of firms and workers, the properties of the *matching* function and the wage determination mechanism are crucial to determine whether the unemployment rate will be above or below the socially efficient level.

☐ APPENDIX A5: STRATEGIC INTERACTIONS AND MULTIPLIERS

This appendix presents a general theoretical structure, based on Cooper and John (1988), which captures the essential elements of the strategic interactions in the models discussed in this chapter. We will discuss the implications of strategic interactions in terms of the multiplicity of equilibria and analyze the welfare properties of these equilibria.

Consider a number I of economic agents ($i = 1, ..., I$), each of which chooses a value for a variable $e_i \in [0, E]$ which represents the agent's "activity level," with the objective of maximizing her own *payoff* $\sigma(e_i, e_{-i}, \lambda_i)$, where e_{-i} represents (the vector of) activity levels of the other agents and λ_i is an exogenous parameter which influences the payoff of agent i. Payoff function $\sigma(\cdot)$ satisfies the properties $\sigma_{ii} < 0$ and $\sigma_{i\lambda} > 0$. (This last assumption implies that an increase in λ raises the marginal return of activity for the agent.)

If all other agents choose a level of activity $\bar{e}$, the payoff of agent i can be expressed as $\sigma(e_i, \bar{e}, \lambda_i) \equiv V(e_i, \bar{e})$. In this case the optimization problem becomes

$$\max_{e_i} V(e_i, \bar{e}), \tag{5.A1}$$

from which we derive

$$V_1(e_i^*, \bar{e}) = 0, \tag{5.A2}$$

where V_1 denotes the derivative of V with respect to its first argument, e_i. First-order condition (5.A2) defines the optimal response of agent i to the activity level of all other agents: $e_i^* = e_i^*(\bar{e})$. Moreover, using (5.A1), we can also calculate the slope of the reaction curve of agent i:

$$\frac{de_i^*}{d\bar{e}} = -\frac{V_{12}}{V_{11}} \lessgtr 0, \text{ if } V_{12} \lessgtr 0. \tag{5.A3}$$

By the second-order condition for maximization, we know that $V_{11} < 0$; the sign of the slope is thus determined by the sign of $V_{12}(e_i, \bar{e})$. In case $V_{12} > 0$, we can make a graphical representation of the marginal payoff function $V_1(e_i, \bar{e})$ and of the resulting reaction function $e_i^*(\bar{e})$. The left-hand graph in Figure 5.12 illustrates various functions V_1, corresponding to three different activity levels for the other agents: $\bar{e} = 0$, $\bar{e} = e$, and $\bar{e} = E$.

Assuming $V_1(0, 0) > 0$ and $V_1(E, E) < 0$ (points A and B) guarantees the existence of at least one *symmetric decentralized equilibrium* in which $e = e_i^*(e)$, and agent i chooses exactly the same level of activity as all other agents (in this case $V_1(e, e) = 0$ and $V_{11}(e, e) < 0$). In Figure 5.12 we illustrate the case in which the reaction has a positive slope, and hence $V_{12} > 0$, and in which there is a *unique* symmetric equilibrium.

In general, if $V_{12}(e_i, \bar{e}) > 0$ there exists a *strategic complementarity* between agents: an increase in the activity level of the others increases the marginal return of activity for agent i, who will respond to this by raising her activity level. If, on the other hand, $V_{12}(e_i, \bar{e}) < 0$, then agents' actions are *strategic substitutes*. In this case agent i chooses a lower activity in response to an increase in the activity level of others (as in the case of a Cournot duopoly situation in which producers choose output levels). In the latter case there exists a unique equilibrium, while in the case of strategic complementarity there may be multiple equilibria.

Before analyzing the conditions under which this may occur, and before discussing the role of strategic complementarity or substitutability in determining the characteristics of the equilibrium, we must evaluate the problem from the viewpoint of a social planner who implements a *Pareto-efficient* equilibrium.

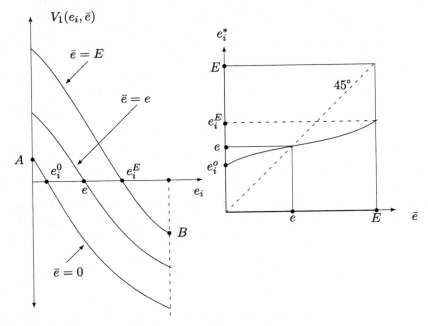

Figure 5.12. Strategic interactions

The planner's problem may be expressed as the maximization of a representative agent's welfare with respect to the *common* strategy (activity level) of all agents: the optimum that we are looking for is therefore the symmetric outcome corresponding to a hypothetical *cooperative equilibrium*. Formally,

$$\max_{e} V(e, e), \tag{5.A4}$$

from which we obtain

$$V_1(e^*, e^*) + V_2(e^*, e^*) = 0. \tag{5.A5}$$

Comparing this first-order condition[49] with the condition that is valid in a symmetric decentralized equilibrium (5.A2), we see that the solutions for e^* are different if $V_2(e^*, e^*) \neq 0$. In general, if $V_2(e_i, \bar{e}) > (<)0$, there are *positive (negative) spillovers*. The externalities are therefore defined as the impact of a third agent's activity level on the *payoff* of an individual.

A number of important implications for different features of the possible equilibria follow from this general formulation.

1. *Efficiency* Whenever there are externalities that affect the symmetric decentralized equilibrium, that is when $V_2(e, e) \neq 0$, the decentralized equilibrium is inefficient. In particular, with a positive externality ($V_2(e, e) > 0$), there exists a symmetric *cooperative equilibrium* characterized by a common activity level $e' > e$.

2. *Multiplicity of equilibria* As already mentioned, in the case of *strategic complementarity* ($V_{12} > 0$), an increase in the activity level of the other agents increases the marginal return of activity for agent i, which induces agent i to raise her own activity level. As a result, the reaction function of agents has a positive slope (as in Figure 5.12). Strategic complementarity is a necessary but not a sufficient condition for the existence of multiple (non-cooperative) equilibria. The *sufficient* condition is that $de_i^*/d\bar{e} > 1$ in a symmetric decentralized equilibrium. If this condition is satisfied, we may have the situation depicted in Figure 5.13, in which there exist three symmetric equilibria. Two of these equilibria (with activity levels e_1 and e_3) are stable, since the slope of the reaction curves is less than one at the equilibrium activity levels, while at e_2 the slope of the reaction curve is greater than one. This equilibrium is therefore *unstable*.

3. *Welfare* If there exist multiple equilibria, and if at each activity level there are positive externalities ($V_2(e_i, \bar{e}) > 0 \, \forall \bar{e}$), then the equilibria can be ranked. Those with a higher activity level are associated with a higher level of welfare. Hence, agents may be in an equilibrium in which their welfare is below the level that may be obtained in other equilibria. However, since agents choose the optimal strategy in each of the equilibria, there is no incentive for agents to change

---

[49] The second-order condition that we assume to be satisfied is given by $V_{11}(e^*, e^*) + 2V_{12}(e^*, e^*) + V_{22}(e^*, e^*) < 0$. Furthermore, in order to ensure the existence of a cooperative equilibrium, we assume that $V_1(0, 0) + V_2(0, 0) > 0$, $V_1(E, E) + V_2(E, E) < 0$, which is analogous to the restrictions imposed in the decentralized optimization above.

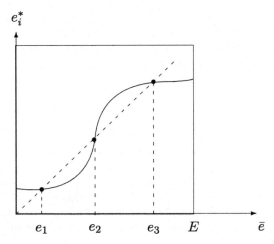

Figure 5.13. Multiplicity of equilibria

their level of activity. The absence of a mechanism to coordinate the actions of individual agents may thus give rise to a *"coordination failure,"* in which potential welfare gains are not realized because of a lack of private incentives to raise the activity levels.

Exercise 52 *Show formally that equilibria with a higher $\bar{e}$ are associated with a higher level of welfare if $V_2(e_i, \bar{e}) > 0$. (Use the total derivative of function $V(\cdot)$ to derive this result.)*

4. *Multipliers* Strategic complementarity is *necessary* and *sufficient* to guarantee that the aggregate response to an exogenous shock exceeds the response at the individual level; in this case the economy exhibits "multiplier" effects. To clarify this last point, which is of particular relevance for Keynesian models, we will consider the simplified case of *two* agents with *payoff* functions defined as $V^1 \equiv \sigma^1(e_1, e_2, \lambda_1)$ and $V^2 \equiv \sigma^2(e_1, e_2, \lambda_2)$, respectively. All the assumptions about these payoff functions remain valid (in particular, $V_{13}^1 \equiv \sigma_{13}^1 > 0$). The reaction curves of the two agents are derived from the following first-order conditions:

$$V_1^1(e_1^*, e_2^*, \lambda_1) = 0, \qquad (5.A6)$$

$$V_2^2(e_1^*, e_2^*, \lambda_2) = 0. \qquad (5.A7)$$

We now consider a "shock" to the *payoff* function of agent 1, namely $d\lambda_1 > 0$, and we derive the effect of this shock on the equilibrium activity levels of the two agents, e_1^* and e_2^*, and on the aggregate level of activity, $e_1^* + e_2^*$. Taking the total derivative of the above system of first-order conditions (5.A6) and (5.A7), with $d\lambda_2 = 0$, and dividing the first equation by V_{11}^1 and the second by V_{22}^2, we have:

$$de_1^* + \left(\frac{V_{12}^1}{V_{11}^1}\right) de_2^* + \left(\frac{V_{13}^1}{V_{11}^1}\right) d\lambda_1 = 0,$$

$$\left(\frac{V_{21}^2}{V_{22}^2}\right) de_1^* + de_2^* = 0.$$

The terms V_{12}^1/V_{11}^1 and V_{21}^2/V_{22}^2 represent the slopes, with opposing signs, of the reaction curves of the agents which we denote by ρ (given that the *payoff* functions are assumed to be identical, the slope of the reaction curves is also the same). The term V_{13}^1/V_{11}^1 represents the response (again with oppositing signs) of the optimal equilibrium level of agent 1 to a shock λ_1. In particular, keeping e_2^* constant, we have

$$V_1^1(e_1^*, e_2^*, \lambda_1) = 0 \quad \Rightarrow \quad \frac{\partial e_1^*}{\partial \lambda_1} = -\frac{V_{13}^1}{V_{11}^1} > 0.$$

We can thus rewrite the system as follows:

$$\begin{pmatrix} 1 & -\rho \\ -\rho & 1 \end{pmatrix} \begin{pmatrix} de_1^* \\ de_2^* \end{pmatrix} = \begin{pmatrix} \frac{\partial e_1^*}{\partial \lambda_1} \\ 0 \end{pmatrix} d\lambda_1,$$

which yields the following solution:

$$\frac{de_1^*}{d\lambda_1} = \frac{1}{1-\rho^2} \frac{\partial e_1^*}{\partial \lambda_1} \tag{5.A8}$$

$$\frac{de_2^*}{d\lambda_1} = \frac{\rho}{1-\rho^2} \frac{\partial e_1^*}{\partial \lambda_1} = \rho \frac{de_1^*}{d\lambda_1}. \tag{5.A9}$$

Equation (5.A8) gives the total response of agent 1 to a shock λ_1. This response can also be expressed as

$$\frac{de_1^*}{d\lambda_1} = \frac{\partial e_1^*}{\partial \lambda_1} + \rho \frac{de_2^*}{d\lambda_1}. \tag{5.A10}$$

The first term is the "impact" (and thus only partial) response of agent 1 to a shock affecting her payoff function; the second term gives the response of agent 1 that is "induced" by the reaction of the other agent. The condition for the additional induced effect is simply $\rho \neq 0$. Moreover, the actual induced effect depends on ρ and $de_2^*/d\lambda_1$, as in (5.A9), where $de_2^*/d\lambda_1$ has the same sign ρ: positive in case of strategic complementarity and negative in case of substitutability. The induced response of agent 1 is therefore always positive.

This leads to a first important conclusion: the interactions between the agents *always* induce a total (or equilibrium) response that is larger than the impact response. In particular, for each $\rho \neq 0$, we have

$$\frac{de_1^*}{d\lambda_1} > \frac{\partial e_1^*}{\partial \lambda_1}.$$

For the economy as a whole, the effect of the disturbance is given by

$$\frac{d(e_1^* + e_2^*)}{d\lambda_1} = \left(\frac{1}{1 - \rho^2} + \frac{\rho}{1 - \rho^2}\right)\frac{\partial e_1^*}{\partial \lambda_1} = \frac{1}{1 - \rho}\frac{\partial e_1^*}{\partial \lambda_1}$$

$$= (1 + \rho)\frac{de_1^*}{d\lambda_1}. \tag{5.A11}$$

The relative size of the aggregate response compared with the size of the individual response depends on the sign of ρ: if $\rho > 0$ (and limiting attention to stable equilibria for which $\rho < 1$), then aggregate response is bigger than individual response. *Strategic complementarity* is thus a necessary and sufficient condition for Keynesian multiplier effects.

Exercise 53 *Determine the type of externality and the nature of the strategic interactions for the simplified case of two agents with payoff function (here expressed for agent 1) $V^1(e_1, e_2) = e_1^a e_2^a - e_1$ (with $0 < 2a < 1$). Furthermore, derive the (symmetric) decentralized equilibria and compare these with the cooperative (symmetric) equilibrium.*

REVIEW EXERCISES

Exercise 54 *Introduce the following assumptions into the model analyzed in Section 5.1:*

(i) *The (stochastic) cost of production c has a uniform distribution defined on $[0, 1]$, so that $G(c) = c$ for $0 \leq c \leq 1$.*

(ii) *The matching probability is equal to $b(e) = b \cdot e$, with parameter $b > 0$.*
   (a) *Determine the dynamic expressions for e and c^* (repeating the derivation in the main text) under the assumption that $\gamma < 1$.*
   (b) *Find the equilibria for this economy and derive the stability properties of all equilibria with a positive activity level.*

Exercise 55 *Starting from the search model of money analyzed in Section 5.2, suppose that carrying over money from one period to the next now entails a storage cost, $c > 0$. Under this new assumption,*

(a) *Derive the expected utility for an agent holding a commodity (V_C) and for an agent holding money (V_M), and find the equilibria of the economy.*

(b) *Which of the three equilibria described in the model of Section 5.2 (with $c = 0$) always exists even with $c > 0$? Under what condition does a pure monetary equilibrium exist?*

Exercise 56 *Assume that the flow cost of a vacancy c and the imputed value of free time z in the model of Section 5.3 are now functions of the wage w (instead of being exogenous).*

In particular, assume that the following linear relations hold:

$$c = c_0\, w, \qquad z = z_0\, w.$$

Determine the effect of an increase in productivity ($\Delta y > 0$) on the steady-state equilibrium.

Exercise 57 *Consider a permanent negative productivity shock ($\Delta y < 0$) in the matching model of Sections 5.3 and 5.4. The shock is realized at date t_1, but is anticipated by the agents from date $t_0 < t_1$ onwards. Derive the effect of this shock on the steady-state equilibrium and describe the transitional dynamics of u, v, and θ.*

Exercise 58 *Consider the effect of an aggregate shock in the model of strategic interactions for two agents introduced in Appendix A5. That is, consider a variation in the exogenous terms of the payoff functions, so that $d\lambda_1 = d\lambda_2 = d\lambda > 0$, and derive the effect of this shock on the individual and aggregate activity level.*

⬚ FURTHER READING

The role of externalities between agents that operate in the same market as a source of multiplicity of equilibria is the principal theme in Diamond (1982a). This article develops the economic implications of the multiplicity of equilibria that have a Keynesian spirit. The monograph by Diamond (1984) analyzes this theme in greater depth, while Diamond and Fudenberg (1989) concentrate on the dynamic aspects of the model. Blanchard and Fischer (1989, chapter 9) offer a compact version of the model that we studied in the first section of this chapter. Moreover, after elaborating on the general theoretical structure to analyze the links between strategic interactions, externalities, and multiplicity of equilibria, which we discussed in Appendix A5, Cooper and John (1988) offer an application of Diamond's model. Rupert *et al.* (2000) survey the literature on search models of money as a medium of exchange and present extensions of the basic Kiyotaki–Wright framework discussed in Section 5.2.

The theory of the decentralized functioning of labor markets, which is based on search externalities and on the process of stochastic matching of workers and firms, reinvestigates a theme that was first developed in the contributions collected in Phelps (1970), namely the process of search and information gathering by workers and its effects on wages. Mortensen (1986) offers an exhaustive review of the contributions in this early strand of literature.

Compared with these early contributions, the theory developed in Section 5.3 and onwards concentrates more on the frictions in the matching process. Pissarides (2000) offers a thorough analysis of this strand of the literature. In this literature the base model is extended to include a specification of aggregate demand, which makes the interest rate endogenous, and allows for growth of the labor force, two elements that are not considered in this chapter. Mortensen and Pissarides (1999a, 1999b) provide an up-to-date review of the theoretical contributions and of the relevant empirical evidence.

In addition to the assumption of bilateral bargaining, which we adopted in Section 5.3, Mortensen and Pissarides (1998a) consider a number of alternative assumptions about wage determination. Moreover, Pissarides (1994) explicitly considers the case of on-the-job search which we excluded from our analysis. Pissarides (1987) develops the dynamics of the search model, studying the path of unemployment and vacancies in the different stages of the business cycle. The paper devotes particular attention to the cyclical variations of u and v around their long-run relationship, illustrated here by the dynamics displayed in Figure 5.11. Bertola and Caballero (1994) and Mortensen and Pissarides (1994) extend the structure of the base model to account for an endogenous job separation rate s. In these contributions job destruction is a conscious decision of employers, and it occurs only if a shock reduces the productivity of a match below some endogenously determined level. This induces an increase in the job destruction rate in cyclical downturns, which is coherent with empirical evidence.

The simple Cobb–Douglas formulation for the aggregate matching function with constant returns to scale introduced in Section 5.3 has proved quite useful in interpreting the evidence on unemployment and vacancies. Careful empirical analyses of flows in the (American) labor market can be found in Blanchard and Diamond (1989, 1990), Davis and Haltiwanger (1991, 1992) and Davis, Haltiwanger, and Schuh (1996), while Contini et al. (1995) offer a comparative analysis for the European countries. Cross-country empirical estimates of the Beveridge curve have been used by Nickell et al. (2002) to provide a description of the developments of the matching process over the 1960–99 period in the main OECD economies. They find that the Beveridge curve gradually drifted rightwards in all countries from the 1960s to the mid-1980s. In some countries, such as France and Germany, the shift continued in the same direction in the 1990s, whereas in the UK and the USA the curve shifted back towards its original position. Institutional factors affecting search and matching efficiency are responsible for a relevant part of the Beveridge curve shifts. The Beveridge curve for the Euro area in the 1980s and 1990s is analysed in European Central Bank (2002). Both counter-clockwise cyclical swings around the curve of the type discussed in Section 5.4 and shifts of the unemployment–vacancies relation occurred in this period. For example, over 1990–3 unemployment rose and the vacancy rate declined, reflecting the influence of cyclical factors; from 1994 to 1997 the unemployment rate was quite stable in the face of a rising vacancy rate, a shift of the Euro area Beveridge curve that is attributable to structural factors.

Not only empirically, but also theoretically, the structure of the labor force, the geographical dispersion of unemployed workers and vacant jobs, and the relevance of long-term unemployment determine the efficiency of a labor market's matching process. Petrongolo and Pissarides (2001) discuss the theoretical foundations of the matching function and provide an up-to-date survey of the empirical estimates for several countries, and of recent contributions focused on various factors influencing the matching rate.

The analysis of the efficiency of decentralized equilibrium in search models is first developed in Diamond (1982b) and Hosios (1990), who derive the efficiency conditions obtained in Section 5.5; it is also discussed in Pissarides (2000). In contrast, in a classic paper Lucas and Prescott (1974) develop a competitive search model where the decentralized equilibrium is efficient.

☐ REFERENCES

Bertola, G., and R. J. Caballero (1994) "Cross-Sectional Efficiency and Labour Hoarding in a Matching Model of Unemployment," *Review of Economic Studies*, 61, 435–456.

Blanchard, O. J., and P. Diamond (1989) "The Beveridge Curve," *Brookings Papers on Economic Activity*, no. 1, 1–60.

———— (1990) "The Aggregate Matching Function," in P. Diamond (ed.), *Growth, Productivity, Unemployment*, Cambridge, Mass.: MIT Press, 159–201.

——— and S. Fischer (1989) *Lectures on Macroeconomics*, Cambridge, Mass.: MIT Press.

Contini, B., L. Pacelli, M. Filippi, G. Lioni, and R. Revelli (1995) *A Study of Job Creation and Job Destruction in Europe*, Brussels: Commission of the European Communities.

Cooper, R., and A. John (1988) "Coordinating Coordination Failures in Keynesian Models," *Quarterly Journal of Economics*, 103, 441–463.

Davis, S., and J. Haltiwanger (1991) "Wage Dispersion between and within US Manufacturing Plants, 1963–86," *Brookings Papers on Economic Activity*, no. 1, 115–200.

———— (1992) "Gross Job Creation, Gross Job Destruction and Employment Reallocation," *Quarterly Journal of Economics*, 107, 819–864.

———— and S. Schuh (1996) *Job Creation and Destruction*, Cambridge, Mass.: MIT Press.

Diamond, P. (1982*a*) "Aggregate Demand Management in Search Equilibrium," *Journal of Political Economy*, 90, 881–894.

——— (1982*b*) "Wage Determination and Efficiency in Search Equilibrium," *Review of Economic Studies*, 49, 227–247.

——— (1984) *A Search-Equilibrium Approach to the Micro Foundations of Macroeconomics*, Cambridge, Mass.: MIT Press.

——— and D. Fudenberg (1989) "Rational Expectations Business Cycles in Search Equilibrium," *Journal of Political Economy*, 97, 606–619.

European Central Bank (2002) "Labour Market Mismatches in Euro Area Countries," Frankfurt: European Central Bank.

Hosios, A. J. (1990) "On the Efficiency of Matching and Related Models of Search and Unemployment," *Review of Economic Studies*, 57, 279–298.

Kiyotaki, N., and R. Wright (1993) "A Search-Theoretic Approach to Monetary Economics," *American Economic Review*, 83, 63–77.

Lucas, R. E., and E. C. Prescott (1974) "Equilibrium Search and Unemployment," *Journal of Economic Theory*, 7, 188–209.

Mortensen, D. T. (1986) "Job Search and Labor Market Analysis," in O. Ashenfelter and R. Layard (eds.), *Handbook of Labor Economics*, Amsterdam: North-Holland.

——— and C. A. Pissarides (1994) "Job Creation and Job Destruction in the Theory of Unemployment," *Review of Economic Studies*, 61, 397–415.

———— (1999*a*) "New Developments in Models of Search in the Labor Market," in O. Ashenfelter and D. Card (eds.), *Handbook of Labor Economics*, vol. 3, Amsterdam: North-Holland.

———— (1999*b*) "Job Reallocation, Employment Fluctuations and Unemployment," in J. B. Taylor and M. Woodford (eds.), *Handbook of Macroeconomics*, Amsterdam: North-Holland.

Nickell S., L. Nunziata, W. Ochel, and G. Quintini (2002) "The Beveridge Curve, Unemployment and Wages in the OECD from the 1960s to the 1990s," Centre for Economic Performance Discussion Paper 502; forthcoming in P. Aghion, R. Frydman, J. Stiglitz, and M. Woodford (eds.), *Knowledge, Information and Expectations in Modern Macroeconomics: In Honor of Edmund S. Phelps*, Princeton: Princeton University Press.

Petrongolo B., and C. A. Pissarides (2001) "Looking into the Black Box: A Survey of the Matching Function," *Journal of Economic Literature*, 39, 390–431.

Phelps, E. S. (ed.) (1970) *Macroeconomic Foundations of Employment and Inflation Theory*, New York: W. W. Norton.

Pissarides, C. A. (1987) "Search, Wage Bargains and Cycles," *Review of Economic Studies*, 54, 473–483.

—— (1994) "Search Unemployment and On-the-Job Search," *Review of Economic Studies*, 61, 457–475.

—— (2000) *Equilibrium Unemployment Theory*, 2nd edn. Cambridge, Mass.: MIT Press.

Rupert P., M. Schindler, A. Shevchenko, and R. Wright (2000) "The Search-Theoretic Approach to Monetary Economics: A Primer," *Federal Reserve Bank of Cleveland Economic Review*, 36(4), 10–28.

☐ ANSWERS TO EXERCISES

Solution to exercise 1

When $\lambda = 0$ (assuming for simplicity that $y_{t-i} = \bar{y}\ \forall i \geq 0$) the agent has an initial consumption level $c_t = \bar{y}$ and a stock of financial assets at the beginning of period $t + 1$ equal to zero: $A_{t+1} = 0$. In period $t + 1$, we have

$$c_{t+1} = \bar{y} + \frac{r}{1+r}\varepsilon_{t+1}, \qquad s_{t+1} = y_{t+1} - c_{t+1} = \frac{1}{1+r}\varepsilon_{t+1} = A_{t+2}.$$

In subsequent periods (with no further innovations) current income will go back to its mean value $\bar{y}$, and consumption will remain at the higher level computed for $t + 1$. The return on financial wealth accumulated in $t + 1$ allows the consumer to maintain such higher consumption level over the entire future horizon:

$$y_{t+2}^D = y_{t+2} + r A_{t+2} = \bar{y} + \frac{r}{1+r}\varepsilon_{t+1} = c_{t+2} \Rightarrow s_{t+2} = 0.$$

The same is true for all periods $t + i$ with $i > 2$. There is no saving, and the level of A remains equal to A_{t+2}. When $\lambda = 1$, the whole increase in income is permanent and is entirely consumed. There is no need to save in order to keep the higher level of consumption in the future.

Solution to exercise 2

We look for a consumption function of the general form

$$c_t = r(A_t + H_t) = r A_t + \frac{r}{1+r}\sum_{i=0}^{\infty}\left(\frac{1}{1+r}\right)^i E_t y_{t+i},$$

as in (1.12) in the main text. Given the assumed stochastic process for income, we can compute expectations of future incomes and then the value of human wealth H_t. We have

$$E_t y_{t+1} = \lambda y_t + (1 - \lambda)\bar{y}$$

$$E_t y_{t+2} = \lambda^2 y_t + (1 + \lambda)(1 - \lambda)\bar{y}$$

$$\ldots$$

$$E_t y_{t+i} = \lambda^i y_t + (1 + \lambda + \ldots + \lambda^{i-1})(1 - \lambda)\bar{y} = \lambda^i y_t + (1 - \lambda^i)\bar{y}.$$

Plugging the last expression above into the definition of H_t, we get

$$H_t = \frac{1}{1+r} \sum_{i=0}^{\infty} \left(\frac{1}{1+r}\right)^i (\lambda^i y_t + (1-\lambda^i)\bar{y})$$

$$= \frac{1}{1+r} \left[y_t \sum_{i=0}^{\infty} \left(\frac{\lambda}{1+r}\right)^i + \bar{y} \sum_{i=0}^{\infty} \left(\frac{1}{1+r}\right)^i - \bar{y} \sum_{i=0}^{\infty} \left(\frac{\lambda}{1+r}\right)^i \right]$$

$$= \frac{1}{1+r} \left[y_t \frac{1+r}{1+r-\lambda} + \bar{y} \left(\frac{1+r}{r} - \frac{1+r}{1+r-\lambda}\right) \right]$$

$$= \frac{1}{1+r-\lambda} y_t + \frac{1-\lambda}{r(1+r-\lambda)} \bar{y}.$$

The consumption function is then

$$c_t = r(A_t + H_t) = r A_t + \frac{r}{1+r-\lambda} y_t + \frac{1-\lambda}{1+r-\lambda} \bar{y}.$$

If $\lambda = 1$, income innovations are permanent and the best forecast of all future incomes is simply current income y_t. Thus, consumption will be equal to total income (interest income and labor income):

$$c_t = r A_t + y_t.$$

If $\lambda = 0$, income innovations are purely temporary and the best forecast of future incomes is mean income $\bar{y}$. Consumption will then be

$$c_t = r A_t + \bar{y} + \frac{r}{1+r}(y_t - \bar{y}).$$

The last term measures the *annuity value* (at the beginning of period t) of the income innovation that occurred in period t and therefore known by the consumer (indeed, $y_t - \bar{y} = \varepsilon_t$).

Solution to exercise 3

Since $c_2 = w_1 - c_1 + w_2$, from the first-order condition

$$\frac{1}{c_1} = E\left(\frac{1}{c_2}\right)$$

we get

$$\frac{1}{c_1} = \frac{p}{w_1 - c_1 + x} + \frac{1-p}{w_1 - c_1 + y}.$$

Rearranging and writing $px + (1-p)y = z$, we get

$$(w_1 - c_1 - z + y + x) c_1 = (w_1 - c_1 + x)(w_1 - c_1 + y).$$

This is a quadratic equation for c_1, so a closed-form solution is available. Writing $x = z + \Delta$, $y = z - \Delta$, the first-order condition reads

$$(w_1 - c_1 + z)c_1 = (w_1 - c_1 + z + \Delta)(w_1 - c_1 + z - \Delta).$$

In the absence of uncertainty ($\Delta = 0$), the solution is $c_1 = (w_1 + z)/2$. (With discount and return rates both equal to zero, the agent consumes half of the available resources in each period.) For general Δ the optimality condition is solved by

$$c_1 = \frac{3}{4}(w_1 + z) \pm \frac{1}{4}\sqrt{((w_1 + z)^2 + 8\Delta^2)}.$$

Selecting the negative square root ensures that the solution approaches the appropriate limit when $\Delta \to 0$, and implies that uncertainty reduces first-period consumption (for precautionary motives). An analytic solution would be impossible for even slightly more complicated maximization problems. This is why studies of precautionary savings prefer to specify the utility function in exponential form, rather than logarithmic or other CRRA.

Solution to exercise 4

Solving the consumer's problem, we get the following first-order condition (see the main text for the solution in the certainty case):

$$\frac{1 + r}{1 + \rho} E_t \left[\left(\frac{c_{t+1}}{c_t} \right)^{-\gamma} \right] = 1.$$

The assumption $\Delta \log c_{t+1} \sim N\left(E_t(\Delta \log c_{t+1}), \sigma^2\right)$ yields

$$-\gamma \Delta \log c_{t+1} \sim N\left(-\gamma E_t(\Delta \log c_{t+1}), \gamma^2 \sigma^2\right).$$

Using the properties of the lognormal distribution, we can write the Euler equation as

$$\frac{1 + r}{1 + \rho} e^{(-\gamma E_t(\Delta \log c_{t+1}) + (\gamma^2/2)\sigma^2)} = 1.$$

Taking logarithms, the following expression for the expected rate of change of consumption is obtained:

$$E_t(\Delta \log c_{t+1}) = \frac{1}{\gamma}(r - \rho) + \frac{\gamma}{2}\sigma^2.$$

The uncertainty on future consumption levels, captured by the variance σ^2, induces the (prudent) consumer to transfer resources from the present to the future, determining an increasing path of consumption over time.

Solution to exercise 5

(a) The increase of mean income changes the consumer's permanent income. Both permanent income and consumption increase by $\Delta \bar{y}$. Formally,

$$\Delta c_{t+1} = \Delta y_{t+1}^P = \frac{r}{1+r} \sum_{i=0}^{\infty} \left(\frac{1}{1+r}\right)^i (E_{t+1} - E_t) \, y_{t+1+i}$$

$$= \frac{r}{1+r} \sum_{i=0}^{\infty} \left(\frac{1}{1+r}\right)^i \Delta \bar{y} = \Delta \bar{y}.$$

Since the income change is entirely permanent, saving is not affected.

(b) In order to find the change in consumption following an innovation in income, it is necessary to compute the revision in expectations of future incomes caused by ε_{t+1}. Given the stochastic process for labor income, we have

$$(E_{t+1} - E_t) \, y_{t+1} = \varepsilon_{t+1},$$
$$(E_{t+1} - E_t) \, y_{t+2} = -\delta \varepsilon_{t+1},$$
$$(E_{t+1} - E_t) \, y_{t+i} = 0 \qquad \text{for } i > 2.$$

Applying the general formula for the change in consumption, we get

$$\Delta c_{t+1} = r(H_{t+1} - E_t H_{t+1})$$

$$= \frac{r}{1+r} \left(\varepsilon_{t+1} - \frac{1}{1+r} \delta \varepsilon_{t+1} \right) = \frac{r(1+r-\delta)}{(1+r)^2} \varepsilon_{t+1}.$$

The increase in consumption is lower than the increase in income since the latter is only temporary. The higher is δ, the lower is the change in consumption, because a positive income innovation in $t + 1$ (ε_{t+1}) is offset by a negative income change ($-\delta \varepsilon_{t+1}$) in the following period.

(c) The behavior of saving reflects the expectation of future income changes. Given ε_{t+1} and using the stochastic process for income, we obtain

$$y_{t+1} = \bar{y} + \varepsilon_{t+1}$$
$$y_{t+2} = \bar{y} - \delta \varepsilon_{t+1} \qquad \Rightarrow \qquad \Delta y_{t+2} = -(1+\delta)\varepsilon_{t+1}$$
$$y_{t+3} = \bar{y} \qquad\qquad\quad \Rightarrow \qquad \Delta y_{t+3} = \delta \varepsilon_{t+1}.$$

(No income changes are foreseen for subsequent periods.) Saving in $t+1$ and $t+2$ is then

$$s_{t+1} = -\sum_{i=1}^{\infty} \left(\frac{1}{1+r}\right)^i E_{t+1}\Delta y_{t+1+i} = -\left[-\frac{1+\delta}{1+r} + \frac{\delta}{(1+r)^2}\right]\varepsilon_{t+1}$$

$$= \frac{1+r(1+\delta)}{(1+r)^2}\varepsilon_{t+1} > 0,$$

$$s_{t+2} = -\sum_{i=1}^{\infty} \left(\frac{1}{1+r}\right)^i E_{t+2}\Delta y_{t+2+i} = -\frac{\delta}{1+r}\varepsilon_{t+1} < 0.$$

In $t+1$ a portion of the higher income is saved, since the consumer knows its transitory nature and then anticipates further income changes in the two following periods. In $t+2$ income is temporarily lower than average and the agent finances consumption with the income saved in the previous period: in $t+2$, then, saving is negative.

Solution to exercise 6

For each period from t onwards, the consumer must choose both the consumption of non-durable goods c_{t+i} (which coincides with expenditure), and the expenditure on durable goods d_{t+i} (which adds to the stock and starts to provide utility in the period after the purchase). The utility maximization problem is then solved for c_{t+i} and d_{t+i}. Besides the constraints in the main text, we must consider the transversality condition on financial wealth A and the non-negativity constraint on the stock of durable goods S and on consumption c (though we will not explicitly use these additional constraints in the solution below). Following the solution procedure already used in the main text, we substitute the two constraints into the utility function to be maximized. Combining the constraints, we can write consumption as

$$c_{t+i} = (1+r)A_{t+i} - A_{t+i+1} + y_{t+i} - p_{t+i}[S_{t+i+1} - (1-\delta)S_{t+i}].$$

Plugging the above expression into the objective function, we get the following optimization problem:

$$\max_{A_{t+i}, S_{t+i}} U_t = \sum_{i=0}^{\infty} \left(\frac{1}{1+\rho}\right)^i u((1+r)A_{t+i} - A_{t+i+1} + y_{t+i}$$

$$- p_{t+i}(S_{t+i+1} - (1-\delta)S_{t+i}), S_{t+i}).$$

Expanding the first two terms of the summation (for $i = 0, 1$) and differentiating with respect to A_{t+1} and S_{t+1}, we obtain the following first-order conditions:

$$\frac{\partial U_t}{\partial A_{t+1}} = -u_c(c_t, S_t) + \frac{1+r}{1+\rho}u_c(c_{t+1}, S_{t+1}) = 0,$$

$$\frac{\partial U_t}{\partial S_{t+1}} = -p_t u_c(c_t, S_t) + \frac{1}{1+\rho}p_{t+1}(1-\delta)u_c(c_{t+1}, S_{t+1})$$

$$+ \frac{1}{1+\rho}u_S(c_{t+1}, S_{t+1}) = 0.$$

The consumer makes two decisions. First, he chooses between consumption in the current period and in the next period (and then between consumption and saving). Second, he chooses between spending on non-durable goods and spending on durable goods, which yield deferred utility. The first-order conditions above illustrate these two choices. The first condition captures the choice between consumption and saving, as in (1.5) in the main text,

$$u_c(c_t, S_t) = \frac{1+r}{1+\rho}u_c(c_{t+1}, S_{t+1}),$$

and bears the usual interpretation: the loss of marginal utility arising from the decrease in consumption at time t must be offset by the marginal utility (discounted with rate ρ) obtained by accumulating financial assets with gross return $1 + r$. The choice between spending for non-durable goods and purchasing durables is illustrated by the second condition, rewritten as

$$p_t u_c(c_t, S_t) = \frac{1}{1+\rho}[u_S(c_{t+1}, S_{t+1}) + (1-\delta)p_{t+1}u_c(c_{t+1}, S_{t+1})].$$

One unit of the durable good purchased at time t entails a decrease of spending on (and consumption of) p_t units of non-durable goods with a utility loss measured by $p_t u_c(c_t, S_t)$ on the right-hand side of the above equation. In equilibrium, this loss must be offset, in the following period, by the higher utility stemming from the unitary increase of the stock of durables. This increase in utility, measured on the left-hand side of the equation, has two components (both discounted at rate ρ). The first is the marginal utility of the stock of durables at the beginning of period $t + 1$. The second accounts for the additional resources that an increase in the stock of durables makes available for consumption in $t + 1$ by reducing the need for further purchases, d_{t+1}. These additional resources are measured by $(1-\delta)p_{t+1}$, yielding utility $(1-\delta)p_{t+1}u_c(c_{t+1}, S_{t+1})$.

Solution to exercise 7

(a) In each period, utility is affected positively by consumption in the current period and negatively by consumption in the previous period.

This formulation of utility may capture *habit formation* behavior: a high level of consumption in period t decreases utility in period $t + 1$ (but increases period $t + 1$ marginal utility). Therefore, the agent is induced to increase consumption in period $t + 1$. This effect is due to a consumption "habit" (related to the last period level of c) making the agent increase consumption over time.

(b) Substituting c_{t+i} and c_{t+i-1} from the budget constraints of two subsequent periods into the objective function and differentiating with respect to financial wealth, we obtain the following first-order condition (Euler equation):

$$E_t u'(c_{t+i-1}, c_{t+i-2}) = \frac{1 + r + \gamma}{1 + \rho} E_t u'(c_{t+i}, c_{t+i-1})$$

$$- \frac{(1 + r)\gamma}{(1 + \rho)^2} E_t u'(c_{t+i+1}, c_{t+i}).$$

Setting $i = 0$ and $\rho = r$, and assuming quadratic utility so that $u'(c_{t+i}, c_{t+i-1}) = 1 - b(c_{t+i} - \gamma c_{t+i-1})$, we get

$$1 - b(c_{t-1} - \gamma c_{t-2}) = \frac{1 + r + \gamma}{1 + r}[1 - b(c_t - \gamma c_{t-1})]$$

$$- \frac{\gamma}{1 + r}[1 - b(E_t c_{t+1} - \gamma c_t)],$$

or

$$\gamma E_t c_{t+1} = (1 + r + \gamma + \gamma^2)c_t$$

$$- [(1 + r + \gamma)\gamma + (1 + r)]c_{t-1} + \gamma(1 + r) c_{t-1}.$$

Using first differences of consumption,

$$\gamma E_t \Delta c_{t+1} = \left(1 + r + \gamma^2\right) \Delta c_t - (1 + r)\gamma \Delta c_{t-1}.$$

The change in consumption between t and $t + 1$ depends on past values of Δc and therefore is not orthogonal to all variables dated t. If in each period utility depends on consumption in the current and the last periods, in choosing between c_t and c_{t+1}, the agent considers the effects on utility not only at t and $t + 1$ (as in the case of a time-separable utility function), but also at $t + 2$. This creates an intertemporal link between the marginal utility in three subsequent periods and then, with quadratic utility, between the consumption *levels* in subsequent periods. In this case there is a dynamic relation between c_{t+1} and c_t, c_{t-1} and c_{t-2}, which makes the consumption change Δc_{t+1} dependent on lagged values Δc_t and Δc_{t-1}. Therefore, the orthogonality conditions that hold with separable utility are not valid here.

Solution to exercise 8

(a) The change in permanent income for *agents*, Δy_t^P, is found from the following version of equation (1.6):

$$\Delta y_t^P = \frac{r}{1+r} \sum_{i=0}^{\infty} \left(\frac{1}{1+r}\right)^i [E(y_{t+i} \mid I_t) - E(y_{t+i} \mid I_{t-1})],$$

where the information set used by agents (I) has been made explicit. It is then necessary to compute the "surprises": $y_t - E(y_t \mid I_{t-1})$, $E(y_{t+1} \mid I_t) - E(y_{t+1} \mid I_{t-1})$, etc. Since agents in each period observe the realization of x, using the stochastic process for income, we have

$$E(y_t \mid I_{t-1}) = \lambda y_{t-1} + x_{t-1},$$

from which we obtain

$$y_t - E(y_t \mid I_{t-1}) = \varepsilon_{1t}.$$

Recalling that the properties of x imply that $E(x_t \mid I_{t-1}) = 0$, to compute the second "surprise" we use the following expressions:

$$E(y_{t+1} \mid I_t) = \lambda y_t + x_t,$$

$$E(y_{t+1} \mid I_{t-1}) = \lambda E(y_t \mid I_{t-1}),$$

from which

$$E(y_{t+1} \mid I_t) - E(y_{t+1} \mid I_{t-1}) = \lambda(y_t - E(y_t \mid I_{t-1})) + x_t = \lambda\varepsilon_{1t} + x_t.$$

Iterating the same procedure, we find, for $i \geq 1$,

$$E(y_{t+i} \mid I_t) - E(y_{t+i} \mid I_{t-1}) = \lambda^i(\lambda\varepsilon_{1t} + x_t).$$

The change in permanent income is then given by

$$\Delta y_t^P = \frac{r}{1+r}\left[\varepsilon_{1t} + \sum_{i=1}^{\infty}\left(\frac{1}{1+r}\right)^i \lambda^{i-1}(\lambda\varepsilon_{1t} + x_t)\right]$$

$$= \frac{r}{1+r}\left[\sum_{i=0}^{\infty}\left(\frac{1}{1+r}\right)^i \lambda^i \varepsilon_{1t} + \sum_{i=1}^{\infty}\left(\frac{1}{1+r}\right)^i \lambda^{i-1} x_t\right]$$

$$= \frac{r}{1+r}\left(\frac{1+r}{1+r-\lambda}\varepsilon_{1t} + \frac{1}{1+r-\lambda}x_t\right)$$

$$= \frac{r}{1+r-\lambda}\left(\varepsilon_{1t} + \frac{1}{1+r}x_t\right).$$

Now consider the change in permanent income $(\Delta \tilde{y}_t^P)$ computed by the *econometrician*, who does not observe the realization of x.

The relevant "surprises" are then: $y_t - E(y_t \mid \Omega_{t-1})$, $E(y_{t+1} \mid \Omega_t) - E(y_{t+1} \mid \Omega_{t-1})$, etc. As in the previous case, we get

$$E(y_t \mid \Omega_{t-1}) = \lambda y_{t-1}$$

$$E(y_{t+1} \mid \Omega_t) = \lambda y_t$$

$$E(y_{t+1} \mid \Omega_{t-1}) = \lambda E(y_t \mid \Omega_{t-1}),$$

from which we compute the "surprises":

$$y_t - E(y_t \mid \Omega_{t-1}) = \varepsilon_{1t} + x_{t-1}$$

$$E(y_{t+1} \mid \Omega_t) - E(y_{t+1} \mid \Omega_{t-1}) = \lambda(\varepsilon_{1t} + x_{t-1})$$

$$\dots$$

$$E(y_{t+i} \mid \Omega_t) - E(y_{t+i} \mid \Omega_{t-1}) = \lambda^i(\varepsilon_{1t} + x_{t-1}).$$

Finally, using equation (1.7), we obtain

$$\Delta \tilde{y}_t^P = \frac{r}{1+r} \sum_{i=0}^{\infty} \left(\frac{1}{1+r}\right)^i \lambda^i (\varepsilon_{1t} + x_{t-1})$$

$$= \frac{r}{1+r-\lambda}(\varepsilon_{1t} + x_{t-1}).$$

(b) The variability of permanent income, measured by the variance of Δy_t^P and $\Delta \tilde{y}_t^P$, is

$$\mathrm{var}(\Delta y_t^P) = \psi^2 \left(\sigma_1^2 + \left(\frac{1}{1+r}\right)^2 \sigma_x^2\right),$$

$$\mathrm{var}(\Delta \tilde{y}_t^P) = \psi^2(\sigma_1^2 + \sigma_x^2),$$

where $\psi \equiv r/(1+r-\lambda)$, $\sigma_1^2 \equiv \mathrm{var}(\varepsilon_1)$, and $\sigma_x^2 \equiv \mathrm{var}(x)$. We find then that $\mathrm{var}(\Delta y_t^P) < \mathrm{var}(\Delta \tilde{y}_t^P)$. The variability of permanent income estimated by the econometrician is higher than the variability perceived by agents. Overestimating the unforeseen changes in income may lead to the conclusion that consumption is *excessively smooth*, even though agents behave as predicted by the rational expectations–permanent income theory.

Solution to exercise 9

(a) For the assumed utility function, marginal utility is

$$u'(c) = \begin{cases} a - bc & \text{for } c < a/b; \\ 0 & \text{for } c \geq a/b, \end{cases}$$

As shown in the figure, marginal utility is *convex* in the neighborhood of $c = a/b$ where it becomes zero. Therefore, there exists a precautionary saving motive.

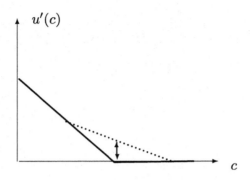

$u'(c)$

c

(b) The optimality condition for c_1 is

$$u'(c_1) = E_1[u'(c_2)].$$

If $\sigma = 0$, we get $c_1 = c_2 = a/b$: in each period income is entirely consumed, there is no saving, and marginal utility is zero. If $\sigma > 0$, with $c_1 = a/b$, in the second period the agent consumes either $a/b + \sigma$ (with zero marginal utility) or $a/b - \sigma$ (with positive marginal utility) with equal probability. The expected value of the second-period marginal utility will then be positive, violating the optimality condition. Therefore, when $\sigma > 0$ the agent is induced to consume *less* than a/b in the first period. Writing the realizations of second-period income and consumption, i.e.

$$c_2 = y_2 + (y_1 - c_1) = \begin{cases} 2a/b - c_1 + \sigma \equiv c_2^H(c_1) & \text{with probability } 0.5 \\ 2a/b - c_1 - \sigma \equiv c_2^L(c_1) & \text{with probability } 0.5 \end{cases}$$

and noting that marginal utility is zero in the first case, the optimality condition becomes

$$a - bc_1 = \frac{1}{2}(a - bc_2^L(c_1))$$

and the value of c_1 is computed as

$$c_1 = \frac{a}{b} - \frac{\sigma}{3}.$$

First-period consumption is *decreasing* in σ: income uncertainty gives rise to a precautionary saving motive.

Solution to exercise 10

If $G(\cdot)$ has the quadratic form proposed in the exercise, then the marginal investment cost $\partial G(K, I)/\partial I = x \cdot 2I$ has the same sign as the investment flow I. Since the optimal investment flow I^* must satisfy the condition $x \cdot 2I^* = \lambda$, where λ is the marginal value of capital, $\lambda > 0$ implies $I^* > 0$. Intuitively, this functional form (whose slope at the origin is zero, rather than unity) implies costs for the firm not only when $I > 0$, but also when $I < 0$. As long as installed capital has a positive value, it cannot be optimal for the firm to pay costs in order to scrap it, and the optimal investment flow is never negative.

The slope at the origin of functions in the form I^β is zero for all $\beta > 0$, and such functions are well defined for $I < 0$ only when β is an integer. If β is an even number, then the sign of $\partial G(K, I)/\partial I = x \cdot \beta I^{\beta-1}$ coincides with that of I and, as in the case where $\beta = 2$, negative gross investment is never optimal. If β is an odd integer then, as in the figure, the derivative of adjustment costs is always positive.

$G(I, \cdot)$

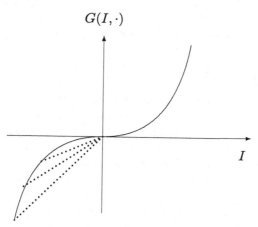

I

Thus, negative investment yields positive cash flows, and may be optimal. The second derivative $\partial^2 G(K, I)/\partial I^2 = x \cdot \beta (\beta - 1) I^{\beta-2}$, however, is not always positive as assumed in (2.4). Rather, it is negative for $I < 0$. This implies that the unit cash flow yielded by negative gross investment is increasingly large when increasingly negative values of I are considered. Hence, the firm would profit from mixing periods of gradual positive investment (of arbitrarily small cost, since the function $G(\cdot)$ is flat for I near zero) with sudden spurts of negative investment. Such functional forms make no economic sense, and also make it impossible to obtain a unique formal characterization of optimal investment. If the adjustment cost function had increasing returns to (negative) investment, the first-order conditions would not characterize optimal policies, and many different intermittent investment policies could yield an infinitely large firm value.

Solution to exercise 11

Employment of the flexible factor N must satisfy in steady state, as always, the familiar first-order condition $\partial R(\cdot)/\partial N = w$. As mentioned in the text, if capital does not depreciate, its steady-state stock must satisfy the similarly familiar condition $\partial F(\cdot)/\partial K = r\,P_k$. Equivalently, since $\partial F(\cdot)/\partial K = \partial R(\cdot)/\partial K - P_k \partial G(\cdot)/\partial K$ and $\partial G(\cdot)/\partial K = 0$ in this exercise,

$$\partial R(\cdot)/\partial K = r\,P_k.$$

Thus, we need to characterize the effects of a smaller w on the pair (K_{ss}, N_{ss}) that satisfies the two conditions. If revenues have the Cobb–Douglas form, the conditions

$$\frac{a}{K_{ss}} K_{ss}^a N_{ss}^\beta = r\,P_k, \qquad \frac{\beta}{N_{ss}} K_{ss}^a N_{ss}^\beta = w,$$

can be solved if $a + \beta < 1$ and the firm has decreasing returns in production. Then, we have

$$K_{ss} = w^{\beta/a+\beta-1}(r\,P_k)^{1-\beta/a+\beta-1} a^{\beta-1/a+\beta-1} \beta^{-\beta/a+\beta-1}$$

and a smaller wage is associated with a higher steady-state capital stock.

Solution to exercise 12

If $G(\cdot)$ has constant returns to K and I, we may write

$$G(I, K) = g\left(\frac{I}{K}\right) K$$

and note that, by the investment first-order condition,

$$g'\left(\frac{I}{K}\right) = q,$$

optimal investment is proportional to K for given q:

$$I = \iota(q)K.$$

The portion of the firm's cash flows that pertains to investment costs,

$$P_k G(I, K) = g(\iota(q))K,$$

therefore has zero second derivative with respect to K. Since revenues (once optimized with respect to N) are also linear in K, $\partial F(\cdot)/\partial K$ does not depend on K, and the $\dot{q} = 0$ locus is horizontal. As for the $\dot{K} = 0$ locus, we noted when tracing phase diagrams that its slope tends to be positive when $\delta > 0$, since a higher q and more intense investment flows are needed to keep a larger capital stock constant. To determine the slope of the $\dot{K} = 0$ locus, however, the derivative of $G(\cdot)$ with respect to K is also relevant when it is not zero (as was convenient to assume when drawing phase diagrams). In the case where $G(\cdot)$ has constant returns, we can write

$$\dot{K} = \tilde{\imath}(q)K - \delta K = (\tilde{\imath}(q) - \delta)K$$

and find that, even when $\delta > 0$, the locus identified by setting this expression equal to zero is horizontal. As is the case in a static environment, the optimal size of a competitive firms with constant returns to scale is undetermined (if the two stationarity loci coincide), or tends to be infinitely large or small (if either locus is larger than the other).

Solution to exercise 13

(a) As shown in the text, an increase in y has two effects on the steady-state value of q: a positive "dividend effect" and a negative "interest rate effect." If the former dominates, the $\dot{q} = 0$ schedule slopes upwards in the (q, y) phase diagram, as in the figure.

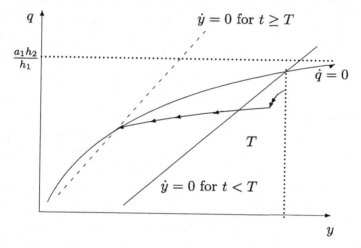

Formally, from (2.35) we get

$$\left.\frac{dq}{dy}\right|_{\dot{q}=0} = \frac{a_1 r - (a_0 + a_1 y)h_1/h_2}{r^2} > 0 \quad \Leftrightarrow \quad a_1 > q\frac{h_1}{h_2},$$

where we used the expression for $q = \pi/r$ which applies along the $\dot{q} = 0$ locus. This schedule crosses the stationary locus for y from above, since

$$\lim_{y\to\infty} \left.\frac{dq}{dy}\right|_{\dot{q}=0} = 0$$

and q approaches the value $a_1 h_2/h_1$ asymptotically from below (for $y \to \infty$). Outside its stationary locus, q retains the same dynamic properties illustrated in the main text: $\dot{q} > 0$ at all points above the curve and $\dot{q} < 0$ below the curve. In this case the saddlepath slopes upwards, reflecting the fact that, when output increases towards the steady state of the system, the stronger influence on q is given by dividends, which are also rising.

(b) Under the new assumption, the effects of the fiscal restriction on the steady-state values of output and the interest rate are similar to those reported in the text: both y and r decrease. However, the effect on the steady-state value of q is different: here q is affected mainly by lower dividends, and attains a lower level in the final steady state. The permanent reduction in output (and dividends) is foreseen by agents at $t = 0$, when the future fiscal restriction is announced. The ensuing portfolio reallocation away from shares and toward bonds determines an immediate decrease in stock market prices, with a depressing effect on private investment, aggregate demand, and (starting gradually from $t = 0$) output. At the implementation date $t = T$ the economy is on the saddlepath converging to the new steady-state position. In contrast with the case of a dominant "interest rate effect," here in the final steady state there is less public spending *and* less private investment; moreover, the (apparently) perverse temporary effect of fiscal policy on output does not occur.

Solution to exercise 14

(a) With $F(t) = R(K(t)) - G(I)$, the dynamic optimality conditions

$$G'(I) = \lambda, \qquad \dot{\lambda} - r\lambda = -F'(K) + \delta\lambda,$$

are necessary and sufficient if $G'(I) > 0$, $F'(K) > 0$, $F''(K) \le 0$, and $G''(I) > 0$. The optimal investment flow is a function $\iota(\cdot)$ of q (or, since $P_k = 1$, of λ), where $\iota(\cdot)$ is the inverse of $G'(\cdot)$. Inserting $I = \iota(q)$ in the accumulation constraint, using the second optimality conditions, and noting that $\dot{q} = \dot{\lambda}$, we obtain a system of two differential equations:

$$\dot{K} = \iota(q) - \delta K, \qquad \dot{q} = (r + \delta)q - F'(K).$$

The dynamics of K and q can be studied by a phase diagram, with q on the vertical axis and K on the horizontal axis. The locus where $\dot{q} = 0$ is negatively sloped if $F''(K) < 0$; the locus where $\dot{K} = 0$ is positively sloped if $\delta > 0$. The point where the two meet identifies the steady state, and the system converges toward it along a negatively sloped saddlepath.

(b) For these functional forms, $F'(K) = a$, $F''(K) = 0$, $G'(I) = 1 + 2bI$. Hence, $\iota(q) = (q - 1)/(2b)$, and the dynamic equations are

$$\dot{K} = \frac{q-1}{2b} - \delta K, \qquad \dot{q} = (r + \delta)q - a.$$

The locus along which capital is constant,

$$(\dot{K} = 0) \quad \Rightarrow \quad q = 1 + 2b\delta K,$$

is positively sloped if $\delta > 0$, while

$$(\dot{q} = 0) \quad \Rightarrow \quad q = \frac{a}{r + \delta}$$

identifies a horizontal line: the shadow price of capital, given by the marginal present discounted (at rate $r + \delta$) contribution of capital to the firm's cash flow, is constant if $\partial^2 F(\cdot)/\partial K^2 = 0$, as is the case here. The saddlepath coincides with the $\dot{q} = 0$ locus, on which the system must stay throughout its convergent trajectory. In steady state, imposing $\dot{K} = 0$, we have

$$K_{ss} = \frac{1}{\delta} \frac{q-1}{2b} = \frac{a - (r + \delta)}{(r + \delta)2b\delta}.$$

The firm's capital stock is an increasing function of the difference between a (the marginal revenue product of capital) and $r + \delta$ (the financial and depreciation cost of each installed unit of capital). If $a > r + \delta$, the steady-state capital stock is finite provided that $b\delta > 0$. As the capital stock increases, in fact, an increasingly large investment flow per unit time is needed to offset depreciation. Since unit gross investment costs are increasing, in the long run the optimal capital stock is such that the benefits $a - (r + \delta)$ of an additional unit will be exactly offset by the higher marginal cost of investment needed to keep it constant. If $a < r + \delta$, revenues afforded by capital are smaller than its opportunity cost, and it is never optimal to invest. If $\delta \to 0$ (and also if $b \to 0$) the $\dot{K} = 0$ is horizontal, like the one where $\dot{q} = 0$, and the steady state is ill-defined: the expression above implies that K_{ss} tends to infinity if $a > r$, tends to minus infinity (or zero, in light of an obvious non-negativity constraint on capital) if $a < r$, and is not determined if $a = r$.

Solution to exercise 15

(a) It must be the case that cash flows are concave with respect to endogenous variables: $a > 0$, $\beta > 0$, $a + \beta \leq 1$, $G(\cdot)$ convex.

(b) The diagram is similar to that of Figure 2.5. Since there is no depreciation, the slope of the $\dot{K} = 0$ locus depends on how the capital stock affects the marginal cost of investment: if a given investment flow is less expensive when more capital is already installed, that is if

$$\frac{\partial^2 G(x, y)}{\partial x \partial y} < 0,$$

then the $\dot{K} = 0$ locus is negatively sloped. If it is steeper than the $\dot{q} = 0$ locus, then the system's dynamics will be globally unstable: when investing, the firm will reduce the cost of further investment so strongly as to more than offset the decline of capital's marginal revenue product. Dynamics are well-behaved if, instead, the $\dot{K} = 0$ schedule meets the $\dot{q} = 0$ from above, in which case a change of P_k relocates the $\dot{q} = 0$ schedule and q jumps on the new saddlepath. A higher P_k decreases K in the new steady state.

(c) As in exercise 10, a quadratic form for $G(\cdot)$ implies that investment is almost costless when it is very small. This is not realistic, and P_k represents the market price of capital net of adjustment costs only if the derivative of adjustment costs is unity at $\dot{K} = 0$. Cubic functional forms are not convex for $\dot{K} < 0$, implying that first-order conditions do not identify an optimum.

(d) As usual, the first-order condition is $g'(\dot{K}(0)) = \lambda(0)$. Since $R(\cdot)$ is linearly homogeneous and $G(\cdot)$ is independent of K, the shadow price of capital does not depend on future capital stocks, and is a convex function of the exogenous wage w:

$$\lambda(0) = \text{constant} \cdot \int_0^\infty e^{-rt} E_0 \left[(w(t))^{\frac{\beta}{\beta-1}} \right].$$

Larger values of ξ increase the variance of w over the period (from T to infinity) when it is positive from the standpoint of time 0. Thus, Jensen's inequality (as in Figure 2.11) associates a larger ξ with higher shadow values, and with larger investment flows between $t = 0$ and $t = T$.

Solution to exercise 16

(a) Cash flows are given by

$$F(t) = a\sqrt{K(t)} + \beta\sqrt{L(t)} - wL(t) - I - \frac{\gamma}{2}I^2,$$

and the optimality conditions are

$1 + \gamma I = \lambda$ (marginal investment cost = shadow price of capital),

$\dfrac{\beta}{2\sqrt{L}} = w$ (marginal revenue product of labor = wage), and

$$\dot{\lambda} - r\lambda = -\frac{a}{2\sqrt{K}} + \delta\lambda.$$

(Capital gains minus the opportunity cost of funds = depreciation costs minus the marginal revenue product of capital.)

Hence, dynamics are described by the

$$\dot{K} = \frac{\lambda - 1}{\gamma} - \delta K, \qquad \dot{\lambda} = (r + \delta)\lambda - \frac{a}{2\sqrt{K}}.$$

Graphically, this can be shown as follows:

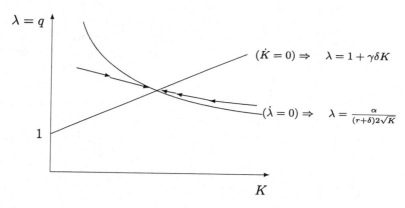

$$(\dot{K} = 0) \Rightarrow \quad \lambda = 1 + \gamma\delta K$$

$$(\dot{\lambda} = 0) \Rightarrow \quad \lambda = \frac{\alpha}{(r+\delta)2\sqrt{K}}$$

(b) Both $\dot{\lambda} = 0$ and $\dot{K} = 0$ move to the left, as shown in the figure.

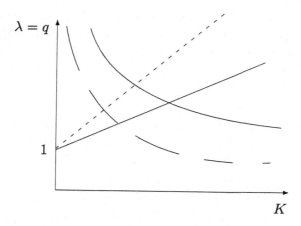

In the new steady state the capital stock is unambiguously smaller; intuitively, a higher marginal product is needed to offset the larger cost of a higher replacement investment flow. The effect on capital's shadow price and on the gross investment flow is ambiguous: in the graph, it depends on the slope of the two curves in the relevant region. Recall that λ is the present discounted value capital's contribution to the firm's revenues: in the new steady state, the latter is larger but it is more heavily discounted at rate $(r + \delta)$.

(c) For the functional form proposed, capital's marginal productivity is independent of L:

$$\frac{\partial Y}{\partial K \partial L} = \frac{\partial}{\partial L} \frac{-a}{2\sqrt{K}} = 0,$$

and therefore the cost w of factor L has no implications for the firm's investment policy. If instead the mixed second derivative is not zero then, as in Figure 2.8, capital's marginal productivity evaluated at the optimal $L^*(w)$ employment of factor L is a convex function of w, implying that variability of w will lead the firm to invest more.

Solution to exercise 17

(a) The dynamic first-order condition is

$$(r + \delta)q = \frac{dR(\cdot)}{dK} \frac{1}{P_k} + \dot{q},$$

or, with $(r + \delta) = 0.5$ and $dR(\cdot)/dK = 1 - K$,

$$0.5q = \frac{1 - K}{P_k} + \dot{q}.$$

The optimality condition for investment flows is $G'(I) = q$. In this exercise, $G'(I) = 1 + I$. Hence, $I = q - 1$, and optimal capital dynamics are described by

$$\dot{K} = q - 1 - 0.25K,$$

or graphically:

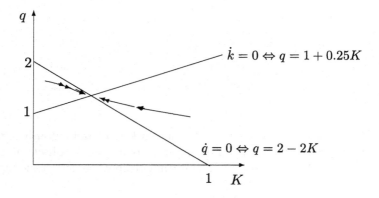

(b) If the price of capital is halved, the $\dot{q} = 0$ schedule rotates clockwise around its intersection with the horizontal axis, and q jumps onto the new saddlepath:

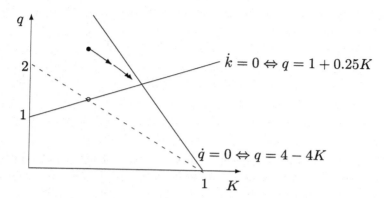

$$\dot{k} = 0 \Leftrightarrow q = 1 + 0.25K$$

$$\dot{q} = 0 \Leftrightarrow q = 4 - 4K$$

(c) From T onwards, the $\dot{q} = 0$ locus returns to its original position. (The combination of the subsidy and higher interest rate is exactly offset in the user cost of capital, and the marginal revenue product of capital is unaffected throughout.) Investment is initially lower than in the previous case: q jumps, but does not reach the saddlepath; its trajectory reaches and crosses the $\dot{k} = 0$ locus, and would diverge if parameters did not change again at T. At time T the original saddlepath is met, and the trajectory converges back to its starting point. The farther in the future is T, the longer-lasting is the investment increase; in the limit, as T goes to infinity the initial portion of the trajectory tends to coincide with the saddlepath:

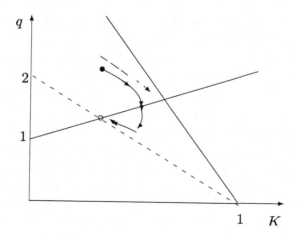

Solution to exercise 18

(a) The conditions requested are

$$K^{1/2}N^{-1/2} = w, \quad 1 + I = \lambda, \quad -K^{-1/2}N^{1/2} + \delta\lambda = -r\lambda + \dot{\lambda}.$$

(b) From $K^{1/2}N^{-1/2} = w$, we have $N = K/w^2$, hence

$$F(t) = 2K^{1/2}N^{1/2} - G(I) - wN = \frac{2}{w}K - G(I) - \frac{1}{w}K,$$

$$\lambda(0) = \int_0^\infty e^{-(r+\delta)t}\frac{\partial F(\cdot)}{\partial K(t)}dt = \int_0^\infty e^{-(r+\delta)t}\frac{1}{w(t)}dt.$$

(c) $\lambda = 1/[r + \delta)\bar{w}]$ is constant with respect to K. The form of adjustment costs and of the accumulation constraint imply that $I = \lambda - 1$ and that $\dot{K} = 0$ if $I = \delta K$, that is, if $\lambda = 1 + \delta K$ as shown in the figure.

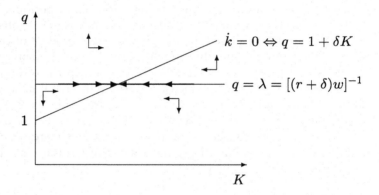

$$\dot{k} = 0 \Leftrightarrow q = 1 + \delta K$$

$$q = \lambda = [(r + \delta)w]^{-1}$$

(d) One would need to ensure that $G(\cdot)$ is linearly homogeneous in I and K. For example, one could assume that

$$G(I, K) = I + \frac{1}{2K}I^2.$$

Solution to exercise 19

Denote gross employment variations in period t by $\tilde{\Delta}N_t$: positive values of $\tilde{\Delta}N_t$ represent hiring at the beginning of period t, while negative values of $\tilde{\Delta}N_t$ represent firings at the end of period $t - 1$. Noting that effective employment at date t is given by $N_t = N_{t-1} + \tilde{\Delta}N_t - \delta N_{t-1}$, we have $\tilde{\Delta}N_t = \Delta N_t + \delta N_{t-1}$ for each t.

If turnover costs depend on hiring and layoffs but not on voluntary quits, we can rewrite the firm's objective function as

$$V_t = E_t \left[\sum_{i=0}^{\infty} \left(\frac{1}{1+r} \right)^i \left(R(Z_{t+i}, N_{t+i}) - w N_{t+i} - G(\Delta N_{t+i} + \delta N_t) \right) \right].$$

Introducing a parameter with the same role as P_k, that is multiplying $G(\cdot)$ by a constant, influences the magnitude of the hiring and firing costs in relation to the flow revenue $R(\cdot)$ and the salary $w_t N_t$. Such a constant of proportionality is not interpretable like the "price" of labor. Each unit of the factor N is in fact paid a flow wage w_t, rather than a *stock* payment; for this reason, the slope of the original function $G(\cdot)$ is zero rather than one, as in the preceding chapter.

In the problem we consider here, the wage plays a role similar to that of user cost of capital in Chapter 2. To formulate these two problems in a similar fashion, we need to assume that workers can be bought and sold at a unique price which is equivalent to the present discounted value of future earnings of each worker. One case in which it is easy to verify the equivalence between the flow and the stock payments is when the salary, the discount rate, and the layoff rate are constant: since only a fraction equal to $e^{-(r+\delta)(\tau-t)}$ of the labor force employed at date t is not yet laid off at date τ, the present value of the wage paid to each worker is given by

$$\int_t^{\infty} w e^{-(r+\delta)(\tau-t)} d\tau = \frac{w}{r+\delta}.$$

The role of this quantity is the same as the price of capital P_k in the study of investments, and, as we mentioned, the wage w coincides with the user cost of capital $(r + \delta) P_k$. The formal analogy between investments and the "purchase" and "sale" of workers—which remains valid if the salary and the other variables are time-varying—obviously does not have practical relevance except in the case of slavery.

Solution to exercise 20

To compare these two expressions, remember that

$$\dot{\lambda} = [\lambda(t + dt) - \lambda(t)]/dt \approx [\lambda(t + \Delta t) - \lambda(t)]/\Delta t$$

for a finite Δt. Assuming $\Delta t = 1$, we get a discrete-time version of the optimality condition for the case of the Hamiltonian method,

$$r \lambda_t = \frac{\partial R(\cdot)}{\partial K} + \lambda_{t+1} - \lambda_t,$$

or alternatively

$$\lambda_t = \frac{1}{1+r} \frac{\partial R(\cdot)}{\partial K} + \frac{1}{1+r} \lambda_{t+1}.$$

This expression is very similar to (3.5). It differs in three aspects that are easy to interpret. First of all, the operator $E_t[\cdot]$ will obviously be redundant in (3.5) in which by assumption there is no uncertainty. Secondly, the discrete-time expression applies a discount rate to the marginal cash flow, but this factor is arbitrarily close to one in continuous time (where $dt = 0$ would replace $\Delta t = 1$). Finally, the two relationships differ also as regards the specification of the cash flow itself, in that only (3.5) deducts the salary w from the marginal revenue. This difference occurs because labor is rewarded in flow terms. (The shadow value of labor therefore does not contain any resale value, as is the case with capital.)

Solution to exercise 21

If both functions are horizontal lines, the shadow value of labor will not depend on the employment level. Without loss of generality, we can then write

$$\mu(N, Z_g) = Z_g, \qquad \mu(N, Z_b) = Z_b,$$

and calculate the shadow values in the two possible situations. In the case considered here, (3.5) implies that

$$\lambda_g = \mu_g - w + \frac{1}{1+r}((1-p)\lambda_g + p\lambda_b),$$

$$\lambda_b = \mu_b - w + \frac{1}{1+r}((1-p)\lambda_b + p\lambda_g),$$

a system of two linear equations in two unknowns whose solution is

$$\lambda_b = \frac{1+r}{r}\frac{(r+p)\mu_b + p\mu_g}{r+2p} - w, \qquad \lambda_g = \frac{1+r}{r}\frac{(r+p)\mu_g + p\mu_b}{r+2p} - w.$$

These two expressions are simply the expected discounted values of the excess of productivity (marginal and average) over the wage rate of each worker. In the absence of hiring and firing costs, the firm will choose either an infinitely large or a zero employment level, depending on which of the two shadow values is non-zero. On the contrary, if the costs of hiring and firing are positive, it is possible that

$$-F < \lambda_D < \lambda_F < H,$$

and thus that, as a result of (3.6), the firm will find it optimal not to vary the employment level. If only one marginal productivity is constant, then it may be optimal for the firm to hire and fire workers in such a way that the first-order conditions hold with equality:

$$\mu(N_g, Z_g) = w + p\frac{F}{1+r}$$

and

$$Z_b = w - (r + p)\frac{F}{1 + r}$$

can be satisfied simultaneously only if the second condition (in which all variables are exogenous) holds by assumption. In this case, the first condition can be solved as

$$N_g = \frac{1}{\beta}\left(Z_g - \beta w - p\frac{F}{1 + r}\right).$$

As in many other economic applications, strict concavity of the objective function is essential to obtain an interior solution.

Solution to exercise 22

Subtracting the two equations in (3.9) term by term yields an expression for the difference between the two possible marginal productivities of labor:

$$\mu(N_g, Z_g) - \mu(N_b, Z_b) = (r + 2p)\frac{H + F}{1 + r}.$$

This expression is valid under the assumption that the firm hires and fires workers upon every change of the exogenous conditions represented by Z_t. However, H and F can be so large, relative to variations in demand for labor, that the expression is satisfied only when $N_b > N_g$, as in the figure.

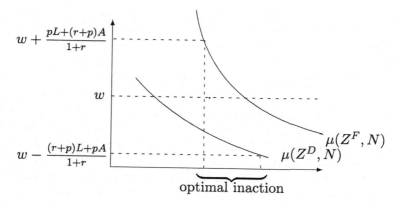

Such an allocation is clearly not feasible: if $N_b > N_g$, the firm will need to fire workers whenever it faces an increase in demand, violating the assumptions under which we derived (3.9) and the equation above. (In fact, the formal solution involves the paradoxical cases of "negative firing," and "negative hiring," with the receipt rather than the payment of *turnover* costs!). Hence, the firm is willing to remain completely inactive, with employment equal to any level within the inaction region in the figure. It is still true that employment takes only two values, but, these values coincide and they are completely determined by the initial conditions.

Solution to exercise 23

A trigonometric function, such as $\sin(\cdot)$, repeats itself every $\pi = 3.1415\ldots$ units of time; hence, the $Z(\tau)$ process has a cycle lasting p periods. If $p = $ one year, the proposed perfectly cyclical behavior of revenues might be a stylized model of a firm in a seasonal industry, for example a ski resort. If the firm aims at maximizing its value, then

$$V_t = \int_t^{\infty} (R(L(\tau), Z(\tau)) - wL(\tau) - C(\dot{X}(\tau))\dot{X}(\tau))e^{-r(\tau-t)}d\tau,$$

where $r > 0$ is the rate of discount and $R(\cdot)$ is the given revenue function. Then with $\partial R(\cdot)/\partial L = M(\cdot)$ as given in the exercise, optimality requires that

$$-f \le \int_t^{\infty} (M(L(\tau), Z(\tau)) - w)\,e^{-r(\tau-t)}d\tau \le h$$

for all t: as in the model discussed in the chapter, the value of marginal changes in employment can never be larger than the cost of hiring, or more negative than the cost of firing. Further, and again in complete analogy to the discussion in the text, if the firm is hiring or firing, equality must obtain in that relationship: if $\dot{X}_t < 0$,

$$-f = \int_t^{\infty} (M(L(\tau), Z(\tau)) - w)\,e^{-r(\tau-t)}d\tau, \qquad (*)$$

and if $\dot{X}_t > 0$,

$$\int_t^{\infty} (M(L(\tau), Z(\tau)) - w)\,e^{-r(\tau-t)}d\tau = h. \qquad (**)$$

Each complete cycle goes through a segment of time when the firm is hiring and a segment of time when the firm is firing (unless turnover costs are so large, relative to the amplitude of labor demand fluctuations, as to make inaction optimal at all times). Within each such interval the optimality equations hold with equality, and using Leibnitz's rule to differentiate the relevant integral with respect to the lower limit of integration yields local Euler equations in the form

$$M(L(t), Z(t)) - w = r\,C(\dot{L}(t)).$$

Inverting the functional form given in the exercise, the level of employment is

$$\left(\left(K_1 + K_2 \sin\left(\frac{2\pi}{p}\tau\right) \right) / (w - rf) \right)^{1/\beta}$$

whenever τ is such that the firm is firing, and

$$\left(\left(K_1 + K_2 \sin\left(\frac{2\pi}{p}\tau\right)\right)/(w+rh)\right)^{1/\beta}$$

whenever τ is such that the firm is hiring. If $h + f > 0$, however, there must also be periods when the firm neither hires nor fires: specifically, inaction must be optimal around both the peaks and troughs of the sine function. (Otherwise, some labor would be hired and immediately fired, or fired and immediately hired, and $h + f$ per unit would be paid with no counteracting benefits in continuous time.) To determine the optimal length of the inaction period following the hiring period, suppose time t is the last instant in the hiring period, and denote with T the first time after t that firing is optimal at that same employment level: then, it must be the case that

$$L(t) = \left(\frac{K_1 + K_2 \sin\left(\frac{2\pi}{p}t\right)}{w + rh}\right)^{1/\beta} = \left(\frac{K_1 + K_2 \sin\left(\frac{2\pi}{p}T'\right)}{w - rf}\right)^{1/\beta}.$$

This is one equation in T and t. Another can be obtained inserting the given functional forms into equations (*) and (**), recognizing that the former applies at T and the latter at t, and rearranging:

$$\int_t^T e^{-r(\tau-t)}\left[\left(K_1 + K_2 \sin\left(\frac{2\pi}{p}\tau\right)\right)(L(t))^{-\beta} - w\right]d\tau = h + fe^{-r(T'-t)}.$$

The integral can be solved using the formula

$$\int e^{\lambda x}\sin(\gamma x)\,dx = \frac{\lambda e^{\lambda x}}{\gamma^2 + \lambda^2}\left(\sin(\gamma x) - \frac{\gamma}{\lambda}\cos(\gamma x)\right),$$

but both the resulting expression and the other relevant equation are highly nonlinear in t and T', which therefore can be determined only numerically. See Bertola (1992) for a similar discussion of optimality around the cyclical trough, expressions allowing for labor "depreciation" (costless quits), sample numerical solutions, and analytical results and qualitative discussion for more general specifications.

Solution to exercise 24

Denoting by $\eta(t) \equiv Z(t)L(t)^{-\beta}$ labor's marginal revenue product, the shadow value of employment (the expected discounted cash flow contribution of a marginal unit of labor) may be written

$$\lambda(t) = \int_t^\infty E_t[\eta(\tau) - w]e^{-(r+\delta)(\tau-t)}d\tau,$$

and, by the usual argument, an optimal employment policy should never let it exceed zero (since hiring is costless) or fall short of $-F$ (the cost of firing a unit of labor). Hence, the optimality conditions have the form $-F \leq \lambda(t) \leq 0$ for all t, $-F = \lambda(t)$ if the firm fires at t, $\lambda(t) = 0$ if the firm hires at t.

In order to make the solution explicit, it is useful to define a function returning the discounted expectation of future marginal revenue products along the optimal employment path,

$$v(\eta(t)) \equiv \int_t^{\infty} E_t[\eta(\tau)]e^{-(r+\delta)(\tau-t)}d\tau = \lambda(t) + \frac{w}{r+\delta}.$$

This function depends on $\eta(t)$, as written, only if the marginal revenue product process is Markov in levels. Here this is indeed the case, because in the absence of hiring or firing we can use the stochastic differentiation rule introduced in Section 2.7 to establish that, at all times when the firm is neither hiring nor firing,

$$d\eta(t) = d[Z(t)L(t)^{-\beta}]$$

$$= L(t)^{-\beta}dZ(t) - \beta Z(t)L(t)^{-\beta-1}dL(t)$$

$$= L(t)^{-\beta}[\theta Z(t)\,dt + \sigma Z(t)\,dW(t)] + \beta Z(t)L(t)^{-\beta-1}\delta L(t)$$

$$= \eta(t)(\theta + \beta\delta)\,dt + \eta(t)\sigma\,dW(t)$$

is Markov in levels (a geometric Brownian motion), and we can proceed to show that optimal hiring and firing depend only on the current level of $\eta(t)$, hence preserving the Markov character of the process. In fact, we can use the stochastic differentiation rule again and apply it to the integral in the definition of $v(\cdot)$ to obtain a differential equation,

$$(r+\delta)v(\eta) = \eta + \frac{1}{dt}\left(\frac{\partial v(\cdot)}{\partial \eta}E(d\eta) + \frac{\partial^2 v(\cdot)}{\partial \eta^2}(d\eta)^2\right)$$

$$= \eta + \frac{\partial v(\cdot)}{\partial \eta}\eta(\theta + \beta\delta) + \frac{\partial^2 v(\cdot)}{\partial \eta^2}\eta^2\sigma^2,$$

with solutions in the form

$$v(\eta) = \frac{\eta}{r - \theta - \delta\beta} + K_1\eta^{\alpha_1} + K_2\eta^{\alpha_2},$$

where α_1 and α_2 are the two solutions of the quadratic characteristic equation (see Section 2.7 for its derivation in a similar context) and K_1, K_2 are constants of integration. These two constants, and the critical levels of the $\eta(t)$ process that trigger hiring and firing, can be determined by inserting the $v(\cdot)$ function in the two first-order and two smooth-pasting conditions that must be satisfied at all times when the firm is hiring or firing. (See Section 2.7 for a definition and interpretation of the smooth-pasting conditions, and Bentolila and Bertola (1990) for further and more detailed derivations and numerical solutions.)

Solution to exercise 25

It is again useful to consider the case where $r = 0$, so that (3.16) holds: if $H = -F$, and thus $H + F = 0$, then wages and marginal productivity are equal in every period, and the optimal hiring and firing policies of the firm coincide with those that are valid if there are no adjustment costs. The combination of firing costs and identical hiring subsidies does have an effect when $r > 0$. Using the condition $H + F = 0$ in (3.9), we find that the marginal productivity of labor in each period is set equal to $w + rH/(1 + r) = w - rF/(1 + r)$. Intuitively, the moment a firm hires a worker, it deducts $rH/(1 + r)$ from the flow wage, which is equivalent to the return if it invests the subsidy H in an alternative asset, and which the firm needs to pay if it decides to fire the worker at some future time.

If $H + F < 0$, then *turnover* generates income rather than costs, and the optimal solution will degenerate: a firm can earn infinite profits by hiring and firing infinite amounts of labor in each period.

Solution to exercise 26

Specializing equation (3.15) to the case proposed, we obtain

$$\frac{1}{2}(f(Z_g) + \beta(N_g) + g(Z_b) + \beta(N_b)) = w,$$

or, alternatively,

$$\frac{1}{2}(\beta(N_g) + \beta(N_b)) = w - \frac{1}{2}(f(Z_g) + g(Z_b)).$$

The term on the right does not depend on N_g and N_b, and hence is independent of the magnitude of the employment fluctuations (which in turn are determined by the optimal choices of the firm in the presence of hiring and firing costs). We can therefore write

$$E[\beta(N)] = \text{constant} = \beta(E[N]) + \xi,$$

where, by Jensen's inequality, ξ is positive if $\beta(\cdot)$ is a convex function, and negative if $\beta(\cdot)$ is a concave function. In both cases ξ is larger the more N varies. Combining the last two equations to find the expected value of employment, we have

$$E[N] = \beta^{-1} \left(w - \frac{1}{2}(f(Z_g) + g(Z_b) + 2\xi) \right),$$

where $\beta^{-1}(\cdot)$, the inverse of $\beta(\cdot)$, is decreasing. We can therefore conclude that, if $\beta(\cdot)$ is a convex function, the less pronounced variation of employment when hiring and firing costs are larger is associated with a lower average employment level. The reverse is true if $\beta(\cdot)$ is concave.

Solution to exercise 27

Since we are not interested in the effects of H, we assume that $H = 0$. The optimality conditions

$$Z_g - \beta N_g = w + p\frac{g}{1+r},$$

$$Z_b - \gamma N_b = w - (r + p)\frac{g}{1+r},$$

imply

$$N_g = \frac{1}{\beta}\left(Z_g - w - p\frac{g}{1+r}\right),$$

$$N_b = \frac{1}{\gamma}\left(Z_b - w + (r + p)\frac{g}{1+r}\right),$$

and thus

$$\frac{N_g + N_b}{2} = \frac{1}{2\beta\gamma}\left[\gamma\left(Z_g - w - p\frac{F}{1+r}\right) + \beta\left(Z_b - w + (r + p)\frac{F}{1+r}\right)\right]$$

$$= \frac{\gamma Z_g + \beta Z_b - (\gamma + \beta)w}{2\beta\gamma} + \frac{\beta - \gamma}{2\beta\gamma}\frac{pF}{1+r} + \frac{\beta}{2\beta\gamma}\frac{rF}{1+r}.$$

The first term on the right-hand side of the last expression denotes the average employment level if $F = 0$; the effect of $F > 0$ is positive in the last term if $r > 0$, but since $\beta < \gamma$ the second term is negative. As we saw in exercise 21, the limit case with $\gamma = 0$ is not well defined unless the exogenous variables satisfy a certain condition. It is therefore not possible to analyze the effects of a variation of g that is not associated with variations in other parameters.

Solution to exercise 28

In (3.17), p determines the speed of convergence of the current value of P to its long-run value. If $p = 0$, there is no convergence. (In fact, the initial conditions remain valid indefinitely.) Writing

$$P_{t+1} = p + (1 - 2p)P_t,$$

we see that the initial distribution is completely irrelevant if $p = 0.5$; the probability distribution of each firm is immediately equal to P_∞, and also the frequency distribution of a large group of firms converges immediately to its long-run stable equivalent.

Solution to exercise 29

As in the symmetric case, we consider the variation of the proportion P of firms in state F:

$$P_{t+1} - P_t = p(1 - P_t) - q P_t = p - (q + p)P_t = p \left(1 - \frac{q + p}{p} P_t \right).$$

This expression is positive if $P_t < p/(q + p)$, negative if $P_t > p/(q + p)$, and zero if P_t corresponds to $P_\infty = p/(q + p)$, the stable proportion of firms in state F. Intuitively, if $p > q$ (if the entry rate into the strong state is higher than the exit rate out of this state), then in the long run the strong state is more likely than the weak state.

Solution to exercise 30

(a) Marginal productivity of labor is

$$\frac{\partial}{\partial l} F(k, l; a) = a - \beta l.$$

When $a = 4$ and the firm is hiring, employment is the solution x of

$$4 - \beta x = 1 + \frac{pF}{1 + r};$$

therefore, with $r = F = 1$ and $p = 0.5$, the solution is $11/4\beta = 2.75/\beta$. When $a = 2$ and the firm fires, it employs x such that

$$2 - \beta x = 1 - \frac{(p + r)F}{1 + r},$$

so employment is $7/4\beta = 1.75/\beta$.

(b) Employment is not affected by capital adjustment for this production function because it is separable; i.e., the marginal product of (and demand for) one factor does not depend on the level of the other. The marginal product of capital is $a - \gamma k$, so setting it equal to $r + \delta = 2$ yields

$$4 - \gamma k = 2 \Rightarrow k = 2/\gamma$$

when $a_t = 4$ and

$$2 - \gamma k = 2 \Rightarrow k = 0$$

when $a_t = 2$.

Solution to exercise 31

(a) The optimality conditions of the firm, analogous to (3.9), are

$$Z_g - \beta N_g = w_g + p\frac{F}{1+r} + (r+p)\frac{H}{1+r},$$

$$Z_b - \beta N_b = w_b - (r+p)\frac{F}{1+r} - p\frac{H}{1+r},$$

from which we obtain

$$N_g = \left(Z_g - w_g - \frac{pF + (r+p)H}{1+r}\right)\frac{1}{\beta},$$

$$N_b = \left(Z_b - w_b + \frac{(r+p)F + pH}{1+r}\right)\frac{1}{\beta}.$$

(b) We know that workers are indifferent between moving and staying if (3.24) holds, that is if, $w_g - w_b = \kappa(2p+r)/(1+r)$. Hence, the given wage differential is an equilibrium phenomenon if the mobility costs for workers are equal to

$$\kappa = \frac{1+r}{2p+r}\Delta w.$$

(c) Given that $\Delta w = \kappa(2p+r)/(1+r)$, and that $w_F = w_b + \Delta w$, we have

$$N_g = \left(Z_g - w_b - \kappa\frac{2p+r}{1+r} - \frac{pF + (r+p)H}{1+r}\right)\frac{1}{\beta},$$

and the full-employment condition $50N_g + 50N_b = 1000$ can therefore be written

$$50\left(Z_g - w_b - \kappa\frac{2p+r}{1+r} - \frac{pF + (r+p)H}{1+r}\right)\frac{1}{\beta}$$

$$+ 50\left(Z_b - w_b + \frac{(r+p)F + pH}{1+r}\right)\frac{1}{\beta} = 1000.$$

Hence the wage rate needs to be

$$w_b = \frac{1}{2}(Z_g + Z_b) - 10\beta - \frac{1}{2}\frac{\kappa(2p+r) + (H-F)r}{1+r}.$$

Solution to exercise 32

Denote the optimal employment levels by N_b and N_g. Noting that $\lambda(Z_g, N_g) = H$ and $\lambda(Z_b, N_b) = -F$, the dynamic optimality conditions are given by

$$H = \pi(Z_g, N_g) - \bar{w} + \frac{1}{1+r} \frac{H - F + \lambda_{(M,G)}}{3},$$

$$-L = \pi(Z_b, N_b) - \bar{w} + \frac{1}{1+r} \frac{H - F + \lambda_{(M,B)}}{3}.$$

In both cases the shadow value of labor is equal to the current marginal cash flow plus the expected discounted shadow value in the next period. The latter is equal to H or to $-F$ in the two cases in which the firm decides to hire or fire workers; and it will be equal to $\lambda_{(.)}$ such that it is optimal not to react if labor demand in the next period takes the mean value. To characterize this shadow value, consider that if $Z_{t+1} = Z_M$—so that inactivity is effectively optimal— then the shadow value $\lambda_{(M,G)}$ satisfies

$$\lambda_{(M,G)} = \mu(Z_M, N_g) - \bar{w} + \frac{1}{1+r} \frac{H - F + \lambda_{(M,G)}}{3}$$

if the last action of the firm was to hire a worker, while the shadow value $\lambda_{(M,B)}$ satisfies

$$\lambda_{(M,B)} = \mu(Z_M, N_b) - \bar{w} + \frac{1}{1+r} \frac{H - F + \lambda_{(M,B)}}{3}$$

if the last action of the firm was to fire workers. The last four equations can be solved for N_g, N_b, $\lambda_{(M,G)}$, and $\lambda_{(M,B)}$. Under the hypothesis that $\mu(Z, N)$ is linear, we obtain

$$N_b = \frac{1}{\beta}\left(Z_b - \bar{w} + L + \frac{1}{1+r}\frac{Z_M - Z_b + H - 2F}{3}\right),$$

$$N_g = \frac{1}{\beta}\left(Z_g - \bar{w} - A + \frac{1}{1+r}\frac{Z_M - Z_g + 2H - F}{3}\right),$$

and the solutions for the two shadow values, which need to satisfy

$$-F < \lambda_{(M,B)} < H, \qquad -F < \lambda_{(M,G)} < H$$

if, as we assumed, the parameters are such that it is optimal for the firm not to react if the realization of labor demand is at the intermediate value.

Solution to exercise 33

Since $\dot{k} = sf(k) - \delta k$,

$$\frac{\dot{Y}}{Y} = \frac{f'(k)\dot{k}}{f(k)} = f'(k)\left(s - \delta\frac{k}{f(k)}\right).$$

The condition $\lim_{k\to\infty} f'(k) > 0$ is no longer sufficient to allow a positive growth rate: also, the limit of the second term, which defines the proportional growth rate of output, needs to be strictly positive. This is the case if $\delta \lim_{k\to\infty}(k/f(k)) < s$. If both capital and output grow indefinitely, the limit required is a ratio between two infinitely large quantities. Provided that the limit is well defined, it can be calculated, by l'Hôpital's rule, as the ratio of the limits of the numerator's derivative—which is unity—and of the denominator's derivative—which is $f'(k)$, and tends to b. Hence, for positive growth in the limit is necessary that

$$\lim_{k\to\infty} f'(k) = b > \frac{\delta}{s} > 0.$$

When a fraction s of income is saved and capital depreciates at rate δ, we get

$$\lim_{k\to\infty} \frac{\dot{Y}}{Y} = b\left(s - \frac{\delta}{b}\right) = bs - \delta.$$

Solution to exercise 34

If $\lambda \le 0$, capital and labor cannot be substituted easily: no output can be produced without an input of L. In fact, the equation that defines factor combinations yielding a given output level,

$$\bar{Y} = (aK^\lambda + (1-a)L^\lambda)^{1/\lambda},$$

allows $\bar{Y} > 0$ for $L = 0$ only if $\lambda > 0$. In that case, the accumulation of capital can sustain indefinite growth of the economy: the non-accumulated factor L may substitute capital, but output can continue to grow even if the ratio L/K tends to zero.

These particular examples both assume that $\delta = g = 0$, and we know already that indefinite growth is feasible if the marginal product of capital has a strictly positive limit. If $\lambda = 1$, the production function is linear, i.e.

$$F(K, L) = aK + aL, \qquad f(k) - ak(1-a),$$

and the requested growth rates are

$$\frac{\dot{y}}{y} = \frac{a\dot{k}}{y} = as, \qquad \frac{\dot{k}}{k} = s\frac{ak + (1-a)}{k} = sa + \frac{1-a}{k}.$$

The growth rate of output equals as, which is constant if agents consume a constant fraction s of income. Capital, on the other hand, grows at a decreasing rate which approaches the same value as only asymptotically.

The case in which $a = 1$ is even simpler: since $y = k$, the growth rate of both capital and output is always equal to s.

Solution to exercise 35

As in the main text, we continue to assume that the welfare of an individual depends on *per capita* consumption, $c(t) \equiv C(t)/N(t)$. However, when the population grows at rate g_N we need to consider the welfare of a representative *household* rather than that of a representative individual. If welfare is given by the sum of the utility function of the $N(t) = N(0)e^{g_N t}$ individuals alive at date t, objective function (4.10) becomes

$$U' = \int_0^\infty u(c(t))N(t)e^{-\rho t}\, dt = \int_0^\infty u(c(t))N(0)e^{-\rho' t}\, dt,$$

where $\rho' \equiv \rho - g_N$: a higher growth rate of the population reduces the impatience of the representative agent. With $g_A = 0$, and normalizing $A(t) = A(0) = 1$, the law of motion for *per capita* capital $k(t)$ is

$$\frac{d}{dt}\frac{K(t)}{N(t)} = \frac{Y(t) - C(t) - \delta K(t)}{N(t)} - \frac{K(t)\dot{N}(t)}{N(t)^2}$$

$$= f(k(t)) - c(t) - (\delta + g_N)k(t).$$

The first-order conditions associated with the Hamiltonian are

$$H(t) = [u(c(t)) + \lambda(t)(f(k(t)) - c(t) - (\delta + g_N)k(t))]e^{-\rho' t}.$$

Using similar techniques as in the main text, we obtain

$$\dot{c} = \left(\frac{u'(c)}{-u''(c)}\right)(f'(k) - (\delta + g_N) - \rho') = \left(\frac{u'(c)}{-u''(c)}\right)(f'(k) - \delta - \rho).$$

The dynamics of the system are similar to those studied in the main text, and tend to a steady state where

$$f'(k_{ss}) = \rho + \delta, \qquad 0 = f(k_{ss}) - c_{ss} - (\delta + g_N)k_{ss}.$$

The capital stock does not maximize *per capita* consumption in the steady state: in each possible steady state $\dot{k} = 0$ needs to be satisfied; that is,

$$c_{ss} = f(k_{ss}) - (\delta + g_N)k_{ss}.$$

The second derivative of the right-hand expression is $f''(\cdot) < 0$. The maximum of the steady state per capita stock of capital is therefore obtained at a value k^* at which the first derivative is equal to zero so that

$$f'(k^*) = \delta + g_N.$$

Hence $f'(k_{ss}) > f'(k^*)$ if $g_N < \rho$, which is a necessary condition to have $\rho' > 0$ and to have a well defined optimization problem. From this, and from the fact that $f''(\cdot) < 0$, we have $k^* > k_{ss}$. The economy evolves not toward the capital stock that maximizes *per capita* consumption (the so-called *golden rule*), but to a steady state with a lower consumption level. In fact, given that the economy needs an indefinite time period to reach the steady state, it would make sense to maximize consumption only if ρ' were equal to zero, that is, if a delay of consumption to the future were not costly in itself. On the other hand, when agents have a positive rate of time preference, which is needed for the problem to be meaningful, then the optimal path is characterized by a higher level of consumption in the immediate future and a convergence to a steady state with $k_{ss} < k^*$.

Solution to exercise 36

Denote the length of a period by Δt (which was normalized to one in Chapter 1), and refer to time via a subscript rather than an argument between parentheses: let r_t denote the interest rate per time period (for instance on an annual basis) valid in the period between t and $t + \Delta t$; moreover, let y_t and c_t denote the flows of income and consumption in the same period but again measured on an annual basis. Finally let A_t be the wealth at the beginning of the period $[t, t + \Delta t]$. Hence, we have the discrete-time budget constraint

$$A_{t+\Delta t} = \left(1 + r_t \frac{\Delta t}{n}\right)^n A_t + (y_t - c_t)\Delta t.$$

Interest payments are made in each of the n subperiods of Δt. Moreover, in each of the subperiods of length $\Delta t/n$, an amount $r_t \Delta t/n$ of interest is received which immediately starts to earn interest. If n tends to infinity,

$$\lim_{n \to \infty} \left(1 + \frac{r_t \Delta t}{n}\right)^n = e^{r_t \Delta t}.$$

Therefore

$$A_{t+\Delta t} = e^{r_t \Delta t} A_t + (y_t - c_t)\Delta t.$$

Rewriting the first-order condition in discrete time denoting the length of the discrete period by $\Delta t > 0$, we have

$$u'(c_t) = \left(\frac{1+r}{1+\rho}\right)^{\Delta t} u'(c_{t+\Delta t}).$$

Recognizing that $(1 + r)^{\Delta t} \approx e^{(s-t)\Delta t}$ and imposing $s = t + \Delta t$, we get

$$u'(c_t) = e^{r(s-t)} e^{-\rho(s-t)} u'(c_s).$$

We can rewrite this expression as

$$\frac{u'(c_t)}{e^{-\rho(s-t)} u'(c_s)} = e^{r(s-t)},$$

which equates the marginal rate of substitution, the left-hand side of the expression, to the marginal rate of substitution between the resources available at times t and s. Isolating any two periods, we obtain the familiar conditions for the optimality of consumption and savings, that is the equality between the slope of the indifference curve and of the budget restriction. In continuous time, this condition needs to be satisfied for any t and s: hence, along the optimal consumption path we have (differentiating with respect to s)

$$-\frac{u'(c_t)}{(e^{-\rho(s-t)}u'(c_s))^2}\left(e^{-\rho(s-t)}\frac{du'(c_s)}{ds} - \rho e^{-\rho(s-t)}u'(c_s)\right) = re^{r(s-t)}.$$

In the limit, with $s \to t$, we get

$$-\frac{1}{u'(c_t)}\left(\frac{du'(c_t)}{dt} - \rho u'(c_t)\right) = r,$$

or, equivalently,

$$-\left(\frac{du'(c_t)}{dt}\right) = (r - \rho)u'(c_t).$$

Given that the marginal utility of consumption $u'(c_t)$ equals the shadow value of wealth λ_t, this relation corresponds to the Hamiltonian conditions for dynamic optimality. Differentiating with respect to Δt and letting Δt tend to 0, we get

$$\frac{dc_t}{dt} = \left(-\frac{u'(c_t)}{u''(c_t)}\right)(r - \rho).$$

In the presence of a variation of the interest rate r (or, more precisely, in the differential $r - \rho$), the consumer changes the intertemporal path of her consumption by an amount equal to the (positive) quantity in large parentheses: this is the reciprocal of the well-known Arrow–Pratt measure of *absolute* risk aversion. As we noted in Chapter 1, the more concave the utility function, the less willing the consumer will be to alter the intertemporal pattern of consumption. With regard to the cumulative budget constraint, we can write

$$\frac{A_{t+\Delta t} - A_t}{\Delta t} = \frac{(e^{r_t\Delta t} - 1)}{\Delta t}A_t + (y_t - c_t)$$

and evaluate the limit of this expression for $\Delta t \to 0$:

$$\lim_{\Delta t \to 0}\frac{A_{t+\Delta t} - A_t}{\Delta t} = \lim_{\Delta t \to 0}\frac{(e^{r_t\Delta t} - 1)}{\Delta t}A_t + (y_t - c_t).$$

On the left we have the definition of the derivative of A_t with respect to time. Since both the denominator and the numerator in the first term on the right are zero in $\Delta t = 0$, we need to apply l'Hôpital's rule to evaluate this limit. This gives

$$\frac{d}{dt}A_t = \lim_{\Delta t \to 0}\frac{(r_t e^{r_t\Delta t})}{1}A_t + (y_t - c_t)$$

or, in the notation in continuous time adopted in this chapter,

$$\dot{A}(t) = r(t)A(t) + y(t) - c(t),$$

which is a constraint, in flow terms, that needs to be satisfied for each t. This law of motion for wealth relates $A(t), r(t), c(t), y(t)$ which are all functions of the continuous variable t. The summation of ($\overset{??}{}$) obviously corresponds to an integral in continuous time. Suppose for simplicity that the interest rate is constant, i.e. $r(t) = r$ for each t, and multiply both terms in the above expression by e^{-rt}; we then get

$$e^{-rt}\dot{A}(t) - re^{-rt}A(t) = e^{-rt}(y(t) - c(t)).$$

Since the term on the left-hand side is the derivative of the product of e^{-rt} and $A(t)$, we can write

$$\frac{d}{dt}(e^{-rt}A(t)) = e^{-rt}(y(t) - c(t)).$$

It is therefore easy to evaluate the integral of the term on the left:

$$\int_0^t \frac{d}{dt}(e^{-rt}A(t))\, dt = [e^{-rt}A(t)]_0^T = e^{-rT}A(T) - A(0).$$

Equating this to the integral of the term on the right, we get

$$e^{-rT}A(T) = A(0) + \int_0^T e^{-rt}(y(t) - c(t))\, dt. \tag{5.A1}$$

If we let T tend to infinity, and if we impose the continuous-time version of the *no-Ponzi-game condition* (1.3), i.e.

$$\lim_{T\to\infty} e^{-rT}A(T) = 0,$$

we finally arrive at the budget condition for an infinitely lived consumer who takes consumption and savings decisions in each infinitesimally small time period:

$$\int_0^\infty e^{-rt}c(t) = A(0) + \int_0^\infty e^{-rt}y(t)\, dt.$$

Solution to exercise 37

If $\dot{K}/K = \dot{A}/A + \dot{N}/N = \dot{L}/L$, then $k \equiv K/L$ is constant. The rate r at which capital is remunerated is given by

$$\frac{\partial F(K,L)}{\partial K} = \frac{\partial [LF(K/L, 1)]}{\partial K} = f'(K/L),$$

and is constant if K and L grow at the same rate. Moreover, because of constant returns to scale, production grows at the same rate as K (and L), and the income share of capital rK/Y is thus constant along a balanced growth path, even if the production function is not Cobb–Douglas.

Solution to exercise 38

The production function

$$F(K, L) = (aK^\lambda + (1 - a)L^\lambda)^{1/\lambda}$$

exhibits constant returns to scale and the marginal productivity of capital has a strictly positive limit if $\lambda > 0$, as we saw on page 150. The income share of labor L is given by

$$
\begin{aligned}
\frac{\partial F(K, L)}{\partial L} \frac{L}{F(K, L)} &= \frac{[aK^\lambda + (1 - a)L^\lambda]^{(1-\lambda)/\lambda}(1 - a)L^{\lambda-1}L}{[aK^\lambda + (1 - a)L^\lambda]^{1/\lambda}} \\
&= [aK^\lambda + (1 - a)L^\lambda]^{-1}(1 - a)L^\lambda \\
&= \left[a\left(\frac{K}{L}\right)^\lambda + (1 - a)L^\lambda \right]^{-1} (1 - a), \qquad (5.\text{A}2)
\end{aligned}
$$

which tends to zero with the growth of K/L if $\lambda > 0$.

Solution to exercise 39

In terms of actual parameters, the Solow residual may be expressed as

$$\frac{\dot{A}}{A} + \mu a \left(\frac{\dot{N}}{N} - \frac{\dot{K}}{K}\right) + (a + \beta - 1)\frac{\dot{K}}{K}.$$

This measure may therefore be an overestimate or an underestimate of "true" technological progress.

Solution to exercise 40

The return on savings and investments is

$$r = \frac{\partial F(K, L)}{K} = aK^{a-1}L^{1-a}.$$

Hence, recognizing that $A = aK/N$, so that $L = NA = aK$,

$$r = aK^{a-1}K^{1-a}a^{1-a} = aa^{1-a},$$

which does not depend on K and thus remains constant during the process of accumulation. If this r is above the discount rate of utility ρ, the rate of aggregate consumption growth is

$$\frac{\dot{C}}{C} = \frac{aa^{1-a} - \rho}{\sigma},$$

where, as usual, σ denotes the elasticity of marginal utility. Since $A(\cdot)N/K$ is constant and production,

$$F(K, L) = K^a N^{1-a} A^{1-a} = K^a N^{1-a}(aK/N)^{1-a} = Ka^{1-a},$$

is proportional to K, the economy moves immediately (and not just in the limit) to a balanced growth path.

Solution to exercise 41

Since the production function needs to have constant returns to K and L, it must be the case that $\beta = 1 - a$; moreover, since the returns need to be constant with respect to K and G, we need to have $\gamma = 1 - a$. Hence, writing

$$\tilde{F}(K, L, G) = K^a L^{1-a} G^{1-a},$$

and substituting fiscal policy parameters from (4.34) we get

$$G = \tau K^a L^{1-a} G^{1-a} \quad \Rightarrow \quad G = (\tau K^a L^{1-a})^{1/a} = (\tau L^{1-a})^{1/a}K.$$

Given that G and K are proportional, the net return on private savings is constant:

$$(1 - \tau)\frac{\partial \tilde{F}(K, L, G)}{\partial K} = (1 - \tau)aK^{a-1}L^{1-a}G^{1-a}$$

$$= (1 - \tau)a\left(\frac{G}{K}\right)^{1-a}L^{1-a}$$

$$= (1 - \tau)a(\tau L^{1-a})^{1/a}L^{1-a}.$$

The growth rate of consumption, which can be obtained by substituting the above expression into (4.35), and that of capital and aggregate production are also constant.

Solution to exercise 42

(a) We know that along the optimum path of consumption the following Euler condition holds:

$$-u''(C)\dot{C} = (F'(K) - \rho)u'(C),$$

which is necessary and sufficient if $u''(C) < 0$, $F''(K) \le 0$. These regularity conditions are satisfied if, respectively, $C < \beta$ and $K < a$. In this case the derivatives are given by $u'(C) = \beta - C$, $u''(C) = -1$, $F'(K) = a - K$, and we can write

$$\dot{C} = (a - K - \rho)(\beta - C).$$

(b) In the steady state,

$$(\dot{C} = 0) \Longleftrightarrow ((a - K_{ss} - \rho)(\beta - C_{ss}) = 0).$$

If $C_{ss} < \beta$ and $K_{ss} < a$ then necessarily $K_{ss} = a - \rho$ (or, as is usual, $F'(K_{ss}) = \rho$). Since

$$(\dot{K} = 0) \Longleftrightarrow (y_{ss} = F(K_{ss}) = C_{ss}),$$

we have

$$Y_{ss} = C_{ss} = F(K_{ss}) = a(a - \rho) - \tfrac{1}{2}(a - \rho)^2 = \tfrac{1}{2}(a^2 - \rho^2).$$

For all this to be valid, the parameters need to be such that $K_{ss} < a$, which is true if $\rho > 0$ and $C_{ss} < \beta$, which in turn requires $(a^2 - \rho^2) < 2\beta$.

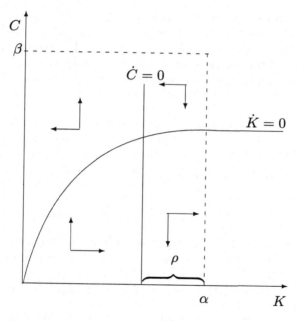

In the diagram, optimal consumption can never be in the region where $C > \beta$, since this would provide the same flow utility as $C = \beta$. If $K > a$, it is optimal to consume the surplus as soon as possible, given that production is independent of K in this region. Hence, the flow consumption needs to be set equal to the maximum utility, $C = \beta$. If that implies that $\dot{K} < 0$, then the system moves to the region studied above. But if the parameters do not satisfy the above conditions, then consumption may remain the same at β with capital above α forever. In this case the maximization problem does not have economic significance. (There is no scarcity.)

(c) Writing

$$\dot{C} = (a - K - \rho)\beta - (a - K - \rho)C,$$

we see that β determines the speed of convergence towards the steady state for given C and K, that is (so to speak) the strength of vertical arrows drawn in the phase diagram, and the slope of the saddlepath.

(d) If returns to scale were decreasing in the only production factor, then, setting $F'(K) = r$ (as in a competitive economy), total income rK would be less than production, $F(K)$. Thus, an additional factor must implicitly be present, and must earn income $F(K) - F'(K)K$. For the functional form proposed in this exercise, we have

$$F(\lambda K, \lambda L) = a\lambda K - g(\lambda L)\lambda^2 K^2, \qquad \lambda F(K, L) = a\lambda K - g(L)\lambda K^2,$$

hence returns to scale are constant if $g(\lambda L)\lambda = g(L)$, i.e. if $g(x) = \mu/x$ for μ a constant (larger than zero, to ensure that L has positive productivity). Setting $\mu = 1$ and $L = 2$, production depends on capital according to the functional form proposed in the exercise, and the solution can be interpreted as the optimal path followed by a competitive market economy.

Solution to exercise 43

(a) For the production function proposed,

$$\dot{Y}(t) = \left(\frac{1}{L + K(t)}\right)\dot{K}(t) = \left(\frac{1}{L + K(t)}\right)sY(t),$$

and the proportional growth rate of income tends to $s/L > 0$. Since consumption is proportional to income, consumption can also grow without limit.

(b) The returns to scale of this production function are non-constant:

$$\ln(\lambda L + \lambda K) = \ln \lambda + \ln(L + K) \neq \lambda \ln(L + K).$$

If both factors were compensated according to their marginal productivity, total costs would be equal to

$$\left(\frac{1}{L + K}\right)L + \left(\frac{1}{L + K}\right)K = 1,$$

while the value of output may be above one (in which case there will be pure profits) or below one (in which case profits are negative if $L + K < 1$). Hence, this function is inadequate to represent an economy in which output decisions are decentralized to competitive firms.

Solution to exercise 44

(a) The returns to scale are constant. Each unit of L earns a flow income

$$w(t) = \frac{\partial Y(t)}{\partial L} = 1 + (1 - a)\left(\frac{K(t)}{L}\right)^a,$$

and each unit of K earns

$$r(t) = \frac{\partial Y(t)}{\partial K(t)} = a\left(\frac{K(t)}{L}\right)^{a-1}.$$

(b) From the optimality conditions associated with the Hamiltonian, we obtain

$$\frac{\dot{C}(t)}{C(t)} = \frac{r(t) - \rho}{\sigma}.$$

Hence, if consumers have the same constant elasticity utility function, the growth rate will not depend on the distribution of consumption levels. Moreover, the growth rate increases with the difference between the interest rate and the rate of time preference and is higher if agents are more inclined to intertemporal substitution (a low σ).

(c) Production starts from L for $K = 0$, is an increasing and concave function of K, and coincides with the locus along which $\dot{K} = 0$. The locus where $\dot{C} = 0$ is vertical above K_{ss}, such that

$$r = f'(K_{ss}) = \rho \quad \Rightarrow \quad K_{ss} = \left(\frac{a}{\rho}\right)^{1/1-a} L.$$

The saddlepath converges in the usual way to the steady state, where

$$C_{ss} = L + L^{1-a} K_{ss}^a = L + \left(\frac{a}{\rho}\right)^{a/1-a} L.$$

(d) The return on investments is constant and equal to one, and so aggregate consumption grows at a constant rate. However, the income share of capital is growing and approaches one asymptotically. Except in the long run, when labor's income share is zero, the growth rate of production is therefore not constant and we do not have a balanced growth path.

Solution to exercise 45

(a) Calculating the total derivative, and using $\dot{K} = sY$ and equation $\dot{A}$, we get

$$\frac{\dot{Y}}{Y} = \frac{\dot{A}}{A} + a\frac{\dot{K}}{K} = L - L_Y + as\frac{Y}{K}.$$

Hence, when the growth rates are constant, Y/K needs to be constant and

$$\frac{\dot{Y}}{Y} = \frac{\dot{K}}{K} = \frac{L - L_Y}{1 - a}.$$

(b) The growth rate of the economy does not depend on s (which determines Y/K) but is instead endogenously determined by the allocation of resources to the sector in which A can be reproduced with constant returns to scale. A can be interpreted as a stock of knowledge (or instructions), produced in a research and development sector.

(c) The sector that produces material goods has increasing returns in the three factors; thus, no decentralized production structure could compensate all three factors according to their marginal productivity.

Solution to exercise 46

(a)

$$F(\lambda K, \lambda L) = [(\lambda K)^\gamma + (\lambda L)^\gamma]^{1/\gamma} = [\lambda^\gamma (K^\gamma + L^\gamma)]^{1/\gamma}$$

$$= \lambda(K^\gamma + L^\gamma)^{1/\gamma} = \lambda F(K, L).$$

(b)

$$y = \frac{1}{L}F(K, L) = [L^{-\gamma}(K^\gamma + L^\gamma)]^{1/\gamma} = \left[\left(\frac{K}{L}\right)^\gamma + 1^\gamma\right]^{1/\gamma}$$

$$= (k^\gamma + 1)^{1/\gamma} \equiv f(k).$$

(c)

$$f'(k) = (k^\gamma + 1)^{(1-\gamma)/\gamma}k^{\gamma-1} = [(k^\gamma + 1)k^{-\gamma}]^{(1-\gamma)/\gamma} = (1 + k^{-\gamma})^{(1-\gamma)/\gamma}.$$

Taking the required limit,

$$\lim_{x \to \infty} (1 + k^{-\gamma})^{(1-\gamma)/\gamma} = \left(1 + \lim_{x \to \infty} k^{-\gamma}\right)^{(1-\gamma)/\gamma}.$$

If $\gamma < 0$, then $k^{-\gamma}$ tends to infinity and the exponent $(1 - \gamma)/\gamma$ is negative; thus, $f'(k)$ tends to zero and $r = f'(k) - \delta$ tends to $-\delta$. If $\gamma > 0$ then $k^{-\gamma}$ tends to zero, and in the limit unity is raised to the power of $(1 - \gamma)/\gamma > 0$. Hence, $f'(k)$ tends to unity, and $r = f'(k) - \delta$ tends to $1 - \delta$.

(d) The economy converges to a steady state if $\lim_{k \to \infty} \dot{k}(t) = 0$. That is (given that a constant fraction of income is dedicated to accumulation), the economy converges to a steady state if net output tends to zero.

(e) For a logarithmic utility function the growth rate of consumption is given by the difference between the net return on savings and the discount rate of future utility: $\dot{C}(t)/C(t) = r(t) - \rho$. In order to have perpetual endogenous growth, this rate needs to have a positive limit if k approaches infinity: $\lim_{k \to \infty} r(t) = 1 - \delta$ if $\gamma > 0$; in addition, $1 - \delta - \rho > 0$ or equivalently $\rho < 1 - \delta$ must hold. (Naturally, ρ needs to be positive, otherwise the optimization problem does not have economic significance.)

Solution to exercise 47

(a) Since capital has a constant price and does not depreciate, there does not exist a steady state in levels: in fact, no positive value of $K(t)$ makes

$$\dot{K}(t) = \bar{P} s Y(t) = \bar{P} s K(t)^a L(t)^\beta$$

equal to zero. If $a = 1$ a balanced growth path exists, where

$$\frac{\dot{K}(t)}{K(t)} = \frac{\dot{Y}(t)}{Y(t)} = \bar{P} s L(t)^\beta.$$

The economy can be decentralized if the production function has constant returns to scale, that is if $a + \beta = 1$.

(b) The proportional growth rate of capital is

$$\frac{\dot{K}(t)}{K(t)} = s P(t) \frac{Y(t)}{K(t)} = s P(t) K(t)^{a-1} \bar{L}^\beta.$$

Hence $\dot{K}(t)/K(t) = g_k$ is constant if

$$\frac{\dot{P}(t)}{P(t)} + (a - 1) \frac{\dot{K}(t)}{K(t)} = 0.$$

The balanced growth rate of the stock of capital is

$$g_k = \frac{1}{1 - a} \frac{\dot{P}(t)}{P(t)} = \frac{h}{1 - a},$$

and the constant growth rate of output is given by

$$\frac{\dot{Y}(t)}{Y(t)} = a \frac{\dot{K}(t)}{K(t)} = \frac{a}{1 - a} h.$$

(c) If $P(t) = K(t)^{1-a}$, the accumulation of capital is governed by

$$\dot{K}(t) = K(t)^{1-a} s Y(t) = K(t)^{1-a} s K(t)^a \bar{L}^\beta = K(t) s \bar{L}^\beta.$$

Hence $\dot{K}(t)/K(t) = s\bar{L}^\beta$ is constant (and depends endogenously on the savings rate, s).

(d) $P(t)$ is the price of output (of savings) in terms of units of capital: if $P(t)$ increases, a given flow of savings can be used to buy more units of capital. In part (b) this increase is exogenous and, like the dynamics of A in the Solow model, allows for perpetual growth even in the case of decreasing marginal returns to capital. In part (c) the price of investment goods depends endogenously on the accumulation of capital: as in models of *learning by doing*, this can be interpreted as assuming that investment is more productive if the economy is endowed with a larger capital stock.

Solution to exercise 48

(a) Inserting $u'(c) = 1/c^2$, $u''(c) = -2/c^3$, and $\rho = 1$ in the Euler equation, we obtain

$$\dot{c}(t) = \frac{r-1}{2}c(t).$$

In words, the growth rate of consumption is independent of its level (since the utility function has CRRA form).

(b) $w(t) = B(t)$, $r(t) = 3$.

(c) The proportional rate of growth of capital is

$$\frac{\dot{K}(t)}{K(t)} = \frac{B(t)}{K(t)}L + 3 - \frac{C(t)}{K(t)},$$

and it is constant if $C(t)/K(t)$ and $B(t)/K(t)$ are constant and capital grows at the same rate as consumption and $B(t)$. In fact, if $r = 3$, consumption does grow at the same rate as $B(t)$: $\dot{c}(t)/c(t) = \dot{C}(t)/C(t) = 1 = \dot{B}(t)/B(t)$. The level of consumption can be such as to ensure also that $\dot{K}(t)/K(t) = 1$:

$$1 = \frac{B(t)}{K(t)}L + 3 - \frac{C(t)}{K(t)} \Leftrightarrow C(t) = B(t)L + 2K(t).$$

(d) The aggregate production function is $Y(t) = (L+3)K(t)$. Hence, the return to capital is $L + 3 > 3 = r$ for the aggregate economy, and it would be optimal for growth to proceed at rate

$$\frac{\dot{C}(t)}{C(t)} = \frac{L+3-1}{2} = L + 1.$$

Solution to exercise 49

From the third row of the table of expected utilities in the text, we can easily see that $V_M^P > V_C^P$, since $x < 1$; then, the commodity holder is willing to trade with a money holder. To check that the latter is also willing to trade, we must show that $U - (V_M^P - V_C^P) > 0$, since after the exchange the agent initially endowed with money enjoys utility from consumption but becomes a commodity holder. Using the appropriate entries of the table and the definition of K given in the text, we have

$$U - (V_M^P - V_C^P) = U - \frac{K}{r + \beta x} r (1 - x)$$

$$= U \left(1 - \frac{\beta x (1 - M)(1 - x)}{r + \beta x} \right).$$

This expression is positive, because the fraction in the large parentheses is less than unity. Hence, a money holder is willing to exchange money for a commodity she can consume.

Solution to exercise 50

Consider a discrete time interval Δt, from $t = 0$ to $t = t_1$, during which θ is constant and therefore $\dot{J} = \dot{V} = 0$. Retracing the argument of Section 5.1, suppose that, when a firm and a worker experience a separation event, the resulting vacant job is not filled again during such an interval. (This assumption is valid, of course, in the $\Delta t \to 0$ limit.) The value of a filled job at the beginning of the interval is thus given by

$$J = \int_0^{t_1} e^{-st} e^{-rt} (y - w) \, dt + e^{-r\Delta t} [e^{-s\Delta t} J + (1 - e^{-s\Delta t}) V]. \qquad (0.1)$$

The first term on the right-hand side denotes the expected production flow during the time interval, net of the wage paid to the worker, discounted back to $t = 0$. (e^{-st} represents the probability that the job is still filled and productive at time t.) The second term represents the (discounted) expected value of the job at $t = t_1$, the end of the interval. (If a separation occurs, with probability $1 - e^{-s\Delta t}$, the job becomes a vacancy, valued at V.) Solving the integral yields

$$J = \frac{1}{r + s} (y - w) + \frac{e^{-r\Delta t}(1 - e^{-s\Delta t})}{1 - e^{-(r+s)\Delta t}} V.$$

The limit as $\Delta t \to 0$ of the second term is $s/(r + s)$, by l'Hôpital's rule. Thus,

$$J = \frac{1}{r + s} (y - w) + \frac{s}{r + s} V \quad \Rightarrow \quad rJ = (y - w) + s(V - J).$$

Solution to exercise 51

Totally differentiating (5.45) and (5.46) around a steady state equilibrium point, we obtain

$$\begin{pmatrix} 1 - (r+s)c\frac{q'}{q^2} & \\ 1 & -\beta c \end{pmatrix} \begin{pmatrix} dw \\ d\theta \end{pmatrix} = \begin{pmatrix} -\frac{c}{q} & 1 \\ 0 & \beta \end{pmatrix} \begin{pmatrix} ds \\ dy \end{pmatrix},$$

and we can compute the following effects of an aggregate productivity shock (recall that $q' < 0$):

$$\frac{dw}{dy} = \frac{\overbrace{-\beta c + \beta(r+s)c\dfrac{q'}{q^2}}^{-}}{\Delta} > 0, \qquad \frac{d\theta}{dy} = \frac{\overbrace{\beta - 1}^{-}}{\Delta} > 0,$$

where the determinant

$$\Delta = -\beta c + (r+s)c\frac{q'}{q^2}$$

is negative. An aggregate productivity shock moves the equilibrium wage in the same direction but, barring extreme cases, by a smaller amount $(0 \le dw/dy \le 1)$; it also induces a change in the same direction of labor market tightness. (Lower productivity is associated with a lower vacancy/unemployment ratio in the new steady state.) As $\beta \to 1$ (and all the matching surplus is captured by workers), different productivity levels affect only the wage, with no effect on θ. For intermediate values of β, the effects of a negative productivity shock are shown in parts (a) and (b) of the figure. The effects on unemployment and vacancy rates are uniquely determined, since productivity variations do not affect the Beveridge curve and only cause the equilibrium point to move along it.

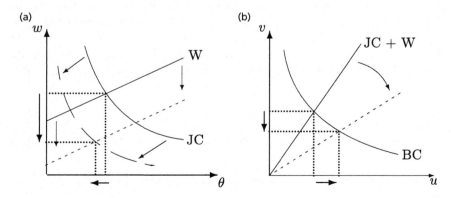

For the case of a *reallocative shock*, we have

$$\frac{dw}{ds} = \frac{\beta \overset{+}{\overbrace{\frac{c^2}{q}}}}{\Delta} < 0, \qquad \frac{d\theta}{ds} = \frac{\overset{+}{\overbrace{c/q}}}{\Delta} < 0(*).$$

An increase in s leads to a reduction in both the equilibrium wage and the labor market tightness through a leftward shift of the curve JC (which is more pronounced for higher values of β). However, at the same time the Beveridge curve shifts to the right, and the effect of s on the number of vacancies v is therefore ambiguous, while the unemployment rate increases with certainty— see parts (c) and (d) of the figure. Totally differentiating the expression for the Beveridge curve and using the result obtained above for θ, we obtain (with $p' > 0$ and $0 \leq \eta \equiv p'\theta/p \leq 1$)

$$du = \frac{p}{(s+p)^2}ds - \frac{sp'}{(s+p)^2}d\theta$$

$$\Rightarrow \frac{du}{ds} = \frac{p}{(s+p)^2}\left(1 - \frac{\eta s}{(r+s)(\eta-1) - \beta p}\right) > 0(**).$$

(The denominator of the last fraction is negative.) Moreover, using the definition for θ, we can express the effect on the mass of vacancies as

$$\frac{dv}{ds} = u\frac{d\theta}{ds} + \theta\frac{du}{ds},$$

which, together with ($*$) and ($**$), yields

$$\frac{dv}{ds} = \frac{s}{s+p}\frac{\theta}{(r+s)(\eta-1) - \beta p} + \theta\frac{p}{(s+p)^2}\left(1 - \frac{\eta s}{(r+s)(\eta-1) - \beta p}\right)$$

$$= \frac{\theta}{(s+p)^2}\frac{s^2 + pr(\eta-1) - \beta p}{(r+s)(\eta-1) - \beta p}.$$

From these equations one can deduce that, starting from a relatively low level of s, a reallocative shock will lead to an increase in the mass of vacancies.

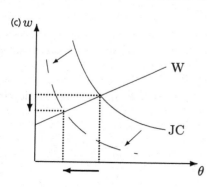

(c) w

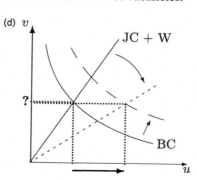

(d) v

Solution to exercise 52

Totally differentiating the payoff function with respect to $\bar{e}$ yields

$$\frac{dV(e_i(\bar{e}), \bar{e})}{d\bar{e}} = V_1(e_i, \bar{e})\frac{de_i}{d\bar{e}} + V_2(e_i, \bar{e}) = V_2(e_i, \bar{e}) > 0,$$

since $V_1(.) = 0$ in an optimum. (This is an application of the envelope theorem.)

Solution to exercise 53

There is a positive externality between the actions of agents, since

$$\frac{\partial V^1}{\partial e_2} = ae_1^a e_2^{a-1} > 0.$$

The reaction function of agent 1 is obtained by maximizing this agents's payoff:

$$\max_{e_1} V^1(e_1, e_2) \Rightarrow ae_1^{a-1}e_2^a - 1 = 0 \Rightarrow e_1 = a^{1/1-a}e_2^{a/1-a},$$

from which we obtain

$$\frac{de_1}{de_2} = \frac{a}{1-a}a^{1/1-a}e_2^{2a-1/1-a} > 0.$$

Hence, there is a *strategic complementarity* between the actions of agents. The symmetric decentralized equilibria are obtained by combining the two (identical) reaction functions with $e_1 = e_2 = e$. There are two equilibria: one with zero activity ($\underline{e}^1 = 0$) and one with a positive activity level ($\bar{e} = a^{1/1-2a}$). The cooperative equilibrium (e^*) is obtained by maximizing the payoff of the representative agent with respect to the common activity level e:

$$\max_e V(e, e) = e^{2a} - e \Rightarrow 2a(e^*)^{2a-1} - 1 = 0 \Rightarrow e^* = (2a)^{1/1-2a}.$$

The fact that $e^* > \bar{e}$ confirms that the decentralized equilibria are inefficient in the presence of externalities.

Solution to exercise 54

(a) Given the assumptions, the expression for the dynamics of e is given by

$$\dot{e} = (1 - e)ac^* - e^2 b,$$

from which, setting $\dot{e} = 0$, an expression for the locus of stationary points is obtained:

$$\dot{e} = 0 \Rightarrow c^* = \frac{e^2 b}{(1-e)a} \Rightarrow \frac{dc^*}{de}\bigg|_{\dot{e}=0} = \frac{2eb + ac^*}{(1-e)a} > 0, \quad \frac{d^2c^*}{de^2}\bigg|_{\dot{e}=0} > 0.$$

The production cost c has an upper limit equal to 1. Hence if c^* exceeds this upper limit there is no need for a further increase in e to maintain a constant level of employment, because for $c^* \geq 1$ all production opportunities are accepted. The locus of stationary points is thus vertical for $c^* > 1$. The dynamic expression for c^* is given by

$$\dot{c}^* = rc^* - be(y - c^*) + a\frac{c^{*2}}{2}.$$

Assuming $\dot{c}^* = 0$, one obtains a (quadratic) expression in c^*. This expression is drawn in the figure and along this curve:

$$\frac{dc^*}{de}\bigg|_{\dot{c}^*=0} = \frac{b(y - c^*)}{ac^* + r + be} > 0e \quad \frac{d^2c^*}{de^2}\bigg|_{\dot{c}^*=0} = -\frac{b^2(y - c^*)}{(ac^* + r + be)^2} < 0.$$

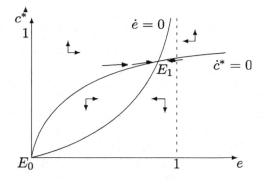

(b) There are two possible equilibria: E_0, in which $c^* = e = 0$, and E_1, which is the only equilibrium with a positive activity level. The stability properties of E_1 can be studied by linearizing the two difference equations around the equilibrium point (e_1, c_1^*) and by determining the sign of the determinant of the resulting matrix:

$$\begin{pmatrix} -(2e_1b + ac_1^*) & (1 - e_1)a \\ -b(y - c_1^*) & ac_1^* + r + be_1 \end{pmatrix}.$$

If the determinant is negative, the equilibrium has the nature of a *saddlepoint*. As in the general case discussed in the main text, this occurs if in equilibrium the curve $\dot{e} = 0$ is steeper than the curve $\dot{c}^* = 0$, as is the case in E_1.

Solution to exercise 55

(a) Restricting our attention to symmetric and stationary equilibria (in which $\pi = \Pi$ and V_C and V_M are constant over time), with $c > 0$, the values of expected utility from holding a commodity and holding money are:

$$V_C = \frac{1}{1+r}\{(1-\beta)V_C + \beta[(1-M)x^2U + (1-M\Pi x)V_C$$
$$+ M\Pi x(V_M - c)]\}$$

$$V_M = \frac{1}{1+r}\{(1-\beta)(V_M - c) + \beta[(1-M)\Pi x(U + V_C)$$
$$+ (1-(1-M)\Pi x)(V_M - c)]\},$$

where c is subtracted from V_M whenever the agent ends the period with money. Using the two equations above, we get

$$V_C - V_M = \frac{\beta(1-M)xU(x-\Pi) + (1-\beta\Pi x)c}{r + \beta\Pi x}.$$

Setting $V_C = V_M$, we find the value of Π, dubbed Π^M, that makes agents indifferent between holding commodities and money:

$$\Pi^M = \frac{\beta(1-M)x^2U + c}{\beta(1-M)xU + \beta xc} = x + \frac{(1-\beta x^2)c}{\beta(1-M)xU + \beta xc} > x.$$

To make agents indifferent, money must be *more* acceptable than commodities: $\Pi^M > x$. The greater acceptability of money compensates money holders for the storage cost they incur in the event of their ending the period still holding money. The agents' optimal strategy and the corresponding equilibria (shown in the figure) are then as follows:

- $\Pi < \Pi^M$: with $V_C > V_M$, agents never accept money and a *non-monetary* equilibrium arises ($\Pi = 0$).
- $\Pi > \Pi^M$: agents always accept money since $V_C < V_M$, and the resulting equilibrium is *pure monetary* ($\Pi = 1$).
- $\Pi = \Pi^M$: in this case $V_C = V_M$ and agents are indifferent between holding commodities and money; the corresponding equilibrium is *mixed monetary* ($\Pi = \Pi^M$).

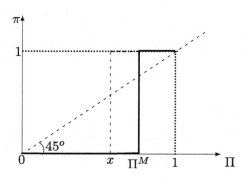

(b) With storage costs for money the *non-monetary equilibrium* always exists, whereas the existence of the other two possible equilibria depends on the magnitude of c. Even when money is accepted with certainty ($\Pi = 1$), agents may not be fully compensated for the storage cost if c is very large. To find the values of c for which a *pure monetary* equilibrium exists, we consider $V_C < V_M$ when $\Pi = 1$:

$$V_C < V_M \Rightarrow \beta(1 - M)xU(x - 1) + (1 - \beta x)c < 0$$

$$\Rightarrow c < \frac{\beta(1 - M)xU(1 - x)}{1 - \beta x}.$$

To ease the interpretation of this condition, consider the case of $\beta = 1$. (Agents meet pairwise with certainty each period.) The above condition then simplifies to $c < (1 - M)xU$. The right-hand term is the expected utility from consumption for a money holder (utility U times the probability of meeting a trader offering an acceptable commodity $(1 - M)x$). Only if the storage cost of money c is lower than the expected utility from consumption does a *pure monetary* (and *a fortiori* a *mixed monetary*) equilibrium exist, as in the case portrayed in the figure.

Solution to exercise 56

The fact that c and z depend on the wage alters the shape of the JC and W curves, as can be seen in the figure. In steady-state equilibrium, using (5.34), we have

$$y - w = (r + s)\frac{c_0 w}{q(\theta)} \quad \Rightarrow \quad w = \frac{1}{1 + (r + s)c_0/q(\theta)}y \, (JC)$$

and

$$w = z_0 w + \beta(y + c_0 w\theta - z_0 w) \quad \Rightarrow \quad w = \frac{\beta}{1 - (1 - \beta)z_0 - \beta z_0\theta}y. \, (W)$$

From (W), which holds in steady-state equilibrium and along the adjustment path, it follows that the wage is proportional to productivity and the factor of proportionality is positively correlated with the measure of labor market tightness θ. Combining both equations, we obtain a result that is different from the one in exercise 51: here θ is independent of the value of productivity in the steady-state equilibrium. Variations in y lead to proportional adjustments in the wage but have no effect on θ or on the unemployment rate u. Hence, in this version of the model, a continuous increase in productivity (technological progress) does not lead to a decrease in the long-run unemployment rate. The unemployment rate is determined by the properties of the *matching* technology (the efficiency of the "technology" that governs the process of meetings between unemployed workers and vacancies) and the exogenous separation rate s.

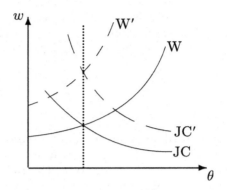

Solution to exercise 57

At t_0 firms anticipate the future reduction in productivity and immediately reduce the number of vacancies: v and θ fall by a discrete amount (see figure). Between t_0 and t_1, the dynamics are governed by the difference equations associated with the initial steady state: v and θ continue to decrease (while the unemployment rate increases) until they reach the new saddlepath at t_1. From t_1 onwards u and v increase in the same proportion, leaving the labor market tightness θ unchanged.

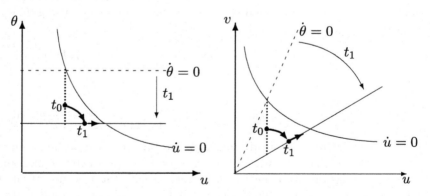

Solution to exercise 58

Following the procedure outlined in the main text, we calculate the total differential of the two first-order conditions, which yields

$$V_{11}^1 de_1^* + V_{12}^1 de_2^* + V_{13}^1 d\lambda = 0,$$
$$V_{21}^2 de_1^* + V_{22}^2 de_2^* + V_{23}^2 d\lambda = 0.$$

Using the same definitions as in the main text, we can rewrite this system of equations as

$$\begin{pmatrix} 1 & -\rho \\ -\rho & 1 \end{pmatrix} \begin{pmatrix} de_1^* \\ de_2^* \end{pmatrix} = \begin{pmatrix} \partial e_1^*(\cdot)/\partial\lambda \\ \partial e_2^*(\cdot)/\partial\lambda \end{pmatrix} d\lambda,$$

from which we obtain the following results:

$$\frac{de_1^*}{d\lambda} = \frac{\partial e_1^*/\partial\lambda + \rho(\partial e_2^*/\partial\lambda)}{1 - \rho^2} = \frac{1}{1 - \rho^2}(1 + \rho)\frac{\partial e_1^*}{\partial\lambda} = \frac{1}{1 - \rho}\frac{\partial e_1^*}{\partial\lambda}$$

$$\frac{de_2^*}{d\lambda} = \frac{\partial e_2^*/\partial\lambda + \rho(\partial e_1^*/\partial\lambda)}{1 - \rho^2} = \frac{1}{1 - \rho}\frac{\partial e_2^*}{\partial\lambda}$$

$$\frac{d(e_1^* + e_2^*)}{d\lambda} = \frac{2}{1 - \rho}\frac{\partial e_1^*}{\partial\lambda} = 2\frac{de_1^*}{d\lambda}.$$

⬜ INDEX

smooth pasting, 88
Solow growth model, 132
stationarity, 16
steady-state, 59, 61, 137
    optimal savings, 140
stochastic process, 3, 82
    ARMA, 16

Taylor expansion, 118
transversality condition, 4, 53, 54, 59, 60, 62, 139, 143

user cost of capital, 61, 77

Wiener process, 82

Printed in the United States
By Bookmasters